Wills and Administrations
of
Southampton County, Virginia
1749-1800

Wills and Administrations of
SOUTHAMPTON COUNTY, VIRGINIA
1749-1800

By Blanche Adams Chapman

Reprinted in an Improved Format
WITH A CONSOLIDATED INDEX

CLEARFIELD

Reprinted for
Clearfield Company by
Genealogical Publishing Co.
Baltimore, Maryland
1998, 2008

ISBN-13: 978-0-8063-0907-1
ISBN-10: 0-8063-0907-5

Made in the United States of America

Originally published in two volumes:
Volume I: 1947
Volume II: 1958
Reprinted, two volumes in one, in an improved
format and with a consolidated index, by
Genealogical Publishing Co., Inc.
Baltimore, 1980
Copyright © 1980
Genealogical Publishing Co., Inc.
Baltimore, Maryland
All Rights Reserved
Library of Congress Catalogue Card Number 80-68126

In
Loving Memory
of
My Mother
Elizabeth C. Carter Adams
(Mrs. William Henry)
1867 - 1945

CONTENTS

Will Book I	1
Will Book II	28
Will Book III	56
Will Book IV	96
Will Book V	155
Index	173

NOTE

THE VOLUME IN HAND contains abstracts of Southampton County's earliest will books (Books I through V), covering the period 1749 to 1800. It was originally published in two mimeographed volumes, Volume I appearing in 1947, Volume II in 1958. Owing to the eleven-year interval in the publication of the two volumes the complete work is rather hard to come by today, even in the larger public libraries. Partly for this reason, and partly to satisfy demand, we have undertaken to reprint it. Our publication, however, is not merely a reprint but an improved edition, consolidated (two volumes in one), re-typed, and re-indexed for the convenience of the researcher.

GENEALOGICAL PUBLISHING CO., INC.

SOUTHAMPTON COUNTY

WILL BOOK I

DUNKLEY, John. Leg.- wife Catherine and her heirs. Wife
Catherine, Extx. D. March 14, 1747/48. R. July 13, 1749.
Wit. William Jones, Edward Doyel. Page 1.

SMITH, George. Inventory of estate returned by Daniel Williams.
Aug. 10, 1749. Page 1.

SIMMONS, John. Leg.- son Charles 180 acres on which I now live
and 725 acres in the low grounds. D. Aug. 25, 1749. R. Nov.
9, 1749. Wit. Daniel Guthrie, Ann Gray, Mary Wainwright.
Page 2.

DUNKLEY, John. Gent. Inventory. Signed, Catherine Dunkley,
Extx. R. Nov. 9, 1749. Page 2.

ADAMS, David. Among items, paid John Adams. Value of estate,
Ŀ118 "II" 3 1/2. Mary Adams and John Adams Adms. D. May 20,
1748. R. Nov. 9, 1749. Audited by James Ridley and Peter
Butts. Page 4.

WILLS, Francis. Of the County of Isle of Wight. Leg.- wife
Temperance; eldest son Thomas; estate among all my children.
Exs. son Thomas and Mathew Wills. D. Jan. 9, 1747/48.
R. Dec. 14, 1749. Wit. Robert Bygrave, James Cary, James
Cary, Jr. Page 4.

SIMMONS, John. Of Isle of Wight, Gent. My water mill on
Cussunkra swamp, 100 acres bought of Henry Clark, 75 acres
bought of John Newton and 280 acres granted me by patent
June 28, 1731 to be sold by my Exs. to pay my debts; wife Mary
the use of the property on which I now live and all other
things provided for my deed of trust with my son Charles on
April 28, 1740; son William my land in Surry County; son
Benjamin 390 acres bought of the Nottoway Indians, adjoining
his own land; son Charles all my land in the low grounds not
already sold to Charles Brown and John Arrington and 180 acres
on which I live, being part of William Cock's patent; daughter
Ann Ruffin and her husband Edmund Ruffin; daughter Lucy Ruffin
and her husband Benjamin Ruffin; daughter Elizabeth Jones and
her husband Elberton Jones; son Henry Simmons. Charles to
divide my wearing apparel between Henry and Benjamin Simmons.
Exs. sons Benjamin and Charles Simmons.
D. June 25, 1746. R. Dec. 14, 1749. Wit. Robert S. Woobank,
Howell Edmunds, Peter Butts, William Little. Page 6.
(Note: Several genealogists have claimed that the above
will and the one on page 2 proved there were two John
Simmons, who died in 1749. I feel after comparing the
text of the two and taking into consideration the
following items from the Order Books of the County that
they were the wills of the same man and the second one
found at a later date and also filed ------- Col. John
Simmons of Southampton County died Sept. 21, 1749.
Virginia Gazette. Mary Simmons was granted administration of the will of her husband John Simmons. Resigned

2

and administration requested by Benjamin Simmons. Will
proven by Mary Wainwright a witness. Security for Adm.
Joseph Gray and Peter Butts. Appraisers appointed,
Benjamin Clements, Peter Butts, Thomas Westbrook and
Charles Barham. Southampton Order Book I, page 22.
------- A writing purporting to be the last will and
testament of John Simons, Gent. was presented and proven
by Howell Edmunds and Peter Butts. 1749 Order Book I,
page 31. ------- Thomas Lee, William Nelson and als.
versus Benjamin Simmons with will annexed of John
Simmons decd. with Charles Simmons and William Simmons
an infant under the age of 21. Frances Simmons of the
County of Surry appointed guardian to deft. William
Simmons. 1750. Order Book I, page 60. B. A. C.)

DREW, Edward of Nottoway Parish. Leg.- son Newitt; grandson
Newitt Harris, son of my daughter Mary Harris; grandson
Thomas Harris; grandson Drew Harris; grandson Nathan Harris;
granddaughters Ann and Martha Harris; daughter Mary, wife of
John Harris; grandson William Turner; granddaughter Frances
Drew; grandson Edward Drew, son of Newitt Drew; granddaughter
Mary Harris, wife of Henry Harris; grandson Joseph Lane;
granddaughter Faith Lane, daughter of Benjamin Lane; daughter
Ann Lain; son Thomas Drew. Ex. Newitt Drew. D. Nov. 24, 1745.
R. March 8, 1749. Wit. Thomas Pursell, John Bavion (?), James
Ridley. Page 8.

HARRIS, Martin. Leg.- cousin James, son of Robert Harris; to
James son of Edward Harris; to Mathew son of Robert Harris; to
John son of Robert Harris; to William son of George Harris; to
James son of James Harris. Exs. John Dunkley, Joseph Jones
and William Jones. D. Feb. 1, 1747. R. April 12, 1750.
Wit. Catherine Dunkley, Joseph Munger. Page 10.

MANNING, Samuel. Leg.- son Richard; son Jonathan; daughter
Elizabeth; daughter Mary; daughter Susannah; daughter Sarah;
daughter Lucy; wife Sarah. Exs. wife Sarah Manning and Thomas
Williamson. D. Feb. 24, 1749. R. April 12, 1750. Wit.
Joseph Dowles, George Summerell, Jonathan Joyner. Page 11.

WILLIAMS, Sarah of Littletown. Leg.- grandson Richard son of my
eldest son John Williams, decd.; son Daniel; son Elisha; son
Joshua; grandson Thomas son of Joshua Williams; son George;
son Solomon; daughter Elizabeth Daughtrey; daughter Mary Carr.
Ex. son Daniel Williams. D. March 24, 1749. R. June 14, 1750.
Wit. Joseph Carle (?), William Barcroft. Page 12.

WILLS, Francis. Appraisal of estate by Bensjamin Johnson,
Nathan Vasser, Phillip Brantley. Signed, Temperance Wills.
R. June 14, 1750. Page 14.

HARRIS, Martin. Appraisal of estate by William Exum, Sampson
Pitman, Joseph Mounger. Signed, Joseph Jones and William
Jones. R. June 14, 1750. Page 15.

BRYAN, Robert. Leg.- to wife; son William, land on Terraro Creek;
daughter Morning; daughter Ann; granddaughter Elizabeth
Garner; son Thomas; son Robert; son John; daughter Alice;
daughter Rebecca; daughter Mary Garner; son Guil (?); daughter
Ann; daughter Sarah; daughter Elizabeth. Exs. sons William
and Thomas Bryan. D. Aug. 28, 1750. R. Nov. 8, 1750. Wit.
Robert Gilliam, Andrew Mackmial, Lewis Bryan. Page 17.

CROCKER, Robert. Leg.- son Benjamin; son Moses; grandson Elisha
Crocker; son Arthur; daughter Elizabeth Jordan; daughter
Sarah Braswell; my housekeeper Mary Hill; daughter Mary
Middleton. Exs son Benjamin Crocker. D. Sept. 24, 1750.
R. Nov. 8, 1750. Wit. William Bynum, John Jones, Alex. Watson.
Page 19.

BRADDY, Margaret. Leg.- son Arthur Crafford; daughter Martha
Phillips; daughter Elizabeth Hays; daughter Mary Crafford; son
Henry Crafford land in Carolina. Ex. son Henry Crafford.
D. July 29, 1750. R. Nov. 8, 1750. Wit. Arthur Pitman,
Chaplain Williams, Jr. Page 20.
Estate appraised by Chaplain Williams, Henry Dawson and
Joshua Dawson. R. Dec. 13, 1750. Page 21.

BRANCH, Elizabeth. Leg.- son George; daughter Lidia; daughter
Ann Tyas; daughter Elizabeth Cord; daughter Mary Brewter;
granddaughter Ann Cord; daughter Jone Williams; daughter
Martha Williamson; daughter Sarah Williams; son Benjamin;
granddaughter Sarah Brewton; daughter Hannah Williamson.
Ex. son Benjamin Branch. D. Oct. 28, 1749. R. Dec. 13, 1750.
Wit. J. Gray, Sarah Gray. Page 22.

HARRIS, Martin. Account of estate audited by William Jarrell
and Richard Kello. R. July 9, 1750. Page 24.

WHITEHEAD, Arthur. Leg.- eldest son Arthur, land adjoining
William Turner; grandson Arthur Whitehead; son Lewis, land
bought of William Powers and land on Pottycassey Creek in
Carolina; son Nathan land on Fishing Creek in Carolina; grand-
son ------- Benjamin Whitehead; daughter Patience Vick, land
adjoining Jacob Vicks plantation on Long Branch; daughter
Catrin Cobb; grandson Jacob Vick; daughter Mary; daughter Ann.
Brother William Whitehead, Capt. Thomas Jarrell and Mr. James
Washington to divide estate. Ex. son Lewis Whitehead.
D. March 12, 1744. R. Jan. 10, 1750/51. Wit. William White-
head, Lazarus Whitehead, William Bock (?). Page 26.

CROCKER, Robert. Estate appraised by William Bynum, John Harris
and Arthur Long. R. Jan. 10, 1750/51. Page 30.

BRANCH, Elizabeth. Inventory returned by Benjamin Branch.
R. Feb. 14, 1750. Page 32.

WILLIAMS, Mathew. Estate appraised by William Pope, James
Gardner and Phillip Brantley. R. Feb. 14, 1750. Page 33.

EDWARDS, William of Nottoway Parish. Leg.- son William; son John;
daughter Elizabeth; wife Elizabeth Ex. son Thomas Edwards.
D. Sept. 30, 1750. R. Feb. 14, 1750/51. Wit. George Gurley,
Jr., John Gurley.. Page 33.

JONES, John. Leg.- son Simon; son Jesse; son Joshua (under 21)
son John (under 21); son Isham land on Buckhorn; son Brittain;
daughter Sarah; daughter Martha. Exs. wife Eleanor and son
Simon Jones. D. Oct. 5, 1750. R. Feb. 14, 1750/51. Wit.
Chaplain Williams, Henry Dawson, Simon Harris. Page 34.

CRUMPLER, William. Leg.- son John land adjoining William Crumpler;
son William; grandson William Crumpler and to his daughter.
Ex. son William Crumpler. D. Oct. 24, 1750. R. Feb. 14,
1750/51. Wit. Page 36.

THORP, Timothy. Leg.- daughter Margaret, wife of James Bruce; daughter Mary, wife of Owen Mirick; granddaughter Mary Harris; granddaughter Ann Harris; granddaughter Mary Barham; son John; son Timothy; son Joseph; daughter Olive Atkinson. Exs. John and Timothy Thorpe. D. Dec. 2, 1750. R. March 14, 1750/51. Wit. Edward Harris, Francis Hilliard, Thomas Ammon. Page 37.

JONES, John. Estate appraised by Henry Crafford, Henry Dawson and Arthur Long. R. April 11, 1751. Page 39.

GRIFFIN, Mathew. Leg.- son Andrew land in Isle of Wight adjoining Arthur Fowler; son Jones land in I. of W. adjoining Hardy Council; son Lot land in I. of W.; son Lemuel to sell a tract of land to pay money I owe Edmund Fowler; daughter Mary; daughter Martha; daughter Sarah; daughter Rebecca. Exs. wife Catherine and son Andrew Griffin. D. Nov. 2, 1750. R. July 11, 1751. Wit. Joseph Jones, Samuel Johnson. Page 40.

BRYANT, Robert. Estate appraised by Epaphroditus Williams, Simon Everett and Benjamin Crocker. R. July 11, 1751. Page 42.

POPE, John. Leg.- son John; son William; daughter Elizabeth; daughter Mary Darden; grandson John son of William Pope; daughter Else Mosley; grandson Henry Darden; daughter Sarah Barnes. Ex. son William Pope. D. Feb. 1, 1748. R. July 14, 1751. Wit. Howel Edmunds, Isaac Johnson, Nathan Pope. Page 46.

WILLIAMS, Sarah, widow. Estate appraised by Joseph Cobb, Thomas Crenshaw, Nathan Vasser. R. July 14, 1750. Page 48.

EDWARDS, William. Estate appraised by Henry Thomas, Joseph Cobb, George Gurley. R. July 11, 1751. Page 41.

JONES, Arthur. Estate appraised by Ambrose Williams, John Browning and John Arrington. D. April 12, 1751. R. Aug. 8, 1751. Page 52.

MANNING, Samuel. Estate appraised by Andrew Sikes, Robert Vasser (?) and Joseph Tanner. Signed by Sarah Manning. R. Aug. 8, 1751. Page 53.

MATTHEWS, Hugh. Leg.- grandson Jonas, son of John Matthews, decd. land on Angelica Swamp, being part of a tract taken up by Capt. William West and now owned by Edward Drew; grandson Ralph son of Ralph Matthews land on Angelica Swamp surveyed by James Baker; grandson Solomon Stephenson; son Edward; son William; wife Ann; son Joseph; grandson Jacob, son of Joseph Matthews; daughter Mary Thorp; daughter Sarah Mackenny; daughter Martha Newsom; son Benjamin; daughter Hester Johnson; grandson Aaron Matthews; daughter Patience Johnson. Exs. wife Ann and son Joseph Matthews. D. Nov. 7, 1747. R. Sept. 12, 1751. Wit. Daniel Sebrell, Thomas Pursell, George Stephens. Page 55.

EVANS, Elizabeth. Leg.- Jesse, Elizabeth, Patience, Sarah and Mathew Womble; daughter Elizabeth Walters; son James. Ex. son James Evans. D. June 7, 1749. R. Nov. 14, 1751. Wit. Benjamin Britt, Edward Jenkins. Page 57.

SIMMONS, Col. John. Account estate audited by James Ridley and Peter Butt. Signed by Benjamin Simmons, Adm. R. Aug. 8, 1751. Page 58.

SMITH, George. Account estate audited by James Ridley and
Timothy Thorp. R. Jan. 10, 1752. Page 65.

PERSON, John. Leg.- son John land purchased of John Blair, Esq.
and land in Northampton Co., in N.C., whereon Benjamin Person
now lives; son Henry land in Granville Co., N.C., bought of
John Lyles and Daniel Flugunion (?); son Thomas land on the
Meherrin River recovered in the General Court from Edward
Jacquelin's Executors; son William; daughter Hannah; daughter
Prescilla; grandson John the son of John and Dorcas Person
land in Surry Co.; land bought of John Ledbetter in Granville
Co., N.C. to be sold; daughter Sarah; daughter Mary; daughter
Rebeccah; daughter Elizabeth. Exs. sons John and Henry
Person. D. Aug. 31, 1751. R. Feb. 13, 1752. Wit. Amos
Garris, William Bowers, John Inman, Sr. Page 66.

GRIFFIN, Mathew. Estate appraised by Joseph Joyner, William
Crumpler and William Bulls. R. Feb. 13, 1752. Signed Exum
Scott, Adm. Page 69.

CLARK, Thomas. Leg.- wife Sarah; daughter Frances; son John;
son James land on Allen's Creek in Lunenburg County; son Jesse
land on Caton's Creek in Lunenburg County; son Jordan Thomas
Clark land on aforesaid Creek; son Carter Clark. Exs. wife
Sarah and daughter Frances Clark. D. Dec. 1, 1750. R. Feb.
13, 1752. Wit. John Person, Thomas Clifton, Benjamin Blunt.
Page 72.

WHITEHEAD, Arthur. Estate appraised by John Edwards and Harris
Taylor. Signed Lewis Whitehead. R. April 9, 1752. Page 77.

BRYANT, Robert. Account of estate examined by Howell Edmunds,
Chaplain Williams and Henry Crafford. Signed Mary Bryant,
Adm. R. April 9, 1752. Page 79.

GRIFFIN, Mathew. Account of estate examined by A. Jones, James
Jordan Scott and Joshua Pretlow. Signed Exum Scott, Adm.
R. April 9, 1752. Page 80.

BLUNT, Benjamin. Leg.- son William (under 21), land bought of
Samuel Davis; son John land bought of John Chapman; son
Benjamin land in North Carolina. My brothers Henry Blunt and
Henry Thomas and John Person, Sr. and John Person, Jr. to
divide my land. Ex. wife Priscilla Blunt. D. July 4, 1751.
R. May 14, 1752. Wit. John Person, Jr., Edward Windham, Elias
Foster, Alex. Watson. Page 81.

WOODWARD, Samuel. Leg.- to Henry Johnson the plantation on which
he now lives if he pays 35ь to my estate; son Rueben; son
Charles; wife Martha. Exs. wife Martha Woodward and Henry
Johnson. D. March 25, 1752. R. May 14, 1752. Wit. Daniel
Johnson, Jacob Johnson. Page 84.

SCOTT, William. Leg.- brother John Scott; brother John Mundell.
Ex. John Mundell. D. Dec. 28, 1751. R. May 14, 1752. Wit.
Robert Deane, Mary Bowers, Francis Sharp, John Sharp. Page 84.

KINDRED, Mary. Leg.- son Samuel; daughter Faith. Extx. daughter
Faith Kindred. D. Feb. 19, 1740. R. June 11, 1752. Wit.
Howell Edmunds, Raman Ennis. Page 86.

EVERETT, Simon. Nuncupative will. Leg.- brother Joseph; sister
Sarah Turner; sister Patience Turner. D. Feb. 17, 1752. R.
June 11, 1752. Wit. William Bynum, Elizabeth Bynum. Page 87.

CLARK, Thomas. Estate appraised in Lunenburg County by
Nicholas Major, James Coleman and John Speed. Estate
appraised in Southampton by John Person, Thomas Clifton and
Joshua Claud. R. July 9, 1752. Page 88.

WHITEHEAD, Arthur. Paid Ann Whitehead's dower. Audited by
Howell Edmunds and Jesse Brown. Signed Lewis Whitehead.
R. July 9, 1752. Page 91.

JONES, Arthur. Account estate audited by Charles Simmons and
Richard Kirby, Jr. Signed Phillip Jones. R. July 9, 1752.
Page 92.

WOODWARD, Samuel. Estate appraised by A. Washington, Henry
Blunt and Benjamin Clifton. R. Aug. 13, 1752. Page 93.

JOHNSON, Benjamin. Leg.- wife Anne; son Jesse; son Joshua;
daughter Martha; daughters Elizabeth and Anne. Exs. wife
Anne and brother Jacob Johnson. D. May 18, 1752. R. Aug. 13,
1752. Wit. James Scott, Mary Johnson, Sarah Speed. Page 94.

GRIFFIN, Mathew. Account estate. R. Aug. 13, 1752. Page 95.

KINDRED, Mary. Estate appraised by William Kirby, Raman Ennis
and Henry Vaughan. R. Aug. 21, 1752. Page 95.

MATTHEWS, Hugh. Estate appraised by Newit Drew, Timothy Thorp
andJames Jones. R. Oct. 12, 1752. Page 96.

JOHNSON, Benjamin, Jr. Estate appraised by Job Wright, George
Speed and Arthur Edwards. R. Oct. 12, 1752. Page 97.

MOUNGER, Robert of Nottoway Parish. Leg.- son Joseph; daughter
Amy Pitman; grandson Henry Mounger; grandson Jethro Mounger.
Exs. son Joseph and Samson Pitman. D. Sept. 18, 1752. R.
Nov. 9, 1752. Wit. Joseph Jones, Benjamin Joyner, Ruth Moore.
Page 98.

SCOTT, William. Estate appraised by John Person, Henry Harrison
and Francis Sharp. R. Nov. 11, 1752. Page 100.

JONES, Mathew. Appraisal of estate unadministered by Elizabeth
Jones, decd., by Benjamin Johnson, Phillip Brantley and Job
Wright. Signed A. Jones. R. Dec. 14, 1752. Page 102.

THOMAS, Richard. Appraisal of estate ordered Nov. 9, 1752, by
John Person, Henry Harris and Jacob Harris. R. Dec. 14, 1752.
Page 102.

BAXTER, David. Appraisal of estate ordered Nov. 9, 1752 by
Phillip Brantley, John Brantley and Mathew Wills. R. Dec. 13,
1752. Page 103.

MOUNGER, Robert. Inventory of estate, signed by Joseph Mounger
and Samson Pitman. R. Jan. 11, 1753. Page 104.

FORT, John. Leg.- son Elias; son John; son Henry; son Joshua;
son Arthur; grandson Henry Thomas; daughter Lucy Grisard;
daughter Betty; wife Rebecca. D. Jan. 10, 1753. R. March 8,
1753. Wit. Peter Butts, John Forster, Arthur Forster, David
Newsom. Page 105.

MATTHEWS, Hugh. Estate settled by J. Ridley, James Jones and
Timothy Thorp. R. March 8, 1753. Page 108

STEPHENSON, Katherine. Leg.- son George; son William; daughter Elizabeth Mathews; Sarah the wife of Solomon Stephenson. Ex. son Solomon Stephenson. D. Aug. 31, 1750. R. March 8, 1753. Wit. Timothy Thorp, Charles Spence. Codicil. Bequest to daughter Mary Mathews. Page 109.

SMITH, Virgus. Leg.- grandson Joseph Smith; grandson Arthur Smith; daughter Patience; daughter Martha. Ex. son Arthur Smith. D. R. March 8, 1753. Wit. John Bowin, Thomas Jones. Page 110.

THOMAS, Richard. Estate audited by J. Gray, Ben Ruffin and Micajah Edwards. Signed Thomas Pylent. R. March 8, 1752. Page 111.

POPE, John. Inventory presented by William Pope. R. April 12, 1753. Page 112.

SMITH, Virgus. Inventory presented by Arthur Smith. R. April 12, 1753. Page 112.

JOYNER, Jonathan. Leg.- wife Drusilla; daughter Patience; son Thomas; son Alexander; daughter Mary; son David. Exs. wife Drusilla and brother-in-law John Boykin. D. Jan. 10, 1750. R. Nov. 9, 1752. Wit. Samson Pitman, Catherine Dunkley. Page 113.

BLUNT, Benjamin. Estate appraised by James Turner, Sr., James Turner, Jr. and Simon Turner. Also filed account of estate in North Carolina. R. May 10, 1753. Page 115.

STORY, Daniel. Appraisal ordered Jan. 11, 1753 by Henry Thomas, Thomas Crenshaw and George Gurley. R. May 10, 1753. Page 117.

WILLIAMSON, Joseph. Leg.- son Absolom; son William; son Burwell; wife Hannah; daughter Averilla; daughter Ann; daughter Elizabeth, daughter Silviah; daughter Mary. Brothers Arthur and Benjamin Williamson to divide my estate. Exs. wife Hannah and son Burwell Williamson. D. Feb. 6, 1742. R. May 10, 1753. Wit. Thomas Williamson, Burwell Williamson. Page 119.

RIDLEY, Nathaniel. Leg.- son Nathaniel; son Day; son Thomas; daughter Anne; daughter Pamilla; wife Priscilla. Exs. wife Priscilla and her brother Arthur Applewhite and brother James Ridley. D. Oct. 20, 1752. R. May 10, 1753. Wit. James Ridley, Robert Bygrave, George Stephenson. Page 120.

FORT, John. Estate appraised by Charles Barham, Benjamin Barham and Thomas Westbrook. R. July 12, 1753. Page 122.

DRAKE, John. Leg.- eldest daughter Mary; daughter Ann; daughter Esther Pully; son Joshua; son Thomas; son Barnaby; son Timothy; to daughters at wife's decease. Extx. daughter Mary Drake. D. March 15, 1753. R. July 12, 1753. Wit. Thomas Oberry, Thomas Drake, George Gurley, Jr. Page 124.

BAXTER, David. Estate audited by William Haynes and Benjamin Westray. Signed A. Jones, Adm. R. Aug. 9, 1753. Page 126.

DRAKE, John, Sr. Inventory returned Aug 8, 1735. Page 127.

EXUM, Francis. Leg.- friend Simon Turner land in Brunswick County; sister Elizabeth Smith; nephew Exum Williamson, son of Arthur Williamson; sister Ann Williamson; sister Olive

Williamson; sister Mary Jordan land in Isle of Wight on which
she lives. Ex. brother-in-law Thomas Williamson. D. April 30,
1753. R. Sept. 13, 1753. Wit. Joshua Claud, John Person,
John Mundell. Page 127.

STEPHENSON, Catherine. Inventory of estate returned by Solomon
Stephenson. R. Sept. 13, 1753. Page 129.

WOODARD, Samuel. Estate audited by Charles Cosby and Charles
Briggs. R. Sept. 13, 1753. Page 130.

JARRELL, Thomas. Leg.- son Thomas; son John; son Benjamin;
daughter Ann Ricks; daughter Elizabeth; grandson Thomas Jarrell;
wife Martha. Exs. wife Martha, son Thomas and Richard
Rickards. D. July 9, 1753. R. Sept. 13, 1753. Wit. John
Pleasants, Richard Ricks, Elizabeth Miles, William Francis and
Martha David. Page 130.

JARRELL, William. Estate appraised by Joseph Cobb, Henry Thomas
and Micajah Edwards. Ordered Sept. 13, 1753. R. Oct. 11,
1753. Page 133.

JOHNSON, John. Estate appraised by Joshua Joyner, Bridgman
Joyce and Job Wright. Signed John Johnson. R. Oct. 11, 1753.
Page 133.

ROTCHELL, John. Leg.- son-in-law Raman Ennis; son George;
daughter Elizabeth Salls (?); son John; wife. D. March 20,
1753. R. Nov. 8, 1753. Wit. William Bynum, Samuel Atkinson,
Ann Portear (?), Ann Rotchell, widow qualified as Extx.
Page 135.

JOHNSON, John. Leg.- son Daniel; son Lazarus; son Joseph; son
Henry; daughters Sarah, Martha and Ester; deceased son John's
heirs; wife Lucy. Ex. son Lazarus Johnson. D. Nov. 29, 1752.
R. March 14, 1754. Wit. Richard Murfee, John Pope, James
Fowler. Page 136.

WASHINGTON, John. Leg.- son Arthur; daughter Elizabeth; son
John; son Thomas; daughter Faith; daughter Mary; son Jesse.
Extx. wife Elizabeth Washington. D. March 4, 1747/48.
R. March 14, 1754. Wit. Charles Cosby, Thomas Washington.
Page 137.

GRIFFIN, Mary. Leg.- son Epenetus; daughter Henerilear (?)
Joyner; daughter Constant Bennett; daughter Sarah Jones;
Robert Carr; granddaughter Martha Revel; grandson Andrew, son
of Epenetus Griffin; grandson Andrew son of Martha Griffin
decd. Ex. grandson Andrew Griffin. D. May 21, 1753. R. March
14, 1754. Wit. Benjamin Wester, Christopher Wade. Page 139.

RICKS, Elizabeth. Leg.- son Robert; daughter Elizabeth Scott;
granddaughter Elizabeth Scott; daughter Mary Pretlow; grand-
son Robert Ricks; grandson Thomas Ricks; granddaughter
Elizabeth Ricks. Ex. son Richard Ricks. D. July 25, 1753.
R. March 14, 1754. Wit. Thomas Langley, Dennis Herne.
Page 140.

ROTCHELL, John. Estate appraised by Benjamin Crocker, Joshua
Dawson and William Bynum. R. March 15, 1754. Page 141.

JOHNSON, John. Inventory. Signed by Lazarus Johnson. R. May
9, 1754. Page 142.

EDWARDS, Arthur. Estate appraised by Henry Blunt, Benjamin Barnes, Richard Johnson. R. May 9, 1754. Page 142.

JARRELL, Thomas. Estate appraised by Micajah Edwards, Henry Thomas and Joseph Cobb. R. June 15, 1754. Page 144.

PERSON, Thomas. Estate appraised by Thomas Clifton, Joseph Claud and William Westbrook. R. July 11, 1754. Page 146.

JOYNER, Bridgman. Leg.- son Jacob; son Bridgman; son Jesse; daughter Sarah; daughter Ann; daughter Patience Bunn; granddaughters Ann and Sarah Bunn. Exs. sons Bridgman and Jacob Joyner. D. April 4, 1754. R. July 11, 1754. Wit. James Jordan Scott, John Lewis, John Brantley. Page 148.

WASHINGTON, John. Estate appraised by Joseph Phillips Charles Calthorp and Benjamin Williamson. Signed Arthur Washington. R. Aug. 8, 1754. Page 149.

GARNER, James. Leg.- son James; son Joshua land in Nansemond County; son Mathew; son-in-law John Lawrence; daughter Penelope; son-in-law James Vick; wife. (The name of Juda Garner is included in a list of the above in the division of a piece of property); son John Garner. Exs. son-in-law James Vick and son Joshua Garner. D. Oct. 9, 1747. R. Aug. 8, 1754. Wit. Thomas Sharp, Carr Darden, John Garner. Page 152.

SMITH, James. Leg.- wife Mary; son John; grandson James Smith; daughter Mary. Exs. wife Mary and son John Smith. D. R. Sept. 13, 1754. Wit. Robert Lancaster, John Lithgee. Page 154.

GARNER, James. Estate appraised by Mathew Wills, Phillip Brantley and John Pope. R. Nov. 14, 1754. Page 155.

TAYLOR, Thomas. Leg.- wife Katherine; son Hermon, land in Northhampton County, N.C.; son James land adjoining John Thomas and the widow Norfleet; son John; son Edward; son Harris; son Thomas; daughter Elizabeth Strickland; daughter Olive; daughter Hannah; daughter Margret. Exs. wife Katherine and son Hermon Taylor. D. Aug. 7, 1754. R. Nov. 14, 1754. Wit. John Pitman, Arthur Pitman, James Taylor. Page 156.

BARRETT, Edmond. Leg.- son Edmond; son Simon; wife Sarah. Exs. wife Sarah and son Edmond Barrett. Wit. Samuel Davis, William Fowler, Jacob Barrett. Page 157.

SAUL, Elizabeth. Leg.- son William Broom. Ex. son William Broom. D. Nov. 7, 1754. R. Dec. 12, 1754. Wit. Nathaniel Ridley, Ann Ridley. Page 158.

JARRELL, Col. Thomas. Second appraisal by Micajah Edwards, Joseph Cobb, Henry Thomas. D. Feb. 13, 1753. Page 159.

EXUM, Francis. Inventory presented by Thomas Williamson. R. March 13, 1755. Page 160.

TAYLOR, Thomas. Inventory. R. March 13, 1755. Page 161.

RIDLEY, Nathaniel. Estate appraised by James Jones, Newit Drew and Simon Turner. R. March 14, 1755. Page 162.

BARRETT, Edmond. Estate appraised by John Edwards, Epaphroditus Williams and Thomas Davis. R. April 10, 1755. Page 165.

HATFIELD, William. Leg.- wife Mary; cousin Tillaman Hatfield; cousin John Hatfield; cousin David Hatfield; cousin Philemon Hatfield. Exs. wife Mary and cousin Philemon Hatfield. D. March 11, 1785. R. April 10, 1755. Wit. Joseph Cobb, John Drake, George Gurley. Page 166.

JOHNSON, John. Account current of estate. Signed John Johnson. R. April 10, 1755. Page 167.

JOYNER, John. Estate appraised by Joseph John Hollemon, Robert Messer and Joseph Doles. R. May 8, 1755. Page 168.

PHEASANT, John. Leg.- Daniel Lubree; William Edmunds; Brumfield Ridley; Betty Farrow; Charles the son of Charles Travis; Jeremiah Drew; William Dean; Betty Dean (?); Arthur Long's wife; Mary Long; John Smith's wife; widow Atkins' lame son; children of William Tanner; John Hilliard. Ex. Capt. Howell Edmunds. D. Aug. 23, 1755. R. June 12, 1755. Wit. Howell Edmunds, Sr., Howell Edmunds, Jr. Page 169.

SCOTT, Elizabeth. Leg.- son James Jordan Scott; daughter Elizabeth Williams; daughter Sarah Pinner; grandson Jesse Weatherley. Ex. son James Jordan Scott. D. Nov. 9, 1748. R. June 12, 1755. Wit. Josiah Jordan, Mourning Jordan, Martha Surkett (?). Page 170.

HATFIELD, William. Estate appraised by Joseph Cobb, George Gurley, Thomas Crenshaw. R. June 12, 1755. Page 171.

SCOTT, Elizabeth. Inventory signed by James Jordan Scott. R. July 10, 1755. Page 172.

JARRETT, William. Paid to Thomas Jarrell, Adm. and to William Eldridge. Audited by Micajah Edwards and William Taylor. R. Aug. 14, 1755. Page 173.

JOYNER, Jonathan. Estate audited by J. Gray, Thomas Williamson and R. Kello. Signed, Drusilla Joyner and John Boykin. R. July 13, 1755. Page 174.

NEWSUM, Elizabeth of Nottoway Parish. Leg.- son Jacob; son Thomas; son Moses; son Sampson; son Solomon; son Nathan; son Amos; daughter Ann Holt; daughter Sarah Barham; son David. Ex. son David Newsum. D. Sept. 18, 1751. R. Aug 14, 1755. Wit. Peter Butts, Charles Barham, James Barham. Page 175.

HARRISON, Henry. Estate appraised by Joshua Claud, Thomas Day and James Turner. D. Aug. 20, 1755. R. Sept. 11, 1755. Page 176.

SAUL, Elizabeth. Estate appraised by Henry Vaughan, David Edmunds and Simon Turner. R. Oct. 9, 1755. Page 178

PHAESANT, John. Estate appraised by Henry Vaughan, David Edmunds and Simon Turner. R. Oct. 9, 1755. Page 178.

GARDNER (Garner ?), James. Account estate examined by M. Edwards and Benjamin Ruffin. Signed James Vick and Joshua Gardner. R. Oct. 9, 1755. Page 180.

SANDEFUR, William. Leg.- son Hill; son Samuel; son William; to unborn child. Ex. wife Mary Sandefur. D. May 27, 1755. R. Nov. 13, 1755. Wit. Joseph Jones, Richard Pond, Martha Pond, Ruth Sweney. Page 181.

TAYLOR, Etheldred of Nottoway Parish. Leg.- wife; son Henry the
plantation on which James Railey lives; son Kinchen; son
Etheldred the plantation called "Howells"; son John plantation
called Indian Town; son James land on the Meherrin; son
Richard the plantation on which William Drewry lives; son
William; daughter Elizabeth Cary; daughter Mary. Exs. wife,
son William and son-in-law Miles Cary. D. June 18, 1755.
R. Nov. 13, 1755. Wit. Robert Bygrave, James Moore. Page 182.

SANDEFUR, William. Estate appraised by Arthur Arrington,
Joseph Vasser and Richard Pond. Signed, Mary Sandefur.
R. Dec. 11, 1755. Page 185.

SMELLY, Giles. Leg.- Joseph son of Joshua Joyner; Giles son of
William Joyner; John son of Joseph Joyner; Robert Durdan;
Moses son of William Joyner; Lewis son of William Joyner and
Joshua Whitney. Ex. Joshua Whitney. D. Nov. 25, 1755.
R. Dec. 11, 1755. Wit. William Haynes, John Lawrence, Elenor
Joyner. Page 187.

JARRELL, Colonel Thomas. Account estate signed by Martha Thomas,
Thomas Jarrell and Richard Ricks. Audited by Micajah Edwards,
Henry Thomas and Joseph Cobb. R. Dec. 11, 1755. Page 189.

STORY, Daniel. Account estate signed by Mary Story. Audited
by M. Edwards, Joseph Cobb and Henry Thomas. D. Dec. 11,
1755. R. Jan. 8, 1756. Page 190.

EDWARDS, Arthur. Account estate signed by Admtx., Alice Edwards.
R. Feb. 13, 1756. Page 193.

JOYNER, Bridgman. Estate appraised by Job Wright, Mathew Wills
and John Bryant. Signed Bridgman and Jacob Joyner. R. Dec.
12, 1756. Page 194.

DAWSON, John. Leg.- grandson John Dawson; son-in-law Abraham
Johnson; daughter Ann Joyner's children; daughter Mary Worrell;
wife Mary; grandson Demse, with reversion to his brother
Solomon Dawson. Ex. cousin Joshua Dawson. D. April 6, 1755.
R. Feb. 12, 1756. Wit. James Jordan Scott, Thomas Dreaper,
Francis Denson. Page 196.

DAVIS, Thomas. Inventory signed by John Davis. R. March 11,
1756. Page 198.

BLUNT, Benjamin. Division of slaves among his children;
William, Ann Turner, John, Mary, Priscilla, Elizabeth and
Sarah Blunt by Henry Blunt, Henry Thomas and John Person.
Signed Priscilla Blunt. D. Feb. 16, 1756. R. April 8, 1756.
Page 199.

HARRISON, Henry. Account current. Signed by William Harrison.
Audited by Joshua Claud and John Mundell. R. April 7, 1756.
Page 200.

NEWSUM, Elizabeth. Account estate signed by James Barham,
Charles Barham and Benjamin Barham. R. April 9, 1756.
Page 203.

DAVIS, John. Leg.- son William the plantation bought of Thomas
Wiggons; daughter Sarah; daughter Martha; Hannah Steward; Mary
Steward. Exs., Mary Steward and Solomon Newsum. D. Dec. 24,
1747. R. July 8, 1756. Wit. Thomas Pursell, James Ridley.
Page 204.

HATFIELD, William. Estate appraised by Joseph Cobb, George Gurley and Thomas Crenshaw. R. Aug. 12, 1756. Page 205.

SMELLY, Giles. Inventory signed by Joshua Whitney. R. Aug. 12, 1756. Page 206.

COBB, Nicholas of Nottoway Parish. Leg.- son Nicholas; son Henry; grandson William the tract on which his father William Cobb lived, adjoining his uncle Henry Cobb; son Samuel land belonging to old Phillip Brantley; son Lazarus, daughter Deborah Cobb. Exs., sons Samuel and Lazarus Cobb. D. May 24, 1752. R. Nov. 11, 1756. Wit. A. Jones, Phillip Brantley, John Vinkles. Page 208.

SMITH, Turner John. Leg.- David Edloe Disto; James Hook with reversion of bequest to Newit Harris and Newit Foster; wife Sarah Smith. Ex., David Edloe Disto. D. Oct. 31, 1756. R. Dec. 9, 1756. Wit. Christopher Foster, Alse Foster, Amy Foster. Page 208.

EXUM, William of Nottoway Parish. Leg.- wife Patience; son Parnel Robert Pursell (?) Exum; to my wife and ten children, Joseph, Barneby, William, Moses, Michael, Elizah, Mary, Arthur, Sarah and Parnel Robert Pursell (?) Exum. Ex., son William Exum. D. Oct. 17, 1756. R. Jan. 13, 1757. Wit. Joseph Gray, Martha Pursell (?). Page 210.

COBB, William of Nottoway Parish. Leg.- daughter Sarah; son Michael; loving wife. Ex. son Michael Cobb. D. Oct. 8, 1756. R. Jan. 13, 1757. Wit. Charles Calthorpe. Page 211.

COBB, Nicholas. Estate appraised by William Cooper, James Gardner and Richard Williams. R. Jan. 13, 1757. Page 212.

JORDAN, John. Inventory signed by Jesse Brown, Sheriff. D. Dec. 21, 1754. R. Jan. 13, 1757. Page 214.

PATE, Edward. Leg.- son Thomas; son Samuel; daughter Milly; daughter Mary Johnson; wife Ann Pate. Ex., wife Ann Pate and Travis Pate. D. Dec. 19, 1755. R. Jan. 15, 1757. Wit. Joseph Larke, Richard Rose, Abrams Wiggins, Charles Spence. Page 215.

JORDAN, John. Estate in the hands of Jesse Brown, late Sheriff. R. Jan. 13, 1757. Page 217.

JARRELL, John. Nuncupative will proven by Thomas Burgess and Henry Thomas. Leg.- two sisters and brother Benjamin Jarrell. Adm. Henry Thomas. D. Jan. 7, 1757. R. Feb. 10, 1757. Page 217.

JONES, William. Leg.- daughter Grace Revel; daughter Sely; granddaughter Elizabeth Jones; wife Sarah; son Britten Jones. Exs., wife and son Britten Jones. D. R. Feb. 10, 1757. Wit. Mary Benet, Thomas Jones, John Bowen. Page 218.

JARRELL, Colonel Thomas. Account estate, signed by Henry Thomas and Richard Ricks. Audited by Micajah Edwards, Joseph Cobb and Henry Blunt. R. Feb. 11, 1757. Page 218.

PATE, Edward. Estate appraised by Henry Applewhaite, Joseph Harwood and John Thorpe. R. May 12, 1757. Page 219.

JARRELL, John. Estate appraised by Newit Drew, Timothy Thorpe and James Jones. R. May 12, 1757. Page 221.

DAVIS, John. Estate appraised by Timothy Thorpe, Newit Drew and James Jones. R. May 12, 1757. Page 223.

NEWSUM, Robert. Leg.- daughters Mary, Elizabeth, Sarah, Julian and Ann Little; son Thomas; wife Elizabeth; son Robert; son Joseph. Exs., sons Robert and Joseph Newsum. D. Feb. 16, 1750/51. R. June 9, 1757. Wit. George Gurley, Sr., Thomas Edwards, George Gurley, Jr. Page 224.

HATFIELD, William. Account estate signed by Philemon Hatfield. Audited by Joseph Cobb, George Gurley and Thomas Crenshaw. R. July 14, 1757. Page 225.

COBB, William. Estate appraised by William Bailey, John Bailey, and Joseph Phillips. Signed J. Gray. R. July 14, 1757. Page 226.

PORTEOUS, John. Estate appraised by Moses Phillips, Samson Pitman and Joseph Munger. Ordered Sept. 3, 1755. R. July 15, 1757. Page 228.

POPE, Elizabeth of Nottoway Parish. Leg.- cousin Rebecca Gatling; cousin Benjamin Pope; Elizabeth daughter of Edward Barnes in North Carolina; Andrew McMial; cousin Henry Darden; cousin John son of William Pope. Ex., brother William Pope. D. July 12, 1757. R. Aug. 11, 1757. Wit. Anne Faircloth, George Gurley, Jr. Page 230.

SMITH, Turner John. Estate appraised by Charles Barham, Jacob Newsom and David Newsom. R. Sept. 8, 1757. Page 231.

JONES, Thomas. Estate appraised by William Cooper, Nicholas Cobb and James Gardner. Ordered July 16, 1757. R. Oct. 13, 1757. Page 232.

SIMMONS, Stephen. Inventory. R. Nov. 10, 1757. Page 233.

WILLIAMSON, Joseph. Estate appraised by John Harris, Benjamin Britt and Alex Murry. R. Dec. 9, 1757. Signed, Hannah Williamson. Page 235.

NEWSUM, Robert. Estate appraised by M. Edwards, Henry Thomas and George Gurley. R. Jan. 12, 1758. Page 236.

JORDAN, John. Estate audited by R. Kello and Samuel Blow. Signed by William Jordan. R. Nov. 22, 1757. Page 238.

SMITH, Jane. Leg.- daughter Faith Harris; son Joseph; son Flood; son Absolom; daughter Jane; son Lawrence; daughter Hannah; daughter Sarah; estate to be divided by son Joseph and James Turner, Jr. Ex. son Joseph Smith. D. Nov. 21, 1757, R. Feb. 9, 1758. Wit. James Turner, Jr., William Bynum. Page 239.

SPENCE, William of Nottoway Parish. Leg.- daughter Mary; to John Spence; Lucy Powell and John McLemore. Mary Bass to live on my plantation her lifetime. Ex., Simon Turner, Sr. D. Jan. 12, 1758. R. Feb. 9, 1758. Wit. John Rawlings, James Bass, Middy Bass. Page 240.

POPE, Elizabeth. Estate appraised by Joseph Newsum, Etheldred Holt and Stephen Pope. R. Feb. 9, 1758. Page 241.

INGRAHAM, William. Leg.- son John; son William; to wife and my three sons and two daughters. Extx. wife. D. Feb. 6, 1758. R. March 9, 1758. Wit. Josiah John Holloman, Thomas Atkinson, Timothy Atkinson. Will presented by Mary Ingraham. Page 243.

WEBB, Charles. Leg.- son Charles; son John; son Micajah; daughter Elizabeth; wife Elizabeth Webb. D. Feb. 21, 1758. R. April 13, 1758. Wit. Benjamin Clements, Thomas Caple, Arthur Gilliam. Page 245.

JARRELL, Thomas. Estate examined by Joseph Cobb, Jr. John Thomas and Micajah Edwards. R. April 13, 1758. Page 246.

WASHINGTON, Elizabeth. Estate appraised by William Bailey, John Bailey and Joseph Phillips. Signed Arthur Washington. R. May 11, 1758. Page 248.

WASHINGTON, Thomas. Estate appraised by William Bailey, John Bailey and Joseph Phillips. Ordered Nov. 10, 1757. R. May 11, 1758. Page 249.

DAVIS, John. Estate appraised by John Pope, Simon Pope and Joseph Delk. R. May 11, 1758. Page 251.

SMITH, Turner John. Estate audited by Benjamin Simmons, Benjamin Lewis and Charles Barham. R. May 11, 1758. Page 253.

DRAKE, Thomas of Nottoway Parish. Leg.- wife Anne; son John; son Thomas; son William; son Lazarus; daughter Mary the wife of William Williams. Exs., sons Thomas and William Drake. D. Oct. 3, 1757. R. May 11, 1758. Wit. Benjamin Williams, Jacob Williams, Britten Drake. Page 254.

HATFIELD, William. Account estate audited by Joseph Cobb and George Gurley. Signed, Philemon Hatfield. R. July 11, 1758. Page 255.

PITMAN, Arthur. Estate appraised by Henry Dawson, Chaplin Williams and John Edwards. R. July 11, 1758. Page 256.

WHITEHEAD, Arthur. Leg.- brother William; brother Jesse; brother Thomas; brother Lazarus; rest of estate between all my brothers and sisters, viz.- Thomas Boone; Lazarus, William, Selah, Jesse and Thomas Jones. Ex., Richard Vick. D. April 4, 1758. R. May 11, 1758. Wit. William Boon, Thomas Boon, Eday Boon. Page 257.

COBB, William. Estate account signed by Joseph Gray. Michael Cobb and Simon Stephens paid an equal share. R. Aug. 10, 1758. Page 258.

VICK, Richard of Nottoway Parish. Leg.- son Josiah; daughter Patty; wife Martha; son Arthur; son Jacob; son Richard; son William; son Joshua. Exs., friends Jesse Brown and Albridgton Jones. D. July 23, 1757. R. Aug. 10, 1758. Wit. Joseph Newsum, Henry Johnson, George Gurley, Jr. Page 260.

GILLIAM, Walter. Leg.- son Arthur; sons Drury and Ephraim the plantation bought of Abel Mabry; wife Sarah. Extx., wife Sarah Gilliam. D. April 28, 1758. R. Aug. 10, 1758. Wit. Burrell Gilliam, William Hutchings, Arthur Foster. Page 261.

INGRAHAM, William. Estate appraised by Timothy Atkinson and
Benjamin Britt. Signed Sarah Ingraham. R. Sept. 14, 1758.
Page 263.

SMITH, Jane. Estate appraised by James Turner, John Little and
William Person. Signed, Joseph Smith. R. Sept. 14, 1758.
Page 266.

JONES, John. Estate appraised by John Edwards, John Wilkinson
and William Person. R. Sept. 14, 1758. Page 268.

BLUNT, Henry of Nottoway Parish. Leg.- son Thomas; daughter
Mary; wife Sarah. Exs., wife Sarah and son Thomas Blunt.
D. Jan. 16, 1758. R. Sept. 14, 1758. Wit. Samuel Blow,
Elizabeth Edwards. Page 270.

PHEASANT, John. List of debts due his estate. Signed H.
Edmunds. R. Sept. , 1758. Page 271.

CHITTY, Edward. Estate appraised by Simon Pope, John Davis and
Joseph Delk. R. Oct. 12, 1758. Page 272.

JOYNER, William. Leg.- daughter Elizabeth Underwood; son William;
son Israel; daughter Ann Vick; son Lewis; son Moses land
bought of Benjamin Bradshaw; son Giles; wife Ellinor. Ex.,
son Giles Joyner. Wit. William Haynes, Joseph Joyner, John
Joyner. D. Oct. 25, 1757. R. Nov. 9, 1758. Page 274.

DUNKLEY, Katherine. Leg.- brother-in-law Moses Dunkley; Ralph
son of Moses Dunkley, the plantation which my late husband
purchased of John Hodges; Thomas son of Jonathan Joyner;
brother Thomas Joyner; uncle Benjamin Joyner; sister Elizabeth
the wife of John Boykin; sister Cherry the wife of John Boykin
of North Carolina: sister Patience Hodges; to Alexander, Mary,
David, Patience and Jonathan the children of Jonathan Joyner;
Mathew Joyner. Exs., brothers Thomas Joyner, Mathew Joyner
and John Boykin of Southampton County. D. April 12, 1758.
R. Nov. 9, 1758. Wit. Richard Kello, Joseph Mounger, Edward
Doyle. Page 276.

POPE, Henry. Leg.- wife Mary; son Henry at twenty one; son
Richard; daughter Sarah; daughter Mary; daughter Mourning
Pope. Exs., son Richard Pope and son-in-law Hodges Council.
D. Oct. 23, 1758. R. Dec. 14, 1758. Wit. John Matthews,
Jones Griffin. Page 278.

JOYNER, William. Inventory of estate. R. Dec. 14, 1758.
Page 279.

HOLLIMAN, James. Estate appraised by Thomas Chappel, Richard
Pond, Daniel Pond. Ordered Oct. 12, 1758. R. Dec. 14, 1758.
Page 279.

VASSER, Jacob. Estate appraised by Robert Newsum, Henry Thomas
and George Gurley. R. Dec. 12, 1758. Page 280.

SCOTT, John. Estate appraised by William Person, Henry Harris
and Jacob Harris. Signed, John Mundell. R. Dec. 12, 1758.
Page 281.

JOHNSTON, Benjamin. Estate settled by George Gurley, Jr., James
Jordon Scott and Samuel Brown. R. Jan 12, 1759. Page 283.

DRAKE, Thomas. Account estate. R. Jan. 12, 1759. Page 284.

POPE, Henry. Estate appraised by Richard Worrell, Henry Joyner and William Joyner. R. Feb. 8, 1759. Page 286.

BOWIN, John. Leg.- daughter Sarah Bennett; granddaughter Betha Bennett; son John; daughter Beck Griffin; grandson Roche (?) Griffin; housekeeper Elizabeth Bradsha; son Arthur; daughter Mary Branch; daughter Martha Driver. Exs., son John Bowin and William Bennett. D. R. Feb. 8, 1759. Page 289.

WHITEHEAD, Arthur. Estate audited by Thomas Crenshaw and Joseph Cobb. R. Feb. 8, 1750. Page 291.

PERSON, Henry. Estate appraised by Edward Harris, Henry Harris and William Womack. Signed Mary Person. Ordered Oct. 12, 1754. R. Feb. 8, 1759. Page 291.

HOLLIMAN, James. Estate audited by Samuel Blow and Thomas Chappell. Signed by Joseph Vasser. R. March 8, 1759. Page 295.

VICK, Richard. Estate appraised by Micajah Edwards, Joseph Cobb, Henry Thomas and George Gurley, Jr. R. April 12, 1759. Page 296.

DAWSON, John. Estate appraised by Sampson Pitman, John Wellings (WELLONS ?) and Joseph Mounger. R. April 12, 1759. Page 298.

DAVIS, John. Account estate audited by James Ridley, Timothy Thorpe and James Jones. R. April 12, 1759. Page 300.

PORTIS (PORTEOUS), John. Account audited by Peter Butts and Charles Simmons. R. April 10, 1759. Page 301.

SIMMONS, John. Estate appraised by Benjamin Clements, Richard Kirby and Ambrose Williams. R. June 14, 1759. Page 302.

WEST, James. Estate appraised by John Bowin, Moody Kirby and John Kirby. R. July 12, 1760. Page 305.

SAVAGE, Moses. Nuncupative will. Died at the home of Thomas Davis, Jr. Proven by Thomas Davis, Hannah Davis and Thomas Davis Jr. Leg.- brothers Joshua and Aaron Savage. R. July 12, 1759. Page 306.

SPENCE, William. Estate appraised by Henry Harris, Joshua Harris and John Mundell. R. July 12, 1759. Page 307.

DUNKLEY, Katherine. Estate signed by John Boykin, Mathew Joyner and Thomas Joyner. R. July 12, 1759. Page 309.

BOWIN, John. Inventory signed by John Bowin and William Bennett. R. Aug. 9, 1759. Page 311.

DRAKE, Richard. Leg.- son Francis; son Mathew; son Nathaniel; son Tristrom; son William; son Britten; son Richard; son Edmond; daughter Martha wife of Jacob Williams wife Margaret with reversion of bequest to my four children Richard, Edmond, Elizabeth and Margaret. Exs. sons Mathew and Richard Drake. D. Feb. 28, 1759. R. Sept. 13, 1759. Wit. Thomas Gray, Benjamin Williams. Page 313.

WILLIAMS, Thomas of Nottoway Parish. Leg.- son Thomas; son
Chaplin; son Benjamin; Rebecca the wife of Nathan Williams,
deceased; grandson Thomas the son of Nathan Williams; son
Joseph; daughter Elizabeth Jones; daughter Anne Pitman;
daughter Mary Baisden; to Francis Gregory; grandson Bly
Williams; rest of estate to my eight children with Patience
Gregory decd. expected. D. Oct. 6, 1758. R. Nov. 8, 1759.
Exs., son William Williams, Chaplin Williams Sr. and Chaplin
Williams, Jr. Wit. James Basden Jr., Richard Maning,
William Dunn. Page 314.

WHITEHEAD, Lewis. Leg.- wife Mary the land granted deceased
father Arthur Whitehead in 1743; daughter Isabel the land which
I had of Daniel Oquin; daughter Mary; daughter Elizabeth;
daughter Patty; son John; son --------. Exs., wife and friend
Nicholas Maget. D. June 19, 1759. R. Nov. 8, 1759. Wit.
Simon Everett, Charles Traverse, Joseph Curl; Jesse Brown.
Page 316.

DAVIS, Gideon. Estate appraised by Edward Harris, Edward
Lundy and Robert Lundy. D. July 14, 1757. R. Dec. 13, 1759.
Page 317.

BOOTH, Robert. Leg.- son Arthur land bought of Robert Barham; son
Robert; grandson John Booth; grandson James Booth; grandson
Beverley Booth; son Shelly the land I bought of John Drew; son
Moses; daughter Faith; daughter Sary; granddaughters Sarah
and Patience Booth. Ex., son Moses Booth. D. Oct. 6, 1757.
R. Jan. 10, 1760. Wit. Mary Hase, Barnaby Bailey. Page 318.

MASON, Isaac. Estate appraised by William Simmons, Benjamin
Clifton and Arthur Joyner. R. Jan. 10, 1760. Page 320.

BOOTH, Robert. Inventory signed by Moses Booth. R. March 13,
1760. Page 323.

SOUTHWORTH, Thomas. Account estate audited by Edward Harris
and Henry Holt. R. March 13, 1760. Signed, John Southworth.
Page 323.

LOVE, Elias. Leg.- friend Samuel Slade; son Henry; son Silas;
wife Eleanor; son Thomas; son Elias; daughter Betty Campbell.
Exs., Benjamin Denson and Samuel Slade. D. Nov. 17, 1759.
R. April 14, 1760. Wit. John Denson, John Forgueson, Eleanor
Power. Page 325.

WILLIAMS, Capt. Thomas. Estate appraised by John Boykin, Simon
Stevenson and John Summerell. R. April 10, 1760. Page 326.

POWELL, Joseph. Inventory signed by Elizabeth Powell. R. April
10, 1760. Page 329.

BLUNT, Henry. Inventory signed by Thomas Blunt. R. April 8,
1760. Page 330.

SANDIFUR, William. Estate signed by William Hasty and his wife,
the Extx. of said deceased. Audited by J. Gray, Charles Cosby
and R. Kello. R. May 8, 1760. Page 330.

BARHAM, Robert. Leg.- son Charles; son Robert; son Johnson;
daughter Martha; son Thomas; son Benjamin; daughter Elizabeth;
daughter Mary; daughter Sarah. Exs., son Charles and daughter
Elizabeth Barham. D. Jan. 18, 1748. R. Aug. 14, 1760. Wit.
Henry Hart, Benjamin Bailey. Page 331.

POPE, Henry. Account estate signed by Hodges Council and
Richard Pope. Audited by William Haynes, Joseph Denson and
Benjamin Denson. R. Aug. 14, 1760. Page 332.

LEWIS, Joshua. Leg.- loving wife; daughter Joanna; daughter
Catherine; daughter Sarah; daughter Martha; daughter Mille;
son James; son Edmond. Exs., wife and son James Lewis. Wit.
Charles Travers, Joseph Holden, Thomas Westbrook Jr. D.
April 9, 1757. R. Page 334.

JONES, John. Account estate signed by Eleanor Jones. Audited
by John Person, John Wilkinson and Henry Crafford. R. May 8,
1760. Page 334.

BRITTAIN, John. Estate appraised by Charles Cosby, Edward
Boyle and Sampson Pitman. Signed Benjamin Bradshaw. R.
May 8, 1760. Page 335.

WHITEHEAD, Lewis. Estate appraised by Simon Pope, Thomas
Crenshaw and Nathan Vasser. R. May 8, 1760. Page 336.

DRAKE, Richard. Estate appraised by Nicholas Williams,
Benjamin Williams and Thomas Blunt. R. May 8, 1760. Page 338.

MACY, Jane. Estate appraised by Charles Simmons, William
Andrews, Benjamin Clements Jr. R. June 12, 1760. Page 341.

CHARLES, Rebecca. Leg.- son Mathew Charles; son Thomas Marks.
Exs. sons Mathew Charles and Thomas Marks. D. Sept. 20, 1755.
R. June 12, 1760. Wit. John Bowin, William Joyner. Page 341.

BITTLE, John. Leg.- daughter Lucy; daughter Mary Saul; wife
Sarah Bittle. Ex., brother William Bittle. D. June 26,
1760. R. July 10, 1760. Wit. Henry Vaughan, Joseph Delk,
Jr., William Bittle, Sr. Estate appraised by David Edmunds,
William Kirby and William Kinnebrew. R. Sept. 11, 1760.
Page 342.

FRANCIS, William. Estate appraised by Henry Vaughan, William
Kinnebrew and William Kirby. Signed by David Edmunds.
R. Sept. 11, 1760. Page 344.

CHITTY, Edward. Account estate, among items many to Ruth
Chitty. Audited by Joseph Cobb, Cordall Norfleet and John
Edwards. R. Sept. 11, 1760. Page 345.

POPE, Stephen. Leg.- Israel Joyner land adjoining his own land
and that of Arthur Pope; son Brittain; daughter Ann; daughter
Charity; wife Martha Pope. Exs., wife and neighbor Howell
Edmunds. D. June 24, 1760. R. Sept. 11, 1760. Wit. John
Pope, William Pope, Jesse Pope. Page 347.

WHITEHEAD, Arthur. Estate audited by Nicholas Maget and Joseph
Cobb. R. Oct. 10, 1760. Page 348.

LEWIS, Joshua. Estate appraised by Thomas Westbrook, Joshua
Fort and William Taylor. Signed Martha Lewis. R. Oct. 9,
1760. Page 349.

DUNKLEY, Catherine. Estate audited by Charles Cosby, Thomas
Williamson and John Clayton. R. Oct. 9, 1760. Page 350.

VASSER, Jacob. Estate audited by John Wilkinson, Thomas Gray
and Charles Cosby. Signed Robert Williams. R. Oct. 9, 1760.
Page 351.

BOWIN, John. Estate audited by R. Kello and Joseph Jones.
Signed John Bowin and William Bennett. R. March 20, 1760.
Page 353.

SIMON, Augustine of Isle of Wight County. Leg.- son John land
in Nansemond County, being part of a patent granted Thomas
Mason in 1666 and by him sold to Edward Thelwell; son Jacob;
wife Sarah; to daughters.   D. Jan. 25, 1745. Wit. William
Bynum, Simon Everett, Joseph Everett. Reaffirmation of will,
March 6, 1756. Wit. Richard Vick, Jr. William Simmons,
Benjamin Williams. R. Nov. 13, 1760. Page

HAZLEWOOD, Richard. Estate appraised by John Clayton, Mathew
Harris and William Boykin. R. Dec. 11, 1760. Page 356.

JOHNSON, Richard. Leg.- wife Patty; son Joseph; son James a
helpless cripple; son Richard; daughter Mary Davis; daughter
Charity; daughter Ann; daughter Penelopy; daughter Rebecca;
grandson Beal (?) Johnson. Ex. son Richard Johnson.
D. Sept. 30, 1760. R. Feb. 12, 1761. Wit. Richard Ricks,
Barneby Drake. Page 356.

BARHAM, Robert. Inventory signed by Charles Barham. R. Feb.
12, 1761. Page 357.

FOSTER, Elias. Estate appraised by Charles Barham, Solomon
Deloach and David Newsum. R. Feb. 12, 1761. Page 358.

DELK, Joseph. Leg.- wife Hannah; son John; son Jacob Delk.
Extx. wife Hannah Delk. D. Feb. 6, 1758. R. Feb. 12, 1761.
Wit. Nicholas Maget, Samuel Maget, Michael Rogers. Page 359.

STEPHENSON, Peter. Appraised by John Clayton, Joseph Lancaster,
Mathew Harris. R. Feb. 12, 1761. Page 360.

SIMON, Augustine. Estate appraised by John Edwards, John
Wilkinson and Benjamin Crocker. R. Feb. 12, 1761. Page 363.

DAVIS, John. Leg.- sister Martha; nephew Benjamin Whitehead;
sister Mary Whitehead; sister Judah D------ sister Alce
Bryant. Ex., friend Nicholas Maget. D. Jan. 16, 1761.
R. Feb. 12, 1761. Wit. Jacob Barnes, Lewis Davis, Edward
Barnes, Rachel Davis. Page 364.

DAVIS, Martha of the Parish of Nottoway. Leg.- sister Alse
Briant. Ex., friend William Briant. D. Jan. 16, 1761.
R. Feb. 12, 1761. Wit. Nicholas Maget, John Barnes, Jacob
Barnes. Page 365.

KIRBY, Moody. Leg.- wife Frances Kirby. Ex., wife Frances
Kirby. D. Feb. 9, 1757. R. April 9, 1761. Wit. William
Simmons, John Ingram, John Watkins. Page 366.

WILLIFORD, John. Leg.- wife Mary; son Nathan; son Thomas; son
William land bought from Lawrence Lancaster; grandson
Benjamin Williford; daughter Elizabeth Jones; daughter Mary
Boasman; daughter Lucy; daughter Mourning. Ex., sons Thomas
and William Williford. D. Nov. 15, 1760. R. April 9, 1761.
Wit. Samuel Bailey, Thomas Williford, John Stephenson, Lucy
Williford. Page 367.

WILLIAMS, Arthur. Leg.- daughter Priscilla Edwards; daughter
Mary Carrell the plantation on which John Artice lately lived;
daughter Ann; wife Anne; son William; son-in-law William

Edwards at death of his mother; Lila Lucas. Estate to be
divided by friends, Job Wright, James Fowler, John Bryant
and Bridgman Joyner. Exs., wife Anne and son William
Williams. D. Jan. 19, 1761. R. April 9, 1761. Wit. James
Jordan Scott, Job Wright, John Brantley. Page 368.

CLARKE, Peter. Estate appraised by John Clayton, John Harris
and Mathew Harris. R. April 9, 1761.

POPE, Stephen. Will refused by his wife Martha Pope. Estate
appraised by William Thomas, Henry Vaughan and John Underwood.
Signed R. Kello and Jonathan Godwin. R. May 14, 1761.
Page 372.

KIRBY, Richard of the Parish of Nottoway. Leg.- wife Judith;
son William; son John; son Richard; daughter Ann Porter with
reversion to her children; daughter Mercy West with reversion
to the children of John Porter; daughter Judith Bittle with
reversion to her children; at death of wife estate to be
divided between William Kirby, Moody Kirby, John Kirby and
Elizabeth Ingram. Exs., sons William and John Kirby.
D. June 9, 1761. R. May 14, 1761. Page 374.

WHITEHEAD, Lewis. Additional appraisal of estate by Thomas
Crenshaw, Simon Pope and Nathan Vasser. Page 376.

KIRBY, Moody. Estate appraised by Charles Simmons, Ambrose
Williams and William Andrews. R. June 11, 1761. Page 376.

CROCKER, Elisha. Leg.- sister Sarah; sister Mary; to Mary the
daughter Samuel Kindred. Ex., father Benjamin Crocker.
D. March 6, 1761. R. June 11, 1761. Wit. Samuel Barlow,
Jesse Jones, Thomas Edmunds. Page 377.

ARLINGTON, John of Nottoway Parish. Leg.- wife Ann; son Benjamin;
daughter Ann Holt; grandson Jesse Arrington; grandson John
the son of Benjamin Arrington. Ex., son Benjamin Arrington.
D. April 26, 1761. R. June 11, 1761. Wit. Charles Simmons,
John Simmons, Benjamin Simmons. Page 378.

CROCKER, Moses. Leg.- father Benjamin Crocker; sister Mary
Crocker. Exs., sister Mary and father Benjamin. D. April 2,
1761. R. June 11, 1761. Wit. John Wilkinson, Benjamin Bynum,
Lewcy Bynum. Page 379.

DAVIS, Martha. Estate appraised by Nathan Vasser, Simon Pope
and Thomas Crenshaw. Signed by William Bryant. R. June 11,
1761. Page 380.

NEWTON, William. Estate appraised by David Edmunds, Benjamin
Bynum and Joseph Everett. Ordered May 30, 1761. R. June 11,
1761. Page 382.

JOHNSON, Richard. Estate appraised by Benjamin Williams,
Benjamin Barnes and Stephen Johnson. R. June 11, 1761.
Page 384.

DELK, Joseph. Estate appraised by Robert Gilliam, Jacob
Barrett and Robert Lawrence. R. June 11, 1761. Page 385.

MATTHEWS, Edward. Sale. Signed Amos Harris. R. July 9, 1761.
Page 387.

ARRINGTON, John. Leg.- wife Ann; son Jesse (not eighteen); daughter Patience; daughter Elizabeth. Exs., wife and father John Arrington. D. April 5, 1761. R. July 9, 1761. Wit. John Croney (?), Arthur Arrington, Lucy Bennett. Page 388.

WESTBROOK, Samuel. Leg.- son James with reversion of bequest to grandson Jacob Westbrook; son William; daughter Ann; daughter Mary Turner; daughter Martha Lowe; daughter Mansfill Gray; daughter Mary Gray; granddaughter Martha Gray; son Samuel. Ex., son Samuel Westbrook. D. May 17, 1755. R. Aug. 13, 1761. Wit. Joshua Claud, Joshua Harris, Benjamin Rowell. Page 390.

WESTBROOK, John. Leg.- wife Honour; son Gray (not twenty one); son Thomas; son William; son Moses land bought of Thomas Day; son James; son Elias; son Burwell. Exs., wife and brother James Ramsey. D. April 7, 1761. R. Aug. 13, 1761. Wit. John Person, Joshua Claud, Richard Taylor, Jr. Page 391.

SIMMONS, Stephen. Estate audited by J. Gray and R. Kello. Signed by Moses Bennett and wife Lucy the Admtx. of said Stephen Simmons. R. Aug. 13, 1761. Page 393.

JARRELL, John. Account estate. Paid Richard Ricks for a proportional part of a decree against Jarrell's legatees. Audited by M. Edwards and Henry Taylor. R. Aug. 13, 1761. Page 395.

WESTBROOK, John. Estate appraised by David Edmunds, William Person and John Mundell. Signed by Honour Westbrook and James Ramsey. R. Sept. 10, 1761. Page 396.

ARRINGTON, John. Estate appraised by Charles Simmons, Ambrose Williams and John Brown. R. Sept. 10, 1761. Page 398.

DENSON, John. Leg.- wife; son Joseph; son Benjamin; daughter Mary Johnson; daughter Betty Porter; grandson Jethro, son of Benjamin Denson; son Hollowell Denson. Ex., son Benjamin Denson. D. Oct. 23, 1756. R. Sept. 10, 1761. Wit. Elias Love, Elenor Love, John Council, Thomas Dreaper. Page 400.

CHARLES, Rebecca. Inventory. R. Oct. 8, 1761. Page 401.

CROCKER, Benjamin. Estate appraised by Henry Crafford, John Edwards and John Wilkinson. R. Oct. 8, 1761. Page 402.

HICKMAN, William. Leg.- son Joseph; daughter Sarah; daughter Martha; daughter Elizabeth; daughter Tamer Washington; son John Hickman. Exs., friends Albridgton Jones and Jobe Wright. D. April 3, 1760. R. Oct. 8, 1761. Wit. Mathew Wills, William Pope, Thomas Lawrence, James Cooper. Page 404.

NORSWORTHY, Joseph. Estate appraised by Lewis ----, John Gardner and James Kitchen. R. Nov. 12, 1761. Ordered April 10, 1760. Page 406.

DENSON, John. Account estate audited by Charles Briggs and Robert Andrews. Signed by Joseph Denson and Benjamin Denson. R. Nov. 12, 1761. Page 407.

CROCKER, Elisha. Estate appraised by Jacob Barnes, John Fort and Daniel Barrow. R. Dec. 10, 1761. Page 407.

WASHINGTON, Arthur. Leg.- wife Sarah; son George; daughter
Sarah; daughter Mary; daughter Elizabeth wife of John Abraham;
granddaughter Martha Abraham; granddaughter Sarah Abraham.
Exs., wife Sarah and friend Joseph Nowsum. D. Oct. 22, 1758.
R. Dec. 10, 1761. Wit. A. Jones, H. Vaughan, Benjamin
Denson. Page 408.

TURNER, Simon. Leg.- son Simon land in Brunswick County; son
William land left me in will of Francis Exum and land in
Brunswick Co.; son Arthur and Thomas land in Johnson County,
N. C.; Turner Bynum the tract on which my daughter Jennett
Bynum lives and to her children, Mille, Turner, Benne and
Sugars Bynum; son John land in Brunswick Co.; daughter Milla
land in Northampton Co., N. C.; son Thomas bond owed me by
William Taylor of Johnson Co., N. C.; daughter Dorcas Person;
Lucy Person; Turner Person. Exs., John Person and son Simon
Turner. D. July 7, 1761. R. Dec. 10, 1762. Wit. Thomas
Clifton, John McLemore, Elizabeth McLemore, Mary Spence.
Page 410.

WILLIAMS, Arthur. Inventory, signed by Ann Williams and
William Williams. R. Jan. 14, 1762. Page 414.

KIRBY, Richard. Estate appraised by Charles Simmons, Benjamin
Clements and Ambrose Williams. R. Feb. 14, 1762. Page 415.

SCOTT, John. Account estate audited by John Person and David
Edmunds. John Mundell late Adm. R. Jan. 14, 1762. Page
417.

EDWARDS, Elizabeth of Nottoway Parish. Leg.- son Micah; son
Joseph; daughter Patty; son William; daughter Ann; daughter
Patience; son Benjamin; daughter Martha Edwards. Exs., sons
Thomas and William Edwards. D. Dec. 31, 1761. R. Jan. 14,
1762. Wit. George Gurley, Jr., Mary Gurley, Mary Peden.
Page 418.

NEWSUM, Nathan. Estate appraised by John Gilliam and James
Jones. R. March 11, 1762. Page 419.

GILLIAM, Walter. Estate appraised by John Gilliam, Thomas Holt
and Charles Barham. R. March 11, 1762. Page 422.

ARRINGTON, John. Estate appraised by Miles Cary, John Brown
and Ambrose Williams. R. March 11, 1762. Signed by
Benjamin Arrington. Page 424.

HICKMAN, William. Inventory, signed by A. Jones. R. March 11,
1762. Page 429.

EDMUNDS, Jeremiah. Leg.- daughter Sarah Fowler; daughter
Elizabeth Bryant; daughter Judith Channel; daughter Mary;
grandson Jonas Edmunds; son David land bought of Benjamin
Croker (Crocker ?). Ex., son David Edmunds. D. Feb. 25,
1762. R. March 11, 1762. Wit. John Wilkinson, M. Norton.
Page 430.

LOVE, Elias. Estate appraised by James Hitchings, Lewis Joyner
and Joseph Denson. R. March 11, 1762. Page 431.

MATTHEWS, John. Leg.- daughter Pherriby; daughter Abigail;
cousin William Kitching; wife Lydia Matthews. Ex., friend
Benjamin Bailey. D. Dec. 14, 1761. R. March 11, 1762. Wit.
Edmund Tyler, James Basden, John Summerell. Page 432.

BRYANT, Mary. Leg.- to Hardy Atkinson and Amy his wife. Ex., Hardy Atkinson. D. April 28, 1761. R. March 11, 1762. Wit. Howell Adkins, Mial Adkins. Page 433.

EVANS, Benjamin. Estate appraised by John Underwood, Henry Thomas and M. Edwards. R. March 11, 1762. Page 433.

LUMBLEY, Thomas. Leg.- daughter Elizabeth Taylor; daughter Rebecca Williams; daughter Sarah Bittle; daughter Lucy Williams; daughter Mary Cotis (?); son Thomas; son Jesse; wife Elizabeth; son Richard; unnamed child. D. Oct. 25, 1760. R. March 11, 1762. Wit. Henry Vaughan, Joseph Delk, Benjamin Saul. Page 435.

KITCHING, James. Leg.- son Joseph; son Benjamin the plantation called "Bryants"; to sons James and Mathew land when they become twenty; daughter Martha (?); daughter Lydia; daughter Mary; daughter Ann; son William; daughter Elizabeth; daughter Christian; daughter Patience; daughter Melicent; wife Elizabeth Kitching. Ex., James Jordan Scott. D. Jan. 17, 1762. R. March 11, 1762. Wit. Page 437.

EDWARDS, John. Leg.- son Jacob three-fourths of estate, one-fourth to Jesse Braswell. Ex., Thomas Edwards. D. R. March 11, 1762. Wit. William Edwards, Patience Edwards, Ann Newsum. Page 438.

GURLEY, Nicholas of the Parish of Nottoway. Leg.- son Benjamin; son Nicholas; son William; wife Ann Gurley. Exs., friends George Gurley, Jr. and Joseph Cobb. D. April 23, 1761. R. March 11, 1762. Wit. George Gurley Sr., Mary Gurley Jr., Thomas Edwards. Page 439.

POPE, Benjamin. Leg.- son Thomas the land John Mackmiles and I had an agreement about; wife Meley; daughter Meley; daughter Elizabeth; son Thomas; daughter Mary. Exs., father William Pope and wife Meley Pope. D. Oct. 21, 1751. R. March 11, 1762. Wit. Robert Vick, William Pope, Jesse Pope. Page 440.

BARNES, Edward. Leg.- son Jacob; son Joshua; son James; son Burwell; daughter Mary Barrett; daughter Priscilla; daughter Elizabeth; daughter Martha; wife Elizabeth. Ex., son Jacob Barnes. D. July 16, 1761. R. March 11, 1762. Wit. Epaphroditus Williams, Richard Kemp, Richard Vick. Page 441.

KIRBY, Moody. Account estate signed by Fanny Foster, Extx. R. March 11, 1762. Page 443.

SPEED, George. Estate appraised by William Cooper, Mathew Wills, William Grimmer. R. March 11, 1762. Page 444.

DENSON, John. Estate appraised by Samuel Slade and Lewis Joyner. R. March 11, 1762. Page 446.

JOYNER, Joseph. Leg.- son Joseph; son John land purchased of Mary Clother (?); daughter Margaret Whitney; daughter Mary Mackey; grandson Joseph Mackey; daughter Elizabeth; daughter Ann; daughter Amey Joyner. Exs., sons Joseph and John Joyner. D. Oct. 25, 1760. R. April 8, 1762. Wit. William Haynes, Giles Joyner, Charles Lawrence. Page 450.

WASHINGTON, Arthur. Estate appraised by William Cooper, Mathew Wills and William Greamer. R. March 11, 1762. Page 452.

VASSER, Benjamin of the Parish of Nottoway. Leg.- wife Dolly; unborn child; nephew William son of Joseph Vasser; nephew Joel son of Jacob Vasser; to Patience and Elizabeth the daughters of John Arrington. Ex., wife Dolly Vasser. D. Jan. 5, 1762. R. April 8, 1762. Wit. Samuel Blow, John Mitchell, Richard Kello. Page 455.

DAVIS, Nathaniel of the Parish of Nottoway. Leg.- son Etheldred; son Joel; wife Sarah; son Charles; son Edwin. Exs., wife Sarah and Thomas Davis. D. Feb. 1, 1762. R. April 8, 1762. Wit. Samuel Blow, Joseph Phillips, John Mitchell. Page 456.

WEST, Joseph. Leg.- daughter Ann Tharpe; wife Ann; son Josias; daughter Mary West. Exs., wife Ann and son Josias West. D. 7th of the 9th mo. R. April 8, 1762. Wit. Joseph Vick, Patience Vick, Jacob Vick, Richard Vick. Page 458.

POWELL, Joseph. Estate audited by John Clanton and John Poykin. R. April 8, 1762. Page 459.

THORP, John. Estate appraised by Charles Briggs, Thomas Davis and Benjamin Sebrell. R. April 8, 1762. Page 460.

EDMUNDS, Jeremiah. Estate appraised by Joseph Everett, Benjamin Bynum and Jacob Simons. R. April 8, 1762. Page 462.

WILLIFORD, John. Estate appraised by John Clayton, Thomas Atkinson and Joseph Lancaster. R. April 8, 1762. Page 463.

GURLEY, Benjamin. Estate appraised by John Drake, Nathan Vasser and Thomas Edwards. R. May 13, 1762. Page 465.

GURLEY, Nicholas. Estate appraised by John Drake, Nathan Vasser and Thomas Edwards. R. May 13, 1762. Page 467.

POPE, Stephen. Estate audited by David Edmunds and Henry Vaughan. Signed, Howell Edmunds, Ex. R. May 13, 1762. Page 468.

NEWTON, WILLIAM. Estate audited by John Wilkinson and Cordall Norfleet. R. May 13, 1762. Page 469.

BRYANT, Lewis. Leg.- son John; son William; son Lewis; wife Elizabeth Bryant. Ex., son John Bryant. D. Nov. 16, 1761. R. May 13, 1762. Wit. James Jordan Scott, Benjamin Beel, Jr., Benjamin Beel, Sr. Page 470.

MACKEY, Daniel of Nottoway Parish. Leg.- son William the plantation bought of Joseph and William Harris; daughter Ann; daughter Sally (not sixteen); wife Hope; son John; daughter Hope Joyner; daughter Diana Bradshaw; daughter Frances Armistead; my executors to acknowledge a deed to Joseph Bradshaw. Exs., Robert Carr and Charles Powers. D. Dec. 29, 1761. R. May 13, 1762. Wit. Hardy Pope, Simon Harris, Joseph Bradshaw. Page 471.

LUMBLEY, Thomas. Estate appraised by Newit Drew, Simon Turner and Henry Vaughan. R. May 13, 1762. Page 474.

DAVIS, Nathaniel. Estate appraised by Benjamin Ruffin, Benjamin Sebrell and James Atkins. R. May 13, 1762. Page 475.

EDWARDS, Elizabeth. Estate appraised by Henry Thomas, William Thomas and Benjamin Williams. R. May 13, 1762. Page 475.

25

EDWARDS, John. Estate appraised by James Story, George Gurley, Jr. and William Thomas. R. May 13, 1762. Page 478.

POPE, Richard. Appraisal recorded May 13, 1762. Page 479.

POPE, Benjamin. Appraisal recorded May 13, 1762. Page 481.

DAVIS, John. Estate appraised by Thomas Crenshaw, Simon Pope and Nathan Vasser. R. May 13, 1762. Page 482.

THARPE, Joseph. Leg.- wife Ann with reversion of estate to all my children. Exs., wife Ann and my father-in-law Joseph West. D. 10 of 12th mo. 1761. R. May 13, 1761. Wit. James Long, John Long. Page 484.

HOLLIMAN, Thomas. Leg.- wife Ann with reversion at her death to Arthur, Benjamin, Nathan and Jesse Holliman; to Lucy Holliman and Mary Clayton the daughters of my brother Josias John Holliman; John son of Howell Holliman; William son of William Holliman my brother. Exs., wife Ann and Nathan Holliman. D. Nov. 29, 1760. R. May 13, 1762. Wit. Charles Cosby, Averiller Cosby. Page 485.

BRADSHAW, Joseph. Leg.- son Arthur; son Joseph; son Thomas; daughter Mary; daughter Ann; daughter Martha; daughter Elizabeth; daughter Honour Bradshaw. D. Jan. 20, 1762. R. May 13, 1762. Page 486.

MORGAN, William of Nottoway Parish. My land to be sold by my friend Henry Ivey, Jr. and the proceeds of the sale to go to my wife and at her decease to all my children. Ex. Captain Timothy Thorpe. D. April 29, 1762. R. May 13, 1762. Wit. John Ivey, Francis Hilliard, William Morgan, Jr. Page 488.

EDWARDS, Benjamin. Leg.- to all my sisters and brothers; to mother; brother William; brother Thomas; brother John. Exs., brothers Thomas and John Edwards. D. George Gurley, Jr., Mary Gurley, Mary Peden. Page 489.

GURLEY, Benjamin. Account estate audited by Micajah Edwards and Joseph Cobb. R. May 13, 1762. Page 490.

EDWARDS, Benjamin. Estate appraised by George Gurley, Jr. Robert Newsum and Will Thomas. R. June 13, 1762. Page 491.

HOLLIMAN, Thomas. Estate appraised by Joseph Phillips, Arthur ----- and Benjamin Williamson. R. June 10, 1762. Page 491.

DOYLE, Edward. Leg.- son Hardy; son Edmund; wife Elizabeth; son Daniel; son William; son Josiah; son Jacob; son Carr; daughter Dorcas and her husband Hardy Burn; daughter Elizabeth. Exs., wife and son Hardy Doyle. D. Feb. 22, 1762. R. June 10, 1762. Wit. Sampson Pitman, Charles Cosby. Page 494.

NORTON, Joseph, Jr. Leg.- sister Sarah Norton. D. Feb. 9, 1762. R. June 10, 1762. Wit. Benjamin Bynum, Ann Faircloth. Page 496.

DUNN, William. Estate appraised by Charles Cosby; Moses Phillips and Benjamin Warren. Ordered Jan. 14, 1762. R. June 10, 1762. Page 496.

DOYLE, Edmund. Estate appraised by Charles Cosby, Edmund Taylor and Samuel Pitman. Signed Lydda Doyle, Adm. R. June 10, 1762. Page 498.

MACKEY, John. Estate appraised by Henry Joyner, Christopher Wade and Mathew Charles. R. Aug. 12, 1762. Page 499.

JOYNER, Joseph, Jr. Estate appraised by Henry Joyner, Christopher Wade and Mathew Charles. R. Aug. 12, 1762. Page 500.

NORTON, Joseph. Estate appraised by Benjamin Bynum, Joseph Everett and Benjamin Faircloth. R. Aug. 12, 1762. Page 501.

JOYNER, Joseph, Sr. Estate appraised by Henry Joyner, Christopher Wade and Mathew Charles. R. Aug. 12, 1762. Page 503.

JOYNER, Henrietta. Leg.- son Arthur; daughter Martha; daughter Mary Tines; daughter Prudence Long; son Henry. Ex., son Henry Joyner. D. Nov. 1, 1750. R. Aug. 12, 1762. Wit. John Joyner, Bridget Lewis. Page 504.

WEST, Josiah. Appraised by Nathan Vasser, Thomas Crenshaw and Jesse Drake. R. Aug. 12, 1762. Page 505.

WEST, Joseph. Estate appraised by Nathan Vasser, Jesse Drake and John Drake. R. Aug. 12, 1762. Page 506.

THARPE, Joseph. Estate appraised by Jesse Drake, John Drake and Nathan Vasser. R. Aug. 12, 1762. Page 508.

MATTHEWS, John. Estate appraised by Kinchen Taylor, Aaron Phillips and John Summerell. R. Agu. 12, 1762. Page 509.

DOYLE, Edward. Estate appraised by Charles Cosby, Moses Phillips and Edmund Taylor. R. Aug. 12, 1762. Page 511.

WRIGHT, James. Leg.- wife Martha; son John (under age); daughter Mary Wright. Extx., wife Martha Wright. D. Dec. 25, 1761. R. Aug. 12, 1762. Wit. Simon Woodward, Elizabeth Gurley, Mary Woodward. Page 512.

BRYANT, Lewis, Jr. Inventory, signed John Bryant, Ex. R. Aug. 12, 1762. Page 512.

MATTHEWS, Edward. Account signed Amos Harris, Adm. R. Aug. 12, 1762. Page 513.

COOPER, William. Leg.- son James; son Benjamin; wife; son Demsey; son John; son Jesse. Extx., wife Mary Cooper. D. March 9, 1762. R. Aug. 12, 1762. Wit. John Hatfield, Mathew Wills, Francis Wills. Page 515.

NEWSUM, Benjamin. Estate appraised by Henry Westbrook, Jacob Newsum and John Watkins. R. Agu. 12, 1762. Page 515.

DAVIS, Gideon. Estate audited by William Thweatt and William Blunt. Signed, George Eppes, Adm. R. Aug. 12, 1762. Page 519.

HOLT, Joseph. Fstate appraised by Elias Fort, William Kinnebrew and Robert Bittle. R. Aug. 12, 1762. Page 520.

BRYANT, Mary. Estate appraised by Henry Vaughan, John Powell and Samuel Kindred. R. Sept. 9, 1762. Page 521.

BOWEN, John. Leg.- son Jonathan; daughter Bethia Vasser; son Benjamin; daughter Martha; daughter Mary; daughter Rebecca; son Arthur. Extx., wife Mary Bowen. D. Jan. 19, 1762. R. Sept. 9, 1762. Wit. Joseph Bradshaw, Benjamin Bradshaw, Daniel Doyle. Page 522.

BRADSHAW, Joseph. Estate appraised by William Bennett, Benjamin Bradshaw and Daniel Doyle. R. Sept. 9, 1762. Page 523.

COUNCIL, Hodges, Jr. Estate appraised by Samuel Slade, Giles Joyner and William Joyner. R. Sept. 9, 1762. Page 525.

WRIGHT, James. Estate appraised by Robert Carr, Thomas Jones and William Joyner. Signed, Martha Wright. R. Sept. 9, 1762. Page 526.

JOYNER, John. Leg.- wife Bridget Joyner. Extx., wife Bridget Joyner. D. Oct. 13, 1757. R. Sept. 9, 1762. Wit. William Haynes, William Rowe, Martha Rowe. Page 527.

JOYNER, Henrietta. Inventory, signed Henry Joyner. R. Dec. 9, 1762. Page 528.

COOPER, William. Estate appraised by Nathan Vasser, Thomas Lawrence and Joseph Hickman. R. Dec. 9, 1762. Page 528.

DRAKE, Timothy. Estate appraised by Thomas Oberry, John Beal and John Joyner. R. Nov. 11, 1762. Page 532.

DAUGHTRY, Robert. Estate appraised by Joseph Cobb, James Story and John Willson. R. Nov. 11, 1762. Page 534.

SOUTHAMPTON COUNTY

WILL BOOK II

SUMMERELL, Gwin. Inventory. R. Sept. 9, 1762. Page 1.

BARROW, Thomas. Leg.- wife Elizabeth; grandson Thomas the son of Simon Barrow; estate to my seven children, son John; son Thomas' part to his children; son Simon; daughter Elizabeth's part to her children; daughter Jane; daughter Sarah; daughter Fortune. Exs., Richard Avery, Joseph Phillips and wife Elizabeth. D. Nov. 26, 1761. R. Oct. 14, 1763. Wit. David Edmunds, Thomas Day, Howell Edmunds. Page 2.

WHITNEY, Joshua of Nottoway Parish. Leg.- son Joshua land adjoining George Lawrence, Charles Lawrence, Elisha Ballard and Bennett Hilsman; son Elisha land bought in Isle of Wight of George Brewer and land in Southampton adjoining Giles Joyner; son Giles; wife Margery; daughter Amy Whitney. Executors to acknowledge deed in Isle of Wight to Thomas Lankford for land adjoining John Lankford and William Bulls. Ex. wife Margery and friend John Joyner. D. May 18, 1762. R. Oct. 14, 1762. Wit. Charles Lawrence, Joshua Miniard, Mary Bland. Page 3.

BARNES, Joshua. Leg.- wife Lucy; son Brittain; daughter Edee; daughter Chastity; son Burwell; son Buxton; son Bailey; daughter Sally; son Benjamin; daughter Phereby. Exs., son Brittain and cousin Benjamin Barnes. D. Aug. 12, 1762. R. Oct. 14, 1762. Wit. Job. Wright, Sarah Oberry, James Jordan Scott. Page 3.

KITCHING, James. Estate appraised by William Worrell, John Johnson and William Bryant. R. Oct. 14, 1762. Page 6.

CROCKER, Elisha. Account estate. Paid a legacy left Mary Kindred. Signed, Sarah Crocker. Audited by John Wilkinson and Cordall Norfleet. R. Nov. 11, 1762. Page 7.

BOWEN, John. Estate appraised by Richard Worrell, William Joyner and Thomas Marks. R. Nov. 11, 1762. Page 9.

EVANS, Benjamin. Account estate signed, Hannah Evans. Audited by William Taylor and Micajah Edwards. R. Nov. 11, 1762. Page 10.

JOYNER, John. Inventory signed by Bridget Joyner. R. Nov. 11, 1762. Page 11.

CROCKER, Benjamin. Account estate signed, Sarah Crocker. Audited by John Wilkinson and Cordall Norfleet. R. Nov. 11, 1762. Page 11.

NEWSUM, Priscilla. Account Estate, Benjamin Lewis and Gregory Rawlings Adms. Examined by Miles Cary, Henry Taylor and Benjamin Simmons. R. Jan. 13, 1763. Page 12.

WASHINGTON, William. Leg.- sister Mary Hart; niece Elizabeth Hart; cousin Robert Hart, Jr.; cousin John Washington; cousin Joseph son of George Washington; wife Sarah Washington. Ex. cousin, Joseph Washington. D. Dec. 30, 1762. R. Jan. 13,

1763. Wit. J. Gray, Aaron Phillips, Jesse Browne. Page 14.

EDWARDS, Elizabeth. Account estate examined by Henry Thomas, Micajah Edwards and William Thomas. R. Jan. 14, 1763. Page 15.

EDWARDS, John. Account estate audited by Micajah Edwards, Henry Thomas and William Thomas. R. Jan. 14, 1763. Page 16.

NEWSUM, Nathan. Account estate audited by Miles Cary, Henry Taylor and Benjamin Simmons. R. Jan. 13, 1763. Page 17.

NORMAN, William of Nottoway Parish. Whole estate to friend Joshua Whitney, my children having proven to be undutiful and disobedient. Ex., Joshua Whitney. D. Dec. 11, 1761. R. Jan. 13, 1763. Wit. Lewis Joyner, George Lawrence, Charles Lawrence. Page 18.

JOHNSON, Richard, Sr. Account estate audited by Benjamin Williams and James Jordan Scott. Signed, Richard Johnson. R. March 10, 1763. Page 20.

BARROW, Thomas. Estate appraised. R. March 10, 1763. Page 20.

BARNES, Joshua. Estate appraised by Benjamin Williams, Thomas Oberry and Barnaby Drake. R. March 10, 1763. Page 24.

FOSTER, Elias. Account estate audited by James Ridley and James Jones. R. March 10, 1763. Page 25.

NORTON, Joseph. Estate appraised by Benjamin Bynum, Jacob Simons and John Wilkinson. Signed Nicholas Magett. R. March 10, 1763. Page 26.

DAUGHTRY, Robert. Account estate audited by Joseph Cobb and George Gurley, Jr. R. March 10, 1763. Page 27.

WASHINGTON, William. Sarah Washington renunciated will and demanded what the law provided for her. Wit. Jesse Browne, George Branch. D. Jan. 15, 1763. R. March 10, 1763. Page 27.

DUNN, William. Paid, James Basden, Hugh Basden and Martha Williamson. Audited by Edmund Tylaer and Charles Cosby. Signed, John Summerell. R. March 10, 1763. Page 28.

KIRBY, Richard. Account estate audited by H. Edmunds and Henry Vaughan. R. May 12, 1763. Page 29.

HARRIS, Jacob. Leg.- wife Mary; son James; son Drury Harris. Exs., Mary Harris and Amos Harris. D. Oct. 11, 1762. R. March 10, 1763. Page 29.

CALTHORPE, Charles of the Parish of Nottoway. Leg.- son Edward land bought of William Deloach and Leonard Oney; son Anthony; son James Butts Calthorpe land bought from Benjamin Clifton; daughter Mary Bayley; daughter Frances Jones; unborn child my land in Charles Parish, York County, Va., reversion if a daughter to son Edward; daughter Sarah; daughter Elizabeth; daughter Martha; daughter Anne; wife. Exs., sons-in-law John Bayley and Jesse Jones. D. Nov. 8, 1756. R. April 14, 1763. Wit. J. Gray, Michael Cobb. Edmund Tyler qualified as executor the named Exs. and the widow Sarah Calthorpe having refused. Page 30.

HARRIS, Jacob. Estate appraised by Henry Mounger, James Lundy and John Britt. R. May 12, 1763. Page 32.

WHITNEY, Joshua. Estate appraised by William Joyner, Giles Joyner and Christopher Wade. R. May 12, 1763. Page 34.

POPE, William. Leg.- daughter Priscills; son John; son William; daughter Sarah Bracey; daughter Anne Cobb; daughter Mary Westray; John Lewis. Ex., son John Pope. D. May 10, 1758. R. May 12, 1763. Wit. James Jordan Scott, Abigail Scott. Page 36.

BEELE, Thomas. Inventory, signed by Martha Beele. R. Aug. 11, 1763. Page 37.

PITMAN, Arthur. Estate audited by John Wilkinson and Benjamin Bynum. Signed, John Edwards. R. May 12, 1763. Page 38.

BEEL, Thomas. Leg.- wife Martha; son Richard land adjoining Richard Kello; daughter Mary. Friends, Richard Beel, Jr., John Bryant, Bridgman Joyner and James Jordan Scott to divide my estate. Exs., wife Martha and cousin Richard Beel. D. John Beel, Richard Beel, Jr., James Jordan Scott. Page 39.

WASHINGTON, William. Estate appraised by George Branch, Edmund Tyler and Joseph Phillips. Signed by Joseph Washington. R. July 14, 1763. Page 40.

POPE, William. Estate appraised by Bridgman Joyner, Richard Beal and John Beal. Signed, John Pope. R. June 14, 1763. Page 42.

MACKIE, Daniel. Estate appraised by William Bennett, Mathew Charles and Hardy Pope. R. July 14, 1763. Page 43.

EXUM, William. Estate appraised by Samuel Pitman, Joseph Mounger and Moses Phillips. R. Aug. 11, 1763. Page 44.

BARNES, Edward. Estate appraised by Henry Turner, Epaphroditus Williams and Robert Lawrence. R. Aug. 11, 1763. Signed, Jacob Barnes. Page 45.

THWEATT, William of St. Lukes Parish. Leg.- wife; land in Prince George, Southampton and Halifax Counties; daughter Rebecca; nephew Jacob son of Joseph Godwin; nephews James and Peterson sons of James Thweatt, decd.; land in Brunswick to Nathaniel Parham. Exs., wife and Nathaniel Parham. D. March 16, 1763. R. Aug. 11, 1763. Wit. John   , Thomas   , James Day Ridley. Will presented by Jean Thweatt. Page 47.

VASSER, Benjamin. Estate appraised by Daniel Pond, Robert Andrews and John Cobb. R. Aug. 11, 1763. Page 50.

DUNN, William, Jr. Estate appraised by George Branch, William Deloach and Moses Phillips. R. Sept. 8, 1763. Page 52.

ROBINS, James Francis. Estate appraised by George Branch, William Deloach and Moses Phillips. R. Sept. 8, 1763. Page 52.

GURLEY, Nicholas. Account estate audited by Henry Thomas and M. Edwards. Signed Nicholas Gurley, Jr. R. Sept. 8, 1763. Page 53.

JOHNSON, Jacob. Leg.- wife Mary; son Demsey land adjoining
Robert Tyler, Francis Denson and Samuel Eley; son Josiah;
daughter Miriam; daughter Penina Johnson. Extx., wife Mary
Johnson. D. Aug. 8, 1761. R. Sept. 8, 1763. Wit. James
Jordan Scott, James Kitching, Tooke Denson. Page 54.

WOOD, Benjamin. Estate appraised by Benjamin Oney, Benjamin
Exum and Richard Pond. Ordered Jan. 29, 1763. R. Oct. 13,
1763. Page 55.

WASHINGTON, George. Leg.- son George land adjoining Richard
Johnston and James Jordan Scott; son Joseph. Exs., sons
George and Joseph Washington. D. Sept. 11, 1763. R. Oct. 13,
1763. Wit. James Jordan Scott, John Beal, Joshua Beal.
Page 56.

CARR, Robert of Nottoway Parish. Leg.- eldest son Robert; son
John; daughter Ann Jones; daughter Elizabeth Johnson; daughter
Rebecca; daughter Grace; eldest daughter Martha Revil; wife
Sarah Carr. D. June 19, 1763. R. Oct. 13, 1763. Exs., sons
Robert and John Carr. Wit. Arthur Smith, Virgus Smith, David
Johnson, George. Page 58.

THORPE, Timothy of Parish of St. Luke. Leg.- wife Martha land
to be laid off by James Jones and Henry Taylor; son Peterson
the land on which Jesse Newsom is now overseer; son Timothy
my plantation on which William Drury is now overseer; daughter
Betty Atherton; daughter Mary Person; daughter Patty; daughter
Lucy Simmons; daughter Temperance; daughter Silva; granddaughter
Martha Jarrell. Exs., son Peterson Thorpe and son-in-law
William Person. D. Sept. 3, 1763. R. Oct. 13, 1763. Wit.
James Ridley, James Jones, Henry Taylor, James Day Ridley.
Page 59.

HOWELL, William. Leg.- John son of William Bailey land adjoining
Barnaby Bailey. Ex., John Bailey. D. Oct. 7, 1760. R. Oct.
13, 1763. Wit. Charles Calthorpe, Michael Cobb, John Phillips,
Jr. Page 62.

WESTBROOKE, John. Estate appraised by William Person, David
Edmunds and John Mundell. R. Oct. 13, 1763. Page 63.

GRAY, Thomas. Estate appraised by Thomas Chappell, D. Fisher
and William Simmons. R. Nov. 10, 1763. Page 64.

SUMMERELL, Gwin. Estate account audited by Charles Cosby and
R. Kello. Signed, John Summerell, Adm. R. Dec. 8, 1763.
Page 66.

COBB, Michael of Nottoway Parish. Leg.- wife Sarah; daughter
Anne; Godson William Stephenson. Exs., wife, John Bailey and
Simon Stephenson. D. March 24, 1763. R. Dec. 8, 1763. Wit.
Kinchen Taylor, Ridley Taylor, Aaron Phillips. Page 67.

COBB, Michael. Estate appraised by Joseph Phillips, Barnaby
Bailey, Jr., Barnaby Bailey, Sr. R. Jan. 12, 1764. Page 69.

KITCHEN, James. Estate appraised by Job Wright, John Brantley
and Thomas Brantley. Signed, A. Jones, Adm. R. Jan. 12, 1764.
Page 70.

JOHNSON, Jacob. Estate appraised by Henry Joyner, John Johnson
and William Denson. R. Jan. 12, 1764. Page 71.

WASHINGTON, Arthur. Estate account audited by John Blow, George Gurley, Jr. and William Thomas. R. Jan. 12, 1764. Page 73.

HOWELL, William. Estate appraised by Robert Booth, Arthur Booth and Moses Booth. R. Feb. 9, 1764. Page 75.

CALTHORPE, Charles. Estate appraised by Barnaby Bailey, Joseph Phillips and William Deloach. R. Feb. 9, 1764. Page 76.

JOHNSON, Stephen. Leg.- wife Anne; son Mathew; son Henry land bought of John Oney; daughter Rebecca. Ex., friend James Jordan Scott. D. Jan. 23, 1764. R. March 8, 1764. Wit. James Jordan Scott, Anne Johnson. Page 78.

NORMAN, William. Estate appraised by William Denson, Christopher Wade and Henry Joyner. R. April 12, 1764. Page 80.

BYNUM, William. Estate appraised by John Edwards, Joseph Everett and Jacob Simons. Ordered Dec. 9, 1762. R. April 12, 1764. Page 81.

SIMMONS, John. Estate account audited by Charles Briggs and Thomas Williamson. Signed, William Simmons, Adm. R. April 12, 1764. Page 82.

JOHNSON, Stephen. Estate appraised by Job Wright and John Beal. Signed, Anne Johnson. R. June 14, 1764. Page 83.

WASHINGTON, William. Account estate audited by Charles Cosby, Edmund Tyler and Aaron Phillips. Signed, Joseph Washington. R. July 12, 1764. Page 86.

CARR, Robert. Estate appraised by Thomas Jones, Robert Johnson and Hardy Pope. Signed, Robert and John Carr. R. July 12, 1764. Page 87.

MACKIE, Daniel. Estate account audited by Charles Cosby, Mathew Jones and Edmund Tyler. Signed, Charles Powers. R. July 12, 1764. Page 89.

THORPE, Joseph. Account estate audited by Joseph Cobb and Jesse Clark. Paid John Forgason and wife Ann for acting as executors. R. July 12, 1764. Page 90.

WESTBROOK, John. Account estate audited by Joshua Claud, David Edmunds and Will Person. Among items, paid Demsey Westbrook's guardian for his part of Jesse Westbrook's estate. Signed, James Ramsey and Honour Westbrook. R. July 12, 1764. Page 91.

WASHINGTON, George. Estate appraised by Benjamin Williams, Job Wright and John Beal. R. July 12, 1764. Page 92.

LITTLE, John of St. Luke Parish. Leg.- wife Lucy land to be laid off as I have instructed John Blunt, Baker White and William Person; son William land bought of John Inman, Jr.; son John Little. Friends William Person, William Blunt and Absalom Smith to divide my negroes when son William becomes twenty one. Exs., wife Lucy and friend William Person. D. June 24, 1764. R. Aug. 9, 1764. Wit. Jacob Barnes, Edward Windham, Robert Bittle. Page 94.

ARRINGTON, John. Account estate audited by Edwin Gray, Behjamin Ruffin, Jr. and John Simmons. R. Aug. 9, 1764. Signed Benjamin Arrington, Ex. Page 94.

BARNES, Joshua. Account estate audited by Richard Ricks and James Jordan Scott. R. Aug. 9, 1764. Signed Benjamin Barnes and Britten Barnes. Page 96.

IVY, Joseph. Estate appraised by Joshua Thorpe, Henry Applewhite and John Ivey, Sr. R. Sept. 13, 1764. Page 97.

TURNER, William. Estate appraised by Henry Harrison, William Harrison and John Maclemore. R. Sept. 13, 1764. Page 99.

HOWELL, William. Account estate audited by Edwin Gray, John Hay and John Simmons. R. Sept. 13, 1764. Signed, John Bailey Ex. Page 99.

WEST, Josiah. Account estate audited by Jesse Drake, Nathan Vasser and John Drake. R. Sept. 13, 1764. Page 100.

COLLIAR, George of Nottoway Parish. Leg.- wife Jane; daughter Rebeccah; daughter Ann; daughter Sarah; Godson George Lankford son of sister Mary Lankford with reversion of bequest to his brother Thomas Lankford; brother-in-law Thomas Lankford. Extx., wife Jane Colliar. D. July 6, 1757. R. Sept. 13, 1764. Wit. Hardy Lawrence, George Lawrence, Thomas Lankford Jr. Page 100.

BITTLE, William. Leg.- wife Elizabeth; son William; son Drewry; son Robert; daughter Lucy Little; daughter Sarah Barnes. Exs., son William and Jacob Barnes. D. Aug. 12, 1764. R. Sept. 13, 1764. Wit. Henry Vaughan, John Powell, Joseph Delk. Page 102.

RICKS, Robert. Leg.- wife Mary; son Richard; son Joseph; son Thomas; son Robert; daughter Mary; daughter Millicent; daughter Anne Ricks. Exs., wife Mary and son Thomas Ricks. D. 25th day of 7 mo. R. Oct. 12, 1764. Wit. Henry Thomas, Martha Thomas, Richard Ricks, Ann Ricks. Page 103.

POPE, Richard. Account estate audited by William Haynes, Henry Joyner and John Joyner. R. Oct. 11, 1764. Signed Hardy Pope, Adm. Page 105.

WASHINGTON, George. Account estate audited by Benjamin Williams, A. Jones and James Jordan Scott. Signed George Washington. R. Dec. 13, 1764. Page 107.

HARRIS, John. Leg.- son Drew; son Nathan; son John; wife; son Newit; son Thomas; daughter Ann; daughter Martha. Exs., son Nathan and Edward Drew. D. March 21, 1764. R. Dec. 13, 1764. Wit. Simon Harris, Jesse Jones. Page 108.

POPE, William? Sr. Account estate-legacies paid the following, John Pope, William Pope, Francis Bracey, Henry Cobb, William Westray and John Lewis. Audited by A. Jones, James Jordan Scott and Job Wright. Signed, John Pope, Ex. R. Jan 10, 1765. Page 109.

HARRIS, John. Estate appraised by Cordall Norfleet, Henry Crafford and Arthur Long. R. Jan. 10, 1765. Page 110.

BROWNE, Thomas. Leg.- daughter Mourning; daughter Holland; son Jesse; daughter Sarah Mial if she dies without heirs by her husband Thomas Mial reversion to her daughters Tabitha and Martha Exum; daughter Martha Allen; daughter Mary Allen. Exs., son Jesse and James Allen. D. Nov. 28, 1764. R. Jan. 11, 1765. Wit. Thomas Stephenson, Simon Stephenson, Arthur Allen. Page 112.

WORRELL, William. Leg.- son Richard; son Benjamin; son Nathan; daughter Celah Council; son William; daughter Elizabeth; son John; wife Ann Worrell. Exs., wife Ann and friend John Johnson. D. March 14, 1762. R. Jan. 10, 1765. Wit. Joseph Bradshaw, Daniel Doyle, William Doyle. Page 113.

BASS, James. Account estate audited by Nicholas Maget and James Jones. Signed, William Blunt. R. Feb. 14, 1765. Page 115.

CALTHORPE, Charles. Account estate audited by Thomas Williamson and Charles Cosby. Signed, Edmund Tyler. R. Feb. 14, 1765. Page 115.

WOOD, Benjamin. Account estate audited by John Simmons and James Jordan Scott. Signed, Hannah Wood. R. Feb. 14, 1765. Page 117.

COUNCIL, Hodges, Jr. Account estate audited by Joseph Denson, Benjamin Denson and John Johnson. Signed, Sarah Council, Admtx. R. March 14, 1765. Page 118.

WORRELL, William. Estate appraised by William Joyner, Thomas Marks and Benjamin Hasty. R. March 14, 1765. Page 119.

WASHINGTON, John. Account estate audited by J. Gray and R. Kello. Signed, Arthur Washington. R. March 14, 1765. Page 122.

COLLIER, George. Estate appraised by Robert Johnson, John Johnson and Giles Joyner. R. April 11, 1765. Page 123.

FORT, Arthur. Leg.- mother Rebecca Fort; sister Betty; Priscilla and Joshua the children of brother Joshua Fort; Rebecca, daughter of brother Henry Fort. Exs., brother Joshua Fort and Benjamin Simmons. D. Feb. 19, 1765. R. April 11, 1765. Wit. Benjamin Simmons, William Kellam, Amey Foster. Page 125.

GILLIAM, John of St. Luke Parish. Leg.- wife Lucy; son Jeremiah (under age); son Thomas Clemons (under age); daughter Judy when eighteen; daughter Mary when Sixteen. Exs., father Thomas Gilliam, friend Benjamin Clements, Jr. and wife Lucy Gilliam. D. Feb. 25, 1765. R. April 11, 1765. Wit. Samuel Peete, Ann Holt, Arthur Gilliam. Page 126.

BARROW, Thomas. Account estate audited by Will Person and James Jones. The following were paid the same amount from the estate: - John Barrow, Simon Barrow, Jean Barrow, Sarah Crocker; Joseph Phillips, William Kinnebrough guardian of Hosea, orphan of Thomas Barrow, Richard Avery and Elizabeth Barrow. Signed Richard Avery and Jos. Phillips. R. May 9, 1765. Page 128.

HOWELL, Edmund. Account estate audited by William Blunt, James Ridley and John Sturgeon. R. May 9, 1765. Signed, Burwell Atkinson and wife Olive, Admtx. Page 129.

LITTLE, John. Appraisal estate by William Blunt, John Sturgeon and Absalom. R. May 9, 1765. Page 129.

JOHNSON, Jesse. Estate appraised by John Beal, Richard Johnston and William Speed. R. June 13, 1765. Signed, Sarah Johnston. Page 130.

BARNES, Thomas. Estate appraised by James Best, William Williams, Job Wright and John Beal. R. June 13, 1765. Page 131.

NICHOLSON, Joshua of Nottoway Parish. Leg.- daughter Elizabeth Rivers; daughter Sarah Steward; daughter Fanny at twenty one; daughter Lucy Edmunds; wife Sarah; son Joshua Nicholson. Exs., wife Sarah and son Joshua Nicholson. Overseers, Col. Howell Edmunds and Major Richard Kello. D. Sept. 16, 1762. R. June 13, 1765. Wit. Elisha Milton, Miles Railey, Mary Railey. Page 132.

BITTLE, William. Estate appraised by Henry Vaughan, Will Kirby and William Kinnebrew. R. July 11, 1765. Page 133.

IVY, Joseph. Account estate audited by James Ridley, James Jones and Joshua Nicholson. R. June 11, 1765. Page 134.

BARNES, Thomas. Account estate audited by Mathew Wills, James Jordan Scott and Job Wright. Signed, John Beal, Adm. R. July 11, 1765. Page 135.

HOLLIMAN, Josiah John. Leg.- wife Ann; daughter Mary Clayton; daughter Lucy Andrews; daughter Sarah Moody; daughter Martha Hough. Exs., son-in-law John Clayton and Thomas Williamson. D. Oct. 3, 1763. R. March 14, 1765. Wit. William Urquhart, George Fearn, Mathew Fearn, Herbert Haynes. Page 136.

JOYNER, Joseph. Account estate audited by Edmund Tyler, Elias Herring and John Joyner. Signed, Hope Joyner. R. Aug. 8, 1765. Page 137.

BRITAIN. John. Account estate audited by R. Kello and Charles Cosby. Signed, Benjamin Bradshaw, Adm. R. Aug. 8, 1765. Page 138.

FORT, Arthur. Estate appraised by Benjamin Lewis, Benjamin Simmons and John Simmons. R. Aug. 9, 1765. Page 139.

TAYLOR, Katherine. Leg.- granddaughters Sarah and Olive Pope; son Edmund Taylor. Ex., son Edmund Taylor. D. March 9, 1765. R. Sept. 12, 1765. Wit. John Pitman, Joseph Pope. John Edwards qualified to serve as executor until Edmund Taylor became twenty one. Page 139.

KITCHEN, James. Account estate audited by Benjamin Bailey and John Simmons. Paid the following legatees: widow, Ann Kitchen, David Davis, Jesse Pinner and Trial Bailey. Signed, James Jordan Scott. R. Sept. 12, 1765. Page 140.

CARR, Robert. Account estate audited by Charles Cosby, Elias Herring and Edmund Tyler. R. Oct. 10, 1765. Signed, Robert Carr and John Carr. Page 142.

SAULS, John. Estate appraised by David Edmunds, Thomas Day and William Kirby. Ordered June 28, 1765. R. Oct. 10, 1765. Page 142.

BROWNE, Thomas. Estate appraised by Burwell Williamson, Benjamin Williamson and Arthur Williamson. R. Oct. 10, 1765. Page 143.

MANNING, Samuel. Account estate audited by R. Kello and Charles Cosby. Among items, - paid the Extx. for expense in traveling to Gloucester Count. R. Oct. 10, 1765. Signed William

Hatfield and wife Sarah, Extx. Page 145.

SCOTT, John. Account of estate with Henry Harrison's administrators. Audited by Will Person, William Blunt and David Edmunds. R. Oct. 10, 1765. Page 145.

ROSE, Richard of St. Luke Parish. Leg.- wife; son Burrell; daughter Mary Rose. Exs., son Burrell Rose and Amos Harris. D. July 5, 1765. R. Oct. 10, 1765. Wit. James Jones, Will Drury, Ralph Matthews. Probation granted James Jones. Page 146.

FRANCIS, Thomas. Leg.- son John; son Sterling (under age); son Frederick; son Benjamin Francis. Exs., wife Ann and son William Francis. D. Oct. 3, 1760. R. June 12, 1766. Wit. David Edmunds, Ann Edmunds. Page 148.

WARREN, John. Leg.- daughter Celia Womble; daughter Sarah Branch; daughter Elizabeth; son Benjamin Warren. Ex., son Benjamin Warren. D. Jan. 28, 1766. R. June 12, 1766. Wit. Ann Dunn, Charles Shield, Joseph Gray. Page 148.

JENKINS, Valentine of Nottoway Parish. Leg.- daughter Elizabeth Poynter; grandchildren Theophilus and Unity Poynter; grandson Valentine Owlet; son Edmund; grandsons Robert and Thomas Freeman; to daughter Lucy Freeman's son whose christian name I do not know; wife Jean Jenkins. Ex. son Edmund Jenkins. D. Aug. 18, 1764. R. June 12, 1766. Wit. James Bridger, Leighborn Lowe, Robert Williamson. Page 149.

NEWSOM, Joseph of St. Luke Parish. Leg.- wife Patience; daughter Patty; daughter Sally; son Benjamin; son Jacob; son Joel; daughter Ann; daughter Patience; son-in-law Thomas Jones. D. March 16, 1766. R. June 12, 1766. Exs., friends George Gurley, Jr., William Thomas and wife Patience Newsom. Wit. Robert Newson, Benjamin Williams, Etheldred Holt. Page 150.

TURNER, William, Sr. Leg.- wife Elizabeth; son John; son William; son Simon; son Benjamin; son Mathew; son Thomas; daughter Mary; daughter Ann; Jesse son of John Turner; Benjamin son of Simon Turner. Exs., son Benjamin and Benjamin the son of Simon Turner. D. Sept. 6, 1763. R. Aug. 14, 1766. Wit. John Barrow, John Barrow, Jr. Page 152.

VASSER, Benjamin. Account estate audited by Edwin Gray, Benjamin Ruffin and Benjamin Ruffin, Jr. Signed William Spivey and wife Dorothy, Extx. R. Aug. 14, 1766. Page 153.

NICHOLSON, Joshua. Inventory signed by Sarah and Joshua Nicholson. R. Aug. 14, 1766. Page 154.

TAYLOR, Patience. Widow of Etheldred Taylor. Leg.- son John; daughter Mary Peterson; son James; son Richard; daughter Elizabeth Cary; grandchildren, Anna Taylor, Elizabeth Cary, Ann Peterson, Sarah Taylor and Etheldred Taylor. Ex., son John Taylor. D. April 5, 1766. R. Aug. 14, 1766. Wit. Miles Cary, Charles Taylor. Page 155.

VICK, Richard. Account estate examined by R. Kello and D. Fisher. The same amount was paid to Alice, Jesse and Thomas Edwards. The widow Martha Vick was paid her part of the estate. Signed, Albridgton Jones, Ex. R. Aug 14, 1766. Page 156.

BENNET, John. Leg.- son John; son William; daughter Mary Ingles; daughter ------ Bradshaw; daughter Sarah Jones; daughter Elizabeth Council; wife Constance Bennet. Exs., wife and son John Bennet. D. R. Aug. 14, 1766. Wit. David Johnson, John Carr, Joseph Bradshaw. Page 158.

GILLIAM, John. Estate appraised by W. Andrews, Drewry Parker and Benjamin Simmons. R. Aug. 14, 1766. Page 159.

BROWNE, Thomas. Account estate audited by Thomas Williamson and Mathew Jones. R. Aug. 14, 1766. Page 161.

DAVIS, Nathaniel. Account estate examined by Charles Taylor and Benjamin Jarrell. R. Aug. 14, 1766. Signed, Thomas Davis and wife Sarah, Extx. Page 162.

COBB, Michael. Account estate audited by Mathew Jones and Joshua Nicholson. R. Aug. 14, 1766. Page 163.

GRAY, Thomas. Estate audited by Richard Kello and Daniel Fisher. R. Aug 14, 1766. Page 165.

HOLT, Jesse. Account estate audited by Benjamin Lewis and John Simmons. R. Aug. 14, 1766. Page 166.

BLOW, Samuel. Leg.- wife Martha; son Richard; daughter Elizabeth Briggs; daughter Martha; daughter Lucy; daughter Mary Blow. Exs., son Richard and son-in-law Charles Briggs. D. June 6, 1766. R. Sept. 1, 1766. Wit. Joseph Gray, Edwin Gray, John Cobb. Charles Briggs qualified, Richard Blow under age. Page 167.

WARREN, John. Inventory signed by Benjamin Warren. R. Sept. 11, 1766. Page 168.

COLLIER, George. Account estate audited by Thomas Lankford and Hardy Pope. R. Oct. 9, 1766. Page 169.

COUNCIL, Hodges. Account estate audited by Mathew Jones and James Jordan Scott. The following paid a proportional part of estate, - John Council, widow Sarah, Mathew Vick, Mial Brewer, James Council and John Brewer. Signed Benjamin Denson, Adm. R. Oct. 9, 1766. Page 169.

DENSON, John. Account estate audited by Mathew Jones and James Jordan Scott. The following were paid proportional part of the estate. - Joseph Denson, Mary Johnson, Benjamin Denson, John Porter, Hollowell Denson and Jethro Denson. Signed, Benjamin Denson. R. Oct. 9, 1766. Page 170.

THORPE, John. Account estate audited by Benjamin Ruffin, Jr. and Benjamin Jarrell. The following were paid the estate, Susannah Thorpe, Olive Thorpe and John Thorpe, the elder. Page 171.

WILLIAMS, George. Estate account audited by Benjamin Barnes, John Beal. Signed Benjamin Williams. R. Oct. 9, 1766. Page 172.

DAUGHTRY, James. Estate appraised by John Pope, James Gardiner and William Wester. R. Oct. 9, 1766. Signed, James Jordan Scott. Page 173.

COUNCIL, Hodges. Inventory signed by Benjamin Denson. R. Oct. 9, 1766. Page 174.

WORRELL, William. Account estate audited by Mathew Jones and Edmund Tyler. The following were paid legacies, Benjamin Worrell, William Worrell, John Council for wife, Dempsey Johnson for wife, Richard Worrell and Nathaniel Worrell. Signed, John Johnson. R. Oct. 9, 1766. Page 175.

WILLIAMS, Thomas of Nottoway Parish. Leg.- son Benjamin; son Jacob; daughter Sarah; daughter Prudence Rogers; son Thomas Williams. Ex., son Robert Williams. D. March 19, 1761. R. Nov. 13, 1766. Wit. John Blow, Jeremiah Ellis, John Johnson. Page 176.

FRANCIS, Thomas. Estate appraised by Henry Vaughan, David Edmunds and William Kirby. R. Nov. 13, 1766. Page 177.

POPE, Henry of Nottoway Parish. Leg.- son Arthur; son James; son Lazrus; daughter Martha Johnson; daughter Mary Barret; granddaughter Mary Barret; son Henry Pope. Ex., son Henry Pope. D. May 12, 1766. R. Nov. 13, 1766. Wit. Nathan Barnes, Sarah Griffing, Ann Vick. Page 178.

CARY, Miles. Attorney at law. Leg.- wife; son Miles land in Warwick County; land in Southampton County to son Nathaniel Cary. Exs., brother Richard Cary of Warwick County, Rev. Miles Selden of Henrico County, Benjamin Watkins of Chesterfield County and Henry Taylor of Southampton County. D. July 3, 1766. R. Dec. 11, 1766. Wit. Page 179.

GRAY, Benjamin. Leg.- wife Catherine; son James; son Richard; daughter Mary; son Jesse; son Benjamin. Exs., sons Benjamin and Jesse Gray. D. Dec. 28, 1764. R. Dec. 11, 1766. Wit. Thomas Pretlow, Thomas Newby, Mary Pretlow. Page 180.

WASHINGTON, John. Leg.- brother Jesse; sister Faith; sister Mary Washington. Ex., brother Jesse Washington. D. Oct. 10, 1757. R. Jan. 8, 1767. Wit. Benjamin Bailey, Joseph Phillips, Aaron Phillips. Page 181.

BATTLE, William. Estate account audited by Benjamin Simmons and John Blow. Signed, Jacob Barnes and William Bittle. D. 1765. R. Jan. 8, 1767. Page 182.

NEWSOM, Joseph. Estate appraised by Thomas Crenshaw, Henry Thomas and Micajah Edwards. R. Jan. 8, 1767. Page 183.

COGGAN, John. Estate appraised by William Kirby, William Kinnebrew and Henry Vaughan. Ordered Nov. 1, 1766. R. Feb. 12, 1767. Page 184.

JOYNER, Joshua. Leg.- wife Mary; son John; son Nathan; son Jonas; son Britain; daughter Judith; daughter Elizabeth Williams; grandson Walton Williams; daughter Mary Joyner. Exs., son John and friend Job Wright. D. Jan. 6, 1763. R. Feb. 12, 1767. Wit. James Jordan Scott, Job Wright, John Oberry. Page 186.

JOHNSTON, Benjamin. Leg.- wife Mary; son Joseph; son Job; son Stephen; son Jacob; daughter Mary Godwin; son John; son William; daughter Ann Wooten; daughter Sarah Barret; grandson Jesse Johnston; between my three children, Lucy, Stephen and Henry Johnston; daughter Lydia Beel. D. March 29, 1764. R.

BROWN, John. Leg.- daughter Elizabeth Day and all her children, both Fosters and Days; daughter Jane; grandchildren, John, Richard, Mary, Sarah and Lucy Foster; wife Olive; son John Brown. Exs., friends Benjamin Clements, Sr. and Joseph Jones. D. March 19, 1765. R. March 12, 1767. Wit. William Spivey, Benjamin Spivey, Martha Spivey. Page 188.

JACKSON, William. Leg.- wife Patience; son Kindred. Ex., John Edwards. D. Feb. 22, 1767. R. March 12, 1767. Wit. Thomas Boon, William Boon, Valentine Simmons. Page 189.

BULLS, William. Leg.- wife Martha; son Jesse; son William; son Benjamin; son John; daughter Patty; grandson Thomas Gwin. Exs., friend Joshua Whitney and Jessee Bulls. D. Dec. 23, 1760. R. March 12, 1767. Wit. John Joyner, Hardy Pope, Joshua Miniard. Page 189.

BLOW, Samuel. Inventory signed, Charles Briggs. R. March 12, 1767. Page 190.

FOSTER, Christopher. Leg.- son John; grandson Richard son of Elias Foster; son Moses; daughter Amy; wife Alice; son Newit. I resign guardianship of John Westbrook's orphans. Exs., sons Newit and Moses Foster. D. Nov. 17, 1766. R. March 12, 1767. Wit. Arthur Foster, John Fort, John Westbrook. Page 191.

PERSON, John. Leg.- wife Dorcas; son Presley; sons Philip, Colin and Turner my land in North and South Carolina. All children under age. Exs., wife, brother William Person and cousin Benjamin Person of Bute County, N.C. D. Feb. 10, 1767. R. April 9, 1767. Wit. Allen Jones, Willie Jones, Ea. Haynes. Page 193.

ANDREWS, Robert. Estate appraised by Edwin Gray, Samuel Drewry and Benjamin Ruffin, Jr. Ordered Nov. 2, 1766. R. April 10, 1767. Page 195.

JOHNSON, Demsy. Estate appraised by Joseph Bradshaw, Hardy Doyle and Thomas Jones. Signed, Robert Johnson. Ordered in 1766. R. May 14, 1767. Page 197.

DOYLE, Daniel. Estate appraised by Edmund Tyler, Thomas Marks and Benjamin Bradshaw. R. May 14, 1767. Page 198.

BULLS, William. Estate appraised by Hardy Doyle, Robert Johnson and Thomas Jones, Jr. R. May 14, 1767. Page 199.

WESTBROOK, Thomas. Leg.- wife Hilvia; son Benjamin; daughter Hilvia; son Mial land adjoining John Reid; William Laugn (?); son Thomas; daughter Mary; daughter Celia Westbrook. Ex., James Ramsey. D. Oct. 26, 1766. R. May 14, 1767. Wit. Davis Edmunds, Henry Turner, Nathan Turner. Page 201.

WESTBROOK, William. Leg.- wife Elizabeth; son Samuel land bought of my brother James Westbrook; son Joshua; daughter Widdia; daughter Priscilla; daughter Anne; daughter Beckey. Exs., brother Samuel Westbrook and wife Elizabeth. D. April 17, 1767. R. June 11, 1767. Wit. Jesse Harris, Drury Long, Joshua Claud. Page 202.

DENSON, Joseph. Estate appraised by Thomas Chappel, Lewis L. Joyner and William Simmons. R. June 11, 1767. Page 203.

VICK, Joshua of St. Luke Parish. Leg.- wife Elizabeth; daughter Ann land adjoining William Thomas bought of Thomas Blunt; daughter Beda; son William Vick. D. March 11, 1767. R. June 11, 1767. Wit. Patience Newsom, Arthur Vick, William Thomas. Exs., wife Elizabeth, brother Jacob Vick and Arthur Vick. Page 206.

HOWELL, Nathaniel. Account of sales. Among purchasers were Hartwell Howell and Henry Howell. R. June 11, 1767. Page 207.

EPPES, George. Account sales of estate. Among purchasers were Edward Eppes, William Eppes and Mary Eppes. R. July 11, 1767. Signed, Edward Eppes. Page 208.

JOINER, Joshua. Estate appraised by John Beal, Joseph Johnston and Job Wright. Signed, John Joiner, ex. R. July 9, 1767. Page 208.

FOSTER, Newit. Leg.- wife Anthany; daughter Dolly. Exs., wife Anthany and Moses Foster. D. March 19, 1767. R. July 9, 1767. Wit. George Rawlings, John Harper, Tabitha Newsom. Page 212.

SEBRELL, Benjamin. Inventory. R. Aug. 13, 1767. Page 212.

WESTBROOK, Thomas. Estate appraised by William Blunt, John Blunt and John Mundell. R. Aug. 13, 1767. Page 213.

JOHNSON, Benjamin. Estate appraised by Job Wright, George Washington and John Joyner. R. Aug. 13, 1767. Page 215.

KITCHEN, Thomas. Leg.- wife Rebecca; son Thomas; son Dickson; daughter Silvia Kitchen. Ex., wife Rebecca Kitchen. D. R. Sept. 10, 1767. Page 217. Wit. Richard Hamlin, Arthur Exum, Sarah Exum.

WASHINGTON, John. Estate appraised by John Bailey, Joseph Phillips, Sr. and Aaron Phillips. R. Oct. 8, 1767. Page 218.

GRAY, Benjamin. Estate appraised by Joseph Hart, Arthur Holliman and Jesse Womble. R. Oct. 8, 1767. Part 219.

JACKSON, William. Appraisal. R. Oct. 8, 1767. Page 221.

SAUL, John. Estate account audited by Ben Clements and Cordall Norfleet. R. Oct. 8, 1767. Page 222.

LONG, Arthur of St. Luke Parish. Leg.- son John; son Drewry land bought of James Stanley; son Davis; son Arthur; son Littleton land bought of John Wright; daughter Mary Dawson; daughter Lucy; daughter Sarah; wife Elizabeth Long. Exs., wife and sons John and Drewry Long. D. Oct. 23, 1766. R. Oct. 8, 1767. Wit. Britian Jones, John Sauls, Cordall Norfleet. Page 223.

JENKINS, Valentine. Estate appraised by John Boykin, Simon Boykin and Arthur Pursell. R. Oct. 8, 1767. Page 226.

FORT, Rebecca. Leg.- son Henry, reversion to his children; Arthur son of my son Henry; granddaughter Rebecca Turner; Rebecca daughter of my son Joshua; daughter Betty Turner. Ex., son Joshua Fort. D. Oct. 21, 1767. R. Dec. 10, 1767. Wit. Benjamin Simmons, John Fort, Mary Land. Page 227.

JOHNSON, Jesse. Estate appraised by John Beal, William Speed and Richard Johnson. D. 1764. Account estate audited by James Jordan Scott and A. Jones. Among items, paid one-third to widow and to children two-thirds. Signed Sarah Johnson, Admtx. Page 228.

TURNER, Simon, Sr. Leg.- son William; son Benjamin; daughter Hannah; daughter Edith Barrow; daughter Mary; son Thomas land bought of William Pope. Land in Hartford Co., N. C. to be sold. Exs., sons William and Benjamin Turner. D. Nov. 5, 17. R. Oct. 10, 1767. Wit. Benjamin Turner, Mary Drew, John Barrow, Newit Drew, Jeremiah Drew. Page 229.

BROWNE, Tabitha. Inventory, signed by Jesse Browne. Ordered March 2, 1765. R. Jan. 14, 1767. Page 231.

VICK, Joshua. Estate appraised by Henry Thomas, Thomas Edwards and William Thomas. R. Feb. 12, 1768. Page 232.

TURNER, Simon. Estate appraised by Henry Vaughan, Robert Bittle and Thomas Day. R. March 10, 1768. Page 232.

GRAY, William Watson. Estate appraised by Samuel Westbrook, Thomas Day and John Mundell. Ordered Nov. 12, 1767. R. March 10, 1768. Page 232.

WESTBROOK, William. Estate appraised by Joshua Cloyd, Thomas Day, John Mundell. R. March 10, 1768. Page 233.

BARRET, Jacob. Estate appraised by John Pope, Jacob Barnes and John Edwards. R. May 12, 1768. Page 236.

TURNER, James. Leg.- son James; son Jacob land in Northampton Co., N. C.; daughter Elizabeth; son William land in Northampton Co., N. C. on which Newit Harris formerly lived; son Thomas; son John; wife Anne Turner. Exs., sons James Turner, Jacob Turner, William Turner. D. July 18, 1763. R. May 12, 1768. Wit. John Person, John Channel, Selah Cockerell. Page 237.

POPE, Henry. Inventory, signed by Henry Pope. Ex. R. May 12, 1768. Page 239.

FORT, Rebecca. Inventory, signed by Joshua Fort. R. May 12, 1768. Page 240.

WILLIAMS, George. Account estate audited by Job Wright and James Jordan Scott. Appraisers paid, Benjamin Williams and Benjamin Barnes. Signed Sion Williams. R. May 12, 1768. Page 241.

POWELL, James. Estate appraised by Cordall Norfleet, William Powell and John Blunt. R. June 9, 1768. Page 242.

DOYEL, Daniel. Account estate audited by Edmund Tyler and Samson Pitman. Signed, William Joiner. R. June 9, 1768. Page 243.

NEWSOM, David of St. Luke Parish. Leg.-wife Mary; son Randolph; son Joel; son Barham; son William; daughter Lucy; son James Newsom. Exs., wife Mary and friend James Barham. D. Nov. 22, 1767. R. July 14, 1768. Wit. Henry Taylor, Temperance Taylor, Jamey Taylor, John Pearce. Page 244.

JOHNSON, Benjamin. Estate appraised by Job Wright, John Joiner and George Washington. Estate audited by Job Wright, John Beal and James Jordan Scott. Signed, Joseph Johnson, Ex. R. July 14, 1768. Page 245.

HANDCOCK, William. Leg.- son Lewis; son-in-law Francis Groce and to each of his children by my daughter Priscilla; son Thomas Handcock. D. Jan. 1, 1768/69. R. July 14, 1768. Administration granted Thomas Hancock. Page 246.

DAUGHTRY, James. Account estate, signed James Jordan Scott. James Gardner and William Westra paid as appraisers. R. July 24, 1768. Page 247.

LITTLE, John. Account estate aduited by William Person and J. Sturgeon. Signed, by Simon Turner and wife Lucy. R. Aug. 11, 1768. Page 24.

SMITH, Absalom. Account sale at which the following bought items; Hannah Smith, Lawrence Smith, Joseph Smith and Flood Smith. Slaves appraised by Will Person, John Blunt and William Blunt. Estate audited by Will Person and William Blunt. Signed, Joseph Smith, Adm. D. Aug. 26, 1766. R. Aug. 11, 1768. Page 252.

BROWN, John. Inventory, signed by James Jones. R. Aug. 11, 1768. Page 252.

OBERRY, Thomas. Leg.- son Henry; son Nathan; son John. Ex., son John Oberry. D. Oct. 17, 1766. R. Aug. 11, 1768. Wit. James Jordan Scott, Jordan Denson, Miriam Scott. Page 260.

JOYNER, Joseph. Account estate audited by Elias Herring and Esmund Tyler. Signed, Hoopy Joyner. R. Sept. 8, 1768. Page 261.

KITCHEN, Thomas. Inventory, signed by Thomas Kitchen. R. Oct. 13, 1768. Page 261.

TURNER, James. Inventory. R. Oct. 13, 1768. Page 262.

JENKINS, Valentine. Slaves appraised in York County by Seymour Powell, John Gibbons and William Cary. Slaves appraised in Southampton County by John Boykin, Simon Boykin and Arthur Pursell. D. July 19, 1766. R. Oct. 13, 1768. Page 263.

HAISTY, James. Leg.- son Benjamin; son Robert; son James; son John; wife Elizabeth; daughter Sarah; daughter Isabel; daughter Elizabeth; son Joshua; son Mathew; son Moses Haisty. Exs., sons John and James Haisty. D. Sept. 1, 1767. R. Nov. 10, 1768. Wit. John Vasser, Rachel Vasse. Page 263.

DAVIS, Samuel. Estate appraised by Joshua Barnes, Mathew Vick and Israel Joyner. Signed, Thomas Ricks, Adm. R. Dec. 8, 1768. Page 264.

PERSON, William. Leg.- wife Mary land adjoining John Sturgeon; son John land adjoining William Blunt and John Person; son Anthony; son William my land in North Carolina. (eldest son not of age) Exs., wife Mary and Day Ridley of Hertford County, N. C. D. Oct. 17, 176. R. Oct. 8, 1768. Wit. Thomas Person, William Blunt, James Jones, John Dawson, Peterson Thorp. Page 267.

HAISTY, James. Estate appraised by Benjamin Bradshaw, Francis Rose, John Gardiner. Signed, James Haisty, Ex. R. Jan. 12, 1769. Page 269.

JOHNSON, Dempsey. Account estate audited by Edmund Tyler, John Council and Sampson Pitman. Signed, Robert Johnson. R. Feb. 9, 1769. Page 271.

SPEED, George. Account estate audited by R. Kello and Daniel Fisher. Signed Mary Speed. R. March 9, 1769. Page 271.

BEEL, John. Leg.- son John land adjoining James Jordan Scott and Francis Bracey, including the land on which George Williams formerly lived, adjoining Stephen Johnson; son Joshua; daughter Patience; daughter Lydia; daughter Abigail; daughter Temperance Woodard; son-in-law-William Fowler; son-in-law Richard Beel. My estate to be divided by friends, Albridgton Jones, Job Wright and James M. Scott. Ex., son Joshua Beel. D. Jan. 20, 1769. R. March 9, 1769. Wit. Shadrack Lewis, Jordan Denson, James Jordan Scott. Page 272.

OBERRY, Thomas. Estate appraised by Benjamin Beal, John Beal and Job Wright. March 9, 1769. Signed, John Oberry, Ex. R. March 0, 1769. Page 273.

NEWSOM, Joseph. Account estate audited by Nicholas Maget, Samuel Maget, Jr. and Micajah Edwards. R. April 13, 1769. Page 274.

HARRIS, Simon. Leg.- son William; son Simon; son Jacob; wife Ruth Harris. Exs., wife Ruth, sons Simon and Jacob Harris. D. Oct. 9, 1767. R. May 11, 1769. Page 275. Wit. Joseph Channel, Priscilla Reaves, Baker White.

JARREL, Benjamin. Leg.- wife Mary; daughter Elizabeth; daughter Ann; son William Jarrel. Exs., wife Mary and Albridgton Jones. D. Feb. 25, 1769. R. May 11, 1769. Wit. Henry Thomas; Richard Ricks, Benjamin Barham. Page 276.

HARRIS, Simon. Inventory, signed by Jacob Harris. R. June 8, 1769. Page 277.

COOPER, William. Account of estate audited by Simmons Jones and Henry Briggs. Among items, paid for Demsey Cooper's schooling to William Pope. R. June 8, 1769. Page 277.

SIMMONS, Charles. Estate appraised by Will Andrews, Benjamin Ruffin, Jr. and Benjamin Clements, Jr. R. June 8, 1769. Page 278.

LONG, Arthur. Estate appraised by William Blunt, John Blunt and Cordall Norfleet. R. June 8, 1769. Page 283.

JONES, Thomas. Estate appraised by Hardy Doyle, Moses Johnson and Mathew Smith. R. July 13, 1769. Page 286.

BRANCH, William. Leg.- wife Ruth and her heirs. Extx., wife Ruth Branch. D. Sept. 10, 1766. R. July 13, 1769. Wit. J. Gray, John Deloach, Lucy Bennet. Page 287.

DOYLE, Edward. Account estate audited by Edmund Tyler, Samson Pitman and William Jones. Among items legacy paid to John Oberry. Signed, Hardy Doyle, Ex. R. July 13, 1769. Page 288.

EDWARDS, John. Estate appraised by William Blunt, John Blunt and John Suter (Luter?). R. Aug. 10, 1769. Page 290.

BRANCH, William. Estate appraised by William Lane, Bailey Branch, Benjamin Doles. R. Aug 10, 1769. Page 292.

GILLIAM, John. Estate account audited by John Wilkinson and Charles Briggs. R. Aug. 10, 1769. Page 293.

FOSTER, Christopher. Estate appraisers, Charles Barham, Joshua Fort and James Barham. R. Aug. 10, 1769. Page 294.

BROWN, John. Account estate audited by William Blunt and Nicholas Maget. Signed, Joseph Jones. R. Aug. 10, 1769. Page 29.

VAUGHAN, William. Leg.- son William; daughter Hannah Sharpe, son Ephraim; daughter Lucy Taylor; wife Sarah; daughter Mary; daughter Fathe; daughter Amy; daughter Dorcas; daughter Elizabeth Vaughan. Exs., wife Sarah and son-in-law Nathan Turner. D. May 13, 1769. R. Oct. 12, 1769. Wit. John Mundell, Thomas Francis, Isom Smith. Page 298.

PURSELL, Arthur. Leg.- son John; son Peter; son Arthur; daughter Mary my land in Isle of Wight County. Exs., Thomas Carrell and John Pursell. D. July 29, 1769. R. Oct. 12, 1769. Wit. Joseph Rite, Robert Williamson, Christian Roberts. Page 298.

WILLIAMS, Thomas, Sr. Inventory. R. Oct. 12, 1769. Page 300.

HANDCOCK, William. Estate appraised. R. Oct 12, 1769. Page 300.

POPE, Joshua. Leg.- sons Josiah and Micajah my land which is to be divided between them by Nathan Pope, Isaac Johnson and Howell Edmunds; son Reuben; loving wife; daughter Ennis; daughter Savia; daughter Fanny Pope. Exs., wife, Nathan Pope, Shadrack Newton and son Josiah. Wit. Isaac Johnson, John Newton, Samuel Kindred. D. Sept. 15, 1769. R. Nov. 9, 1769. Will presented by Sarah Pope. Page 301.

POPE, Nathan. Leg.- loving wife; son Jonathan; son Elijah; son John (under age) daughter Phoebe; son Joel (under age); son Nathan; son Richard land between Joseph Warren and Isaac Johnson. Exs., wife and brother Isaac Pope. D. March 29, 1766. Wit. Jacob Johnson, Joshua Pope, Nathan Johnson. Codicil; to two daughters Patience and Charity, born since date of will. Wit. Howell Edmunds, Isaac Johnson. Will presented by Patience Pope. R. Sept. 26, 1769. Page 303.

DOYEL, Edmund. Account estate audited by Charles Cosby and Edmund Tyler. Estate in account with Hardy Doyel, security for Lindy Bull. R. Dec. 14, 1769. Page 303.

THOMAS, John. Leg.- John Thomas Blow, son of Richard Blow, decd. land on which Arthur Sellers formerly dwelt, other bequests upon the death of Elizabeth Inman; Martha, daughter of Richard Blow, Jr. decd.; to Richard, son of Richard Blow, Jr. decd., the plantation on which William Stanford dwells; James son of Henry Vaughan when twenty-one; to Henry son of Henry Vaughan at twenty-one; Mary Briggs Vaughan, daughter of Henry Vaughan at eighteen or marriage; Thomas son of Henry Vaughan land adjoining Benjamin Evans at twenty-one; to

Elizabeth Inman for maintenance of herself and family, reversion at her death to John Thomas Blow. Exs., John Thomas Blow and Elizabeth Inman. In case of death of said Elizabeth Inman, Henry Vaughan is to made trustee. D. April 9, 1763. R. March 8, 1770. Wit. George Gurley, Jr., Charles Taylor, Joseph Newsom, Jeremiah Ellis, Robert Williams. Page 304.

EDMUNDS, Howell. Leg.- wife Mary land bought of Raman Ennis and Joshua Pope and land formerly granted William Barnes; unmarried daughters, Sarah, Mary, Ann, Martha and Lucy; son Samuel under age; son Thomas land adjoining John and Andrew Pope; Henry Edmunds; Charles son of Henry Edmunds; son Howell land bought of Benjamin Williams; son William land in Halifax County, N.C.; son John land bought of James Craven in Northampton County, N. C.; daughter Elizabeth Williamson cash loaned Stephen Williamson; granddaughters, Nanney and Elizabeth Williamson; negroes left daughters, Martha and Lucy and son Samuel to be divided between them by my sons, Howell, Thomas, William and John; the aforesaid children are to be under the direction and care of my son Thomas without the formality of a guardianship. Exs., son Thomas and wife Mary Edmunds. D. Jan. 1, 1770. R. March 8, 1770. Wit. George Gurley, Jr., William Whitehead, Holliday Revel. Page 306.

ADAMS, Henry. Leg.- beloved wife; son Henry; daughter Martha; daughter Mary; son John; daughter Agnes Killegrew; daughter Ann Rollings. Exs., wife Elizabeth and son Henry Adams. D. Sept. 4, 1767. R. March 8, 1770. Wit. Edward Harris, Henry Ivey, Reuben Adams. Page 311.

HART, Henry. Leg.- wife Elizabeth, son Henry; son Joseph; son John; daughter Jane; daughter Sarah Hart. Exs., David Andrews and Joseph Hart. D. July 20, 1767. R. Feb. 8, 1770. Wit. Thomas Brock, Richard Andrews, Henry Andrews. Page 313.

STEPHENSON, Thomas, Sr. Leg.- son William; daughter Esther, wife of Jesse Browne; daughter Celah; son Simon; wife Elizabeth; son Mathew; son James; son Thomas, Jr.; daughter Jane wife of George Summerrell; Stephen son of John Summerrell; daughter Celah Stephenson; daughter Elizabeth, wife of Thomas Summerrell. Exs., wife Elizabeth and son Simon. D. Dec. 7, 1768. R. Feb. 8, 1770. Wit. Benjamin Turner, Samson Turner, Arthur Allen. Page 314.

NEWSOM, David. Appraisal. R. March 8, 1770. Page 316.

POPE, Joshua. Estate appraised by Robert Bittle, Hardy Atkinson and Benjamin Blunt. R. March 8, 1770. Page 318.

JELKS, William of St. Luke Parish. Leg.- wife Anne; son Lemuel; son William; daughter Mary; daughter Tabby; daughter Betty Jelks. Exs., wife Anne and son Lemuel Jelks. D. Oct. 9, 1766. R. April 12, 1770. Wit. Gregory Rawlings, River Barker. Page 319.

VASSER, Nathan of St. Luke Parish. Leg.- wife Lyda; son Robert; son Jesse land on which my brother lived; daughter Elizabeth Carr; daughter Ann; daughter Margaret; daughter Mary Vasser. Exs., wife and son-in-law Robert Carr. D. Nov. 30, 1769. R. April 12, 1770. Wit. Simon Everett, Jesse Drake, Will Thomas. Page 320.

POPE, Nathan. Estate appraised by Arthur Foster, Joseph Delk and William Turner. Signed, Patience Pope. R. April 12, 1770. Page 321.

BYNUM, William. Account estate audited by Cordall Norfleet, John Wilkinson and John Edwards. The account of Benjamin Bynum was approved. Signed, Ea. Bynum. R. June 10, 1770. Page 232.

BARNES, Thomas. Leg.- wife Martha; daughter Mary; son Nathan, to all my children. Exs., wife and son Nathan Barnes. D. May 18, 1769. R. June 14, 1770. Wit. Edmund Day, Jr., Israel Joyner, Charles Joyner. Page 323.

HARRIS, Joshua. Estate appraised by Joseph Claud, Thomas Day and Samuel Westbrooke. R. June 14, 1770. Page 324.

VAUGHAN, William. Estate appraised by David Edmunds, Jacob Turner and William Kirby. R. June 14, 1770. Page 325.

VICK, Joseph. Leg.- daughter Priscilla Joyner; daughter Margaret Joyner. D. March 2, 1769. R. June 14, 1770. Wit. Job Wright, Robert Vick, James Jordan Scott. Page 326.

ADAMS, Henry. Estate appraised by James Lundy, Edward Lundy, Jr. and Edward Harris. R. July 12, 1770. Page 326.

JOHNSTON, Henry. Estate appraised. R. July 12, 1770. Page 32.

VICK, Joseph. Inventory. R. July 12, 1770. Page 330.

RICKS, Robert. Estate appraised by Thomas Blunt, Henry Johnson and Benjamin Williams. R. July 12, 1770. Page 330.

MAGET, Micajah. Estate appraised by Richard Blow, James Jones and John Cobb. Ordered Oct. 4, 1769. R. Aug. 9, 1770. Page 333.

JELKS, William. Estate appraised by James Barham, Drewry Parker and Jacob Newsom. R. Aug. 9, 1770. Page 334.

JARREL, Benjamin. Estate appraised by Henry Taylor, Benjamin Barham and Robert Jones. Additional appraisal by Benjamin Barham, Robert Jones and Peterson Thorpe. Signed, Albridgton Jones. R. Sept. 13, 1770. Page 338.

EDMUNDS, Howel. Inventory. Signed, H. Edmunds. R. Aug. 9, 1770. Page 336.

HART, Henry, Sr. Estate appraised by Aaron Phillips, Jesse Washington and Arthur Holliman. R. Sept. 13, 1770. Page 341.

WOOD, George of Nottoway Parish. Leg.- wife Mary; daughter Mary Bailey; son Joshua; son Moses; grandson George son of Moses Wood; grandson Richard Bailey; grandson Thomas son of Benjamin Wood, decd.; granddaughter Lucy Bailey; granddaughter Mary, daughter of Benjamin Wood, decd. Exs., son Joshua and son-in-law Barnaby Bailey. D. Aug. 6, 1770. R. Sept. 13, 1770. Wit. Edwin Gray, Nicholas Morris, Benjamin Oney. Page 342.

HART, Elizabeth. Leg.- son Joseph; son John; daughter Jane; daughter Sarah Hart. Exs., sons Joseph and John Hart. D. Feb. 6, 1770. R. Oct. 12, 1770. Wit. Robert Hart, Jesse Hart, Henry Andrews. Page 343.

JONES, William of Nottoway Parish. Leg.- daughter Mary Hargrave; son Mathew; son Joseph; wife Elizabeth to live with my son Lemuel Jones. Ex., son Lemuel Jones. D. May 30, 1769. R. Oct. 12, 1770. Wit. Boaz G. Summerrell, William Doyel, James Basden, Jr. Page 343.

JONES, Joseph. Inventory. Signed, John Bailey. R. Oct. 12, 1769. Page 344.

PURSELL, Arthur. Estate appraised by Robert Williams, Robert Mercer and Edward Britt. R. Nov. 8, 1770. Page 345.

BRANCH, George. Leg.- son Bailey; son Howel land bought of John Holden; son Henry land bought of Samuel Holden; son Benjamin; wife Martha; daughter Lucy; granddaughter Mary, daughter of son Edmund Branch; son Newsom. Exs., sons Bailey and Newsom Branch. D. Sept. 14, 1770. R. Nov. 8, 1770. Wit. R. Kello, Moses Phillips. Page 347.

BOOTH, Arthur. Leg.- son James; son William G. Booth land in Sussex County; son Michael; my brother Moses Booth to have charge of son Arthur until he is twenty-one; daughter Lucy; daughter Sarah; daughter Martha Booth. Exs., son James and brother Moses Booth. D. April 14, 1769. R. Nov. 8, 1770. Wit. Edwin Gray, Joseph Lane, Jesse Lane, Charles Briggs. Page 348.

VASSER, Nathan. Estate appraised by Thomas Crenshaw, William Thomas and Henry Briggs. R. Dec. 13, 1770. Page 350.

HART, Elizabeth. Estate appraised by Jesse Womble, Jesse Washington and Thomas Brock. R. Dec. 13, 1770. Page 352.

HART, Robert. Leg.- son Thomas land adjoining Robert Atkinson; son Jesse; son Robert; daughter Sarah; daughter Elizabeth; daughter Mary; daughter Lucy Hart. Ex., son Jesse Hart. D. June 25, 1770. R. Dec. 13, 1770. Wit. Joseph Hart, John Hart, Richard Andrews. Page 352.

EDWARDS, Micajah of Nottoway Parish. Leg.- wife Elizabeth; son William (under age); son Micahah; son Richard; son Benjamin; daughter Mary Butts; daughter Lucy; daughter Elizabeth; daughter Anne; to unbaptised daughter. Exs., wife Elizabeth and friends Benjamin Blunt and John Thomas Blow. D. Nov. 17, 1770. R. Dec. 13, 1770. Wit. Henry Thomas, Benjamin Evans, M. Edwards. Page 354.

DENSON, Joseph. Account estate audited by Peter Butts and Benjamin Clements, Jr. R. Dec. 13, 1770. Signed, Mathew Jones, Adm. Page 355.

BROWNE, Jesse of St. Luke Parish. Leg.- beloved wife; son Samuel; grandson Jesse Browne land in Hertford County, N. C. and land bought of Joseph Strickling, which was patented by Oliver Woodward, also all my books of physic and surgery and my instruments of surgery; to my executors the slaves bought of William Taylor and the plantation on which Kinchen Taylor now lives to be used for the benefit of my daughter

Ridley Taylor and in case her husband should survive her to be divided among all her children; whereas Francis Wills left the reversion of a plantation in trust for the use and benefit of my daughter Ridley and her husband Kinchen Taylor and their heirs, to Thomas Wills his son after the death of his mother Temperance on condition that said Thomas should pay fifty pounds to his brothers and sisters upon the death of his mother, in case the said Thomas should fail to perform the said condition, it is my will and desire that it be paid from my estate; my friend George Williams land in Nansemond adjoining his line and the Carolina line; grandson Jesse Taylor at twenty-one; to my six daughters, Jack, Atkinson, Dickins, Parsons, Parthenia and Jenny Browne. Exs., son Samuel and sons-in-law John Atkinson, Thomas Jack and Benjamin Parsons. D. Nov. 29, 1770. R. Dec. 13, 1770. Wit. A. Jones, Abraham Mitchell, Nicholas Maget, Lemuel Riddick, Benjamin Crocker. Will presented by Thomas Jack. Page 357.

DRAKE, John of St. Marks Parish. Leg.- son Jesse; daughter Mary Grimer (Grimmer), wife of Robert Grimmer; daughter Martha, wife of William Battle; son Thomas; son John; daughter Penelope, wife of Joseph Barrow; my seven youngest children, Joel, Molly, Zellah, Isaac; Honor, Jurden and Jonah; beloved wife. Ex., William Thomas. D. Sept. 14, 1767. R. Dec. 13, 1770. Wit. William Drake, James Story, Sarah Story. Page 361.

GURLEY, George, Sr. of St. Luke Parish. Leg.- loving wife; son George; son John; daughter Mary West; daughter Fathey Sellers; grandson George Edwards; residue of estate to George Gurley, Jr. and Ann Edwards. Ex., son George Gurley. D. Aug. 12, 1768. R. Jan. 10, 1771. Wit. William Thomas, Jesse Braswell, James Peding. Page 362.

STEPHENSON, Thomas, Sr. Estate appraised by William Boykin, Richard Manning and Jacob Summerell. R. Jan. 10, 1771. Page 363.

WEBB, Charles. Estate audited by Thomas Holt and Charles Barram. Signed, Elizabeth Webb. R. Feb. 14, 1771.

BARNES, Thomas. Inventory. R. Feb. 14, 1771. Page 366.

DRAKE, John. Estate appraised by Thomas Crenshaw, John Crenshaw and Thomas Edwards. R. Feb. 14, 1771. Page 366.

SPEED, William. Estate appraised by Mathew Wills, Thomas Lawrence and Joseph Johnson. R. Feb. 14, 1771. Signed, Henry Briggs, Adm. Page 367.

GRISWITT, Thomas of Nottoway Parish. Leg.- son William; wife Elizabeth; daughter Mary Cobb; son Anthony; son Thomas; daughter Elizabeth; daughter Martha; son George; son James. Exs., wife, eldest son William and Samuel Cobb. D. Dec. 10, 1770. R. Feb. 14, 1771. Page 369.

DAVIS, Samuel. Account estate examined by Nicholas Maget, William Thomas and Thomas Edwards. Signed, Thomas Ricks, Adm. R. Feb. 14, 1771. Page 370.

COGGIN, John. Account estate examined by Henry Vaughan, Benjamin Blunt and William Blunt. Signed, David Edmunds. R. Feb. 14, 1771. Page 370.

FRANCIS, William. Account estate, among items paid to Drury and John Francis their part of father's estate. Feb. 14, 1771. Signed, David Edmunds. Page 371.

PURSELL, Arthur. Account estate examined by William Urquhart and John Clayton. Signed, Thomas Carrell, Ex. R. Feb. 14, 1771. Page 372.

BOOTH, Arthur. Account estate examined by Joshua Wood, Barnaby Bailey and Nathaniel Coker. R. Feb. 14, 1771. Page 373.

KING, Katherine. Leg.- Benjamin Evans; Rebecca Thompson; sister Hannah Evans; my clothes to be divided between Mary Pope, Martha Pope and Frances Evans by Martha Thomas and Mary Blow. D. Dec. 4, 1770. R. Feb. 14, 1771. Wit. Henry Thomas, Newit Crizard. Administration granted Benjamin Evans. Page 375.

GARRIS, Amos. Leg.- William son of Joshua Garris a tract of land bought of William Arrington in Northampton, N. C.; my money to be divided among the following, John, Amos, Joshua, Benjamin and Hannah Garris, Susannah the wife of Haley Dupree and Lidea, the daughter of Hannah Garris. Exs., son John Garris and John Sturgeon. Wit. Simon Harris, William Bowin, William Harrison. Page 376.

ATKINSON, Thomas. Leg.- wife Patience my estate with reversion to my children, Thomas, James, Ann, Nathan, Celia, Sarah, Easter, Lucy, Michael and Priscilla Atkinson. Exs., wife Patience and son Thomas Atkinson. D. Dec. 21, 1762. R. April 11, 1771. Wit. Edwin Gray, William Urquhart, Abraham Maer. Page 378.

TURNER, Thomas. Leg.- son Thomas (under age); my three other sons. Exs., Capt. Nicholas Maget and William Kirby. D. Oct. 4, 1770. R. April 11, 1771. Wit. John Edwards, Joseph Everett, John Taylor. Page 379.

DAVIS, Lewis. Leg.- mother Elizabeth Davis; sister-in-law Rachel Davis; Britian, son of Nathan Barnes land I had by the death of my brother John Davis, decd.; to Jacob son of Jacob Barrett, decd.; Benjamin son of William Bryant; Josiah son of Jacob Barnes; land in Nansemond to be sold and money to go to mother and sister-in-law. Ex., Nicholas Maget. D. March 24, 1771. R. April 11, 1771. Wit. John Gilliam, Keton Everet, Joseph Gilliam. Page 380.

KING, Katherine. Estate appraised by Henry Thomas, William Thomas and William Millar. R. April 11, 1771. Page 381.

DENSON, Francis. Leg.- son David; son William; wife Elizabeth; daughter Sarah; daughter Ann; daughter Elizabeth; son Thomas; son Took; daughter Dority; son James Denson. Exs., wife Elizabeth and daughters Sarah and Ann Denson. D. Jan. 28, 1771. R. May 9, 1771. Wit. Thomas Draper, Jesse Draper, Patience Draper. Page 383.

GATHON, John. Estate appraised by Thomas Crenshaw and Jesse Drake. R. May 9, 1771. Page 386.

WOOD, George. Inventory signed by Joshua Wood and Barnaby Bailey. R. May 9, 1771. Page 386.

PERSON, John. Estate appraised by William Blunt, John Blunt and Joshua Nicholson. R. May 9, 1771. Page 388.

WILLIAMS, Jonah. Leg.- wife Martha; daughter Martha; son Isaac; son-in-law James Moore; grandsons James and Jesse Williams Moore, when they become of age; son Wilson; son Jesse; son Eley Williams. Exs., sons Wilson, Jesse, Eley and Isaac Williams. D. April 1, 1769. R. May 9, 1771. Wit. Jacob Williams, William Drake, Benjamin Williams and Lewis Williams. Page 389.

RAMSEY, James. Leg.- wife Catherine; son James; daughter Catherine; daughter Temppy; son Henry; daughter Lidia; daughter Mary; son William; son John; son David. Exs., wife Catherine and daughter Lidia Ramsey. D. Feb. 11, 1771. R. May 9, 1771. Wit. John Mundell, William Bowers, Amos Garris. Page 399.

BRANCH, George. Estate appraised by John Bailey, Aaron Phillips and Moses Phillips. Signed, Bailey Branch and Newsom Branch. R. June 13, 1771. Page 401.

HART, Robert. Estate appraised by Jesse Womble, Aaron Phillips and Burwell Williamson. R. June 13, 1771. Page 403.

STORRS, Thomas. Estate appraised by Henry Thomas and John Thomas Blow. R. June 13, 1771. Page 406.

THOMAS, John. Inventory of estate signed by John Thomas Blow. R. June 13, 1771. Page 408.

JONES, William. Inventory of estate signed by Lemuel Jones. R. June 13, 1771. Page 409.

GRAY, Joseph. Leg.- wife Sarah; son James; son Edwin; daughter Mary Fanning; daughter Ann Blunt; daughter Sarah Wall; daughter Lucy Gray. Exs., sons James and Edwin Gray. D. Aug. 30, 1769. R. June 13, 1771. Wit. Thomas Carrell, John Pursell, Will Hamlin. Page 411.

DENSON, Francis. Inventory of estate signed by Elizabeth, Sarah and Ann Denson. R. July 11, 1771. Page 413.

TAYLOR, James. Appraisal of estate, ordered Feb. 18, 1771. Not signed. R. July 11, 1771. Page 413.

GRESWITT, Thomas. Estate appraised by Henry Briggs, Abraham Mitchell and Mathew Wills. R. July 11, 1771. Page 415.

DAY, Thomas of St. Luke's Parish. Leg.- wife Elizabeth, daughters, Elizabeth Briggs Francis, Ann, Frances Dupree and Mary; son Thomas; granddaughter Sarah Francis; when daughter Rebecca is eighteen certain parts of estate to be divided between my five daughters, Rebecca, Priscilla, Elizabeth Brown Day, Phebe and Charlotte Day. Exs., wife and friend George Gurley. D. May 22, 1771. R. July 11, 1771. Wit. John Barrow, Jr., Thomas Day, Jr., Richard Forster. Page 416.

EDWARDS, Michael, Gent. Estate appraised by Henry Thomas, William Thomas and William Millar. R. July 11, 1771. Page 418.

BOOTH, Faitha of Nottoway Parish. Leg.- sister Sarah Wellons; neice Patience James; Pamelia daughter of Moses Wood; Mary wife of Moses Wood; Sarah daughter of Arthur Booth, decd. Ex., brother Moses Booth. D. July 2, 1771. R. Aug. 8, 1771. Wit. Edward Gray, Barnaby Bailey, James Booth. Page 424.

PHILLIPS, Aaron. Leg.- wife Elizabeth; son Lemuel; son Edwin; daughter Mary; daughter Sarah Phillips. Exs., John Bailey, Sr., Anthony Calthorp. D. Aug. 22, 1771. R. Sept. 12, 1771. Wit. Benjamin Bailey, Dianah Calthorpe. Page 425.

MYRICK, John. Leg.- son William land bought of Joseph Harwood; son Owen the plantation on which his grandfather lived, except a small tract formerly belonging to William Smith; son John land purchased of Thomas Barrow, William Lee and William Lee, Jr.; son Howel; daughter Sarah Jones; daughter Elizabeth Barnes; daughter Amy; loving wife. Exs., wife and sons William and Owen Myrick. D. Sept. 27, 1764. R. Sept. 12, 1771. Wit. Joshua Nicholson, Jr., Drewry Parker, Howel Edmunds. Will presented by Ann Myrick and Owen Myrick. Page 426.

BROWNE, Jesse. Estate appraised by William Thomas, Henry Briggs and Abraham Mitchell. R. Sept. 12, 1771. Page 429.

SPEED, William. Account estate signed Henry Briggs. (people by the name of Speed mentioned: paid Mary Speed, Charles Speed and Robert Speed). Examined by A. Jones, James Jordan Scott and Abraham Mitchell. R. Sept. 12, 1771. Page 432.

CALTHORP, Charles. Inventory recorded, Sept. 12, 1771. Estate appraised in York County, Nov. 22, 1763, by Edward Tabb, James Dickson and Bennet Tompkins. R. Sept. 12, 1771. Page 433.

BOOTH, Shelly. Leg.- son Phillip; son John; daughter Patience the wife of John James. D. Aug. 17.1771. R. Sept. 12, 1771. Wit. Moses Wood, William Booth, Charles Briggs. Ex., son John Booth. Page 435.

CRAFFORD, Henry. Leg.- wife Elizabeth; granddaughter Priscilla Pitman; son John; daughter Sarah Edwards; daughter Winnefred Davis; daughter Martha Bynum. Ex., son John Crafford. D. March 19, 1771. R. Nov. 14, 1771. Wit. Howell Edmunds, Milly Grizzard. Page 436.

CRUMPLER, William. Leg.- son Bessant; son William; son Benjamin; daughter Dorothy Brock; daughter Sarah; daughter Elizabeth Woodard; daughter Ann Turner; daughter Lucy; daughter Cherry; daughter Mary Crumpler. Exs., wife Elizabeth and son Bessant Crumpler. D. Aug. 7, 1761. R. Nov. 14, 1771. Wit. John Buskin, Edward Doyel. Page 437.

JONES, Thomas. Account estate examined by Charles Cosby, Samson Pitman and Edmund Tyler. Signed, Thomas Jones. R. Nov. 14, 1771. Page 438.

RAMSEY, James. Estate appraised by John Blunt, Joseph Claud and David Edmunds. R. Nov. 14, 1771. Page 439.

BOOTH, Faitha. Inventory signed by Moses Booth. R. Nov. 14, 1771. Page 441.

WILLIAMS, Jonah. Appraisal of estate signed by Jesse, Eley, Wilson and Isaac Williams. R. Nov. 14, 1771. Page 441.

VASSER, Nathan. Account estate examined by William Thomas, Samuel Brown and Henry Briggs. Signed, Lydia Vasser. R. Dec. 12, 1771. Page 442.

DRAKE, John. Account estate examined by John Thomas Blow and Henry Briggs. Signed, William Thomas. R. Dec. 12, 1771. Page 443.

CRAFFORD, Henry. Estate appraised by John Wilkinson, Cordall Norfleet and John Suitin (?). R. Dec. 12, 1771. Page 443.

VICK, Joseph. Account estate examined by Elias Herring and Benjamin Blunt. Signed, James and Mathew Vick. R. Dec. 12, 1771. Page 446.

PHILLIPS, Aaron. Estate appraised by Barnaby Bailey, Bailey Branch and Joseph Washington. R. Jan. 9, 1772. Page 447.

EDWARDS, John. Account estate, among items paid Winifred Pitman in full her part of her father's estate which the deceased held in his hands; paid to Michael Bynum, guardian of Priscilla and Lucy Pitman the same amount. Signed, Sarah Edwards, Adm. Examined by William Blunt and John Blunt. R. Nov. 14, 1771. Page 449.

BOOTH, Shelly. Estate appraised by Barnaby Bailey, John Bailey and Joseph Phillips. R. Feb. 13, 1771. Page 451.

SIMMONS, Charles. Leg.- Mary, Sarah, Ann, Catherine, John and Mason Simmons. D. Jan. 29, 1755 and Sept. 20, 1757. R. Dec. 12, 1771. Wit. John Simmons, Sarah Butts. This writing proved by Sarah Butts now Sarah Simmons and on motion of Benjamin Kirby is ordered recorded. Page 453.

BRANCH, George. Account estate examined by R. Kello, Charles Cosby and W. Urquhart. Signed by Bailey V. Newsom. R. Jan. 9, 1772. Page 453.

STEPHENSON, Thomas. Account estate examined by Charles Cosby and Edmund Tyler. Signed, Simon Stephenson. R. Feb. 13, 1772. Page 455.

EDMUNDS, Ann. Leg.- mother Mary Edmunds. D. Nov. 20, 1771. R. March 12, 1772. Wit. Mary Edmunds, Thomas Edmunds. Page 456.

THORPE, John of St. Luke Parish. Leg.- Phebe Thorpe, relict of son Aaron Thorpe, decd., land between Three Creeks and George Branch, which I bought of John Junnicutt, with reversion of request to grandson Henry Thorpe, son of said Aaron; his other children being Anne, Thomas, Edith and Phebe Thorpe; son Moses land bought of James Bass; son Jeremiah land adjoining Charles Bass; son John land adjoining Charles Bass; daughter Media Spence land bought of James Westbrook adjoining William Johnson and Arthur Mathews; to Drucilla Thomas with reversion to granddaughter Tamer Barlow; daughter Sarah Harris; daughter Mary Reese; daughter Olive Reese; grandson Randolph Harris; son-in-law Lewis Harris; granddaughter Anne Thorpe; my tract of land adjoining William Taylor, Nathaniel Howel, Edward Lundy, John Myrick

and Edward Harris to be sold and proceeds to be divided
between all my children, including Anne, Thomas, Edith,
Henry and Phebe the children of Aaron Thorpe; Moses Thorpe;
Jeremiah Thorpe; John Thorpe; Media Spence; Drucilla
Thompson (?); Sarah Harris; Mary Reese and Olive Reese.
Ex., son John Thorpe. D. May 6, 1771. R. Feb. 13, 1772.
Wit. Joseph Nicholson, Clabay Johnson, Hardy Harris. Page
457.

JOHNSON, Lazarus. Leg.- wife Christian; son David; daughter
Elizabeth; daughter Martha Johnson. Ex., Job Wright. D.
Dec. 28, 1771. R. Feb. 13, 1772. Wit. Job Wright, Sarah
Fowler, James Jordan Scott. Page 459.

THOMAS, Henry. Leg.- wife Martha; son William; daughter Ann,
wife of James Exum; daughter Elizabeth; daughter Mary;
daughter Sarah Thomas. Exs., son William Thomas and friend
Thomas Blunt. D. Feb. 24, 1771. R. Feb. 13, 1772. Wit.
John Thomas Blow, William Francis, James Hook. Page 460.

POPE, Nathan. Estate appraised by Arthur Foster, Joseph Delk,
William Turner. Signed, Patience Pope. D. Jan 13, 1770.
R. March 12, 1772. Page 462.

VICK, Richard. Account current, with Albridgeton Jones, Ex.
Paid Arthur Edwards his part of his father's estate, due the
said Edwards from the said Vick. Examined by Charles Cosby
and Rickard Kello. R. March 13, 1772. Page 463.

SIMMONS, Charles. Whereas I am informed that instruments of
writing were proved in Court in November or December last,
said or thought to be a will of Charles Simmons decd., my
former husband. This is to inform the said Court that I
disclaim, renounce and refuse any benefit or advantage by
from or under it, the said will or writing, but that I do
expect to have and receive the same advantage and benefit
as the law doth provide for widows. Signed, Mary Jones.
Wit. Simmons Jones, Mathew Meacom. R. March 12, 1772.
Page 463.

DAVIS, Lewis. Inventory signed by Nicholas Maget, Ex. R.
April 9, 1772. Page 464.

HINES, John. Parish of Nottoway. Leg.- son Peter; son
Joshua; son David; son Steven; daughter Mary; son Richard
land adjoining Richard Parker and William Hines; son John;
son William; son Thomas; wife Elizabeth Hines. Extx. wife
Elizabeth Hines. D. Oct. 15, 1771. R. April 9, 1772. Wit.
Peter Butts, John Brown, William Foster, Howell Bosman.
Page 464.

MARKS, Thomas. Parish of Nottoway. Leg.- daughter Mary, wife
of Benjamin Bradshaw; to Elizabeth Spivey, sister of my
deceased wife, until she marries; daughter Rebecca, wife of
William Mackey; daughter Honour, wife of Richard Worrell,
daughter Marget, wife of William Doyel; land adjoining John
Hastey, William Spivye and land formerly Robert Mongers
to be sold and proceeds to be divided between Richard
Worrell and William Mackey. Exs., my two sons-in-law
Richard Worrell and William Mackey. D. April 20, 1771. R.
April 9, 1772. Wit. Francis Rose, Charity Spivey, William
Spivye, the son of Aaron Spivye. Page 466.

HART, Elizabeth. Division of estate, each paid the same amount: David Andrews, Henry Hart, Joseph Hart, John Hart and Jesse Carrell. Ex., Joseph Hart. Examined by John Bailey and James Gray. R. April 9, 1772. Page 467.

HART, Henry. Division of estate, each paid the same amount: Henry Hart, Jane Andrews, Joseph Hart, John Hart and Sarah Carrell. Examined by John Bailey and J. Gray. R. April 9. 1772. Page 468.

WILLIAMSON, Benjamin. Northampton County, N.C. Leg.- son Stephen; son Lewis; son Mathew; daughter Elizabeth; daughter Lucy Bynum; daughter Sally Peterson; son James Williamson. Ex., son James Williamson. D. March 4, 1771. R. April 9, 1772. Wit. Mary Wilkinson, Howell Jones, William Stephens. Page 469.

JONES, James. Leg.- wife Martha the land on which Captain Timothy Thorpe lived; son Robert; daughter Susanna Simmons; daughter Elizabeth Barnes; daughter Lucresy; son James land bought of Thomas Ridley, adjoining John Cooper; daughter Mary; son Abram Parham Jones, land bought of Fathy Lane; son Richard; son David Jones. Exs., sons Robert and James Jones and son-in-law John Simmons. D. Dec. 15, 1771. R. April 9, 1772. Wit. Thomas Jarrell, Jordan Waller, John Cooper, Winifred Cooper. Page 469.

MOORE, Thomas. Leg.- wife Sarah; son Thomas; daughter Maray Blow; daughter Sarah; son William land in North Carolina; son John land in North Carolina; daughter Elizabeth; daughter Rebecca Moore. D. Nov. 10, 1767. R. April 9, 1772. Wit. Thomas Storrs, Edmund Gray. Administration granted Sarah Moore, James Moore and Richard Blow. Page 472.

BRANCH, Martha. Leg.- son Benjamin; granddaughter Mary Deloach Branch. Ex., son Benjamin Branch. D. Aug. 25, 1771. R. April 9, 1772. Wit. J. Gray, Thomas Griffin. Page 473.

POPE, John. Leg.- grandson Robert Turner; grandson Kitchen Turner; grandson John Turner; granddaughter Sally Turner. Exs., daughter Sarah Turner and Richard Beel. D. Feb. 11, 1772. R. April 9, 1772. Wit. Thomas Coffield, William Williamson, Richard Beel. Upon motion of John Turner, husband of Sarah Turner, the Extx. named, the said Joseph (?) Turner is granted probation. Page 474.

SIMMONS, Benjamin. Leg.- son John; son Benjamin all my land in Brunswick County; daughter Mary Newsom; daughter Elizabeth; daughter Lucy; daughter Sarah; daughter Keziah; daughter Martha; son Spratley a mare bought of Richard Hamlin; son Henry Simmons. Not dated or signed. R. May 14, 1772. Wife Elizabeth Simmons refused to qualify, administration granted John Simmons the heir at law. Page 475.

BEAL, John. Inventory, signed by Joshua Beal, Ex. D. April 4, 1769. R. May 14, 1772. Page 476.

DAY, Thomas. Estate appraised by David Edmunds, Joshua Cloud, Henry Vauhan (?). R. May 14, 1772. Page 477.

GRAY, Joseph. Inventory, signed Edwin Gray. R. May 14, 1772. Page 480.

THORPE, Aaron. Estate appraised by James Jones, Nathaniel
Ridley, Henry Applewhite. D. May 28, 1771. R. June 11,
1772. Adm. Joshua Nicholson. Page 486.

RIDLEY, Nathaniel. Estate account. Adm. James Ridley. To
balance of wife's part of her mother's estate to which said
Nathaniel Ridley was Adm.; to Thomas Holt the balance of his
wife's part; to Mary Jones the balance of her part of her
mother's estate; to Albridgeton Jones the balance of his
father's and mother's estates; to Hugh Vance the balance of
his wife's part of her mother's estate. Paid James Ridley
for settling the account current of Elizabeth Jones' estate.
Examined by Henry Taylor and Charles Taylor. Ordered June
13, 1771. R. June 11, 1772. Page 489.

DUNFORD, Thomas. Leg.- friend William Turner all my crops in
the possession of Mrs. Martha Turner. Ex., friend William
Turner. D. Oct. 20, 1771. R. June 4, 1772. Wit. Baker
White, John Channell. Page 491.

ARTISS, Abraham. Estate appraised by William Vick, William
Thomas, Benjamin Newsum. Ordered April 18, 1772. R.
June 11, 1772. Page 492.

TURNER, Thomas. To cash received of William Turner of North
Carolina. Estate appraised by Henry Taylor, Lewis Bryant,
John Williamson. Exs., Nicholas Maget, William Kerby. D.
May 31, 1772. R. June 9, 1772. Page 494.

THORPE, Captain Timothy. Estate appraised by John Ridley and
William Taylor. R. July 9, 1772. Page 496.

EDMUNDS, Ann. Inventory, signed by Mary Edmunds, Extx.
Ordered March 1, 1772. R. July 9, 1772. Page 502.

TAYLOR, James. Estate examined by Thomas Edmunds and Day
Ridley. Signed, John Wilkinson, Adm. R. July 9, 1772.
Page 503.

WILLIAMSON, Arthur. Parish of Nottoway. Leg.- wife Ann;
daughter Mary land bought of Benjamin Williamson; to my three
grandchildren, Mary Ann; Turner and John Williamson, the
children of Exum Williamson; son Arthur; son Jesse; grandson
Francis Williamson the son of Exum Williamson. Exs., sons
Jesse and Arthur Williamson. D. Dec. 9, 1772 (?). R.
July 9, 1772. Wit. Burwell Williamson, John Harris, Charles
Williford. Page 504.

THOMAS, Henry. Inventory, signed William Thomas and Thomas
Blunt. R. June 9, 1772. Page 507.

WIGGONS, John. Parish of St. Luke. Leg.- son William; son
James; son John; daughter Sarah Spence; son Richard; son
Abraham. Exs., sons Richard and Abraham Wiggons. D. Oct.
19, 1769. R. Sept. 10, 1772. Wit. Joshua Nicholson,
Henry Applewhite, Mathew McKiney. Page 508.

SOUTHAMPTON COUNTY

WILL BOOK III

WILLIAMS, Jacob. Estate appraised by Job Wright, Nicholas Williams and George Washington. R. Sept. 10, 1772. Page 1.

EDWARDS, Micajah. Account current, estate. Paid Benjamin Evans, overseer. Paid George Williamson; paid Herman Harris, overseer. Paid Thomas Butts his wife's legacy; paid Elizabeth Edwards board for five of her children. Examined by Charles Taylor, Thomas Blunt and William Thomas. R. Sept. 1, 1772. Page 2.

HART, Robert. Account estate. Paid legacies to Sarah, Elizabeth and Mary Hart. Ex., Jesse Hart. Examined by Burwell Williamson and J. Gray. R. Sept. 10, 1772. Page 3.

REED, Alexander. Estate appraised by John Lutter, John Blunt, John Wilkinson. D. July 18, 1772. R. Sept. 10, 1772. Page 3.

ANDREWS, William. Parish of Nottoway. Leg.- son John; son Thomas; son Drury; daughter Elizabeth Bryan Andrews; daughter Sarah; wife Ann; grandson Robert Andrews. Exs., sons William and John Andrews. D. 1771 R. Oct. 8, 1772. Wit. Benjamin Clements, Jr., John Simmons, Jr., Jesse Arrington. Page 4.

WHITNEY, Joshua. Exs., Margery Whitney and John Joyner. Paid the levy for Semour Sweny, who lived a year with the said Whitney; paid William Joyner, Jr. in right of his wife, her part of her father's estate for whom the said Whitney was administrator; paid Jesse Minard his part as above; paid legacies to Joshua, Elisha and Giles Whitney. Examined by Lemuel Jones and Henry Joyner. R. Oct. 8, 1772. Page 5.

GARRIS, Amos. Estate examined by William Blunt and Joel Avery. Ex., John Sturgeon. R. Oct. 8, 1772. Page 7.

CLIFTON, Benjamin. St. Lukes Parish. Leg.- eldest sons, John, Thomas and Benjamin; son Samuel land, part of which has been sold James Martin; grandson John Clifton; sons, Richard, Jesse and William Clifton. Ex., son Richard Clifton. D. Feb. 10, 1770. R. Oct. 8, 1772. Wit. William Claud, John Claud, Joshua Claud. Page 10.

TAYLOR, William. Leg.- brother Etheldred Taylor; daughter Nancy Browne; son William the plantation on which John Morgan is overseer which I purchased of Henry Adams; daughter Mary Mason Taylor; daughter Martha and son Robert Taylor. Exs., wife and brother Henry Taylor. D. Aug. 10, 1772. R. Nov. 12, 1772. Wit. Charles Taylor, John Taylor, Denham Foord (?). Page 10.

BOOTH, Arthur. Estate examined by John Bailey and James Gray. Signed, James Booth, Ex. R. Aug. 13, 1772. Page 12.

THORPE, Timothy. Estate examined by J. Ridley, Henry Taylor and Charles Taylor. Signed, Day Ridley, Administrator R. Aug. 13, 1772. Page 13.

KIRBY, William. Parish of St. Luke. Leg.- son William land bought of Thomas Gilliam, when he is 21; son John; son Turner when he is 21; daughter Milly Drew; daughter Elizabeth Howell; daughter Edith Kinnebrew; daughter Mary Nicholson; granddaughter Mason Holt; wife Mary Kirby Exs., son John Kirby and Joshua Nicholson. D. Sept. 26, 1772. R. Nov. 12, 1772. George Gurley, David Edmunds, Robert Bittle. Page 15.

CRUMPLER, William. Estate appraised by Frederick Holt, Robert Williamson and Edmund Jenkins. R. Dec. 10, 1772. Page 16.

JOHNSON, Robert. Leg.- son Robert land bought of James Kitchen; daughter Sarah; daughter Seley; daughter Ann; daughter Martha; grandson Kinchen Johnson at 20; grandson Esmond Johnson; daughter Mary Doyels; wife Martha; son Britain Johnson. Exs., son Robert Johnson and Council Johnson. D. Sept. 4, 1772. R. Dec. 12, 1772. Wit. Joseph Bradshaw, Hardy Doyel. Page 16.

BRANCH, Martha. Estate appraised by Benjamin Griffen, Robert Shields and Moses Phillips. R. Dec. 8, 1772. Page 17.

KINNEBREW, William. Parish of St. Luke. Leg.- son Edwin; wife Ann; son Lot; son Jacob; son Shadrack. Exs., wife and sons Jacob and Shadrack Kinnebrew. D. Nov. 19, 1772. R. Dec. 8, 1772. Wit. Elias Fort, Robert Bittle. Page 18.

TURNER, Sampson. Estate appraised by John Clayton, John Summerell and Richard Manning. D. Dec. 10, 1772. R. Jan. 11, 1773. Page 19.

TURNER, Sampson. Leg.- wife Celia; son Joseph. Exs., wife Celia Turner and Arthur Allen. D. Oct. 28, 1772. R. Dec. 10, 1772. Wit. Arthur Allen, Thomas Stephenson, Benjamin Turner. Page 20.

BOOTH, Shelly. Estate appraised by John Simmons, Thomas Edmunds and Benjamin Booth. R. Dec. 11, 1772. Page 20.

HARRIS, John. Leg.- wife Avis, my six children, Harmon, Howel, Lucy, Elizabeth, Joel and Benjamin Harris. Ex., son Howel Harris. D. May 11, 1771. R. Feb. 11, 1773. Wit. Arthur Holleman, Micajah Holleman, William Holleman. Page 21.

ELZEY, John. Parish of St. Luke. Leg.- wife Kezia; son William, provision for unborn child; neice Priscilla Adams. Ex., Joseph Tooke. D. Nov. 2, 1772. R. Feb. 11, 1773. Wit. Day Ridley, Drury Lundy, William Rawlings. Page 22.

BAILEY, William. Leg.- wife Sharah; son John; daughter Mary Wellons; son Barnaby; daughter Sarah Booth; daughter Lucy Lane; my grandchildren, James Booth, Lucy Blow, William Booth, Michael Booth, Sarah Booth, Patty Booth, Arthur Booth and Peter Bailey. Exs., sons Barnaby and John Bailey. D. Dec. 26, 1772. R. Feb. 11, 1773. Wit. James Freeman, Charles Bailey, J. Gray. Page 22.

HARRIS, Simon. Parish of Nottoway. Leg.- wife Rebecca; son Joseph land purchased of Hardy Pope; son William; daughter Patience; daughter Molly Harris. D. Sept. 1, 1771. R. Feb. 11, 1773. Ex., wife Rebecca Harris. Wit. John Johnson and Henry Pope. Page 23.

FOSTER, Alis. Leg.- son Moses; daughter Amey Foster; grandson Elias Westbrook. Ex., son Moses Foster. D. Aug. 7, 1770. R. Feb. 11, 1773. Wit. Arthur Foster, Joshua Fort. Page 24.

JOHNSON, Job. Leg.- wife Elizabeth; provision for unborn child. Ex., friend John Beale. D. Jan. 13, 1773. R. Feb. 11, 1773. Wit. George Washington, Benjamin Waller, Stephen Johnson. Page 25.

KINNEBREW, William. Exs. Jacob and Shadrack Kinnebrew. R. Feb. 11, 1773. Page 26.

BRANCH, Martha. Account estate examined by Charles Cosby and Samuel Kello. Signed by Benjamin C. Deloach, appointed as Adm. during the infancy of Benjamin Branch, her Ex. Paid legacy to Mary Deloach Branch. R. Feb. 11, 1773. Page 26.

CLIFTON, Benjamin. Estate appraised by John Mundell, Joshua Claud and William Andrews. R. Feb. 11, 1773. Page 27.

BEAL, John. Account estate examined by Lemuel Jones and James Jordan Scott. Paid Peter Beal, Samuel Woodard for his wife Lydia, Abigail Beal and Joshua Beal. Signed, Joshua Beal, Ex. R. Feb. 11, 1773. Page 28.

JOHNSON, Robert. Estate appraised by Samuel Pitman, Edmund Tyler and John Council. R. Feb. 11, 1773. Page 29.

HARRIS, John. Estate appraised by John Clayton, Burwell Williamson and Thomas Brock. R. Feb. 11, 1773. Page 29.

TAYLOR, Charles. Leg.- cousin John, son of Etheldred Taylor, if he pays the balance of my account due to Mrs. Elizabeth Cary and Benjamin Turner; brother-in-law Samuel Smith McCroskey in lieu of my sister's legacy; Charles Taylor, son of John Taylor; sister Chanette McCroskey. Exs., Samuel Smith McCroskey and cousin John Taylor. D. Feb. 3, 1773. R. Wit. Enos James, James Sterling, Richard Pond, Henry Taylor. Page 31.

EDMUNDS, Col. Howell. Estate examined by George Gurley, John Thomas Blow and William Thomas. Legacies paid to William, Sarah, Mary, Anne, Martha, Lucy, Samuel and Charles Edmunds and Stephen Williamson and my Mother. Signed Thomas Edmunds, Ex. R. March 11, 1773. Page 32.

EVERETT, Joseph. Leg.- daughters, Ann Dawson; Polly Pope; Elizabeth Dawson; Patience Pope; Sarah and Jenett Everett. Exs., son-in-law.David Dawson and friend John Wilkinson. D. March 5, 1773. R. March 11, 1773. Wit. Ferebo Barnes, Harris Taylor, James Williamson. Page 32.

JONES, Honor. Leg.- nephew John Brown; brother Joseph; brother Jesse; sister Olive Brown. Exs., brothers Joseph and John Jones, brother-in-law John Brown. D. Sept. 18, 1766. R. April 8, 1773. Wit. Anne Wellons, Mary Wellons, Elenor Love. Page 35.

WILLIAMS, Nathan Robert. Leg.- son Robert; son Gilstrap; wife Elizabeth; daughter Dorcas; son Joshua; son Jethro. Exts., wife Elizabeth Williams. D. Oct. 4, 1772. R. March 11, 1773. Wit. John Bassett, William Bynum, John Spence. Page 36.

MARKS, Thomas. Estate appraised by Jethro Denson, Charles Powers and William Joyner. R. April 8, 1773. Page 37.

LUNDY, Edward. Of St. Luke Parish. Leg.- son James; son Drewry; son John; son Edward; son Byrd land in Sussex County; daughter Elizabeth Harris; daughter Christian Reese (written Rose in another place); grandson James Holt; granddaughter Clerimont Holt; grandson Henry Holt. Exs., sons Edward and Drewry Lundy. D. Oct. 24, 1770. R. March 11, 1773. Wit. Henry Pritchette, John Poythress, James Day Ridley. Page 38.

POPE, John. Estate appraised by Job Wright, Richard Beal, Jr., Will Williams. R. April 8, 1773. Page 39.

KIRBY, William. Estate account examined by David Edmunds, Cordall Norfleet, Robert Bittle. Legacies paid to Elizabeth Howell, William Kirby; Turner Kirby; Milly Drew; Mary Nicholson and Edith Kinnebrew. Signed, John Kirby and Joseph Nicholson, Exs. R. April 8, 1773. Page 40.

DAWSON, Henry. Leg.- son David and my five daughters; son Britain; son John; daughter Dorcas; daughter Elizabeth; daughter Hannah Smith. Ex., son David Dawson. D. April 23, 1768. R. April 8, 1773. Wit. John Edwards, John Bassett, Solomon Dawson. Page 42.

EVERETT, Joseph. Estate appraised by John Edwards, John Drake, Michael Brown. R. April 8, 1773. Page 44.

HINES, John. Estate appraised by John Simmons, Jr., Jesse Arrington, William Forster. R. May 13, 1773. Page 45.

WOOTTEN, Richard. Estate appraised by Benjamin Beal, John Beal, Jonah Edwards. Signed, Job Wright. R. May 13, 1773. Page 46.

JOHNSON, Lazarus. Estate appraised by John Beal, Joshua Beal, Jonah Edwards. R. May 13, 1773. Page 46.

MYRICK, John. Estate appraised by James Barham. Solomon Deloach, Henry Applewhaite. R. May 13, 1773. Page 49.

WHITE, Baker. Estate appraised by William Blunt, Thomas Luter, John Luter. R. May 13, 1773. Page 50.

DRAKE, Jesse. Leg.- wife Ann and my child. Wife Exts. D. Nov. 25, 1768. R. May 13, 1773. Wit. Samuel Sebrell, William Standford, John Grimmer. Page 51.

ARTIS, Abraham. Estate account, examined by Will Thomas and George Gurley. Signed William Scott, Adm. R. May 13, 1773. Page 51.

HARRIS, Simon. Estate appraised by Giles Johnson, John Joyner, William Joyner. R. May 13, 1773. Page 53.

CASHELL, John. Sale, signed by Thomas Ridley, Deputy Sheriff. R. May 14, 1773. Page 54.

DRAKE, Jesse. Estate appraised by Thomas Crenshaw, William Thomas, William Gwaltney. R. June 10, 1773. Page 54.

MYRICK, John. Inventory, signed by Ann and Owen Myrick. R. June 10, 1773. Page 55.

CLAUD, Philip. Leg.- son Newitt, son Joshua, wife Elizabeth Claud. Exs. Wife, John Claud and Jeremiah Drew. D. Jan. 25, 1773. R. June 10, 1773. Wit. Thomas Gilliam, Jr., Robert Wilkins, Mathew Morrell. Page 57.

STEPHENSON, Thomas. Account estate examined by Edmund Tyler and Charles Cosby. R. June 10, 1773. Page 59.

GRISWITT, Thomas. Account estate examined by Abraham Mitchell and Mathew Wills. R. June 10, 1773. Page 60.

THORPE, Timothy. Account estate examined by Henry Taylor and James Sterling. Paid William Person for his wife Mary's portion; ditto to John Simmons for his wife Lucy; ditto to Day Ridley for his wife Martha; ditto to Philip Person for his wife Tempy; to James Jones, guardian for Silvia Thorpe; paid Martha Jarrell's legacy; paid Peterson Thorpe his portion; paid Timothy Thorpe, ditto. Signed Day Ridley. R. June 10, 1773. Page 62.

BYNUM, Elizabeth. Leg.- son William; son Benjamin; daughter Abigail Williamson; my grandchildren Colin, Temperance and Priscilla Whitehead; grandson Robert Mickleberry Williamson; daughter Colia Bryant; son Michael; grandsons Cordall Norflect Bynum and Bennett Bynum; granddaughter Milly Bynum. Exs., William and Michael Bynum and friend William Blunt. Dated July 3, 1771. R. July 8, 1773. Wit. John Wilkinson, H. Stevens, J. Williamson. Page 64.

MACKIE, John. Account estate examined by Henry Pope and John Council. R. July 8, 1773. Page 65.

BAILEY, William. Estate appraised by Moses Booth, J. Gray, Jesse Carrell. R. Aug. 12, 1773. Page 67.

JOHNSTON, Job. Estate appraised by William Williams, James Wright and David Wright. Signed John Beal, Ex. R. Aug. 12, 1773. Page 68.

PERSON, John. Leg.-William Blunt, Sr., land on Orange, Granville and Bute Counties and the tract in Southampton on which William Morgan lives. Exs., William Blunt, Sr., and John Blunt. D. July 20, 1773. R. Sept. 9, 1773. Wit. Henry Harris, William Womack, Juliana Womack, Priscilla Blunt. Page 69.

BLOW, Samuel. Account estate examined by John Wilkinson and Thomas Clements. R. Sept. 9, 1773. Page 71.

FOSTER, Alse. Inventory returned by Moses Foster. R. Sept. 9, 1773. Page 71.

WILLIAMSON, Arthur. Inventory returned by Jesse and Arthur Williamson. R. Sept. 9, 1773. Page 71.

ATKINSON, Thomas, Sr. Estate account examined by John Clayton and William Urquhart. R. Sept. 9, 1773. Page 72.

DRAKE, Jesse. Inventory returned by Anne Drake. R. Sept. 9, 1773. Page 73.

PHILLIPS, Aaron. Account estate examined by Barnabey Bailey and J. Gray. Signed, John Bailey and A. Calthorp. D. Oct. 14, 1773. Page 74.

ANDREWS, Robert. Estate account examined by Peter Butts and
Benjamin Clements, Jr. Page 74.

BYNUM, Michael. Leg.- brother Benjamin; nephew Turner Bynum;
to Collin and Cordall Norfleet Bynum; to Polly Bryant;
daughter Elizabeth Sugars Bynum land I bought from Richard
Blow; my brothers and sisters, William and Benjamin Bynum and
Abigail Williamson and Selah Bryant. Exs., brother William
Bynum and friend John Wilkinson. D. Aug. 2, 1773. R. Oct.
14, 1773. Wit. James Denson, Jesse Jones, Nathan Bryant,
William Bryant. Page 75.

WESTBROOK, James. Of St. Luke Parish. Leg.- wife Diana; to my
children, Henry; Jacob; James; Mary; Fason; Arthur; Phebe;
Thomas and child in esse. Ex., Joshuah Nicholson. D. April
26, 1773. R. Oct. 14, 1773. Wit. Amos Harris, John
Westbrook, Arthur Mathews. Page 77.

MAGET, Micajah. Account estate audited by Will Urquhart, Daniel
Merring, Jr. Paid Sarah Davis, orphan of Nathan her part of
her father's estate. R. Oct. 14, 1773. Page 77.

WIGGONS, John. Inventory signed by Richard Wiggons and Abraham
Wiggons. R. Oct. 14, 1773. Page 78.

ADAMS, John. Estate account audited by Edward Lundy, James
Lundy and Joshua Nicholson. Signed John Ivey. R. Nov. 11,
1773. Page 79.

MORGAN, John. Estate appraised by William Andrews, Samuel
Westbrook, Sr., Thomas Turner. R. Nov. 11, 1773. Page 79.

BURNELL, Charity. Leg.- Ralph Farrer (?); granddaughter Nanny
Burnell, with the request that Mrs. Anne Taylor shall have
the care of her. Ex., John Blunt. D. Nov. 13, 1773. R.
Dec. 9, 1773. Wit. John Blunt, Alexander Watson. Page 80.

TURNER, William. Estate appraised by Day Ridley, Newit Drew,
Thomas Day. R. Dec. 9, 1773. Page 81.

CLAUD, Philip. Estate appraised by Samuel Westbrook Sr. Samuel
Westbrook, Jr., James Wommack. Signed, Jeremiah Drew and John
Claud, Exs. R. Dec. 9, 1773. Page 82.

WOOD, Hannah. Estate appraised by Thomas Davis, Henry Davis,
Benjamin Doles. R. Dec. 9, 1773. Page 83.

TAYLOR, Charles. Estate appraised by John Simmons, Arthur
Foster, Benjamin Lewis. R. Jan. 13, 1774. Page 84.

WESTBROOK, James. Estate appraised by Lewis Harris, John
Sharpe, Amos Harris. R. Jan. 13, 1774. Page 86.

TURNER, Joseph. Leg.- son Mathew; son Benjamin; grandson
Joseph son of Sampson Turner; daughter Roger, wife of Jonathan
Rogers; daughter Mary, wife of Joel Dickenson; daughter Polly;
daughter Caty; wife Catherine Turner. Exs., wife and son
Benjamin Turner. D. March 6, 1773. R. Jan. 13, 1774. Wit.
Arthur Allen, Brittain Britt, Mathew Britt. Page 87.

POWELL, James. Account estate audited by Benjamin Blunt,
Cordall Norfleet and Thomas Edmunds. Signed, Martha Powell,
Extx. R. Jan. 13, 1774. Page 88.

BYNUM, William. Of St. Luke Parish. Leg. son William; daughter Ann; son John; wife Martha Bynum. Exs. William Blunt and John Blunt. D. Nov. 12, 1773. R. Jan. 10, 1774. Wit. James Day Ridley, John Crafford, Joshua Sebrell, Ann Wall. Page 88.

WILLIAMSON, Ann. Estate appraised by John Clark, Burwell Williamson, William Urquhart. Signed, Micajah Holliman, Adm. R. March 14, 1774. Page 89.

WOMBWELL, Jesse. Leg.- wife Selah; son Joseph, land bought of Arthur Holleman; son Jesse; son Joshua; daughter Nancy; daughter Sarah Wombwell. Exs. Joseph Washington and his brother George Washington. D. Jan. 16, 1774. R. March 10, 1774. Wit. B. Bailey, Thomas Brooks, Jesse Hart. Page 90.

VICK, Joshua. Estate account examined by William Thomas and Henry Briggs. Among items, paid Elizabeth Vick; Ann Vick; Beda Vick and William Vick. R. April 10, 1774. Page 91.

BYNUM, William. Estate appraised by John Wilkinson, John Edwards and Cordall Norfleet. Signed, Elizabeth Bynum. Page 92.

BAILEY, William. Estate account examined by Samuel Kello, Will Salter Jr., and J. Gray. Paid legacies, Robert, Mary, Michael, Sarah, Arthur, James and William Booth; John Wellons, Thomas Laine; John Blow. Signed Barnabey Bailey and John Bailey, Exs. R. April 10, 1774. Page 92.

ATKINSON, Elizabeth. Estate appraised by Samuel Kindred, John Powell and Joseph Powell. R. April 10, 1774. Page 93.

HARRIS, Benjamin. Leg.- son Benjamin with reversion of bequest to grandson West Harris and to his next youngest brother; son Absalom; son Hardy, a tract bought of John Person, with reversion of bequest to son Michael, the said son to have also the land bought of Jesse Boykin; wife Sathy Harris. My estate is to be divided by my friends, Joseph Smith, William Blunt and John Blunt; daughter Mary; son Absalom. Exs. wife and son Absalom Harris. D. July 7, 1771. R. April 10, 1774. Wit. William Blunt, Joseph Smith, Will Harris. Page 93.

TURNER, John. Of St. Luke Parish. Leg.- son Jesse, the negroes hired to the widow Nicholson; daughter Selah Alsobrook; son James, the money he owes me, which can be proven by Michael Wilkins; son John; son Jacob; daughter Mary; son William; daughter Charlotte Claud; daughter Elizabeth Exum; son Amos; son Joseph; son David Turner. Ex., Joshua Nicholson. D. Jan. 28, 1774. R. April 14, 1774. Wit. Abraham Johnson, Harris Johnson, Isaac Harris. Page 95.

TATUM, John. Estate appraised by Lewis Joyner, Isaac Williams and John Davis. R. April 14, 1774. Page 97.

BYNUM, William. Estate appraised by Thomas Luter, John Luter and William Turner. R. June 9, 1774. Page 97.

STEPHENSON, George. Estate appraised by Amos Harris, John Barrow, Jeremiah Drew. R. June 9, 1774. Page 98.

MECOM, Mathais. Leg.- father, John Mecom; wife Mary. Ex., William Simmons. D. April 20, 1774. R. July 14, 1774. Wit. Elizabeth Drewry, Samuel Drewry, Jr., William Simmons. Page 99.

TURNER, John. Inventory signed Joshua Nicholson. R. July 14, 1774. Page 100.

BURNELL, Charity. Estate appraised by Thomas Luter, John Luter and William Turner. R. July 14, 1774. Page 101.

HARRIS, Simon. Account estate examined by Elias Herring and John Council. R. July 14, 1774. Page 101.

COOPER, John. Estate appraised by Robert Jones, James Jones and Thomas Fitzhugh. R. July 14, 1774. Page 102.

PHILLIPS, Joseph. Account estate, examined by Jesse Carrell and Joseph Washington. R. Aug. --, 1774. Page 103.

WOMBWELL, Jesse. Estate appraised by Micajah Holleman, William Holleman and Burwell Williamson. R. Aug. --, 1774. Page 104.

WOOD, George. Account estate examined by Charles Briggs, Edwin Gray and Benjamin Ruffin, Jr. R. Aug. --, 1774. Page 105.

TURNER, William. Account estate examined by Henry Taylor, James Sterling and John Simmons. Paid to the following,- William Turner, Simon Turner, Benjamin Turner, Mathew Turner, Jesse Turner, William Kirby and Elias Fort. R. Aug. --, 1774. Page 105.

TURNER, Simon. Account estate examined by Henry Taylor, James Sterling and John Simmons. Paid to the following,- William Turner, Hannah Westbrook, Edith Barrow, Benjamin Turner and Mary Harris. R. Aug. 11, 1774. Page 105.

WILLIAMS, Sarah. Of Parish of St. Luke. Leg.- son Robert Williams. Ex., son Robert Williams. D. Nov. 25, 1773. R. Sept. 8, 1774. Wit. William Thomas, Michael Williams. Page 107.

STEPHENSON, Ann. Leg.- son Benjamin; granddaughter Ann Clary; daughter Martha, wife of James Clary. Ex., son-in-law James Clary. D. April 7, 1773. R. Oct. 13, 1774. Wit. Benjamin Bailey, Elizabeth Bailey. Page 107.

IVY, Henry. Of St. Luke Parish. Leg.- son George land adjoining Mrs. Sarah Nicholson and Dr. James Day Ridley; son John; son Robert; daughter Ruth Dortch, nothing for I have paid Moses Thorpe money for her husband John Dortch; refers to son Joseph, who is deceased; wife Phillis had a marriage contract; daughter Sarah and her daughter Phebe Ivy; son Henry; son Charles; daughter Mary Adams. Exs., sons Henry and Robert Ivy. D. Feb. 15, 1774. R. Oct. 13, 1774. Wit. Joseph Reese, William Rawlings, Joshua Nicholson. Page 108.

KIRBY, Mary. Of St. Luke Parish. Leg.- son Turner; son William; granddaughter Mason Holt; daughter Milly Drew; son John; daughter Mary Nicholson; daughter Elizabeth Howell; daughter Edith Kinnebreww. Ex. D. March 24, 1774. R. Oct. 13, 1774. Wit. John Barrow, Jr., M. Wo------(?). Page 109.

BAILEY, Sarah. Leg.- son Barnaby; daughter Mary Wellons; granddaughter Barbary Bailey; granddaughter Patty Booth; grandsons, Charles and Hartwell Bailey; granddaughter Sarah Bailey. Ex., son John Bailey. D. March 12, 1774. R. Oct. 13, 1774. Wit. J. Gray. Page 110.

DAY, Thomas. Account of estate examined by Benjamin Blunt and Thomas Edmunds. Among items, paid Robert Duprey's legacy, paid Michael Hargraves, ditto; paid Mary Day, ditto. R. Oct. 13, 1774. Page 110.

CARROLL, Thomas. Leg.- son Samuel; son Thomas land adjoining John Bailey; daughter Lucy; wife Priscilla; daughter Charity; daughter Elizabeth; daughter Patty; daughter Priscilla Carroll. Exs., wife Priscilla and John Clayton. D. Jan. 15, 1774. R. Nov. 10, 1774. Wit. Bly Williams, Jacob Turner, James Summerell. Page 111.

IVY, Henry. Inventory signed by Henry and Robert Ivy. R. Nov. 24, 1774. Page 112.

JONES, Honour. Inventory. Among items, paid cash for keeping Sarah Sherrard. R. Dec. 8, 1774. Page 113.

KIRBY, Mary. Inventory. R. Dec. 8, 1774. Page 114.

MOORE, Thomas. Estate appraised by Joshua Nicholson, Hardy Harris, Owen Myrick and Robert Jones. Legacies paid to Mrs. Sarah Moore and William, Rebecca, Sarah, Thomas, John and Elizabeth Moore. Signed, Sarah Moore, Adm. R. Dec. 8, 1774. Page 114.

CALTHORPE, Elener. Leg.- daughter Elener Clifton Calthorpe; daughter Diana; grandson Charles Butts Bowen; son Edward; son Anthony Calthorpe. Exs., Edward and Anthony Calthorpe. D. April 7, 1772. R. Jan. 12, 1775. Wit. Joshua Bailey, Benjamin Bailey, Sarah Bailey. Page 118.

TURNER, Simon. Estate appraised by John Sturgeon, John Blunt and John Suitor. R. Jan. 12, 1775. Page 119.

FORT, Elias. Estate appraised by Jeremiah Drew, Robert Bittle and Jacob Kinnebrew. R. March 9, 1775. Page 121.

JOHNSON, Robert. Account estate audited by Edmund Tyler and Benjamin Griffin. Among items, paid William Doyle his legacy; paid Edmund Tyler Kinchen Johnson's legacy; paid grandson Dempsey Johnson; paid Martha, Celah and Robert Johnson. R. March 9, 1775. Page 122.

WHITE, Mary. Account estate examined by William Blunt and John Blunt. Signed Thomas Luter, Adm. R. March 9, 1775. Page 122.

JONES, Honour. Account estated audited by Samuel Kello and Moses Phillips. Signed. Thomas Lane, Adm. R. March 9, 1775. Page 123.

CHILDS, Joseph. Estate appraised by Robert Jones, James Jones and Benjamin Barham. R. March 9, 1775. Page 124.

GLOVER, George. Leg.- wife Margarett my estate to rear our child. I should be glad if some of my brothers would come here,- Jonathan Glover, Samuel Glover and James Andrews all of Salem in New England in Boston Government in the County of Essex and Province of Mashattuth Bay. D. Aug. 3, 1774. R. March 9, 1775. Wit. John Crenshaw, Philemon Hatfield, Amey Crenshaw. Page 124.

TATUM, Joshua. Leg.- mother Elizabeth; sister Rebecca. Extx. mother Elizabeth Tatum. D. Sept. 5, 1774. R. March 9, 1775. Wit. Thomas Peete. Page 125.

STEPHENSON, Elizabeth. Estate appraised by Mathew Boykin, Richard Manning and Jacob Summerell. R. April --, 1775. Page 126.

BAILEY, Robert. Leg.- daughter Lucy; son Walter; son Robert Bailey. Ex. Benjamin Ruffin, Jr. D. Jan. 17, 1775. R. April --, 1775. Wit. Anselm Jones, Benjamin Ruffin, Thomas Butts. Page 126.

ELLZEY, John. Estate appraised by John Myrick, Drury Lundy and Byrd Lundy. R. April --, 1775. Page 127.

EXUM, Patience. Estate appraised by Sampson Pitman, Charles Wellons and Moses Phillips. R. April --, 1775. Page 128.

GRIZARD, Ambrose. Of St. Luke Parish. Leg.- son John; son Ambrose; to Hannah Lewter; son Hardy; daughter Betty; daughter Sarah; daughter Mille; daughter Priscilla Grizard. D. March 11, 1775. R. May 11, 1775. Ex., son Hardy. Wit. John Blunt, John Luter; Samuel Tanner. Page 129.

TATUM, Joshua. Estate appraised by Nicholas Williams, Lewis Joyner and Isaac Williams. James Jordan Scott, Adm. R. May 11, 1775. Page 129.

MERCER, Robert. Leg.- son-in-law Joseph Holleman; son-in-law Arthur Holleman; Micajah Holleman son of Arthur Holleman; brother John Mercer and his son John Mercer, Jr.; Robert Williamson. Ex. son-in-law Joseph Holleman. D. Sept. 9, 1773. R. July 13, 1775. Wit. John Pursell, James Mercer, Edmund Crumpler. Page 130.

BAILEY, Sarah. Inventory. R. July 7, 1775. Page 131.

JOHNSON, John. Leg.- son Moses; son David; daughter Patty Doyel; daughter Sarah Doyel; daughter Charity; son James; grandson Shadrack, son of Josiah Doyel; grandson Rawls, son of Moses Johnson; wife Rebecca Johnson. Ex. son Moses Johnson. D. Feb. 23, 1771. R. Aug. 10, 1775. Wit. Bly Williams, Thomas Jones, Joseph Crenshaw. Page 131.

DREW, Newitt. Of St. Luke Parish. Leg.- son Edward, who is deceased; son Jeremiah land bought of Elisha Melton, adjoining John Turner; son Jesse; daughter Patience Smith; daughter Priscilla Fitzhugh; daughter Selah Figures, surviving children; daughter Olive Harris. Exs., Jeremiah and Jesse Drew. D. Sept. 10, 1774. R. Aug. 10, 1775. Wit. Abraham Johnson, Jesse Clifton, Thomas Ridley. Page 132.

DRAKE, Ann. Leg.- Ridley and Cordial, sons of Barnaby Drake, Jr., all the land on which Timothy Drake and I now live; to Burgess, Baker and Eaton Joyner; to Baldy Drake; Mary Drake the wife of Barnaby Drake, Jr.; sister Mary Drake; to Tabitha Joyner. Ex., Barnaby Drake, Jr. D. June 27, 1775. R. Aug. 10, 1775. Wit. J. Donson, Mourning Joyner, Jonas Joyner. Page 133.

HARRIS, Benjamin. Estate appraised by Jacob Turner, Thomas Luter and John Luter. R. Aug. 10, 1775. Page 134.

RAY, William. Leg.- loving wife; son Reuben; son James; daughter Sally Ray. Exs., wife and friend Lewis Bryant. D. May 8, 1775. R. Aug. 10, 1775. Wit. James Williamson, James Bryant. Page 135.

MERCER, John. Leg.- son John; daughter Patty Lowe; son James; daughter Patience; daughter Betty; daughter Grace Mercer. Exs., John Mercer and John Pursell. D. July 25, 1775. R. Dec. 14, 1775. Wit. Benjamin Crumpler, John Crumpler, John Britt. Page 136.

DRAKE, Ann. Estate appraised by Joseph Mountfortt, Thomas Mountfortt and Thomas Lankford, Jr. R. Dec. 14, 1775. Page 137.

VASSER, Elijah. Estate appraised by Daniel Pond, Richard Pond and Thomas Lane. R. Dec. 14, 1775. Page 138.

SCOTT, James Jordan. Leg.- wife Miriam; son Joseph son James; son Robert; daughter Anne; daughter Sarah Scott. Estate to be divided by friends, Joseph Scott, Lemuel Jones, Thomas Draper and Jordan Denson. Exs., Joseph Scott and Jordan Denson. D. Oct. 20, 1774. R. Dec. 12, 1775. Wit. Shadrack Lewis, Jesse Council, Thomas Coffield. Page 139.

CLAUD, Joshua. Leg.- son John; son William; son Joshua; daughter Phoebe Lundy; daughter Elizabeth Mundell; to my grandchildren, the children of John Clifton and my daughter Lydia; grandson Joshua Claud, son of Philip Claud, decd.; daughter Mary Williamson at a great distance, reversion of bequest to her children. Exs., Sons William and John Claud and Joshua Nicholson. D. Oct. 16, 1773. R. Dec. 14, 1775. Wit. Samuel Westbrook, Sr., Samuel Westbrook, Jr., John Westbrook.

Transaction of Joshua Claud, dated Saturday Nov. 4, 1775, witnessed by John Pierce, Britain Brantley and John Blake. R. Dec. 22, 1775. Page 141.

CLAUD, Joshua. Dec. 22, 1775. Estate appraised by Joshua Nicholson, Amos Harris and John Barrow. R. Jan. 11, 1776. Page 144.

BYNUM, Elizabeth. March 10, 1774. Estate appraised by Jacob Newsum, Nathan Harris and John Drake. R. Feb. 8, 1776. Page 144.

AVERY, Richard. Leg.- son Joel; son Thomas; son Edward the part of estate already paid for him to John Wilkinson; daughter Martha; son Etheldred when twenty one; wife Fortune; daughter Elizabeth Avery. Ex. Howell Edmunds. D. July 27, 1773. R. Feb. 8, 1776. Wit. David Edmunds Sr., David Edmunds, Jr., Benjamin Turner. Page 145.

IVY, Henry. Account estate. 1774. Audited by James Ridley and Joshua Nicholson. Exs. Henry Ivy and Robert Ivy. R. Feb. 8, 1776. Page 146.

BYNUM, Elizabeth. Account Current. Ex., John Wilkinson. Paid the heirs of William Bynum as per account, returned by Elizabeth Bynum. Audited by John Thomas Blow and John Crafford. R. Feb. 8, 1776. Page 147.

JOHNSON, John. Appraisal estate by Benjamin Griffin, Hardy Doyel and John Worrell. R. April 11, 1776. Page 148.

STEPHENSON, Elizabeth. Estate account. Ex., William Stephenson. Audited by Simon Boykin, John Clayton and John Summerell. R. May 9, 1776. Page 148.

HARRISON, Samuel. Parish of St. Luke. Leg.- wife Amima; son Joseph; son William when twenty one; to my children Olive, Rebecca, Elizabeth, Anne, Joseph, Charlotte, Solomon, Harmon, Hannah Richardson and Mary. Ex., Edward Lundy and Joshua Nicholson. D. March 19, 1775. R. May 9, 1776. Wit. James Lundy Jr., Moses Harris, Joel Atkinson, William Morgan. Page 149.

VASSER, Lydia. Parish of St. Luke. Leg.- son Jesse land purchased of Nicholas Gurley, when of age; daughter Anne; daughter Mary; daughter Elizabeth; daughter Margaret. Ex., son-in-law Robert Carr. D. Oct. 10, 1773. May 9, 1776. Wit. George Gurley, Abraham Mitchell, William Edwards. Page 150.

TAYLOR, Lucy. Leg.- daughter Mary Mason Taylor; daughter Martha; son Robert; daughter; Ann Brown. Exs. brother-in-law Henry Taylor, son-in-law William Brown. D. April 5, 1776. R. July 11, 1776. Wit. Temperance Taylor, Henry Taylor. Page 151.

RIDLEY, Nathaniel. Leg.- wife Sarah; son Mathew when of age, reversion to nephew Nathaniel the son of Day Ridley; negroes to be divided among the children of Day Ridley, his son Nathaniel excepted, Ann Holliday and Pamelia Coffield. Exs., wife Sarah and brothers Day and Thomas Ridley. D. Jan. 7, 1776. Wit. Jeremiah Drew, Faith Lane, James Ridley. Page 152.

GLOVER, George. May 29, 1776. Estate appraised by John Crenshaw, James Story, Philemon Hatfield. R. July 11, 1776. Page 153.

EVANS, Benjamin. June 21, 1776. Estate appraised by Arthur Foster, Enos James, William Francis. R. Sept. 12, 1776. Page 154.

WRAY, William. Inventory. May 26, 1775. Anne Wray, Extx. R. Oct. 10, 1776. Page 155.

STEPHENSON, Ann. Inventory. 1774. Martha Clary, Extx. R. Oct. 10, 1776. Page 155.

DAY, Edmund. July 19, 1776. Estate appraised by John Thomas Blow, John Taylor and William Miller. R. Oct. 10, 1776. Page 155.

JOYNER, Bridgman. Leg.- wife Mary, plantation bought of Jesse Council; nephew Lewis Joyner; to Jacob the son of Jacob Joyner; brother Jacob Joyner; brother Jesse Joyner. Friends Jacob Beale, James Fowler and Absalom Tallaugh to divide my estate. Ex., brother Jacob Joyner. D. July 26, 1776. R. Nov. 14, 1776. Wit. J. Denson, Jacob Beale, Absalom Tallough. Page 156.

BAILEY, Robert. Estate appraised by Henry Davis and Joel Davis. R. Nov. 14, 1775. Page 157.

DAVIS, Thomas, Jr. Leg.- daughter Anne; son Phillip; daughter Elizabeth; wife Hannah. Ex., son Phillip Davis. D. Sept. 17, 1776. R. Nov. 14, 1776. Wit. Edwin Davis, Sally Riggan. Page 158.

WESTBROOK, Elias. Leg.- Aunt Amey Foster and uncle Moses
Foster. Ex., uncle Moses Foster. D. July 9, 1776. R. Jan.
9, 1777. Wit. John Simmons, Joshua Fort. Page 159.

BOWERS, William. Leg.- son Britain; daughter Middey Exs., Jacob
Turner and son Randolph Bowers. D. Dec. 18, 1776. R. Jan.
9, 1777. Wit. Randolph Bowers, William Barmer, Jacob
Turner. Page 159.

TAYLOR, Etheldred. St. Luke's Parish. Leg.- cousin Charles
Taylor, son of my brother John Taylor. Ex., brother John
Taylor. D. April 15, 1776. R. Jan. 9, 1777. Caveat entered
by James Taylor. Wit. Batt Peterson, John Peterson. Page
160.

MERCER, Robert. Inventory. Jan. 9, 1777. Ex., Joseph
Holleman. Page 161.

KINNEBREW, Ann. Leg.- son Edwin; son Lot; granddaughter
Prissy Kinnebrew. Ex., friend Benjamin Blunt. D. Nov. 12,
1776. R. Jan. 9, 1777. Wit. Mary Bittle, Benjamin Blunt.
Page 161.

JOHNSON, Jesse. Estate appraised by John Mitchel, William
Branch, John Cell(?). Adm. Samuel Cooper. R. Jan. 9, 1777.
Page 162.

BARROW, John. Leg.- eldest son William; son Daniel; son John;
granddaughter Phebea Hill Barrow; daughter Anne Kinnebrew;
daughter Hannah Pitman; daughter Martha Frizzell. Exs. son John
Barrow and Benjamin Turner. D. John Blake, Henry Stephenson,
Lucy Stephenson. D. July 29, 1776. R. Jan. 9, 1777. Page
162. Inventory. March 13, 1777. Page 166.

JARRELL, Thomas. Estate appraised by William Miller, Richard
Blow, William Thomas. R. Feb. 13, 1777. Page 163.

JOYNER, Bridgman. Estate appraised by David Wright, John
Joyner and Etheldred Drake. R. Feb. 13, 1777. Page 164.

KINNEBREW, Lot. Inventory. Feb. 13, 1777. Page 163.

CLAUD, Joshua. Of St. Luke's Parish. Leg. My estate to my
sister Phoebe Lundy's children. Exs., brother-in-law Byrd
Lundy and Drury Lundy. D. Nov. 20, 1775. R. Feb. 15, 1777.
Wit. Edward Harris, Edward Lundy, Solomon Harrison. Page
165.

GAY, Edmund. Leg. Elizabeth Scott, daughter of John Scott;
Godson Edmund Blunt; children of my deceased brother Thomas
Gay; to my brothers and sister, - John Gay; Charles Gay;
Mary Barker, William Gay and Jonathan Gay. Ex., friend
William Scott. D. Oct. 31, 1774. R. May 9, 1776. Wit.
William Scott, James Moore, Richard Johnston, Jacob Randolph.
Page 165.

POPE, Joseph. Estate appraised by Thomas Edmunds, Richard Blow
and Edmund Gay. R. March 12, 1777. Page 167.

DELK, Joseph. Estate Account. 1774. Audited by William Miller
and John Taylor. R. March 13, 1777. Page 168.

DAVIS, Thomas Jr. Estate appraised by Richard Wren, Charles
Briggs and John Cobb. R. March 13, 1777. Page 168.

WESTBROOK, Thomas. Parish of St. Luke. Leg.- wife Hellen; son Henry; son Thomas; daughter Lucy Hunt; daughter Hellen Speed, plantation I had of James Speed; grandson Benjamin Speed; daughter Martha Judkins. Exs., Wife Hellen and son Henry Westbrook. D. Aug. 25, 1775. R. May 8, 1777. Wit. John Simmons, Sr., Susannah Simmons, Benjamin Lewis. Page 169.

FOWLER, James. Of Nottoway Parish. Leg.- son William; son James; my land to be divided by William Williams, Jonas Edwards and David Wright. Wife Sarah Fowler. Ex., son William Fowler. D. Feb. 23, 1777. R. May 8, 1777. Wit. Christian Johnson, Martha Johnson, Thomas Williams. Page 169.

HALE, Joseph. Estate appraised by John Gardner, Samuel Sandiford, James Chappell. D. Feb. 13, 1777. Elizabeth Hale, Admtx. R. May 8, 1777. Page 170.

HARGRAVE, Michael. Estate appraised by John Powell, William Vaughan, Samuel Kindred. R. May 8, 1777. Page 171.

HARRISON, William. Legs.- brother Henry (provided he pay a certain amount to brothers Benjamin, Richard and Nathaniel), reversion of bequest to his son Henry; sister Sarah McLemore. Exs., brothers Henry and Richard Harrison. D. June 4, 1777. R. June 12, 1777. Wit. John Sturgeon, Simon Harris, Celia Sturgeon. Page 172.

POPE, William. Leg.- daughter Christian; son William; my gun at Andrew Pope to be given Thomas Pope at twenty one; Hezekiah Pope; my hand mill at my son John Pope is to be used by Andrew, Jesse, William and John Pope; estate to be sold and the money equally divided between my sons and daughters, viz.- John, William, Hardy, Jesse and Andrew; daughters, Christian, Ann and Martha Pope (widow); daughter Alice Newton. Exs., sons William and Andrew Pope. D. July 8, 1776. R. June 12, 1777. Wit. Thomas Edmunds, Benjamin Blunt, John Porter, Samuel Edmunds. Page 173.

JOYNER, William. Leg.- wife Ann; son William; son William; son Lawrence; son Jethro; Ann Joyner, daughter of my brother Lewis Joyner. Exs., sons William, Lawrence and Jethro Joyner. D. Dec. 31, 1776. R. July 11, 1777. Wit. R. Kello, Micajah Griffin, Charles Council. Page 174.

CATHAN, John. Account estate. W. Gwaltney, Adm. Audited by Henry Briggs and Abraham Mitchell. R. Aug. 14, 1777. Page 175.

LITTLE, John. Account estate. Orphan William Little in account with Lucy Turner, Admtx of Simon Turner, his guardian. R. Aug. 14, 1777. Audited by William Blunt and John Sturgeon (or Stringer). Page 175.

KINNEBREW, Ann. Estate appraised by John Kirby and Kirby Brittle. R. Aug. 14, 1777. Page 175.

VASSER, Lydia. Estate appraised by Henry Briggs, William Thomas, Abram Mitchell. D. June 3, 1776. R. Aug. 13, 1777. Page 176.

ATKINSON, Timothy. Parish of Nottoway. Leg.- wife Elizabeth; son Timothy; daughter Holland; daughter Sally; daughter Patty; daughter Mary; daughter Betty Atkinson. Ex. son Timothy Atkinson. D. Jan. 27, 1777. R. Sept. 11, 1777. Wit. William Urquhart, John Clayton, Benjamin Britt. Page 178.

DREWRY, Thomas. Leg.- wife Elizabeth, reversion to all my children. Extx., wife Elizabeth Drewy. D. April 9, 1777. R. Sept. 11, 1777. Wit. John Davis, Jacob Joyner, Robert Hasty. Page 179.

AVORY, Richard. Estate appraised by Jacob Turner, John Powell and David Edmunds. D. Feb. 16, 1776. R. Sept. 11, 1777. Page 179.

JOYNER, William. Estate appraised by Mathew Charles, Henry Joyner, Joseph Mountfortt. R. Sept. 11, 1777. Page 180.

EDMUNDS, Mary. Leg.- son Howell; son William, son John; son Samuel at twenty one; to Charles, son of Henry Edmunds; daughter Sarah; daughter Mary Nicholson; daughter Martha Myrick; grandchildren Edmunds and Susan Myrick at age; daughter Lucy Nicholson; granddaughter Sarah and Lucy daughters of Howell Edmunds; granddaughter Elizabeth, Mary, Lucy and Martha, daughters of Stephen Williamson; to Etheldred son of Thomas Edmunds. Exs., sons William and Samuel and daughter Sarah Edmunds. Sept. 12, 1777. R. Dec. 11, 1777. Wit. John Pope, Simon Revel. Page 181.

JONES, Nathan. Leg.- brother Thomas Jones; wife Mary with reversion to cousin Mary, daughter of Blyth Wiliams; if without heirs to Ann now the wife of Joshua Whitney. Ex., friend Lemuel Jones. D. Sept. 20, 1777. R. Dec. 11, 1777. Wit., Martha Johnson, Ann Johnson, Mary and William Doyle. Lemuel Jones refused to act as Ex., Mary Jones qualified. Page 182.

WESTBROOK, Thomas. Inventory. Signed by Hellen Westbrook and Henry Westbrook. R. Dec. 11, 1777. Page 183.

DRURY, Thomas. Estate appraised by John Gardner, James Vick and Lewis Joyner. R. Dec. 11, 1777. Signed, Elizabeth Drury. Page 184.

FORT, Ann. Leg.- daughter Sarah Turner; son John; son Howell; son Littleton; son Turner Fort. Exs., William Turner, Jeremiah Drew. D. Oct. 20, 1777. R. Dec. 11, 1777. Wit. Solomon Cooper, Harris Johnson, Thomas Turner. Page 184.

JOYNER, Israel. Parish of St. Luke. Leg.- wife Sarah, what was hers at our marriage and one third of my estate; son Charles tract adjoining Benjamin Worrell; son Amos, tract adjoining Nathan Barnes, Jesse Pope and Robert Newsom; remainder of my estate to my sons Joseph, Giles, Mathew and Jordan and daughter Martha; son John Joyner. Exs., Wife Sarah and son Charles Joyner. D. Nov. --, 1777. R. Dec. 11, 1777. Wit. Samuel Woodard, Temperance Woodward, Robert Washington. Sarah Joyner acknowledged that she was satisfied with the estate left her by her husband. Page 185.

BOOTH, Robert. Leg.- son Beverley, tract bought of Benjamin Phillips; son Moses land given me by my father Robert Booth; daughter Elizabeth; grandson Robert Booth; daughter Lucy Sykes; granddaughter Maze Booth; grandson David Booth. Exs., brother Moses Booth and son Beverley Booth. D. Aug. 27, 1777. R. Dec. 11, 1777. Wit. Moses Booth, Elizabeth Booth, William Salter, Jr. Page 187.

FOWLER, James. Estate appraised by William Williams, Jonah Edwards, David Wright. R. Dec. 11, 1777. Page 189.

POND, Richard. Parish of Nottoway. Leg.- son Richard; son John Hawkins Pond the tract on which James Sedget formerly lived; daughter Elizabeth Moore; daughter Mary; daughter Sarah; daughter Martha; son Thomas; son James; wife Martha Pond. Exs. wife and sons Richard and John Hawkins Pond. D. Sept. 22, 1777. R. Jan. 11, 1778. Wit. Edwin Gray, Joshua Wood, Mary James. Page 189.

EDMUNDS, Mary. Inventory. Jan. 8, 1778. Page 191.

COBB, William. Estate appraised by Abraham Mitchell; Thomas Lawrence and Henry Cobb. D. March --, 1777. Signed J. Denson. R. Jan. 8, 1778. Page 191.

KINNEBREW, Mrs. Ann. Account Current. Paid the accounts of Shadrack and Jacob Kinnebrew. Paid legacies to Shadrack, Edwin and Lot Kinnebrew. Signed, Benjamin Blunt. Audited by Charles Briggs and Arthur Foster. R. Jan. 8, 1778. Page 192.

LUNDY, Byrd. Leg.- wife Pheeba, land bought of Edward Eppes decd. with reversion to the children I leave by her, viz.- Christian, Elizabeth, Edwin, Byrd, Joshua, Claud and James; son Edwin the land I purchased of Robert Wilkins; daughter Milly Lundy. Exs., wife Pheeby, sons Edwin and Byrd Lundy and friend Lewis Thorpe. D. Dec. 29, 1777. R. Wit. D. Fisher, William Claud, John Claud. Page 193.

RIDLEY, James Day. Leg.- my three children, John Edwards Ridley, Rebecca and Elizabeth Ridley; wife Mary Ridley. Ex., wife Mary Ridley. D. Aug. 10, 1776. R. Feb. 12, 1778. Wit. W. Edwards, Charles Portlock, Joseph Reece, Jr. Page 195.

WRIGHT, James. Leg.- grandson John son of James Wright; son Joseph Wright; daughter Martha Connor; grandson James Wright; wife Martha Wright. Ex., son Joseph Wright. D. Jan. 9, 1778. R. Feb. 12, 1778. Wit. John Pursell, Ledbetter Lowe, Saphera Fly. Page 194.

WARREN, Joseph. Parish of St. Luke. Leg.- wife Faith; son Michael; the following children have already received their part of my estate- Henry, Joseph, Sarah Smith; Faith Duprey and Mary Day; daughter Elizabeth Duprey; grandson Hill son of Thomas Day, Jr. Exs., wife and son Michael Warren. D. Aug. 15, 1775. R. Feb. 12, 1778. Wit. John Barrow, Richard Foster, Edith Kinnebrew. Page 196.

JACKSON, Sarah. Parish of St. Luke. Leg.- grandson Nathan Jackson, estate in the hands of James Peden; daughter Mary Gurley. Ex., friend William Edwards. D. June 9, 1777. R. Feb. 12, 1778. Wit. William Edwards, Martha Gurley. Page 196.

BEALL, John. To son Drury land adjoining Dr. Browne and Howell Whittington; son Burwell; son John; wife Liddia. Ex., Joseph Johnson. D. Sept. 13, 1777. R. Feb. 12, 1778. Wit. George Gurley, Thomas Edwards, Jacob Braswell. Page 197.

FOWLER, William. Leg.- wife Ann; son Benjamin; son Charles; son William Fowler. Ex., Burwell Barnes. D. Oct. 8, 1777. R. Feb. 12, 1778. Wit. Edmund Barrett, Epaphroditus Williams, Jacob Williams. Page 199.

BUSKIN, John. Estate appraised by John Johnson, Lawrence Joyner, Mathew Charles. R. Feb. 12, 1778. Page 199.

KITCHEN, Benjamin. Leg.- son Benjamin; son Nathaniel; son Frederick; son Etheldred; son Jesse articles bought of Robert Bailey; daughters- Lucy, Sarah, Martha, Cela, Betsey and Mary; wife Mary Kitchen. Ex., son Frederick Kitchen. D. Jan. 14, 1778. R. Feb. 12, 1778. Wit. Anselm Jones, James Jones, Charles Briggs. Page 200.

BOOTH, Robert. Estate appraised by Barnaby Bailey, Richard Bailey and Charles Bailey. R. March 12, 1778. Page 201.

RIDLEY, Nathaniel. Inventory. R. March 6, 1778. Signed, Sarah Ridley. Page 20-.

WRIGHT, James. Estate appraised by Benjamin Crumpler, Beasant Crumpler, Robbin Williamson. R. March 12, 1778. Page 205.

AUSTIN, William. Leg.- wife Ruth; son Charles, son John; daughter Sarah Jackson; son Richard; daughter Molly. D. Sept. 2, 1770. R. March 12, 1778. Wit. Samuel Bridger Collins, William Barden. Exs., wife Ruth and Edward Drew. Page 206.

POND, Richard. Estate appraised by Joshua Woods, John Cobb and Benjamin Exum. R. March 12, 1778. Page 207.

FOWLER, William. Estate appraised by Jacob Barnes, James Barnes and Edmund Barrett. R. March 12, 1778. Page 208.

HOWELL, Hartwell. Estate appraised by William Millar, Richard Blow and John Fort. R. March 12, 1778. Page 209.

SIMMONS, William. Of Nottoway Parish. Leg.- wife Sarah land bought of Henry Browne, and another tract of Thomas Langley; son John; son Thomas land purchased of Thomas Clifton and another of John Meacum, adjoining Samuel Drewry and one of James Ingraham; son Daniel Simmons. Exs., friends Peter Butts, Edwin Gray, Benjamin Ruffin, Jr. D. Nov. 12, 1775. R. April 9, 1778. Wit. Thomas Butts, Henry Adams, Benjamin Scarborough, William Butts. Page 211.

CARY, Miles. Inventory. Signed, Henry Taylor. March 6, 1767. R. April 9, 1778. Page 212.

KITCHEN, Benjamin. Estate appraised by Joshua Wood, Richard Wren and Moses Wood. R. May 14, 1778. Page 213.

SPEED, Mary. Parish of Nottoway. Leg.- youngest daughter Rebecca; rest of my estate to my other two children, Isham Hill and Croker (Crocker ?) Cobb. Exs.,-son Isham Hill and William Cobb. D. Feb. 15, 1773. R. May 14, 1778. Wit. William Gresswitt, Samuel Cobb, Lazarus Cobb. Page 215.

COBB, Joseph. Inventory. Signed Henry Cobb. D. Aug. 12, 1777. R. May 14, 1778. Page 216.

JONES, Nathan. Estate appraised by Moses Johnson, John Summerell, Benjamin Crumpler. R. March 11, 1778. Page 216.

LUNDY, Edward. Of Parish of St. Luke. Leg.- wife; son Lunsford; daughter Frances, rest of estate between all my children except Frances and son William. Exs. (omitted), but the will was presented by Elizabeth Lundy and William Lundy. D. April 22, 1778. R. June 11, 1778. Wit. Edward Harris, Charles Portlock, John Lundy, James Lundy. Page 217.

HAILE, Joseph. Account estate. Signed Elizabeth Haile.
Audited by Edmund Tyler and Lewis Joyner. R. June 11, 1778.
Page 218.

BYNUM, Michael. Account current. Signed, John Wilkinson.
Legacies paid Benjamin Bynum; Nathan Bryant; to Benja. Bryant
guardian of Eliby Bynum, Turner Bynum and Colen Whitehead
Bynum, also for keeping Betsy Bynum and Michael Bynum. Audited
by Benjamin Blunt and John Powell. Page 218.

THORPE, Aaron. Joshua Nicholson, Adm. Refers to a negro in
duspute with Abram Johnson. Audited by J. Ridley, Henry
Taylor and Timothy Thorpe. R. June 11, 1778. Page 220.

BLUNT, Thomas. Of Parish of Nottoway. Leg.- wife Ann, land
bought of Henry Brownes' Exs.; son Henry; son Joseph Gray;
son Thomas; son Edmund; son William; son James; daughters
Sarah, Elizabeth and Ann Blunt. Exs., friends Edwin Gray and
William Thomas. D. Sept. 26, 1777. R. March 12, 1778. Wit.
Benjamin Williams, William Moore, John Bidgood. Page 221.

TATUM, John. Signed, Elizabeth Tatum, Admtx. Paid Richard
Tatum, Joshua Tatum and Rebecca Tatum. Audited by Lewis
Joyner, Sr. and Lewis Joyner, Jr. R. July 9, 1778. Page 222.

JOYNER, Israel. Inventory. R. July 9, 1778. Page 223.

BRADSHAW, Joseph. Leg.- son Joseph land adjoining Jetrho Joyner;
wife Elizabeth; son Semor; son William; son Elias; daughter
Margaret Love; daughter Mary Boone; daughter Ann Croker; at
wife's death estate left her to Honour, Avey, Semor, William
and Elias Bradshaw. Exs., wife Elizabeth and son Joseph
Bradshaw. D. July 11, 1778. R. Sept. 10, 1778. Wit.
Lawrence Joyner, Thomas Bradshaw, Rebekah Joyner. Page 224.

CALTHORP, Ellennere. Estate appraised by Barnaby Bailey, Henry
Coker and Jesse Harrell. R. Sept. 10, 1778. Page 225.

BLUNT, Thomas. Inventory. Signed, Edwin Gray and William
Thomas. R. Oct. 8, 1778. Page 226.

CLEMENTS, Benjamin. Of the Parish of Nottoway. Leg.- son
George my plantation in Prince George County, on which he now
lives, reversion to his children, Elizabeth, Thomas, Lucy,
George and Richard Clements; son Benjamin; son Thomas;
daughter Anna; grandson Jesse Butts the land bought of Charles
Gilliam; daughter Elizabeth Butts; daughter Sarah Butts; to
the nine children of Peter Butts, my grandchildren, Thomas,
John, Benjamin, William, James, Daniel, Lucy, Mary and Elizabeth
Butts; granddaughter Judith Gilliam; grandson Thomas Clements
Gilliam; to the five children of Thomas Peete, my grandchildren,
Elizabeth, Samuel, Benjamin, Thomas and Alexander Peete; grand-
son Thomas Clement Butts. Exs., Sons Benjamin and Thomas
Clements. D. July 9, 1778. R. Oct. 8, 1778. Wit. John
Knight, John Brown, Thomas Peete. Page 228.

DELOACH, William. Parish of Nottoway. Leg.- grandson John
Hudson Deloach, son of John Deloach; son Benjamin. D. April
11, 1772. R. Oct. 8, 1778. Wit. Eustace Windham, Jesse
Windham, Ann Dunn. Page 229.

WELLONS, John. Parish of Nottoway. Leg.- son John; son Henry;
son Charles; daughter Mary; wife Annemeriah; daughter Elizabeth
the wife of Howell Branch; daughter Barbary, wife of Benjamin

Oney. Exs., sons John and Charles Wellons. D. Dec. 18, 1773. R. Oct. 8, 1778. Wit. Francis Rose, Johnson Barnes. Page 230.

VICK, William. Leg.- wife Elizabeth; son Simon land adjoining Epaphroditus Williams, also part of the tract which I gave Simon Baret, adjoining my son William; son Robert a tract adjoining Mathew Vick, Davis Bryant and Thomas Vick; to granddaughter Rebecca Pope and her mother Mary Pope land adjoining son William, William Fowler and Simon Baret; son Isaac; daughter Elizabeth Pope and daughter Martha Baret. Ex., sons Simon and Robert Vick. D. Feb. 15, 1777. R. June 9, 1778. Wit. Jacob Vick, Mathew Vick, Lewis Bryant. Page 231.

WARREN, Joseph. Inventory. Signed Faith Warren and Michael Warren. R. May 14, 1778. Page 232.

RAWLINGS, John. Of St. Luke Parish. Leg.- daughter Betty Sammons (?); son Isaac; daughter Mary Adams; wife Mary Rawlings. Exs., son Isaac and son-in-law Thomas Adams. D. Sept. 17, 1777. R. Oct. 8, 1778. Wit. Richard Mason, George Bell (Beel ?) Henry Ivy. Page 233.

RAWLINGS, William. Estate appraised by Joshua Thorp, Henry Ivy and Joshua Nicholson. D. Sept. 25, 1777. R. Oct. 8, 1778. Page 234.

LUNDY, Drury. Estate appraised by Joseph Reese, Thomas Turner and John Myrick. R. Oct. 8, 1778. Page 234.

MOORE, James. Leg.- wife; son James; son Jesse; daughter Martha; daughter Elizabeth; daughter Sarah; son Richard Moore. Exs., Richard Pond, Richard Ricks, Edwin Gray. D. March 15, 1775. R. Oct. 8, 1778. Wit. Benjamin Stewart, James Bell, Eliphas Lewis Isaac and Jesse Williams qualified as Exs. Page 236.

DAVIS, Thomas. Of the Parish of Nottoway. Leg.- wife Jeane; daughter-in-law Hannah Davis, relict of my son Thomas; grandson Phillip Davis; son Henry land I bought of my son Drury; daughter Hannah; granddaughter Sarah Long; daughter Lucy Phillips; daughter Mary Tarver; to friend Richard Renn a tract of land for value received adjoining Charles Holt and John Thorpe; to sons of my son Drury, Etheldred, Thomas and James Davis. Ex. son Henry Davis. D. June 4, 1778. R. Nov. 12, 1778. Wit. Charles Briggs, Joel Davis, John Mitchel. Page 236.

TURNER, John. Account estate. Ex., Joshua Nicholson. Legacies paid to son Jacob; son Joseph; son Amos; son Jesse and paid to William Claud, guardian of son David. Received his part of his father's estate from his Exs. Audited by Henry Harris and Timothy Thorpe. R. Nov. 12, 1778. Page 237.

TAYLOR, Harris. Leg.- son Bartin; daughter Mary Sousberry; daughter Nancy Johnson; son Henry; daughter Sarah Lisles; daughter Elizabeth Edwards; son Thomas; wife Lucy Taylor. Ex., son Henry Taylor. D. Nov. 18, 1777. R. Nov. 12, 1778. Wit. James Maddra, Samuel Taylor, Elizabeth Ellis. Page 238.

LONGWORTH, John. Estate appraised by Ben -----, John Cobb and Thomas Butts. R. Nov. 12, 1778. Page 239.

FOGERSON, (?) John. Leg.- son William; son Josiah; Ann Thorpe; wife Ann. 3 of 7 mo. 1778. R. Nov. 12, 1778. Wit. Drury Beal, William Gwaltney, Michael Gwaltney. Page 240.

NEWSUM, Jacob. Parish of St. Luke. Leg.- wife; son Gilliam at twenty one; to my four sons; to all my children. Exs., wife, friends Anselm and Isham Gilliam. D. Oct. 2, 1771. Codicil.- to my three sons, Littleberry, Isham and Jacob Newsum. D. March 9, 1778. R. Nov. 12, 1778. Wit. Thomas Holt, Sr., Etheldred Taylor, Henry Taylor, Temperance Taylor. Page 240.

BEAL, John. Account estate. Legacies paid to Liddia Beal, John Beal and Drury Beal. Auditors, Howell Williamson, Samuel Story and John Crenshaw. R. Nov. 12, 1778. Page 242.

LONGWORTH, Joseph. Inventory. 1777. Signed Benjamin Ruffin Adm. R. Nov. 12, 1778. Page 243.

WELLONS, John. Estate appraised by Charles Powers, Sampson Pitman and Thomas Lane. R. Feb. 14, 1779. Page 243.

FORD, Ann. Estate appraised by Jesse Drew and Thomas Turner. D. Dec. --, 1778. R. Feb. 14, 1779. Page 243.

SPEED, Mary. Inventory. Signed Isham Hill. R. Feb. 14, 1779. Page 244.

VICK, William. Estate appraised by John Edwards, James Bryant and Nathan Barnes. R. Feb. 14, 1779. Page 244.

PHILLIPS, John. (Aged). Leg.- son Joshua; grandson Thomas Phillips; daughter Faithy Ellis; daughter Hannah Davis; grandson Phillip Davis; son John reversion to his daughter Lucy Phillips when she is eighteen; grandson Edwin Ellis; grandson John Phillips at twenty one. Ex., son Joseph Phillips. D. Jan. 10, 1779. R. Feb. 14, 1779. Wit. Howel Jones, Edwin Kinnebrew, Milley Hix. Page 245.

BRADSHAW, Joseph. Estate appraised by Lawrence Joyner and Arthur Bowing. R. Feb. 14, 1779. Page 246.

TAYLOR, Harris. Estate appraised by John Wilkins, John Pitman and Lazarus Cook. R. Feb. 14, 1779. Page 247.

COOPER, John. Account estate. Signed Solomon Cooper. Audited by Hardy Harris, Joshua Nicolson. Page 247.

TUCKER, Benjamin. Leg.- son William; son John; son Henry; son Benjamin; daughter Phebe; daughter Winifred; daughter Elizabeth Tucker. Exs. sons John and Henry Tucker. D. Jan. 13, 1778. R. Feb. 14, 1779. Wit. Henry Tucker, Priscilla Gurley, Sarah Edward. Page 248.

REESE, Joseph. Of Parish of Nottoway. Leg.- son John; wife Mary; son Edward; grandson Joseph Reese, son of Edward; daughter Mary Thomas; son Joseph Reese. Exs., wife and son Edward. D. Nov. 14, 1775. R. Feb. 14, 1779. Wit. John Ivy, Moses Thorp, Robert Ivy, Joshua Nicholson. Page 248.

BEALE, Hardy. Leg.- brother Burwell Beale, land on which Britain Jones lived; sister Sarah Beale with reversion to Thomas Joyner; to Thomas Taylor. Exs. Absolom Joyner and Thomas Joyner. D. Dec. 21, 1778. R. Feb. 14, 1779. Wit. Jesse Joyner, Elizabeth Joyner, Daniel Massingaile. Page 250.

BEALE, William. Leg.- son William; son John; wife Priscilla; daughter Patty; son Burwell Beale. Exs. wife and son William. D. April 17, 1778. R. Feb. 14, 1779. Wit. Benjamin Beale, John Drake, Joseph Turner, William Bridger. Page 250.

ONEY, Leonard. Of the Parish of Nottoway. Leg.- daughters Lucy, Martha and Hannah; son Thomas; son John; son Benjamin; daughter Elizabeth, wife of John Atkinson; daughter Mary, wife of James Atkinson. Ex., son Thomas Oney. D. Sept. 18, 1772. R. Feb. 14, 1779. Wit. Nathaniel Coker, Arthur Exum. Page 251.

JOHNSON, Samuel. Of the Parish of Nottoway. Leg.- son Giles; son John land bought of young John Bowen, adjoining John Parr, Simon Johnson and Giles Johnson, son-in-law William Gwi (Gwin); son Samuel; son Simon; daughter Mary Turner; wife Mary Johnson. Exs., wife Mary and son Giles Johnson. D. May 17, 1767. R. Feb. 14, 1779. Wit. Henry Pope, Simon Harris, Hardy Pope. Page 252.

BRITT, John, Sr. Leg.- son John; son Jesse; son Henry; son James; son William; wife Marthat Britt. D. Feb. 15, 1777. R. Feb. 14, 1779. Exs., sons John and Jesse Britt. Wit. Thomas Turner, John Rogers. Page 253.

JONES, Robert. Leg.- wife; daughter Frances; daughter Elizabeth; son Mathew; son Robey; son James; son Benjamin. Exs. brother James Jones and brother-in-law John Simmons. D. June 23, 1778. R. Feb. 14, 1779. Wit. Benjamin Barram, Lucaucy Jones, David Jones. Page 254.

JOHNSON, Jesse. Account Estate. Jesse Cooper, Adm. Audited by Timothy Thorpe, John Blunt and Mark Nicolson. R. Feb. 14, 1779. Page 255.

DELOACH, William. Inventory. Signed, Benjamin Deloach. R. March 11, 1779. Page 255.

ONEY, Leonard. Inventory. R. March 11, 1779. Page 256.

LUTER, Thomas. Estate appraised by Simon Johnson, Joshua Minard and Toomer Joyner. R. March 11, 1779. Page 256.

RICKS, Richard. Of the Parish of Nottoway. Leg.- wife Ann; nephew Richard Ricks; nephew Joseph Ricks; to Samuel, son of my nephew Thomas Ricks; to Robert and John sons of my nephew Thomas Ricks; nephew Robert Ricks; neice Ann Jones; neice Mary Ricks; to Thomas, Robert, Richard, Joseph, Mary, Milisent and Ann children of my deceased brother Robert Ricks. Exs., friends Thomas Blow and William Thomas and nephews, Robert, Richard and Joseph Ricks. D. Sept. 2, 1778. R. March 11, 1779. Wit. Isaac Williams, Thomas Curney, Richard Johnson, John Bidgood. Page 256.

AUSTIN, William. Inventory. Signed, Ruth Austin. R. March 11, 1779. Page 258.

HINES, Joshua. Estate appraised by John Kirby, Jesse Arrington and John Brown. R. March 11, 1779. Page 259.

WILLIAMS, Jacob. Estate appraised November 9, 1769, by Nicholas Williams, George Washington, Job Wright. R. March 11, 1779. Page 259.

HATFIELD, Josiah. Leg.- father Philemon Hatfield and mother Mary Hatfield; sisters Mary Daughtry, Charity, Selah, Jemimy, Mildred, Tabitha and Elizabeth Hatfield. Exs., friends, Capt. Jesse Whitehead and James Maget. D. March 10, 1778. R. April 9, 1779. Wit. Benjamin Blunt, John Thomas Blow, Thomas Edmunds. Page 260.

WILSON, William. Leg.- sister Pheeby Wilson; brother George Wilson. Ex. Capt. Jesse Whitehead. D. March 10, 1778. R. April 9, 1779. Wit. John Thomas Blow, Benjamin Blunt, Thomas Edmunds. Page 261.

BOOTH, Robert. Account current. Legacies paid to Elizabeth Booth, Beverley Booth and to the guardian of Moses Booth. Audited by Wil Salter, Jr., Richard Bailey, Barnaby Bailey. R. May 13, 1779. Page 261.

RIDLEY, James Day. Estate appraised by Joshua Thorpe, John Myrick and John Blunt. R. May 13, 1779. Page 262.

NIBLETT, James. Inventory. Burwell Williamson Adm. R. May 13, 1779. Page 263.

POPE, Patience. Leg.- son-in-law Jonathan Pope; son-in-law Elijah Pope; son Nathan Pope; to my six other children - Jehu, Phebe, Joel, Richard, Patience and Charity Pope. Ex., Nathan Barnes. D. Nov. 3, 1777. R. May 13, 1779. Wit. Joshua Johnson, Moses Johnson, Josiah Pope. Page 264.

NEWSUM, Sampson. Leg.- wife Mary; son Hartwell; to my three daughters and grandson, Agness Polly Newsum, Joice Moseley, Mary Armstrong and Sampson, son of Jesse Newsum; daughter Martha Johnson. Exs., Robert Andrews and son Hartwell Newsum. D. Sept. 18, 1778. R. May 13, 1779. Wit. William Barham, John Fort, Nathaniel Tamer (?). Page 264.

EDMUNDS, Mary. Account Current. William and Samuel Edmunds, Exs. Legacies paid,- Howell Edmunds and daughters; to William, John, Samuel, Charles and Sarah Edmunds; to Mary Nicolson; to Martha Mirick and child; to Lucy Nicolson; to Elizabeth, Mary, Lucy and Martha, daughters of Stephenson Williamson; to Etheldred son of Thomas Edmunds. Audited by John Wilkinson, William Blunt, Arthur Foster. R. May 13, 1779. Page 265.

REESE, Joseph. Inventory. Signed, Edward Reese. R. May 13, 1779. Page 266.

TURNER, William. Leg.- son Littleton, tract by my wife near Meherrin River; son Arthur; son James; daughter Ann; daughter Fanny Turner. Exs., brother Benjamin Turner and son Littleton Turner. D. Feb. 20, 1779. R. May 13, 1779. Wit. Jacob Barnes, Sarah Barnes, Thomas Edmunds. Page 266.

RAMSEY, James. Account current. Signed, Catherine Ramsey. Audited by William Blunt and John Sturgeon. R. June 10, 1779. Page 267.

DAVIS, Thomas. Account current. Paid Edwin Davis, orphan. Signed, Henry Davis. Audited by Beverley Booth and John Powell. R. June 10, 1779. Page 268.

GRIZARD, William. Parish of St. Luke. Leg.- wife Mary; my land to be laid off by Joh Lewter, Sr., Cordal Norfleet, John Blunt and John Crafford; son William; son Thomas land bought of John Bird; son Hulin; daughter Milly Johnson; daughter Ann Williams;

daughter Priscilla Phillips; daughter Mary Munger; son Isum; son Jerry; daughters Dorcas, Pheba, Celia, Charlotte, Elizabeth and Tabitha Grizard. Exs., Moses Johnson and Henry Mounger. D. April 7, 1779. R. June 10, 1779. Wit. John Luter, John Blunt, Mary James. Page 268.

BARHAM, Benjamin. Of the Parish of St. Luke. Leg.- wife Mary; son William land bought of Joseph Cornett; son John land bought of Nathaniel Newsum; son Benjamin; daughter Lucy; daughter Fanny; daughter Elizabeth Barham. Exs., sons William and John Barham. D. March 30, 1776. R. June 10, 1779. Wit. Henry Taylor, James Ridley, Temperance Taylor. Page 269.

HARRISON, Samuel. Estate appraised by James Lundy, John Rogers and John Ivy. Signed Joshua Nicolson, Ex. R. June 10, 1779. Page 270.

JOHNSON, Samuel. Estate appraised by Micajah Griffin, Hardy Pope, John Council. R. June 10, 1779. Page 271.

BEALE, William. Estate appraised by William Williams, David Wright and Jonah Edwards. Signed William Beale, Ex. R. June 10, 1779. Page 272.

LUTER, Thomas. Account Current. Audited by Elias Herring and Hardy Pope. R. June 10, 1779. Page 272.

THORPE, Peterson. Estate appraised by Benjamin Lewis, Arthur Foster, Alexander Murry. Signed, Timothy Thorpe, Adm. R. June 10, 1779. Page 273.

PHILLIPS, John. Inventory. Signed Joseph Phillips. R. June 10, 1779. Page 275.

COBB, William. Estate appraised by Abraham Mitchell, Thomas Lawrence and Henry Cobb. Signed J. Denson. R. July 8, 1779. Page 275.

SCOTT, James Jordan. Estate appraised by Joseph Mountfortt, Thomas Lankford and Shadrack Lewis. R. July 8, 1779. Page 276.

NEWSUM, Sampson. Estate appraised by Joshua Nicholson, Owen Myrick, John Fort. Signed, Robert Andrews and Hartwell Newsum. R. July -, 1779. Page 277.

MOORE, James. Estate appraised by Samuel Drewry, Thomas Butts and John Kirby. R. July -, 1779. Page 278.

LUNDY, Bird. Estate appraised by Edward Harris, John Mirick and Joseph Reese. Signed, Phebe Lundy and Lewis Thorpe. R. July 8, 1779. Page 279.

BEALE, William. Account estate - paid a legacy to Martha Beale. Signed, William Beale, Ex. Audited by Joseph Mountford and Thomas Lankford. R. July 8, 1779. Page 281.

ONEY, Leonard. Account estate. Signed Thomas Oney. Audited by Benjamin Deloach and Thomas Lane. R. Aug. 12, 1779. Page 281.

RICKS, Richard. Estate appraised by Lewis Joyner, Jr., Isaac Williams, John Johnson. R. Aug. 12, 1779. Page 281.

VASSER, Lydia. Current Account. Among items, paid Jesse, Robert, Margaret and Mary Vasser; to legacy left daughter Mary Vasser. Audited by William Thomas and Jesse Whitehead. R. Aug. 12, 1779. Page 283.

CLIFTON, Thomas. Estate appraised by Benjamin Clements, John Simmons and William Foster. R. Aug. 12, 1779. Page 283.

BASS, Joshua. Leg.- Thomas son of Arthur Bass; Burges son of Hardy Bass. Ex. friend Lewis Thorpe. D. Jan. 30, 1779. R. Sept. 9, 1779. Wit. Arthur Bass, Henry Bass, Selah Bass. Page 284.

BARNES, Benjamin. Leg.- wife Mary; son John; son William land purchased of Joshua Johnson and Richard Ricks adjoining William Thomas and John Thomas Blow, from Robert, Richard and Joseph Ricks, exs. of Richard Ricks, decd.; son Jacob land bought of Richard Johnson, Arthur Allen, and Mathew Johnson, also the plantation on which I live after the death of my wife, adjoining Albridgeton Jones, Jordan Denson, Jacob Jenkins and Lewis Joyner; daughter Mary, wife of Stephen Johnson; daughter Peninah Barnes; daughter Milly Barnes. Exs., wife Mary and friend George Washington (son of George) and son William Barnes. D. --- 20, 1779. R. Sept. 9, 1779. Wit. George Washington, Joseph Johnson, Benjamin Williams, Hardy Johnson. Page 284.

HARRIS, Joshua. Account Estate. Jesse Harris, Adm. Audited by Joshua Nicholson, Hardy Harris. 1775. R. Sept. 9, 1779. Page 286.

ADAMS, Robert. Estate appraised. (Not signed.) R. Sept. 9, 1779. Page 286.

COBB, William. Account estate. Jordan Denson, Adm. R. Sept. 9, 1779. Page 287.

POPE, William, Sr. Inventory. Signed, William Pope and Andrew Pope. R. Sept. 9, 1779. Page 287.

VAUGHAN, William. Leg.- mother Sarah Vaughan; brother-in-law Nathan Turner. Ex., Nathan Turner. D. Oct. 28, 1776. R. Oct. 14, 1779. Wit. John -ort, Thomas Turner. Page 289.

POPE, John. Leg.- son Henson, land adjoining Samuel Edmunds; son John; daughter Temperance; daughter Sally; wife Ann Pope. Exs., wife Ann and her brother Mathew Underwood. D. July 11, 1779. R. Oct. 14, 1779. Wit. Nathan Barnes, Sarah Head. (?). Page 289.

BUFFKIN, John. Account estate. Signed, Tuke Denson, Adm. Audited by Lawrence Joyner, John Johnson. R. Oct. 14, 1779. Page 290.

WILLIAMS, Drury. Estate appraised by Benjamin Williams, George Washington and John Davis. R. Oct. 14, 1779. Page 290.

CURL, Thomas. Leg.- sister Martha Fdwards. Ex., Capt. Jesse Whitehead. D. Oct. 2, 1777. R. Oct. 14, 1779. Wit. Howell Myrick, William Wilson, John Johnston. Page 290.

BURN, David. Of Parish of Nottoway. Leg.- son David; daughter Martha Wheelis (Wheeler ?); daughter Elizabeth Mason; daughter Rebecca Vaughan; daughter Mary Council; son Sampson;

son Hardy; wife Patience; daughter Ann; daughter Sarah Council.
Ex., son-in-law Cutchins Council. D. Oct. 2, 1779. R. Nov.
11, 1779. Wit. Thomas Lankford, Theo Lewis, Joseph
Mountfortt Codicil: to Patience Burn and granddaughter Edith
Council. Nov. 5, 1779. R. Nov. 11, 1779. Wit. Joseph
Mountfortt, Shadrack Lewis. Page 291.

POPE, John. Estate appraised by Nathan Barnes, William
Whitehead and Samuel Edmunds. R. Dec. 9, 1779. Page 292.

POND, Richard. Account. Richard Pond and Martha Pond. Audited
by John Salter and John Pond. R. Dec. 9, 1779. Page 292.

GRIZARD, William. Estate appraised by John Suiter, Cordall
Norfleet, John Blunt. R. Jan. 10, 1780. Page 293.

BASS, Joshua. Estate appraised by John Reese, Edward Reese,
Henry Ivy. R. Jan. 10, 1780. Page 294.

BARNES, Benjamin. Leg.- William Barnes; Jacob Barnes; Pening
Barnes; Milly Barnes. Proved by Benjamin Williams, Abraham
Mitchell, Isaack Williams and John Davis. D. Oct. 17, 1779.
R. Jan. 10, 1780. Page 294.

BREWER, John. Of Hertford County, Province of North Carolina,
Planter. Leg.- loving wife; son John; son Reace; son Jacob;
son Jesse; daughter Pacience; daughter Elizabeth; daughter
Ann; daughter Frances; son Hardy; son Henry Brewer. Exs.,
wife and son Hardy Brewer. D. R. Jan. 10, 1780. Wit.
George Little, Abraham Poter, Rebecca Morgan, Will presented
by Ann and Hardy Brewer. Page 295.

BURN, David. Estate appraised by Thomas Lankford, Henry Joyner
and Thad Lewis. R. 1780. Page 296.

BURN, Patience. Appraisal ordered Nov. 11, 1779. Appraised by
Joseph Mountfortt, Henry Joyner and Thad Lewis. R. 1780.
Page 296.

FORT, Ann. Account current. Signed, William Turner, Ex.
Audited by Joshua Nicolson and Hardy Harris. R. May 11, 1780.
Page 296.

SMITH, John. Leg.- wife Martha, tract bought of Benjamin
Holleman. Exs., wife and Joshua Bailey. D. Jan. 1, 1780.
R. May 11, 1780. Wit. Benjamin Bailey, Micajah Holleman.
Page 296.

WOMBWELL, Jesse. Legacies paid Selah and Nancy Wombwell.
Audited by William Urquhart and Micajah Holleman. R. May 11,
1780. Page 297.

HINES, Joshua. Account estate. Audited by Joshua Nicolson and
Arthur Foster. R. May 11, 1780. Page 297.

MACKEY, Joseph. Of the Parish of Nottoway. Leg.- Joshua
Miniard; Elizabeth Mackey. Exs., Joshua Miniard and Elizabeth
Mackey. D. Sept. 30, 1779. R. May 11, 1780. Wit. Toomer
Joyner, Martha Joyner, Ann Joyner, Elias Herring. Page 297.

AVERY, Fortune. Leg.- daughter Elizabeth Grizard. D. Feb. 18,
1778. R. May 11, 1780. Wit. Mary Coggan, Ann Coggan, David
Edmunds. Page 298.

BUTTS, Peter. Of the Parish of Nottoway. Leg.- sons Thomas, Benjamin, John, William and James; daughter Lucy; daughter Molly; daughter Betty; son Daniel at the death of my wife my plantation on which I live: wife Elizabeth. Exs., Benjamin Clements and sons Thomas and Benjamin Butts. D. March 24, 1780. R. June 8, 1780. Wit. Edwin Gray, Benjamin Kirby, Silas Kirby. Page 298.

SCOTT, James Jordan. Signed Jordan Denson Ex. Account estate. Among items, paid Miriam Scott as the will directed; paid Joseph Scott his specific legacy; paid Miriam Scott guardian of James J. Scott his legacy. Audited by Henry Briggs, Albridgton Jones, Lewis Joyner. R. June 8, 1780. Page 299.

MACKEY, Joseph. Estate appraised by Henry Jones, Giles Johnson, John Johnson. R. June 8, 1780. Page 300.

MILLAR, William. Estate appraised, Feb. 20, 1779 by Arthur Foster, John Taylor, John Fort. R. July 13, 1780. Page 300.

BRITAIN, Elisha. D. Jan. 1, 1780. R. July 13, 1780. Page 300.

FIGURES, Joseph. Leg.- Nephew Richard Mossom; son Thomas, if he should return, reversion of bequest to neice Jane Mossom; wife Elizabeth Lucy Figures; to sons Bartholomew and Thomas if they return, reversion to Thomas and Rebecca Bage, the children of Thomas Bage; Richard Figures, son of William Figures; Richard and Jane Mossom, children of William Mossom. Exs. Jesse Whitehead of Southampton County, Thomas Figures and John Maget of the County of Hertford in N. Car. D. March 27, 1780. R. July 13, 1780. Wit. Nicholas Maget, John Boon, Reuben Hill, Rebeckah Stevenson. Page 301.

STURGEON, John. Parish of St. Luke. Leg.- wife Saley; son John Williams Sturgeon; son William Sturgeon. Exs. Wife and friend William Blunt. D. Oct. 28, 1779. R. Aug. 11, 1780. Wit. Simon Harris, Henry Harrison, Richard Harrison. Page 302.

LUNDY, Drury. Signed, James Lundy, Adm. 1778. Account estate. The same proportional part of the estate paid the following: John Lundy; Elizabeth Lundy, Almtx of Drury Lundy; Joseph Reese, Jr.,; Lewis Thorpe Ex. of Byrd Lundy; Edward Harris; Henry Holt's orphans and James Lundy. R. Sept. 14, 1780. Page 302.

CLEMENTS, Benjamin. of Parish of Nottoway. Leg.- son Thomas land on Angeliaa Swamp and land on Nottoway River bought of Pleasant Cocke; son Francis land on which my father lived and a sword loaned Thomas Butts; cattle on my plantation in St. Luke's Parish to Samuel Clifton; son John; daughters Sarah and Elizabeth my plantation in Brunswick County; wife Elizabeth Clements. Exs., brother Thomas Clements, Thomas Clements Butts and Dr. Thomas Peete. D. Dec. 11, 1778. R. Sept. 14, 1780. Wit. John Simmons, Benjamin Kirby, Thomas Butts, Richard Parker. Page 303.

JENKINS, Edmunds. Leg.- wife Sarah; son Valentine; daughter Sally Bailey. Ex., Son Valentine Jenkins. D. Oct. 6, 1779. R. Dec. 14, 1780. Wit. William Urquhart, Robert Eley. Page 304.

EDMUNDS, David. Leg.- wife Ann, son Howell a tract bought of Benjamin Clements, Cordall Norfleet and William Bowers; daughter Mary Dawson; son William tract purchased of Richard

Taylor; land bought of Sterling Francis to be sold; wife Ann
Edmunds. Exs., sons, Howell, John Dawson and William Edmunds.
D. July 29, 1780. R. Dec. 14, 1780. Wit. Samuel Nicolson,
Molly Taylor, Barham Hines, Hardy Grizzard. Page 305.

VICK, Arthur. Leg. - ------- and his heirs; son Shadrack;
son Arthur; son Samuel. Exs. sons Arthur and Samuel Vick.
D. April 9, 1777. R. Dec. 14, 1780. Wit. George Gurley,
Thomas Edmunds, John Beal. Page 306.

MORGAN, John. Leg.- son Jarret; son Foster; son William the
plantation bought of William Turner; daughters Patience,
Elizabeth, Sarah and Ann Morgan. D. March 24, 1775. R.
Dec. 14, 1780. Exs. William Foster and son Jarret Morgan.
Wit. Lelas Kerby, William Foster, Lucy Hines. Page 306.

BASS, Charles. Leg.- son Henry; son Hardiman, land adjoining
Jeremiah Thorpe reversion to son's wife Ann her widowhood and
then to grandson Roger Bass; to my neighbor Moses Thorp; son
Charles, reversion to said son's wife her widowhood, then to
grandson Edwin son of Charles, with reversion to his brother
Dixon and then to his brother Howell Bass; remainder of
estate to be sold and divided between my sons Arthur and
Newit Bass and daughter Mary Matthews, grandson Jordan Bass,
son of my daughter Tabitha Bass. Exs., sons Henry and Charles
Bass and son-in-law Arthur Matthews. D. Sept. 11, 1780. R.
Dec. 14, 1780. Wit. Joshua Nicolson, Jeremiah Thorp, John
Ivy (son of John). Page 307.

CRENSHAW, Thomas. Leg.- son John land bought of William West
and recorded to belong to Josph West, also land adjoining
James Daughtry; daughter Amey Bailey, land bought of Ralph
Carter; reversion to her son Samuel Maget Crenshaw; daughter
Ann Crenshaw. Exs., John Crenshaw, Nicholas Maget, Jesse
Whitehead. D. Oct. 16, 1778. R. Dec. 14, 1780. Wit. Jacob
Turner, Samuel Maget, John Thorp, William Gwaltney, Etheldred
Holt. Page 308.

HARRIS, John. Leg.- brother Newit Harris; brother Thomas;
brother Nathan; neice Fanny Newsum; neice Lucy Newsum; sister
Martha Newsum. Exs., Cordall Norfleet and brother Nathan
Harris. D. Sept. 15, 1780. R. Jan. 11, 1781. Wit. John
Davis, Nathan Bryant, Jeremiah Grizzard. Page 309.

CLIFTON, Thomas. Leg.- son Benjamin land in Northampton County,
N. Car.; son Cordey; son Claibourn; daughter Dorothy Harrison;
daughter Maria; daughters Sarah, Mary, Ann and Eleanor Clifton.,
(Sarah and Mary may be already married ?). Exs., Wife Sarah
and son Benjamin Clifton. D. Oct. 9, 1779. R. Jan. 11, 1781.
Wit. Thomas Turner, Benjamin Harrison, Simon Harris. Page
309.

PITMAN, John. Leg.- daughter Sarah Boykin all the land I
possess in this state and in N. Car.; daughter Dorcas Stevens;
daughter Susanna Taylor; daughter Elizabeth Williamson;
daughter Mourning Pitman; refers to a note and slaves due him
from John Boykin. Ex., son-in-law John Boykin. D. Dec. 12,
1780. R. Jan. 11, 1781. Wit. Micajah Edwards, William
Newsum, John Wilkinson. Page 311.

LANKFORD, Thomas. Leg.- wife Elizabeth lands bought of William
Hobday and Albridgton Whitley; son Elisha land purchased of
Wade Mountfortt and William Glover; son Jesse tract bought of
William Barrett, whereon James Wilson lives; neice Mary Wakins

(Watkins ?); friend Shadrack Lewis to supervise slaves and extend fatherly care to my children; whereas James Chapple did give to me his one third part of a pair of mill stones, formerly belonging to my father, one half the surplus to said Chapple, remainder to be divided all my children, Elisha, Jesse, Margaret, Rebecca and Ann Lankford; -if my Exs. disagree in interpreting my will to be left to the judgment of Joseph Mountfortt, Benjamin Ruffin, William Urquhart and J. Wm. Hines (son of Thomas) Exs., wife Elizabeth, friend Shadrack Lewis and brother Jesse Lankford. D. Nov. 20, 1780. R. Jan. 11, 1781. Wit. Joseph Mountfortt, Thomas Mountfortt, James Wilson, W. Denson. Page 312.

STEPHENSON, Simon. Estate appraised by John Summerell, James Summerell and William Boykin, Jr. R. Jan. 19, 1781. Page 314.

SMITH, John. Inventory. R. Feb. 8, 1781. Page 315.

HARRIS, John. Inventory. Signed, Nathan Harris. R. Jan. 8, 1781. Page 315.

REVIL, Sampson. Leg.- brother Holliday Revil if he ever returns from the Northward, reversion to my sister's son Jesse Holt; sister Joannah Holt; sister Mourning Revil; sister Charlotte Revil. Ex., friend Samuel Edmunds. D. April 12, 1779. R. Feb. 8, 1781. Wit. Nathan Barnes, Samuel Woodard, Robert Carr. Page 316.

KIRBY, Richard. Of the Parish of Nottoway. Leg.- son Benjamin; daughter Susannah Clifton; son Silas; daughter Patty Pond; son Richard; son Thomas; son Miles. Ex., son Richard Kirby. D. Feb. 24, 1780. R. Feb. 8, 1781. Wit. Benjamin Stewart, John Kirby, Henry Adams. Page 316.

PITMAN, John. Estate appraised by Lazarus Cooke, Charles Joiner, Micajah Edwards. R. March 8, 1781. Page 317.

KENNEBREW, Edwin. Of the Parish of St. Luke. Leg.- to Henry Kennebrew, land on which my father lived; to Priscilla Kennebrew; Shadrack Kennebrew. Exs., friend John Barrow and brother Shadrack Kennebrew. D. Nov. 4, 1780. R. Feb. 8, 1781. Wit. Phoeby H. Barrow, John Denson. Page 319.

LUNDY, James. Leg.- neice Mary, daughter of Byrd Lundy, the plantation on which my father lived, also the part of the land given by my father to Drury Lundy and the land he bought of Isham Lundy; cousin James son of Robert Lundy, said James to allow Solomon Harrison to occupy the house as long as he desires; cousin Sarah, daughter of Robert Lundy; Suckey Morris, sister to Chislin Morris; Creasy daughter of Arthur Bass; to Darling, Edwin and Collen, sons of Mary Adams; my slaves to be divided by my friends, Daniel Fisher, Lewis Thorpe, William Blunt, John Rogers and John Myrick; reversion of the bequests to the Adams boys to James, Molly and Sarah Lundy; Chislin Morris. Exs., James Lundy and Chislin Morris. D. March 14, 1780. R. March 8, 1781. Wit. Daniel Fisher, James Harris, Drury Harris. Page 319.

ATKINSON, Mial. Leg.- wife Mary; son Joseph; son William at twenty one; son John at twenty one; daughter Lucy. Ex., son Joseph Atkinson. D. Dec. --, 1780. R. April 12, 1781. Wit. James Chanel (Channell), Benjamin Kindred. Page 320.

JONES, Martha. Of the Parish of St. Luke. Leg.- son Timothy Thorp; granddaughter Mary Cock Simmons; granddaughter Peggy Ridley; granddaughters Rebecca Simmons, Martha Ridley, Ann Thorp, Martha Thorp, Temperance Atherton; Polly Person, and Martha Person; grandson John Thorp Ricgardson. Ex., son Timothy Thorp. D. Dec. 11, 1780. R. April 12, 1781. Wit. Hardy Harris, Sally Jarrell, Sarah Hasty. Page 321.

BYRD, John. Leg.- son Arthur; Joshua Hunt; Susannah, daughter of Arthur Byrd; son John; son James; son Charles; son Philip; son Moses; son Natah Byrd. Ex., son Arthur Byrd. D. R. April 12, 1781. Wit. John Wood, Elizabeth Williams, William Brooks. Page 322.

LANKFORD, Thomas. Estate appraised by John Oberry, Joseph Mountfortt, Thomas Mountfortt. R. June 14, 1781. Page 323.

MYRICK, Mary. Of the Parish of St. Luke. Leg.- son Edward Harris; son Lewis Harris; son Amos Harris; daughter Mary Lewis; daughter Anne Applewhite; granddaughter Olive Harris wife of Joseph Harris; granddaughter Priscilla Harris; son Hardy Harris. Exs., sons Amos and Hardy Harris. D. June 16, 1775. R. April 12, 1781. William Moore, Mary Nicholson, Joshua Nicolson. Page 324.

BRIGGS, Henry. Of Nottoway Parish. Leg.- son Charles land in Sussex County at twenty one; son Henry land in Southampton County on the Nottoway River; daughter Ann. Trustees, Charles Briggs and John Thomas Blow. D. March 23, 1781. R. June 14, 1781. Wit. Samuel Scarbrough, Robert Barredell, Joseph Johnson, Mathew Wills. Page 325.

TAYLOR, Henry. Of the Parish of St. Luke. Leg.- wife my plantation adjoining Benjamin Lewis, the riding chair and harness now being made by Randolph Newsum and Josiah Jordan; son Etheldred the plantation called "Ridleys" daughter Elizabeth; son John; son Henry (not of age); daughters Charlotte, Mary and Martha Taylor. My Executors to be guardians to my sons, my wife guardian to my daughters. Son Henry to be sent to college. Exs. son Etheldred Taylor and friend Daniel Fisher. D. March 8, 1781. R. June 14, 1781. Wit. Mary Mason Taylor, Robert Taylor, D. Fisher, Kinchen Peterson. Page 326.

WOODDARD, Charles. Leg.- son William; wife Elizabeth; son Jesse Wooddard; refers to money which he owes Jo. Vick. Exs., brothers Josiah Vick and Samuel Woodard. D. Oct. 28, 1780. R. June 14, 1781. Wit. John Pledger, Henry Vaugan, Robert Speed. Page 328.

EDWARDS, Micajah. Of the Parish of St. Luke. Leg.- brother Richard; brother Benjamin; sisters, Elizabeth and Ann Edwards. Exs., brothers William and Richard Edwards. D. April 15, 1781. R. June 14, 1781. Wit. Mary Blow, Susannah Edwards, William Edwards. Page 329.

THORPE, John. Leg.- wife Martha; to wife's daughter Nancy Atkinson (whom I own to be my daughter); provision for unborn child; reversion to my brothers and sisters, Midda Spence, Sarah Harris, Mary Reese, Jeremiah Thorpe, to four of my brother Aaron Thorpe's children- Thomas, Edith, Phebe and Henry Thorpe. Exs., wife Martha and friend Hardy Harris. D. May 15, 1779. R. July 12, 1781. Wit. John Nicholson, Thomas Adams, Jr., Mary Nicholson, Sally Kirby, Howell Adams. Page 329.

NICHOLSON, Joshua. Leg.- son Charles Briggs Nicholson; wife
Mary during my Mother's life; to all my children. Exs.,
brothers-in-law Howell Edmunds, John Kirby and friend Hardy
Harris. D. Jan. 12, 1781. R. July 12, 1781. Wit. Sarah
Moore, Betsey Moore, Rebecca Moore, Edwin Sewardd. Page 330.

EDWARDS, Thomas. Of the Parish of St. Luke. Leg.- son Jordan
hunting gun and brandy, which he had of Joseph Washington as
his substitute in the service; son Newit, long gun, brandy
and 200 L in the hands of Thomas Taylor, being what he was to
receive from him as his substitute in the service; son Benjamin;
daughter Mary; daughter Ann; wife Ann; daughter Lucy; daughter
Elizabeth Edwards. Exs., Wife Ann and son Benjamin Edwards.
Trustees, friends William Thomas and George Gurley. D.
March 26, 1781. R. July 12, 1781. Wit. Thomas Newsum,
James Atkinson, Martha Gurley. Page 331.

REVILL, Sampson. Inventory. Signed Samuel Edmunds. R. July
12, 1781. Page 333.

TURNER, Benjamin. Leg.- son Benjamin my tract of land bought
of David Edmunds, adjoining Thomas Porter; son Henry; son
Nathan; daughter Ann; grandsons Turner and James Newsum;
daughter Phebe Newsum. Exs., sons Nathan and Henry Turner.
D. May 26, 1771. R. Aug. 9, 1781. Wit. Cordall Norfleet,
Elizabeth Crocker, Edith Kinnebrew. Page 333.

MORGAN, John. (alias John Martin) Leg.- sister Celia, alias
Celia Martin my land in Sussex and Southampton Counties
devised to me by my father John Morgan; to brother-in-law
Mathew Morgan. Ex., friend, Littleberry Mason. D. May 8,
1781. R. Aug. 9, 1781. Wit. James Sammons, John Sledge,
Sally Sledge. Salia Morgan qualified. Security, John Ivy.
Page 334.

BROWN, John. Leg.- mother Olive Brown. Extx., mother Olive
Brown. D. Oct. 23, 1780. R. Aug. 9, 1781. Wit. William
Foster, Jane Clements, Lucy Hines. Thomas Lane qualified.
Page 335.

RIGHT, Mary. Leg.- James Right, son of Joseph Right; John
Right, son of Joseph Right. Exs., son Joseph Right and John
Pursell. D. Dec. 22, 1780. R. Sept. 13, 1781. Wit. West
Tines, Mathew Smith. Page 335.

WARREN, Faith. Parish of St. Luke. Leg.- daughter Elizabeth
Dupree; grandson Henry, son of Michael Warren. Exs., friend
Henry Bittle and son Michael Warren. D. Jan. 13, 1781. R.
Sept. 13, 1781. Wit. Joel Harris, John Barrow, Sarah Barrow.
Page 336.

RIDLEY, James. Leg.- daughter Mary Blunt; daughter Jane Parker;
daughter Sarah; son Bromfield; Frances Ridley, wife of son
Bromfield; son William the tract on which I live granddaughter
Rebecca, daughter of my son Arthur Ridley, reversion to
Rebecca Ridley, daughter of James Day Ridley; Elizabeth
Ridley, daughter of James Day Ridley, reversion to Rebecca,
daughter of Arthur Ridley; grandson John Edwards Ridley, son
of James D. Ridley, a tract on the Meherrin River bought of
John Johnson and the land on which the said J. D. Ridley died,
purchased of Joseph Thorp; Elizabeth Ridley, widow of Arthur
Ridley, deceased, bond of Sterling Capel; bond of John Francis
and balance due from Miles Cary and Sterling Francis to support the said Elizabeth and her daughter Rebecca Ridley; Exs.,
sons Bromfield and William Ridley. D. Aug. 20, 1781. Sept.

13, 1781. Wit. Hardy Harris, John Blunt, Benjamin Blunt, Jr. Page 337.

RIDLEY, James. Inventory. Sept. 13, 1781. John Blunt released and forever quit claimed all benefits and advantages to any estate devised me by the last will of James Ridley. R. Sept. 13, 1781. Wit. Hardy Harris, James Jones. Page 339.

DREWRY, William. Leg.- wife Rachel; to my seven children, William, Mary Morgan; Richard; James; Rachel; Nicholas and granddaughter Sarah Drewry. Sons, Richard, James and Nicholas to be bound out until twenty one. Exs., Son William and friend John Blunt. D. Oct. 3, 1780. R. Sept. 13, 1781. Wit. Jesse Cooper, Chrles Ross, Hardy Harris. Page 340.

FRANCIS, Thomas. Leg.- daughter Sally; daughter Elizabeth; daughter Milly Colliar Francis; son Wilie, a tract bought of Benjamin Clements and David Edmunds; daughter Charlotte; daughter Molley; daughter Jane Briggs Francis; wife Elizabeth Francis. Exs., wife and friend Howell Edmunds. D. May 14, 1779. R. Aug. 9, 1781. Wit. Jesse Cooper, John Francis. Page 341.

CLAUD, Philip. Account Current. 1773. Signed, Jeremiah Drew and John Claud, Exs. Audited by Jesse Drew and Thomas Turner. R. Sept. 13, 1781. Page 342.

BROWNE, Jesse. Leg.- daughter Sally; son Henry land adjoining Simon Stevenson at twenty one; son Thomas; wife Esther Browne. Exs., Wife and Bailey Branch. D. Sept. 24, 1777. R. Nov. 8, 1781. Wit. William Stephenson, Patience Stephenson, James Summerell. Page 343.

FORT, Joshua. Of the Parish of St. Luke. Leg.- son Joshua land adjoining Moses Foster; son Joseph land in Brunswick County; son John; son Edwin; wife and all my children. Exs., son Joshua, wife and brothers-in-law Joshua and Lewis Thorpe. D. March 15, 1781. R. Nov. 8, 1781. Wit. John Simmons, Benjamin Lewis, Spratley Simmons. Page 344.

WARREN, Faith. Inventory. Signed Michael Warren. R. Nov. 8, 1781. Page 345.

GRIFFIN, Benjamin. Leg.- son James land adjoining Hary Doyle and John Carstaphney; son Wiley land bought of William Doyle; wife Olive; son Jack; son Benjamin Griffin. Ex., Micajah Griffin. D. March 23, 1781. R. Nov. 8, 1781. W. R. Kello, John Worrell, Hartwell Crocker. Page 345.

BRANCH, Howell. Leg.- wife Elizabeth; son Drewry; son Peter; son Jesse at sixteen; daughter Martha Branch. Exs., Bailey Branch and John Wellons, Sr. D. Oct. 12, 1781. R. Nov. 8, 1781. Wit. Benjamin Branch, Henry Branch, John Summerell. Page 346.

JOHNSTON, Joseph. Leg.- son Henry; wife Charity; son Benjamin; daughter Patty; daughter Molly; daughter Olive Johnston. Exs., Henry Briggs and Drury Beal. D. Feb. 23, 1781. R. Nov. 8, 1781. Wit. Shad Lewis, Thomas Butts, Joshua Beal. Page 347.

CROCKER, Sarah. Leg.- daughter Ann Kindred; daughter Sarah Miller; daughter Phoebe Vaughan. Ex., grandson John Kindred. D. Nov. 19, 1779. R. Nov. 8, 1781. Wit. Benjamin Blunt, Benjamin Kindred, Elisha Kindred. Page 348.

DEMMERY, Frederick. Leg.- Richard, Tempy, Micajah, Day and Collin Demmery. Ex. David Demmery. D. Aug. 28, 1780. R. Nov. 8, 1781. Wit. John Bittle, Richard Griffin, Thomas Holladay. Page 348.

HOLT, Charles. Estate appraised, Oct. 1781, by John Simmons and Benjamin Lewis. R. Dec. 13, 1781. Page 349.

PITMAN, John. Account current. Signed John Boykin, Ex. Audited by John Wilkinson and Lazarus Cook. R. Dec. 13, 1781. Page 349.

WRIGHT, Mary. Estate appraised by John Summerell, John Britt and Lightborn Low. D. Oct. 1781. R. Dec. 13, 1781. Page 350.

CROCKER, Sarah. Inventory. Signed J. Kindred. R. Dec. 13, 1781. Page 350.

FORT, Joshua. Estate appraised by Benjamin Lewis, John Simmons and Mark Nicholson. Signed, Lewis Thorp, Ex. D. Dec. 13, 1781. Page 351.

COKER, Nathaniel. Inventory. Signed, R. Kello, Adm. Slaves appraised by Sampson Pitman and Moses Phillips. R. Dec. 13, 1781. Page 352.

EDWARDS, William. Leg.- wife Sally, children Charlotte and George; provision for child in esse. Ex., my uncle George Gurley. D. March 5, 1681. R. Dec. 13, 1781. Wit. George Edwards, George Gurley, Thomas Edwards. Page 352.

MOORE, James. Account Current. Jesse and Isaac Williams, Adms. 1778. refers to sale of land in N. Car.; paid Elizabeth Moore her specific legacy; Audited by Solomon Shepherd, Richard Ricks and J. Denson. R. Dec. 13, 1781. Page 353.

BARNES, Benjamin. Account Current. Exs., Mary Barnes and William Barnes. Among items, - paid William Barnes his legacy; paid for hiring a substitute for the 44th Division; paid John Powel as guardian to Milly Barnes; paid Mary Barnes; paid William Barnes as guardian of Peninah Barnes; paid Stephen Johnson as guardian to Jacob Barnes. Audited by Solomon Shepherd, Richard Ricks and J. Denson. R. Dec. 13, 1781. Page 354.

WILLIAMS, Michael. Inventory. R. Dec. 13, 1781. Page 354.

EVERITT, Thomas, Sr. Leg.- son Keton; son Thomas land adjoining Robert Gilliam; son Exum; daughter Ann; daughter Elizabeth; daughter Mary; daughter Femby and wife Elizabeth Everitt. D. Oct. 26, 1780. R. Dec. 13, 1781. Wit. John Chitty, John Gilliam, Jacob Barrett. Page 355.

BARKER, William. Of the Parish of St. Luke. Leg.- wife Mary and my six children. Exs., wife, Richard Marks, Joseph Marks. D. R. Dec. 13, 1781. Wit. Richard Marks, Lucy Barker, Nancy Barker. The widow being deceased, Richard and Joseph Marks, qualified. Page 355.

HALL, George. Leg.- son James; daughter Ann Woodard; son George; to wife all the estate, which formerly belonged to Joseph Hail, now in her possession, reversion to her son Obadiah Hail; wife

Elizabeth Hall. Exs., sons James and George Hall. D. Feb. 6, 1781. R. Dec. 13, 1781. Wit. Lawrence Joyner, Benjamin Haisty, John Haisty. Page 356.

TAYLOR, James. Of the Parish of St. Luke. Leg.- all debts to be paid, but the bond Silas Kirby is security to and Jeremiah Tyler has paid and had a receipt for, but lost it; to Charles Taylor, son of John Taylor; to beloved wife. Exts. wife. D. Nov. 13, 1781. R. Jan. 10, 1782. Wit. Mary Murray, Mark Nicholson, John Simmons. Elizabeth Taylor qualified. Page 357.

LUNDY, James. Estate appraised by Thomas Turner, John Freeman and Thomas Porch. R. Jan. 10, 1782. Page 357.

PORTER, John. Estate appraised by Edward Day, John Powel and Nathan Harris. R. Jan. 10, 1782. Page 358.

CRAFFORD, John. Estate appraised by John Wilkinson, Lazarus Cook and John Lutar. R. Jan. 10, 1782. Page 359.

JONES, Richard. Leg.- beloved wife; Willis Joyner, son of Amos Joyner. Ex. friend Jacob Burn. D. Sept. 27, 1781. R. Jan. 10, 1782. Wit. Will Ridley, Lucy Bittle, Mary Barnes. Jacob Barnes, qualified. Page 359.

GEORGE, William. Leg.- daughter Sarah Savage; son John; wife Ann; between all my children. Exs., wife Ann and Benjamin Spratley. D. Sept. 21, 1779. R. Jan. 10, 1782. Wit. William Lane, William Riggan, Burwel Sharp. Page 360.

HATFIELD, Charles. Jemima Hatfield refused to accept the bequest made her in the will of Charles Hatfield and delivered management to David Barrow, who qualified as Ex. R. Jan. 10, 1782. Page 360.

GRESSWIT, William. Of the Parish of Nottoway; Leg.- beloved wife; son Mathew; to wife all I have due me for schoolkeeping; daughter Sarah Gresswit. Exs., wife and Mathew Wills. D. Aug. 13, 1781. R. Jan. 10, 1782. Wit. John Edwards, Thomas Lawrence. Page 360.

EVERITT, Thomas. Inventory. Signed Thomas Everitt, Ex. R. Jan. 10, 1782. Page 361.

GILLIAM, Jesse. Leg.- wife Penelopy and her children. Exs., wife and John Gilliam. D. Oct. 23, 1781. R. Jan. 10, 1782. Wit. Edward Britt, Samuel Mathews. Page 361.

POWERS, Charles. Estate appraised by Edward Tyler, Carr Doyle and Sampson Pitman. Signed Moses Johnson, Adm. R. Jan. 10, 1782. Page 362.

GRESWITT, William. Estate appraised by Abram Mitchel, Thomas Lawrence and John Rochell. R. Feb. 14, 1782. Page 362.

GARDNER, John. Of the Parish of Nottoway. Leg.- son Jesse; daughter Lydia Joyner; wife Ann; daughter Mitty; son John land bought of William Worrel; daughter Ann; son James; daughter Mary; daughter Pheby; son Amos Gardner. Exs., sons Jesse and John Gardner. D. Oct. 21, 1778. R. Feb. 14, 1782. Wit. Henry Love, Silas Love, William Gray. Page 363.

GILLIAM, Joseph. Inventory. Signed John Gillaim. R. Feb. 14, 1782. Page 364.

SCARBOROUGH, John. Leg.- son Benjamin; heirs of Robert Scarborough; to Ann wife of John Hines; Lydia wife of Benjamin Stewart; wife Mary; to Brittain Scarborough; son John, at death of my wife my estate to be divided among my five youngest children, viz.- John, Sukey, Patty, Betsey and Sarah Scarborough. Extx. wife Mary Scarborough. D. Jan. 13, 1778. R. Feb. 14, 1782. Wit. Lewis Joiner, Drury Cotton, Richard Tatem. Page 364.

BROWNE, Jesse. Estate appraised by Joseph Washington, Newsom Branch and William Stephenson. R. Feb. 14, 1782. Page 365.

KINNEBREW, Edwin. Inventory. Signed John Barrow, Ex. R. Feb. 14, 1782. Page 366.

BRANCH, Howell. Estate appraised by James Summerell, Robert Shield and Arthur Doles. R. Feb. 14, 1782. Page 366.

WILLIAMSON, Francis. Of the Parish of Nottoway. Leg.- brother Turner Williamsburg land in Greensville County; sister Polly Williamson; Micajah Holliman; brother John Williamson. Ex., Micajah Holliman. D. Nov. 16, 1781. R. Feb. 13, 1782. Wit. John Woodward, Arthur Williamson, Person Williamson. Page 367.

BARRETT, William, Sr. Of Nottoway Parish. Leg.- son Pressley when he is eighteen; son Hancock; daughter Lucresly Toney (?); son William; son Charles; son Rolley; daughter Suzana Peircy; daughter Lucy Hancock; rest of my estate to my two daughter and four sons. Exs., sons William and Rolley Barrett. I impower them to make a right to the land I sold Giles Joyner. D. Jan. 15, 1782. R. Feb. 14, 1782. Wit. Henry Jones, Toomer Joyner, Joshua Miniard. Page 368.

BAILEY, Robert. Account Current. 1775. Audited by Arthur Foster and Arthur Boykin. R. Feb. 14, 1782. Page 369.

COBB, Hardy. Estate appraised by Abraham Mitchell, Mathew Wills, David Edwards and William Westra. D. Dec. 6, 1781. R. March 14, 1782. Page 370.

WOODARD, Charles. Estate appraised by Joseph Pope, John Benjamin Waller, John Pleger. R. March 14, 1782. Page 371.

CLEMENTS, Benjamin. Appraisal in Southampton not signed, but filed. Appr. in Brunswick County made by Henry Nicholson, Federic Lucas, William Clack, Jr. R. March 14, 1782. Page 372.

CLEMENTS, Benjamin, Jr. Of Nottoway Parish. Estate appraised by Charles Briggs and John Simmons. R. May 9, 1782. Page 374.

WILLIAMS, Michael. Estate appraised by William Thomas, John Thomas Blow, James Martin. R. March 14, 1782. Page 377.

GARDNER, John. Estate appraised by Lewis Joyner, Jr., James Vick and Joseph Vick. R. March 14, 1782. Page 377.

CLEVELAND, William. Leg.- mother; sister Patsey; brother John Cleveland. Exs. friends John Andrews and Stephen Summerell. D. Dec. 16, 1775. R. Feb. 14, 1782. Wit. Armstead Vellins, Lucy Andrews, Silvy Jackson. Page 379.

JONES, Richard. Estate appraised by Thomas Fitzhugh, Jeremiah Drew and Thomas Ridley. R. March 14, 1782. Page 379.

FRANCIS, Thomas. Estate appraised by Hardy Harris, Michael Warren and John Kirby. R. March 14, 1782. Page 380.

HATFIELD, Charles. Estate appraised by Henry Jones, Simon Johnson and John Johnson. R. March 14, 1782. Page 381.

TURNER, William. Inventory. Signed, Thomas Turner. R. March 14, 1782. Page 382.

TURNER, Arthur. Estate appraised by James Wilson, Dempsey Johnson and Henry Joyner. R. March 14, 1782. Page 383.

EDWARDS, Elizabeth. Leg.- son William; son Richard; son Benjamin a tract bought of Richard Ricks; daughter Elizabeth; daughter Ann Edwards. Exs., son William Edwards and brother Benjamin Blunt. D. Feb. 24, 1782. R. March 14, 1782. Wit. John Thomas Blow, Benjamin Spivey. Page 384.

AVERY, Joell. D. July 12, 1779. Estate appraised by Howell Edmunds, Henry Turner and John Powell. R. May 9, 1782. Page 385.

POPE, Patience. Estate appraised by Arhthur Foster and Thomas Edmunds. R. May 9, 1782. Page 386.

BARNES, Burwell. Inventory. 1781. R. May 9, 1782. Page 386.

THORPE, John. Inventory. Signed, Hardy Harris and Martha Thorpe. R. May 9, 1782. Page 387.

BUTTS, Peter. Estate appraised by (not signed) Thomas Butts and Benjamin Butts, Exs. R. May 9, 1782. Page 389.

ATKINS, Mial. Inventory. D. April 24, 1781. R. May 9, 1782. Page 389.

MORGAN, John. Estate appraised by Joshua Thorpe, Henry Ivy and H'y Applewhaite. R. May 9, 1782. Page 390.

NEWSOM, Jacob. Estate appraised by James Battle and Howell Harris. Signed, Isham Gilliam and Tabitha Newsom, Exs. May 9, 1782. Page 390.

BARKER, William. Estate appraised by James Battle, James Barham and Howell Harris. R. May 9, 1782. Page 392.

WILSON, William. Inventory. Signed, Jesse Whitehead. R. May 9, 1782. Page 392.

JOHNSON, Joseph. Estate appraised by Mathew Wills, David Wright and James Wright. R. May 9, 1782. Page 393.

HARRIS, Mary. Leg.- daughter Winney Cheaves (?) Exs., son James Harris and Drewry Harris. D. Aug. 24, 1781. R. March 14, 1782. Wit. Thomas Turner, Priscilla Womack, Rebecca Johnson. Page 394.

PERSON, Philip. Of the Parish of St. Luke. Leg.- brother Turner Person; son Timothy when twenty one; wife Temperance; daughter Patsey and to all my children. Exs., wife and friend William Andrews. D. Aug. 25, 1781. R. May 9, 1782. Wit. John Turner, Richard Clifton, John Westbrook. Page 395.

PERSON, Collier. Leg.- wife Elizabeth; daughter Nancy at
fifteen; to wife Elizabeth and all her children legally
begotten by me. Exs., wife and brother Philip Person. D.
Nov. 18, 1780. R. May 9, 1782. Wit. Thomas Turner, Dorcas
Clifton, John Main. Page 396.

NICHOLSON, Joshua. Estate appraised by William Moore, Timothy
Thorpe and Amos Harris. Signed, Howell Edmunds and John
Kirby, Exs. R. May 9, 1782. Page 397.

BRACY, Francis. Estate appraised by Abraham Mitchell, Mathew
Wills and William Williams. R. May 9, 1782. Page 398.

DREWRY, William. Inventory. Signed, William Drewry, Jr. R.
May 9, 1782. Page 399.

VICK, Arthur. Inventory. Signed, Samuel Vick, Sr. Ex. R.
May 9, 1782. Page 400.

VAUGHAN, William. Inventory. Signed Nathaniel Turner. Ex.
R. May 9, 1782. Page 400.

EDWARDS, William. Inventory. R. May 9, 1782. Page 401.

JONES, Mrs. Martha. Inventory. Signed, Timothy Thorpe. Ex.
R. May 9, 1782. Page 401.

BRIGGS, Henry. Inventory. Signed, John Thomas Blow and
Charles Briggs. R. May 9, 1782. Page 402.

JOHNSON, Elibey. Inventory. Signed, William Johnson. R. May
9, 1782. Page 403.

BIRCHETT, James. June 20, 1772. Estate appraised by Henry
Holt, Edward Lundy, Jr. and James Lundy. Signed, John Rogers,
Adm. R. May 9, 1782. Page 403.

CROCKER, Hartwell. Inventory. Signed, Joseph Bradshaw. R.
May 9, 1782. Page 403.

REESE, Edward. Estate Appraised by -------. Signed, Olive
Bunn, Admtx. D. Dec. 19, 1781. R. May 9, 1782. Page 404.

JOHNSON, Robert. Estate appraised by Hardy Doyle, Carr Doyle
and John Carstaphen. Signed Benjamin Beal, Ex. R. May 9,
1782. Page 405.

ATKINSON, Timothy. Estate appraised by John Andrews, Benjamin
Britt and Philip Moody. R. May 9, 1782. Page 406.

SIMMONS, Joseph. Leg.- wife Oluf; son John; son William;
daughter Katherine Barnes; daughter Silviah; daughter Milly
Taylor Simmons and daughter Lucy Simmons. Exs., wife, son
John Simmons and John Chitty, Sr. D. May 6, 1781. R. Jan.
10, 1782. Wit. Newit Edwards, Joseph Pope, Elizabeth
Jackson, Anne Edwards. Page 407.

FERGUSON, John. May 1, 1779. Inventory. Signed, Jesse
Whitehead, Adm. R. May 9, 1782. Page 407.

CRENSHAW. Thomas. Inventory. Signed Nicholas Maget and Jesse
Whitehead. R. May 9, 1782. Page 408.

BRADSHAW, Arthur. Inventory. Signed, Thomas Bradshaw, Adm. R.
May 9, 1782. Page 408.

FREEMAN, James. Inventory. Signed, Olive Freeman. D. 1781.
R. May 9, 1782. Page 408.

JENKINS, Edmund. Estate appraised by John Pursell, William
Judkins and Benjamin Crumpler. Signed by Valentine Jenkins.
R. May 9, 1782. Page 409.

HANDCOCK, Henry. D. Dec. 30, 1777. Appraised by Edward Harris,
Joseph Reese, Jr. and John Lundy. R. May 9, 1782. Page 410.

PILES, Vincent. D. Nov. 26, 1774. Estate appraised by Edward
Lundy, Edward Harris, Sr., John Lundy. R. May 9, 1782. Page
411.

TAYLOR, Henry. Inventory. R. June 13, 1782. Page 411.

HALL, George. Inventory. Signed, James Hall and George Hall,
Exs. R. June 13, 1782. Page 413.

GRIFFIN, Benjamin. Inventory. Signed, Micajah Griffin, Ex.
R. June 13, 1782. Page 413.

MURPHEE, James. Leg.- wife Susannah; neice Elizabeth Poole;
reversion to James Poole and William Murphee Poole. Extx.
wife Susannah Poole. D. April 21, 1782. R. June 13, 1782.
Wit. Edward Archer, John Archer, William Urquhart. Page 414.

BARRETT, William, Sr. Inventory. Signed, William Barrett and
Rawleigh Barrett, Exs. R. June 13, 1782. Page 415.

SIMPSON, Samuel. Estate appraised by Howell Edmunds, William
Edmunds and William Vaughan. R. June 13, 1782. Page 416.

EDWARDS, Micajah. Inventory. Signed, Richard Edwards. R. May
13, 1782. Page 416.

MORGAN, John. Estate appraised by Thomas Turner, Drury Harris
and Colin Person. R. June 13, 1782. Page 416.

JONES, Thomas. Leg.- daughter Sarah land on which my father
Thomas Lones lived; son Mathew Jones. Ex. son Mathew Jones.
D. Dec. 9, 1781. R. June 13, 1782. Wit. Thomas Bradshaw,
Mary Williams, Edmund Johnson. Page 417.

BITTLE, Drury. D. Feb. 25, 1777. Estate appraised by Samuel
Kindred, William Vaughan and John Powell. Signed, Robert
Bittle, Adm. R. June 13, 1782. Page 418.

JOHNSON, Richard, Sr. D. March 28, 1782. Estate appraised by
A. Jones, Jr. and George Edwards. R. June 13, 1782. Page
419.

TURNER, Thomas. Account current. Paid Robert Gilliam for
schooling Mathew and Thomas Turner; paid John Edwards for
boarding Mathew Turner in 1771; paid board and schooling Lewis
Turner; paid Richard Harris for keeping Jesse and Simon Turner;
paid Simon Harris for keeping Harris Turner; paid Elias Fort
for keeping William Turner; paid Edward Drew for keeping T.
Turner; paid Joshua Nicholson for John Turner. Audited by
Jesse Whitehead and John Whitehead. R. June 13, 1782. Page
419.

WADE, Christopher. Of the Parish of Nottoway. Leg.- son Wilson,
land on which he and his family now dwell; friend Sarah Turner
the use of the plantation on which I now live bought of Samuel

Eley; reversion to grandson John Wade and Samuel Wade; wife Ann; daughter Sarah Wade; daughter Martha Wade. Ex., friend Joshua Brantley. D. Oct. 3, 1781. R. June 13, 1782. Wit. Joseph Mountford, Samuel Turner, Joyner Joyner (?). Page 422.

SUETER, Thomas. Estate appraised by William Andrews, Henry Smith and Michael Harris. R. July 11, 1782. Page 422.

DAVIS, David. Estate appraised by Samuel Bristol, William Holleman and Harmon Harris. Samuel Bailey, Adm. R. July 11, 1782. Page 423.

WINDHAM, Benjamin. D. June 27, 1782. Estate appraised by Richard Bailey, Benjamin Deloach and Thomas Oney. Page 424.

GEORGE, William. Estate appraised by Joshua Wood, Brittain Travis and Thomas Wood. Signed by Benjamin Spratley and Anne George, Exs. R. July 11, 1782. Page 424.

GRESSWITT, William. Account current. Signed, Mathew Wills, Ex. Audited by Benjamin Ruffin, Jr. and John Blunt. R. July 11, 1782. Page 424.

HUTCHINGS, Capt. Daniel. Estate appraised by Jacob Barnes, John Fort, Mark Nicholson. R. Aug. 8, 1782. Page 425.

TAYLOR, James. Inventory. Signed by the Extx. R. Aug. 8, 1782. Page 427.

JONES, Thomas. Estate appraised by Leighbourn Lowe and James Johnson. Signed, Mathew Jones, Ex. R. Aug. 8, 1782. Page 428.

WILLIAMSON, Hannah. Inventory. R. Aug. 8, 1782. Page 429.

WESTBROOKE, Samuel. Of the Parish of St. Luke. Leg.- wife Hannah; son Turner at twenty one, also my land that formerly belonged to William Westbrook; my children- David, Joel, Samuel H. and Phebe Westbrook. Exs., wife and friend John Barrow. April 14, 1781. R. Sept. 12, 1782. Wit. Henry Butler, Samuel Blake, William Claud, John Ivey, George Stephenson. Page 429.

TURNER, William. Inventory. Signed Benjamin Turner. Ex. R. Sept. 12, 1782. Page 430.

MURFEE, Richard, Jr. D. Feb. 27, 1782. Estate appraised by A. Jones, Jr., Brittain Joyner, William Williams. R. Sept. 12, 1782. Page 431.

JARRELL, Benjamin. Account current. Signed, Albridghton Jones. Audited by Timothy Thorpe, Hardy Harris, Thomas Fitzhugh and Benjamin Lewis. R. Sept. 12, 1782. Page 432.

WILLIAMS, Henry. D. July 22, 1782. Estate appraised by Stephen Summerell, John Summerell and Arthur Boykin. R. Aug. 12, 1782. Page 434.

DREW, Jesse. Leg.- Estate to be divided between Jeremiah Drew and Thomas Fitzhugh. Exs., brother Jeremiah Drew and Thomas Fitzhugh. D. Sept. 27, 1776. R. June 13, 1782. Wit. Richard Blow, Timothy Thorpe. Page 434.

BLUNT, Priscilla. Of the Parish of St. Luke. Leg.- son John, the tract bought of Alexander Watson; grandson James Turner, son of Jacob Turner; reversion of bequest to grandson John Blunt, son of John Blunt; son William Blunt; daughter Priscilla Turner; grandson Edmund Turner; granddaughters, Martha, Temperance and Elizabeth Turner. Ex., son John Blunt. D. Feb. 25, 1778. R. Sept. 12, 1782. Wit. Savory Atkins, Nathan Bryant, Celia Bryant. Page 435.

DAY, Thomas. Signed, Elizabeth Day and George Gurley. Account current, audited by John T. Blow, Thomas Edmunds and Howell Edmunds. R. Sept. 12, 1782. Page 436.

ADAMS, Thomas. Of the Parish of Nottoway. Leg.- daughter Betty Sammons; daughter Olive Hubbard; son Thomas. Ex. son Thomas Adams. D. March 23, 1782. R. Sept. 12, 1782. Wit. Charles Sledge, Tamer Adams, Richard Mason. Page 436.

LUNDY, Edward. Estate appraised by Moses Thorpe, Moses Harris and Thomas Turner. R. Sept. 12, 1782. Page 437.

WESTBROOK, Samuel. Inventory. Signed, Hannah Westbrook. R. Oct. 9, 1782. Page 437.

MOSS, Henry. Estate appraised by Thomas Gilliam, Jr. and Henry Westbrrok. D. Oct. 28, 1778. R. Oct. 10, 1782. Page 438.

SIMMONS, Sarah. Inventory. Signed, John Simmons. R. Oct. 10, 1782. Page 439.

BARNES, Benjamin. Account estate. To cash paid Philip Moody for a balance due his late wife;- the late Mary Barnes deceased, as per former accounts returned by Mary and William Barnes. Signed, William Barnes, Ex. R. Oct. 10, 1782. Audited by Joseph Vick and J. Denson. Page 439.

BROWNE, John. Inventory. D. Oct. 12, 1781. Signed, Thomas Lane, Adm. R. Oct. 10, 1782. Page 440.

KINNEBREW, Edwin. Account current. Signed, John Barrow. Audited by Jesse Cooper, Jeremiah Drew. R. Nov. 14, 1782. Page 440.

SALTER, John. Estate appraised by Rice B. Peirce, Richard Pond and William Spivey. R. Nov. 14, 1782. Page 440.

WILLIAMSON, Arthur, Sr. Account estate. Paid T. Phillips for schooling F. Williamson; cash paid Exum Williamson's orphans. Ex., Jesse Williamson. Audited by Beverley Booth and Arthur Foster. R. Nov. 14, 1782. Page 441.

HARRISON, William. Estate appraised by John Sturgeon, Thomas Turner and Simon Harris. R. Nov. 14, 1782. Page 442.

HARRIS, Mary. Inventory. Signed, Drewry Harris. R. Dec. 12, 1782. Page 443.

BEEL, Sarah. Leg.- unbaptised daughter, whom I desire to be called Sallie; with reversion of bequest to Henry Doles and brother Burwell Beel. Ex., friend Henry Doles. D. Nov. 27, 1782. R. Dec. 12, 1782. Wit. Robert Washington, Elizabeth Williams, Annais Randolph. Page 443.

BRACEY, Francis. Signed, Frances Bracey. March 1782. Paid Mary Bracy her part; paid Patience Bracy; paid James Wright for his wife Mary; paid Elizabeth Cobb; paid Ann Bracy; paid Meriam Bracy; paid my own proportion; to balance in my hands, belonging to Sarah Bracy. Audited by Lewis Joyner and Joseph Mountfort. R. Dec. 12, 1782. Page 444.

IVY, John. Leg.- wife Elizabeth; daughter Priscilla Bullock; son James land on the Great Ploughman's Swamp, marked by my neighbors, Thomas and Edward Pate, on the line which divides my land from John Reese and Ambrose Grizzard; son John; son Davy; daughter Anne Morgan; daughter Rebecca Ivy. Ex. friend, Joshua Nicholson. D. March 4, 1780. R. April 12, 1781. Wit. Thomas Pate, Edward Pate, William Pate. Page 445.

TURNER, William. Account estate. Signed, Ben. Turner. Paid John Simmons for schooling James and Nancy Turner. Audited by John Taylor, Thomas Ridley and Mark Nicholson. R. Sept. 12, 1782. Page 446.

SOUTHAMPTON COUNTY

WILL BOOK IV

MURPHREE, James. Inventory. Signed Susanna Murphree. R. Feb. 13, 1783. Page 1.

WILLIAMS, William. Leg.- wife Sarah; son Jacob land on Blunt's Swamp, Barrow's Road and Thomas' Swamp; son Kinchen, land adjoining Isaac Pope; son Elisha; daughter Rhoda. Exs., friends Samuel Edmunds and Thomas Vaughan. D. Dec. 1, 1782. R. Feb. 13, 1783. Wit. Richard Deloach, Mathew Underwood, Thomas Edmunds. Page 1.

DAY, Edmund. Of the Parish of St. Luke. Leg.- wife; son Abner; land at his grandfather's decease, and I wish him bound to a house carpenter; son John the land bought of Faircloth and he is to be kept at an academy until he is twenty one; sister Susanna Day. Exs., friends Thomas Edmunds and William Whitehead. D. Dec. 12, 1782. R. Feb. 13, 1783. Wit. William Wester, Christopher Bromadge, Asa Street. Page 3.

DAY, Edmund. Estate appraised by Nathan Harris, Samuel Edmunds and Nathan Barnes. R. April 10, 1783. Page 4.

DRAKE, Thomas. A deed is to be made to Jordan Denson for fifty acres, which he has paid for, adjoining Absalom and Lewis Joyner and the said Denson's land on which Timothy Drake now lives and I direct that Absalom Joyner is to run the dividing line; wife Sarah; daughter Mary; daughter Celia Joyner; grandson Joseph Joyner is to have an education suitable to his station in life. Exs., wife Sarah and son-in-law Absalom Joyner. D. March 6, 1783. R. April 10, 1783. Wit. Lewis Joyner, Sr., Lewis Joyner, Jr., Joseph Denson, Jr. Page 9.

MOODY, Philip. Leg.- son Samuel land purchased of William Barnes; son West; daughter Elizabeth; among all my children. Exs., friends John Andrews, Josiah Vick; Stephen Johnson, Jordan Denson. D. Feb. 24, 1783. R. April 10, 1783. Wit. John Barnes, William Barnes, Jerry Williams. Page 11.

FOSTER, John. Leg.- son Haley. Exs., son Haley and Richard Foster. D. July 24, 1776. R. April 10, 1783. Wit. John Mundell, John Mundell, Jr., James Black. Page 11.

CRENSHAW, Anne. Leg.- sister Amey Bailey all my estate. Ex., Jacob Bailey. D. April 11, 1783. R. Feb. 14, 1783. Wit. Nicholas Maget, Samuel Maget, Jesse Vick. Page 12.

FIGURES, Joseph. Inventory. Signed, Jesse Whitehead, Thomas Figures, Edmund Barrett and John Edwards, Exs. D. Aug. 24, 1780. R. April 11, 1783. Page 13.

MILLAR, William. Account current, signed Sarah Millar. Audited by John Taylor, Thomas Ridley, Mark Nicholson. R. May 8, 1783. Page 13.

MCLEMORE, John. Leg.- sons John and Joel, with reversion to daughters, Elizabeth, Olive and McKerina; son James to pay my indebtedness to George Ivy; daughter Martha Morgan; daughter Mary Norvill; daughter Priscilla, with reversion to her daughter Elizabeth McLemore; wife Elizabeth. Exs., John Rogers and Thomas Turner. D. Dec. 27, 1782. R. May 8, 1783. Wit. John Gray, Frederick Emmory, Thomas Blake, Thomas Turner. Page 15.

FOSTER, John. Estate appraised by Howell Edmunds, John Rogers, Samuel Blake. R. May 8, 1783. Page 16.

SIMPSON, Samuel. Estate appraised by Howell Edmunds, William Edmunds and William Vaughan. W. May 8, 1782. Page 16.

DRAKE, Thomas. Estate appraised by Lewis Joyner, Jr., John Davis and John Beaton. R. May 8, 1783. Page 17.

WILLIAMS, William. Estate appraised by Arthur Foster, William Francis and William Pope. R. May 8, 1783. Page 18.

JOHNSON, John. Leg.- wife Peninah, land descended to me from my father and tract bought of John Denson; son James; son John land purchased of Benjamin and William Kitchen; son Jacob land bought of Mathew Wills; son Josiah land purchased of Robert Tyler; son Jesse, land bought of David Chalmers; daughters, Rebecca, Ann, Lydia and Alice; to youngest son not yet named. Exs., son James and neighbor Jordan Denson. D. Jan. 30, 1783. R. May 8, 1783. Wit. William Kitchen, Joshua Councill, Dempsey Johnson. Page 19.

POPE, Henry. Account estate. May 1782. Signed, Sarah Lewis, Adm. Audited by Hardy Pope and Mathew Charles (or Clarke). R. May 8, 1783. Page 20.

TURNER, Littleton. May 1, 1783. Estate appraised by John Blunt, Michael Harris and William Drury. D. May 1, 1783. R. June 12, 1783. Page 21.

WOOD, Joshua. Of the Parish of Nottoway. Leg.- wife Sarah land bought of Richardson Riggin, also Hardin's place; son Benjamin the bond due me from John Butts' estate; son Joel, land purchased of Isham Davis; son Edmund; daughter Rebecca; daughter Mary; daughter Anna Wood. D. Dec. 26, 1782. R. June 12, 1783. Wit. Edwin Gray, John Pond, John Cobb. Page 21.

JOHNSON, Joseph. Account estate. Signed Drewry Beale. Audited by George Gurley and William Thomas. R. June 12, 1783. Page 23.

APPLEWHITE, Henry. Of the Parish of St. Luke. Leg.- wife Ann, with reversion to sons Henry and Thomas; son Arthur land bought of Hardy Harris; daughter Salley; son Hardy; son John; son Benjamin; son William; daughters, Priscilla, Janey, Beckey, and Nancy Applewhite; daughter Mary Barham, wife of John Barham; son John to make a deed to William Ealey for the land I have sold him. Exs., wife and sons John and Arthur Applewhite. D. May 11, 1783. R. July 10, 1783. Wit. Richard Mason, Selah Reese, John Reese. Page 23.

BEAL, Priscilla. D. May 1, 1783. Signed William Beal. Estate appraised by Jonas Edwards, William Williams, David Wright. R. July 10, 1783. Page 25.

SIMMONS, Joseph. D. July 2, 1783. Estate appraised by Micajah Edwards, Jacob Williams, Henry Taylor. R. Oct. 10, 1783. Page 26.

BARKER, William. D. Aug. 6, 1783. Signed, Richard Marks and Joseph Marks. Account estate audited by John Simmons, Sr., Benjamin Lewis and Etheldred Taylor. R. Aug. 14, 1783. Page 26.

WILLIFORD, William. Leg.- wife Mary; son Belah the plantation bought of my brother, Thomas Willeford; son Jordan the tract purchased by Jordan Thomas; son Jeremiah; son Johnson, the land my father purchased of Lawrence Lancaster, which I possess by virtue of my father's will; son James; daughter Sarah; daughter Mary Williford. Exs., sons Belah and Jordan Willeford. D. Jan. 6, 1782. R. Aug. 14, 1783. Wit. M. Holliman, Mrs. Boykin, William Holliman. Page 27.

POPE, William. Estate appraised by Mathew Wills, John Johnson and Simon Murfree. R. Aug. 14, 1783. Page 29.

CLARK, John. Of the Parish of Nottoway. Leg.- my children; William, James, Mary, Anne, Warner, Rebecca, Milly Richardson, Sa-ly and Judity Clarke; - son James the land I bought of Alexander Murray in July 11, 1768. wife Rebecca. Exs., Arthur Williamson and Micajah Holleman. D. Nov. 11, 1778. R. Aug. 14, 1783. Wit. John Woodard, Benjamin Harris, Micajah Holleman. Page 29.

COBB, Hardy. Account estate. Signed, Elizabeth Cobb, Admtx. Audited by Josiah Vick and Mathew Wills. D. Feb. 1783. R. Aug. 14, 1783. Page 30.

MORGAN, William. Inventory. Signed, William Andrews. D. April 15, 1782. R. Sept. 11, 1783. Page 31.

JONES, Robert. D. Feb. 25, 1779. Appraisal, not signed. Ex., John Simmons. R. Sept. 11, 1783. Page 31.

SMITH, Martha. Leg.- Exum Bailey, son of Joshua Bailey; Edmund Bailey; Rhoda Sadler, with reversion to her son John Smith Sadler; Tryal Bailey; Martha Bailey, daughter of Absalom Bailey; Burwell Brock, son of Sarah Brock; remainder of my estate to be divided between six of my brothers and William Bailey, son of Elijah Bailey and my four sisters, namely: - Tryal, Joseph, Absalom, Edmund, Abidan and Joshua; Miriam Hargrave, Sarah Brock, Mourning Russell and Rhoda Sadler. Exs. Abidan and Joshua Bailey. D. Aug. 18, 1783. R. Sept. 11, 1783. Wit. M. Holleman, B. White, Sarah Kitchen. Page 33.

EDWARDS, Elizabeth. Estate appraised by Thomas Vaughan, Thomas Edmunds and William Francis. R. Sept. 11, 1783. Page 33.

VICK, William. Account current. Audited by Lewis Vick and Nathan Barnes. R. Sept. 11, 1783. Page 35.

CROCKER, Hartwell. Signed Joseph Bradshaw, Adm. Appraised by Edmund Tyler, Arthur Bowin and Lawrence Joiner. R. Sept. 11, 1783.

DREW, Newit. Inventory. Signed, Jeremiah Drew and Jesse Drew. R. Oct. 9, 1783. Page 36. Account estate audited by John Barrow and Timothy Thorpe. R. Oct. 9, 1783. Page 37.

DOYELL, William. Inventory. R. Oct. 9, 1783. Page 37.

WASHINGTON, George. Of Nottoway Parish. Leg.- wife Sarah; daughter Martha; son David, land adjoining Joseph Washington; provision of unborn child. Exs., wife Sarah Washington and Henry Briggs. D. Nov. 5, 1780. R. Oct. 9, 1783. Wit. Joseph Charity, Mary Johnston. Mary Johnston qualified as Admtx. of will. Page 38.

EDWARDS, Captain Micajah. Account estate. Signed Benjamin Blunt and John Thomas Blow, Exs. 1771. To paid the following their legacies, - Elizabeth Edwards, Micajah Edwards, Richard Edwards, Benjamin Edwards, Mary Butts, Lucy Edwards, Elizabeth Edwards; Ann Edwards, Martha Edwards and William Edwards. Audited by Thomas Holladay and J. Denson. R. Oct. 9, 1783. Page 39.

TURNER, Benjamin. Of Buckhorn. Leg.- son Joel a tract bought of Mary Person and another purchased of Richard Avery; son William; daughter Rebecca Turner. Exs., brother and brother-in-law Thomas Turner and Nathan Harris and John Barrow. D. Aug. 8, 1783. R. Oct. 9, 1783. Wit. John Simmons, Mark Nicholson, Arthur Turner. Page 41.

BAILEY, Barnaby. Leg.- wife Mary; son James; daughter Celia Barlow; daughter Martha Booth; daughter Elizabeth Hayes; son Richard my land in Sussex County; daughter Lucy Calthorpe; with reversion Mary Bailey Calthorpe; granddaughter Lucy Bailey; to my grandchildren, the children of my daughter Ann Coker. Exs., wife Mary and son Richard Bailey. D. Sept. 1, 1783. R. Nov. 13, 1783. Wit. Jordan Judkins, James Gray, Halcott Briggs Pride. Page 42.

WHITNEY, Giles. April 1783. Inventory. R. Nov. 13, 1783. Page 43.

WADE, Christopher. Signed, Joshua Brantley. Estate appraised by Joseph Mountfortt, Thomas Mountfortt, William Joyner. R. Nov. 13, 1783. Page 44.

KIRBY, Turner. D. Sept. 18, 1783. Estate appraised by William Edmunds, Thomas Holladay and John Barrow. R. Nov. 13, 1783. Page 44.

NICHOLSON, Samuel. Leg.- wife Sarah; son Howell (not 21); son John; daughter Rebecca. Exs., wife Sarah Nicholson and Thomas Mason. D. April 20, 1783. R. Nov. 13, 1783. Wit. Howell Myrick, William Prince, John Barham. Page 45.

LUNDY, Robert. Leg.- daughter Elizabeth; son William my land in Halifax County, N. Car.; son James; Drury Harris; grandson Isham, son of my son Isham Lundy; grandson Lunsford Lundy; grandson James, son of William Lundy; grandson Thomas with reversion to my son William; grandson William; son of James Lundy; granddaughters, Mary, Sarah and Winifred, daughters of Isham Lundy; to my four grandchildren, offsprings of said son Isham, decd.; sister Elizabeth Hoof; residue of estate to my three children, William, James and Elizabeth Lundy. Exs., sons William and James Lundy. D. May 1, 1783. R. Oct. 9, 1783. Wit. John Rogers, Solomon Harrison, Thomas Porch, Thomas Morris, Jr. Page 46.

CRENSHAW, Ann. Inventory. D. Feb. 15, 1783. Signed, Jacob Bailey. R. Nov. 13, 1783. Page 48.

EDWARDS, Elizabeth. Account current. Signed, William Edwards.
D. 1782. Paid Richard Edwards, his proportion of his father's;
to same as an Ex. of Micajah Edwards, decd. to Benjamin
Edwards his proportion of his father's estate; to Ann Edwards,
sundries given her; to William Edwards his legacy. R. Nov.
13, 1783. Audited by David Barrow and Mark Nicholson.
Page 48.

EDWARDS, Micajah. Account estate. Nov. 22, 1780. Paid
Elizabeth and Ann Edwards, the proportional part of their
father's estate paid William Edwards and Benjamin Edwards.
Audited by David Barrow and Mark Nicholson. R. Nov. 13, 1783.
Page 49.

BASS, Charles. Account current. D. Dec. 13, 1783. Signed,
Arthur Matthews, Ex. Paid Charles Bass, Jr.; paid Hardy Bass
for a proportion of hire in the service. Audited by James
Lundy and Benjamin Clifton. R. Dec. 13, 1783. Page 50.

APPLEWHITE, Henry. D. Dec. 10, 1783. Inventory. R. March 11,
1784. Page 51.

DREW, Jesse. Estate appraised by William Ridley. Thomas
Turner, Timothy Thorpe. R. March 11, 1784. Page 51.

VAUGHAN, Henry. Leg.- son Thomas; son Howell Vaughan. Exs.,
sons Thomas and Howell Vaughan. D. Jan. 20, 1784. R. March
11, 1784. Wit. Samuel Haisty, Moses Johnson, Thomas Edmunds.
Page 52.

MURRAY, Alexander. Of the Parish of St. Luke. Leg.- daughter
Mary Harwood; daughter Elizabeth Smith; daughter Sarah Murray.
Exs., wife and John Simmons. D. Aug. 15, 1783. R. March 11,
1784. Wit. Jacob Barnes, Mark Nicholson, Jesse Fort. Will
presented by Mary Murray. Page 53.

BEAL, Sarah. Estate appraised by Lazarus Cook, Moses Johnson
and Elijah Crocker. D. March 22, 1783. R. March 11, 1784.
Page 54.

STEPHENSON, Simon. Account current. Jan. 1781. Audited by
James Summerell, Arthur Boykin and William Boykin. R. March
11, 1784. Page 55.

RAY, William. Account current. Audited by Charles Birdsong
and Micajah Edwards. R. May 13, 1784. Page 55.

DAY, Patty. Estate appraised by John Wilkinson and Jonas
Bryant. D. Nov. 12, 1783. R. May 13, 1784. Page 55.

WASHINGTON, George. Estate appraisal. Oct. 1783. Signed,
Sarah Washington, Ex. Appraised by Joshua Beal, Shad Lewis
and Benjamin Beal. R. May 13, 1784. Page 56.

BEALE, Priscilla. Account current. Signed, William Beale,
Adm. Paid to John and Burwell Beale, orphans of William
Beale, decd. R. May 13, 1784. Audited by Joseph Mountford,
Shad Lewis. Page 58.

WELLONS, Henry. Leg.- wife Elenor and all my children. Extx.
wife Elenor Wellons. D. June 10, 1779. R. May 13, 1784.
Page 58. Wit. Thomas Lane, Henry Powers.

MOORE, William. Of the Parish of St. Luke. Leg.- mother Sarah Moore; sisters, Sarah Jarrell, Elizabeth and Rebakah Moore and brother John Moore. D.   R. May 13, 1784. Wit. James Jones, Nancy Jones, Thomas Scott. Page 59.

WILKINSON, John. Leg.- son John; son James, land purchased of Henry, Joshua and Iavid Dawson, Benjamin, John and Henry Crafford Tucker; wife Elizabeth; daughter Sarah. Exs., sons John and James Wilkinson. D. Feb. 24, 1784. R. May 13, 1784. Wit. Simon Everett, Susannah Raley, Thomas Edmunds. Page 59.

WADE, Christopher. Account current. D. 1783. Signed, Joshua Brantley. Paid legacies.- Sarah Turner, John Wade, Ann Wade, Wilson Wade, Sarah Wade and Martha Wade. Audited by Joseph Mountford and Shad. Lewis. R. May 13, 1784. Page 61.

MURFREE, Richard. Account current. Signed, Simon Murfee. D. 1782. Audited by J. Denson and Shad. Lewis. R. May 13, 1784. Page 62.

MURRAY, Alexander. Inventory. Signed, Mary Murray and John Simmons. R. May 13, 1784. Page 63.

BAILEY, Barnaby. Inventory. Signed, Mary Bailey. D. Oct. 10, 1783. R. June 10, 1784. Page 63.

WALLER, John. Estate appraised by George Edwards, James Butts and Charles Speed. D. Dec. 19, 1783. R. July 8, 1784. Page 64.

COOPER, John. Estate appraised by Abraham Mitchell, Thomas Lawrence and Henry Cobb. D. April 24, 1784. R. July 8, 1784. Page 65.

RAWLINGS, John. Estate appraised by Joshua Thorp, Henry Ivy and Mathew M. Kenny. D. Dec. 21, 1778. R. July 8, 1784. Page 65.

WELLONS, Henry. Estate appraised by Samuel Pitman, William Wellons and Thomas Lain. Signed, Elender Wellons. R. July 8, 1784. Page 67.

VAUGHAN, Henry. Estate appraised by Samuel Edmunds, Thomas Turner and Henry Bittle. D. March 27, 1784. R. Aug. 12, 1784. Page 67.

SMITH, Martha. Estate appraised by Benjamin Harris, Burwell Williamson and Thomas Brock. Signed, ----- Bailey and Joshua Bailey. R. Aug. 12, 1784. Page 68.

JOHNSON, John. Estate appraised by Lewis Joyner and William Kitching. D. Aug. 12, 1784. Page 70.

TURNER, Benjamin. Estate appraised by John Barrow, Nathan Harris and Thomas Turner. R. Aug. 12, 1784. Page 71.

LUNDY, Robert. Inventory. Signed, William and James Lundy. R. Oct. 14, 1784. Page 72.

SPENCER, Edmund. Of the Parish of St. Luke. Leg.- son David; son William; son Ezekiel; son-in-law Nathan Jackson and his wife Sarah, land bought of Arthur Vick; son Jesse; wife Mary; son-in-law Drewry Beal; daughter Elizabeth Spencer. Exs., friend George Gurley and son-in-law Drewry Beal. D. Sept. 1,

1784. R. Oct. 14, 1784. Wit. Howell Whittington, John Beal. Page 73.

TURNER, Arthur. Account current. Received of Parrot Turner's guardian, her proportional part of George Washington's estate account versus the estate of Benjamin Turner; due from Gordial Row his wife's part of same. Signed Lewis Joiner and J. Denson. R. Nov. 14, 1784. Page 74.

WILLIFORD, William. D. Sept. 15, 1783. Estate appraised by Burwell Williamson and Harmon Harris. Signed Belah and Jordan Williford. R. Oct. 14, 1783. Page 75.

JOHNSON, Robert. Account estate. 1783. Signed, Benjamin Beale. Audited by J. Denson and Shad. Lewis. R. Oct. 14, 1784. Page 76.

MOORE, William. Estate appraised by Howell Myrick, John Applewhite and John Reese. D. Sept. 30, 1784. R. Oct. 14, 1784. Page 77.

NICHOLSON, Sarah. Leg.- granddaughter Sarah Myrick; daughter Elizabeth Rivers; daughter Fanny Myrick; granddaughters Fanny, Lucy and Matilda, daughters of Joshua Nicholson, decd.; grandson Edwin Seward; granddaughter Sarah Briggs Thorp; granddaughters Sarah and Lucy Edmunds, daughters of my daughter Lucy Edmunds, decd. Exs., sons-in-law Col. Howell Edmunds and Owen Myrick. D. April 7, 1783. R. Nov. 11, 1784. Wit. Henry Thorp, Amos Harris, Hardy Harris. Page 77.

ONEY, John. Leg.- wife Sarah; daughter Mary Gay; daughter Martha King; daughter Sarah Denson; daughter Lucy Martin; daughter Elizabeth and daughter Rebecca Oney. Extx., wife Sarah Oney. D. March 17, 1784. R. Nov. 11, 1784. Wit. John H. Pond, Arthur Exum. Page 78.

ATKINSON, Hardy. D. April 13, 1784. Estate appraised by Nathan Harris, John Kindred and John Powell. R. Nov. 11, 1784. Page 79.

VICK, William. Leg.- son Lewis, land adjoining Robert Newsum, Jr.; son Pilgrim, land adjoining Council Vick and William Newsum; son Joshua, land adjoining Lewis Vick and William Thomas; son Richard, land adjoining Jacob Vick; son Giles, land adjoining John Everett; son Silas, land adjoining Jacob and Mathew Vick; wife Anne; daughter Mildred Newsum; daughter Sally Vick; daughter Piety Vick. Exs., sons Lewis and Pilgrim Vick and John Chitty, Sr. D. May 15, 1782. R. Nov. 11, 1784. Wit. W. Burwell Vick, Patience Vick, Dorcas Vick, John Jackson. Page 80.

TURNER, Jacob, Sr. Leg.- wife; son James (not of age); son John; rest of estate to all my children. D. Oct. 22, 1784. R. Oct. 25, 1784. Wit. John Pursell, Holland Turner, Jacob Turner, Jr. Page 82.

SUMMERELL, John. Leg.- son John; wife Sarah; son George; son Samuel; to my eight children, viz.- Nancy, Stephen, Elizabeth Doles, John, George, Janey, Sarah, Samuel and Lucy Summerell; provision for unborn child. Exs., sons Stephen and John Summerell. D. Jan. 8, 1783. R. Nov. 11, 1784. Wit. James Summerell, Thomas Summerell, Jeremiah Summerell. Page 82.

STORY, James. Leg.- son Daniel, land adjoining Samuel Story and George Gurley; son James; son Lewis; to John, Salah, Nanny, Sally, Elizabeth and Samuel Story; provision for wife. Ex., Wit. Drewry Beal, John Willson. Page 84.

RUFFIN, Benjamin. Leg.- beloved wife; son Benjamin. Ex., wife and son Benjamin Ruffin. D. Jan. 29, 1777. R. Dec. 9, 1784. Wit. Francis Newsum, John Ruffin, Joseph Longworth. Page 85.

ONEY, John. Estate appraised by Thomas Lain, Richard Pond and William Spivy. Signed, Sarah Oney. R. Dec. 9, 1784. Page 86.

MOORE, Sarah. Of the Parish of St. Luke. Leg.- daughter Sarah Jarrell; daughter Elizabeth; daughter Rebecca; son John Moore. Ex., friend, John Simmons. D. May 15, 1784. R. Jan. 13, 1785. Wit. Mary Nicolson, Mary Nicholson, Jr., Sally Applewhite. Page 87.

PORTER, John. Account Current. Signed, William Hines, Sheriff and William Blunt. Paid Etheldred Brantley for keeping the children; paid said Brantley his wife's part of the estate. R. Jan. 14, 1785. Page 88.

BAILEY, Benjamin. Leg.- son Trial; son Absalom; son Joseph land in Sussex County on which he lives, according to a patent granted Henry Sharp; son Edmund, land in Sussex on which he lives; son Abidan, land in Sussex; to Josiah Davis the plantation, whereon his father died; wife Sarah, with reversion at her death to Edmund and Abidian Bailey and daughter Miriam Hargrave; to Elijah Bailey; to son Joshua Bailey; daughter Mourning Russell; daughter Rhoda Sadler; daughter Sarah Brock. Exs., sons Abidian and Joshua Bailey. D. April 18, 1784. R. Feb. 10, 1785. Wit. Thomas Brock, Benjamin Brock, Martha Bailey. Page 89.

RICKS, Mary. Leg.- son Thomas; son Robert; son Richard; son Joseph and daughters, Mary, Milisent and Ann Ricks. D. R. Feb. 10, 1785. Wit. Lemuel Hart, Josiah West Cathen. Page 90.

CHANNELL, James. D. Jan. 25, 1785. Estate appraised by Henry Smith, John Blunt and John Suter. R. Feb. 10, 1785. Page 91.

DELOACH, Benjamin. Leg.- wife Ann; to Mary, Allen, Martha and Thomas Deloach, born before my marriage with said Ann; to Averilla, Ann and Elizabeth the children of Ann Deloach. Exs., Richard Kello the Elder and Samuel Kello. D. Jan. 6, 1785. R. Feb. 10, 1785. Wit. Richard Bailey, Richard Kello, Jr. Page 91.

WOOD, Joshua. Inventory. Signed, Benjamin Wood. R. Feb. 10, 1785. Page 93.

WILKINSON, John. Inventory. R. Feb. 8, 1785. Page 93.

BRADSHAW, Elizabeth. Inventory. Signed, Martha Bradshaw. R. March 10, 1785. Page 94.

REESE, Joseph. Inventory. Signed, John Reese. R. March 10, 1785. Page 94.

BRITT, Benjamin. Leg.- son Britain, land on Tarropin Swamp; son Mathew; son Benjamin; to Jordan Britt; daughter Sally, wife of Edmund Stephenson; daughter Anne, wife of John Coging; daughter Holland; son Joseph; refers to wife, but does not name her. Ex. son Joseph Britt. D. April 14, 1783. R. March 10, 1785. Wit. Arthur Allen, James Allen, Anne Allen. Page 95.

STORY, James. Estate appraised by Howell Whittington, Drewry Beale, Jeremiah Drake. R. March 10, 1785. Signed, Daniel Story. Page 97.

VICK, William. (son of Richard Vick). D. Dec. 11, 1784. Estate appraised by Thomas Newsum, Edmund Barrett, Amos Joyner. R. March 10, 1785. Page 98.

KINDRED, Samuel. Leg.- son Benjamin land adjoining Henry Vaughan; son Elisha (not of age); son Henry (not of age); wife Anne; the interest he is entitled to at the death of Sarah Crocker, to my four children, Mary, Elizabeth, Henry and Sarah Kindred. Ex., friend Benjamin Blunt. D. Aug. 1, 1780. R. March 10, 1785. Wit. Henry Bittle, Howell Vaughan, Joseph Atkinson. Page 99.

SMITH, William. Estate appraised by Mark Nicholson, Miles Cary and Arthur Foster. D. July 24, 1784. Estate appraised in Surry, by William Maget, William Hamlin and John Lane. R. March 10, 1785. Page 102.

MOORE, Sarah. Inventory. Signed, John Simmons. R. March 10, 1785. Page 102.

DELOACH, Benjamin. Estate appraised by Richard Bailey, Franklin Clark, Boaz Gwin Summerell. R. March 11, 1785. Page 103.

JOHNSON, Charity. Leg.- daughter Betty; son Elias. Ex., friend, Josiah Vick. D. Jan. 3, 1785. R. March 11, 1785. Wit. William Barnes, Sarah Johnson, Joseph Vick. Page 104.

SPENCER, Edmund. Estate appraised by Howell Whittington, Jeremiah Drake, William Thomas. Signed, George Gurley and Drewry Beal. R. April 15, 1785. Page 105.

GAY, Edmund. D. July 1776. Signed, William Scott. Account current.- paid Elizabeth Scott's legacy; paid legacy left Thomas Gay's four children; paid legacy left Edmund Blunt of Thomas. Audited by John T. Blow and Thomas Vaughan. R. April 15, 1785. Page 107.

JOHNSON, Abraham. Of the Parish of St. Luke. Leg.- wife Sarah; son Harris; son Jacob; son Josiah; son Micajah; Exs., sons Harris and Josiah Johnson. D. March 19, 1785. R. April 15, 1785. Wit. Joel Harris, John Blake, George Stephenson. Page 109.

JENKINS, Jacob. Account Current. 1775. Signed, Richard Edwards. R. April 15, 1785. Page 110.

BRYANT, Lewis. Leg.- son Lewis; son James; son Jonas; wife Sarah Bryant. Exs., sons Lewis and Jonas Bryant. D. Aug. 29, 1776. R. April 15, 1785. Wit. Nathan Bryant, Jonas Bryant, Seley Bryant. Page 111.

BRANCH, Ogborne. Of Nottoway Parish. Leg.- wife Sarah; son
   Arthur; son Moses; son William Branch. Ex., friend Joshua
   Wood. D. Nov. 23, 1776. R. April 15, 1785. Wit. Charles
   Briggs, John Cobb. Moses Branch qualified as Ex., Joseph
   Wood being deceased. Page 112.

LANCASTER, Joseph. Leg.- wife Mary; son Etheldred; son James
   Lancaster. Exs., sons Etheldred and James Lancaster. Wit.
   Richard Edwards, William White, B. Bailey. D. Sept. 8, 1783.
   R. May 12, 1785. Page 112.

HOLDEN, Benjamin. Leg.- son Benjamin, land adjoining Howell
   Branch; son William; wife Janey Holden. Extx., wife Janey
   Holden. D. March 24, 1781. R. May 12, 1785. Wit. James
   Summerell, George Summerell, Arthur Doles. Page 113.

EXUM, Benjamin. Of Nottoway Parish. Leg.- wife Mary; grandson
   William Salter; daughter Ann Salter; daughter Mary Cobb;
   granddaughter, Ann Salter. Exs. son-in-law John Cobb and
   grandson Exum Cobb. D. March 19, 1785. R. May 12, 1785.
   Wit. Benjamin Ruffin, Michael Cobb, Silve M ----. Page 115.

ATKINSON, Samuel. Leg.- daughter -----; son Samuel; son Isham;
   son Jesse, land adjoining William Whitehead; to Martha Newsum;
   son-in-law Jesse Johnson; daughter Mary Johnson; wife Martha;
   daughter Phebe Atkinson. Ex., son Isham Atkinson. D. March
   12, 1782. Wit. Thomas Edmunds, Samuel Edmunds, William
   Tucker. Page 115.

JONES, Captain James. Inventory. Signed, John Simmons. R.
   May 12, 1785. Page 116.

LUNDY, James. Account current. Signed, James Lundy and
   Chislon Morris, Exs. Audited by William Blunt, Thomas Turner
   and John Myrick. D. March --, 1781. R. May 12, 1785.
   Page 117.

BRYANT, Lewis. Estate appraised by Samuel Maget, James Maget
   and James Wilkinson. R. June 9, 1785. Page 119.

HATFIELD, Josiah. Account Current. Audited by Nicholas Maget
   and Samuel Maget. R. June 9, 1785. Page 120.

FIGURES, Joseph. Account Current. Audited by Nicholas Maget
   and Samuel Maget. R. May 9, 1785. Page 120.

CURLE, Thomas. Account current. D. April 11, 1783. Audited
   by Nicholas Maget and Samuel Maget. R. June 9, 1785. Page
   120.

VICK, Samuel. Leg.- wife Elizabeth; daughter Peggy; brother
   Shadrack Vick; brother Arthur Vick. Exs., brother Shadrack
   and Nathan English. D. Feb. 11, 1785. R. June 9, 1785.
   Wit. Drewry Beal, Edmund Ashley. Page 121.

HOLDEN, Benjamin. Estate appraised by Boaz G. Summerell,
   Robert Sheild, Benjamin Branch. R. July 14, 1785. Page 122.

JOYNER, William. Estate appraised by Shadrack Lewis, Joseph
   Mountfort, Hardy Pope and Micajah Griffin. R. July 14, 1785.
   Page 123.

HATFIELD, Charles. Account current. 1782. Legacy paid Mills
   Hatfield. Audited by Henry Jones and Simmons Johnson. R.
   July 14, 1785. Page 123.

DREW, Jeremiah. Leg.- wife Mary land adjoining Dolphin Drew on Angelica Swamp; son James (not of age); son Newit; son James; daughters, Susanna, Mary, Sarah and Priscilla Drew. Exs., wife Mary and friends William Myrick and Randolph Newsum. D. Nov. 24, 1784. R. July 14, 1785. Wit. Thomas Ridley, Henry Thorp, Anne Drew. Page 124.

RICKS, Richard. Account current. D. 1779. Paid Joseph Ricks his legacy; paid Thomas Ricks the legacies left his sons. Audited by Joseph Vick and Isaac Williams. R. July 15, 1785. Page 126.

BRIOUNT, John. (Probated as Bryant). Of Nottoway Parish. Leg.- son John; wife Mary; daughter Sarah; daughter Mary Bryant. Ex., son John Bryant. D. July 29, 1783. R. Aug. 11, 1785. Wit. Benjamin Beal, William Fowler. Page 129.

SMITH, Mathew. Leg.- wife Mourning; my brothers, Joseph, Arthur, Benjamin and Virgus Smith; father Arthur Smith. Exs., wife and friends Hardy Pope and Lemuel Jones. D. Sept. 19, 1783. R. July 4, 1785. Wit. John Pope, Joseph Wright, William Worrell. Page 130.

SHARPE, Richard. Estate appraised by Micajah Griffin, Henry Jones, Giles Joyner. Signed, D. Barron (Barrow ?). R. Aug. 11, 1785. Page 130.

JOHNSON, Abraham. Estate appraised by John Barron (?), Thomas Turner and Thomas Fitzhugh. R. Aug. 11, 1785. Page 131.

DREWRY, William Sr. Account current. Signed, William Drewry Jr., Ex. Audited by John Blunt and Henry Smith. R. Aug. 11, 1785. Page 133.

EXUM, Benjamin. Inventory. R. Sept. 8, 1785. Page 134.

JOHNSON, Simon Jr. Estate appraised by Giles Johnson, John Johnson and John Luter. D. June 21, 1785. R. Sept. 8, 1785. Page 135.

SALTER, John. Account current. Signed, Ann Salter, Admtx. Audited by Robert Bailey and Howell Edmunds. D. May 1780. R. Sept. 8, 1785. Page 136.

JOHNSON, Jacob. Leg.- wife Anne; son Benjamin Johnson. Extx. wife Anne Johnson. D. 1784. R. Aug. 11, 1785. Wit. Thomas Edmunds, Sarah Johnson; Mary Johnson. Page 137.

REESE, Joseph. Account current. Signed, John Reese. Audited by Jesse Cooper and Arthur Applewhite. R. Sept. 8, 1785. Page 137.

SPENCER, Edmund. Account current. Audited by John Whitehead, Samuel Maget and Jesse Vick. R. Sept. 8, 1785. Page 139.

SUMMERELL, John. Estate appraised by William Stephenson, Arthur Doles and William Boykin. R. Sept. 9, 1785. Page 139.

CLEMENTS, Thomas, Jr. Of the Parish of Nottoway. Leg.- wife Martha; daughter Sally Williamson Clements. Exs., Col. Thomas Williamson, Mr. William Urquhart, Col. John Hartwell Cocke and Mr. Hartwell Cocke. D. July 19, 1784. R. Dec. 9, 1785. Wit. Jacob Faulcon, Richard Cocke, Arthur Sinclair, William Edwards, Hartwell Cocke. Page 141.

THORPE, John. Estate appraised by John Cobb, Joel Davis and
Phillip Davis. D. Oct. 10, 1785. R. Dec. 8, 1785. Page
142.

BRANCH, Ogborne. Inventory. Signed, Moses Branch. R. Dec.
8, 1785. Page 143.

WESTBROOK, Samuel. Leg.- son Burwell, land adjoining Jacob
Westbrook; wife Mary; son John; daughter Patty Newsum; grand-
children, the orphans of son Samuel, decd.- namely, Turner,
David, Joel, Samuel and Phebe Westbrook; children of my
daughter Lucy Andrews, decd.; children of daughter Mary
Wommack, decd. Exs., sons John and Burwell Westbrook. D.
Nov. 13, 1784. R. Dec. 8, 1785. Wit. Arthur Foster,
Henry Collier Foster, James Foster. Page 143.

WESTBROOK, John. Leg.- wife Lucy; daughter Dorcas at eighteen;
son John Person Westbrook at twenty one; brother Burwell
Westbrook. Exs., wife Lucy, Sterling Foster and Thomas
Turner. D. Oct. 31, 1785. R. Dec. 8, 1785. Wit. Daniel
Porter, Ananias Randall, Elizabeth Moore. Page 145.

LANCASTER, Joseph. Inventory. Signed, Etheldred and James
Lancaster. R. Dec. 8, 1785. Page 146.

HARRIS, Nathan. Leg.- wife Mary; son Newit at twenty-one; son
John; son Edwin; son Richard; provision for unborn child;
daughter Charlotte; daughter Nancy; refers to brother John's
estate. Exs., friends Thomas Turner, son of Simon and John
Barrow. D. Sept. 15, 1785. R. Dec. 8, 1785. Wit. John
Kindred, Nathan Bryant, Cordall Bynum. Page 148.

REESE, Edward. Account estate. Signed, Olive Reese, Admtx.
Audited by Jesse Cooper, John Williamson, Arthur Applewhite.
R. Dec. 8, 1785. Page 149.

LANKFORD, Thomas. Account current. Signed, Shadrack Lewis,
Ex. Among items- paid James Chapple his legacy; paid Elisha
Langford ditto; paid Jesse Lankford ditto; paid Elizabeth
Lankford, widow her part of estate; paid Mary Watkins her
legacy; paid Shad. Lewis ditto. Audited by Ja. Denson and
Joshua Beal. R. Dec. 8, 1785. Page 150.

BARRETT, William. Account current. Audited by E. Herring and
Joseph Mountfort. R. Dec. 9, 1785. Page 152.

SMITH, Mathew. Estate appraised by Benjamin Crumpler, James
Johnson, John Worrell. D. Oct. 12, 1785. R. Dec. 9, 1785.
Page 153.

HARRISON, Amy. Leg.- daughter Mary Harrison. Ex., Daniel
Harrison. D. Jan. 10, 1783. R. Jan. 12, 1786. Wit. James
Lundy, Drewry Harris. Page 155.

ATKINSON, Samuel. Estate appraised by John Powell, John
Kindred and Jacam Newsum. R. Jan. 12, 1786. Signed, Isam
Atkinson, Ex. Page 156.

JOYNER, Ann. Leg.- daughter Elizabeth Drake; son Jethro; son
Lawrence; son Eley Eley; grandson William Eley; daughter-in-
law Mary Joyner; grandson Josiah Joyner; granddaughter Catie
Joyner; granddaughter Nanne Joyner; to Ann, daughter of Lewis
Joyner; granddaughter Peggy, daughter of Gethro Joyner; grandsons Gethro and William, sons of William Joyner, decd. Exs.,
son Gethro Joyner and Arthur Bowen. D. May 26, 1785. R.

Jan. 12, 1786. Wit. William Barrett, Giles Joyner, Joshua Miniard, Mary Joyner. Page 157.

JONES, James. Of St. Luke's Parish. Leg.- son Nathan land purchased of my brother Abraham P. Jones; son Howell and wife Ann Jones. Exs., wife and brother-in-law Jesse Vasser. D. Jan. 11, 1784. R. Jan. 12, 1786. Wit. Marget Newsum, John Simmons, Sr., Marget Vasser. Page 159.

KINDRED, Samuel. Estate appraised by Samuel Edmunds, Henry Bittle and John Powell. R. Jan. 12, 1786. Page 160.

JONES, James. Inventory. Signed, Ann Jones. R. Jan. 12, 1786. Page 161.

BARHAM, Thomas. Inventory. Signed, Elizabeth Barham. D. July --, 1784. R. Jan. 12, 1786. Page 162.

BRYANT, John. Estate appraised by William Williams, William Edwards and Richard Beal. Signed, John Bryant, Ex. D. Aug. --, 1785. R. Jan. 12, 1786. Page 162.

WESTBROOK, Samuel, Sr. Estate appraised by John Claud, Joshua Harris, James Womack. R. Jan. 12, 1786. Page 164.

BLUNT, Thomas. Inventory. Signed, Edwin Gray and William Thomas. R. Feb. 19, 1786. Page 166.

JOYNER, Ann. Estate appraised by David Denson, Charles Council and William Denson. Signed, Arthur Bowing, Ex. R. Feb. 9, 1786. Page 168.

POND, Daniel. Of the Parish of Nottoway. Leg.- wife Mary; son John; son Richard; daughter Elizabeth Morris; daughter Mary Wood; son Daniel Pond's surviving children; son Samuel Pond's surviving children. Exs., sons John and Richard Pond. D. Dec. 10, 1785. R. Feb. 9, 1786. Wit. Richard Pond, Elizabeth Pond, Sarah Pond. Page 170.

DOLES, Joseph. Leg.- daughter Olif, wife of Bailey Branch; daughter Sarah, wife of John Summerell; daughter Mary, wife of Stephen Andrews; wife Sarah, son Benjamin; son Arthur, son Jesse. Exs., wife and son Benjamin Doles. D. June 8, 1774. R. Feb. 9, 1786. Wit. Arthur Allen, Richard Manning, Thomas Carrel. Page 171.

VICK, Samuel. Estate appraised by Drewry Beal, John Rochelle and Jeremiah Drake. Signed, Shadrack Vick and Nathan English, Exs. R. Feb. 5, 1786. Page 172.

TURNER, Littleton. Account current. R. Feb. 9, 1786. Page 173.

RICKS, Mary. Inventory. Signed, Richard and Robert Ricks. R. Feb. 9, 1786. Page 174.

HARRIS, Carter. Leg.- mother Elizabeth Harris; friend Anselm Harrison; all my brothers and sisters. Exs., brothers John and James Harris. D. Nov. 20, 1785. R. March 9, 1786. Wit. William Owins, John Pillar. Page 175.

MYRICK, Owen. Leg.- son Henry at twenty one; son Owen land adjoining Richard Jelks, Hartwell Newsum, John Barham and my mother's land; wife Fanny; son John; daughter Sarah; daughter Nancy; daughter Fanny; daughter Lucy Myrick. Exs., brothers

William and Howell Myrick. D. Jan. 6, 1786. R. March 9, 1786. Wit. Thomas Peete, Arthur Applewhite, William Newsum. Page 176.

THORPE, John. Of the Parish of Nottoway. Leg.- daughter Susannah; granddaughter Lucy Thorpe; daughter Hannah Barly (Bailey ?); daughter Sarah Seward; daughter Mary Holt; son Joseph; daughter Olive Thorpe. Exs., daughter Susannah and friend Richard Renn. D. Dec. 30, 1784. R. Sept. 8, 1785 (1786 ?). Wit. William Wrenn, Charles Briggs, Faithy ------. (Richard Wrenn was a Quaker). Page 177.

CHANNEL, James. Account estate. Audited by John Luter and Henry Smith. Signed, Mary Channel, Admtx. D. Sept. 14, 1785. R. March 9, 1786. Page 178.

BLOW, Richard. Of St. Lukes Parish. Leg.- wife Ann the negroes left in Thomas Blunt's will; son Thomas; son Benjamin; son James; son Peter; daughter Ann Blow. Exs., friends John Thomas Blow, Sr., William Thomas and Thomas Vaughan. D. Dec. 19, 1785. R. March 9, 1786. Wit. Thomas Scott, William Vaughan, James Millar. Page 179.

WASHINGTON, George. Account current. Signed, Sarah Washington, Extx. Among items- paid Joshua Beal, David Washington's legacy; paid John Darden his wife Martha's legacy; paid Zebediah Washington's legacy. Audited by Joseph Scott, Jr. and A. Jones. R. July 12, 1786. Page 180.

JOHNSON, John. 1783. Account current. Signed, Peninah Johnson Admtx. Paid Rebeckah, Ann, Lidia, Alice and Jordan Johnson. Audited by Joseph Scott, Jr and A. Jones. R. May 11, 1786. Page 182.

JONES, Albridgton. Leg.- son Mathew, land bought of Charles Binns and that bought of Robert Care, called Cedar Island in Nansemond County; son William when of age land purchased of Thomas Holt and Ann his wife and John Holt; also a tract bought of Richard Williams, adjoining and negroes purchased of Richard Kirby; son Albridgton when of age; refers to married children, who have received their proportion of his estate. Ex., son Albridgton Jones. D. Sept. 22, 1784. Codicil: bequest to Ann Simmons, daughter of Mason Simmons. D. Dec. 12, 1785. Wit. Mathew Calvert, Arthur Williams, Thomas Wainwright. Wit. (to will) Samuel Calvert, Simon Murfee, Benjamin Beal. R. July 19, 1786. Page 183.

BLUNT, Thomas. Account current. Signed, Edwin Gray and William Thomas. Exs. Among items- paid Ann his late widow; division between four sons, remainder of estate divided between the seven children. Audited by Richard Kello and Benjamin Ruffin. R. July 12, 1786. Page 186.

POND, Daniel. Inventory. Signed, John and Richard Pond. Exs. R. Sept. 14, 1786. Page 187.

CARR, John. Leg.- wife Abigail; son Lawrence when of age; son Dickinson; son Robert; son John Carr. Exs., wife and friends Elisha Darden and Lemuel Lawrence. D. May 30, 1786. R. Sept. 14, 1786. Wit. David Edwards, Jesse Carr, Charles Hedgpeth. Page 188.

POND, Daniel. Account current. Signed, John and Richard Pond, Exs. Audited by Benjamin Ruffin and Charles Briggs. R. Oct. 12, 1786. Page 190.

MYRICK, Owen. Estate appraised by Randolph Newsum, Richard Johnson and Thomas Peete. R. Oct. 12, 1786. Page 191.

WESTBROOK, William. 1786. Signed, Samuel Westbrook, Adm. Audited by Thomas Edmunds, Samuel Edmunds and Arthur Foster. R. Oct. 12, 1786. Page 194.

MUNDELL, John. Of St. Luke's Parish. Leg.- son John; son Joseph at twenty one; to Hannah, wife of Samuel Ellis; daughter Lidia; daughter Mary; son William; wife Elizabeth; daughter Elizabeth, slaves at death of Sarah Harrison, which she holds by jointure, made her by John Scott; which descend to me; rest of estate among all my children. Exs., wife and Mr. John Rogers. D. March 29, 1785. R. Oct. 12, 1786. Wit. John Claud, William Claud, Basill Pain. Page 195.

WILLIAMSON, Francis. Cash being his proportional part of his grandmother's estate. Signed, Ned Holleman, Ex. Audited by Burwell Williamson and Absalom Williamson. D. Jan. 2, 1782. R. Oct. 12, 1786. Page 197.

BRYANT, John. Account current. Paid legacies to John Bryant, Mary Bryant, Jacob Wheeler and John Joyner. Signed, John Bryant, Wx. Audited by Joseph Scott, Jr. and A. Jones. R. Oct. 12, 1786. Page 198.

DREW, Jeremiah. Account estate. Audited by Thomas Turner and John Barrow. R. Oct. 12, 1786. Page 199.

WILLIAMS, John. Appraisal of estate, by Etheldred Everett, John Bishop and William Hart. D. July 27, 1786. R. Feb. 8, 1787. Page 200.

BAILEY, Benjamin. Estate appraised by Thomas Brock, Joseph Hart and John Hart. R. Feb. 8, 1787. Page 203.

BEAL, Benjamin, Sr. Leg.- son Benjamin; son John; wife Rachel; daughter Isbel Beal. Exs., David Wright and John Beal. D. March 26, 1786. R. Feb. 8, 1787. Wit. William Williams, Anne Williams. Page 204.

BYNUM, William. Account current. Signed, William Blunt and John Blunt. Audited by Thomas Turner, James Lundy and John Rogers. D. March -, 1786. R. April 12, 1787. Page 205.

MOUNTFORT, Thomas. Of the Parish of Nottoway. Leg.- wife Sarah; son Thomas; son Wade, land bought of Jacob Turner; daughter Francis; daughter Susannah Mountfort. Exs., wife, brother Wade Mountford and friend David Barrow. D. March 10, 1787. R. April 12, 1787. Wit. Lemuel Lewis, Thomas Camps, Presley Barrett. (Error in recording ? for this will is signed, Joseph Mountfortt). Page 206.

PRETLOW, Thomas. Leg.- wife Mary; nephew Thomas, son of Joshua Pretlow, decd.; nephew Benjamin, son of Samuel Pretlow, decd.; land purchased of Jordan Thomas in Isle of Wight County to Joseph the grandson of Joseph Pretlow, decd.; rest of estate to be divided, one-fifth each to children of brother Joseph decd.; children of brother Joshua decd.; children of brother Samuel decd.; children of sister Mary decd.; and brother John Pretlow. Exs., Thomas Pretlow, Jr. and Robert Ricks. D. March 14, 1786. R. June 14, 1787. Wit. Jenney Pretlow, Mary Sebrell, Samuel Bailey. Page 207.

CARY, Ann. Estate appraised by Jeb. Darden, William Hart and
John Bishop. D. Dec. 16, 1786. R. June 14, 1787. Page
208.

WASHINGTON, Arthur. Leg.- son James, land adjoining Benjamin
Blayley (? Bailey), brother Jesse Washington and Joseph
Phillips; son Arthur land given me by my father; son Amos
land descended to me from my brother Thomas Washington decd.;
daughter Olive Washington. Exs., friends Joseph Washington
and James Gray. D. Sept. 6, 1770. R. June 14, 1787. Wit.
J. Gray, Jesse Carrel. Micajah Holleman, qualified as
Executor. Page 209.

CRENSHAW, John. Leg.- wife Elizabeth; children Elijah and
Polly; son Elijah the land adjoining Dr. Browne with reversion
of bequest to Elemuel Darden, son of Benjamin Darden, decd.
Exs., William Thomas, Samuel Maget (of Nich^S), Jacob Turner,
William Maget (of Nich^S). D. Dec. 3, 1784. R. Dec. 14,
1786. Wit. Nicholas Maget, Robert Daughtrey. Page 210.

DOYEL, Kinchen. Estate appraised by Jacob Bradshaw, John
Drewry and Charles Powers. D. March 2, 1787. R. June 14,
1787. Page 211.

BRIGGS, Henry. Account current. Signed, Charles Briggs and
John T. Blow, Exs. Paid Peter Fagon for teaching Charles and
Henry Briggs to dance. Audited by Thomas Edmunds and William
Thomas. R. June 14, 1787. Page 212.

WILLIAMS, William. 1784. Signed, Samuel Edmunds and Thomas
Vaughan, Exs. Audited by John T. Blow and William Thomas.
R. June 14, 1787. Page 217.

IVEY, John. Account estate. Signed, Joshua Nicholson. Ex.
Audited by Thomas Edmunds and Michael Warren. R. July 12,
1787. Page 218.

NICHOLSON, Sarah. Account Current. 1784. Signed, Howell
Edmunds and Owen Myrick, Exs. Among items, paid Fanny
Mirick, her proportional part of her mother's estate; paid
the guardian of Fanny, Lucy and Matilda Nicholson, their
proportional part; paid Edwin Seward and Sarah Briggs their
part; paid Sarah and Lucy Edwards their part; paid Elizabeth
Rivers her proportional part of estate. Audited, by Thomas
Edmunds and Michael Warren. R. July 12, 1787. Page 219.

CARR, John. Estate appraised by Jordan Williams and Jacob
Darden. Signed, Elisha Darden, Ex. R. July 12, 1787.
Page 220.

BOWDEN, Robert. Leg.- wife Mary; son Bille; daughter Elizabeth;
daughter Salley; daughter Milley Bowden. Exs., Thomas Bowdin
and John Pursell. D. Nov. 5, 1783. R. July 12, 1787. Wit.
Elias Bowden, John Powell, Rady Bowden. Page 222.

POPE, John. Estate appraised by Stephen Johnson, John Pledger
and John Rawl (Rawls ?) Signed, Joseph Vick, Adm. D. Dec.
13, 1784. R. July 12, 1787. Page 223.

WILLIAMSON, Thomas. Of the Parish of Nottoway. Leg.- daughter
Elizabeth Clements; grandson John Clements; grandchildren,
Sarah Cocke, Elizabeth Clements, Francis Clements; daughter
Sarah Taylor, land in Northampton County, N. C., purchased of
Anthony Armistead;- her husband, John Taylor Esq.; to Thomas
Turner of Nottoway Parish the land on which he lives. Exs.,

son-in-law John Taylor, Esq. and friend William Urquhart and grandson John Clements. D. June 24, 1787. R. July 12, 1787. Wit. John Andrews, Mary Urquhart, Samuel Kello. Page 225.

MOUNTFORT, Thomas. Estate appraised by Thad Lewis, Micajah Griffin and Joseph Scott, Jr. R. July 12, 1787. Page 227.

BEAL, Benjamin. Estate appraised by David Wright, James Wright and Richard Beal. R. July 12, 1787. Page 228.

JOHNSON, Jacob. Estate appraised by Arthur Foster, Arthur Turner and Jacob Barnes. R. July 12, 1787. Page 229.

WOMACK, James. Estate appraised by John Claud, William Claud and Basel Payne. D. April 4, 1787. R. Sept. 13, 1787. Page 230.

BLUNT, William, Sr. Leg.- wife Mary my land adjoining John Myrick and James Lundy; refers to David Johnson (?); son William all my land in Virginia and N. C., reserving the plantation left wife, also land I have paid Thomas Person for, which was purchased by John Person; grandson Jesse Drew when twenty one, reversion to children of my daughter Ann Wright; daughter Mary; daughter Rebekah Mason. Daughter Ann the wife of William Wright and Rebekah the wife of Littleberry Mason. Friends Benjamin Blunt, Thomas Turner, John Turner and brother John Blunt to divide my estate. Exs., son William Blunt and son-in-law Littleberry Mason. D. June 3, 1787. R. Sept. 13, 1787. Wit. John Blunt, Henry Wright, Susannah Cooper. Page 231.

WESTBROOK, Helen. Of the Parish of St. Luke. Leg.- daughter Lucy Linear; daughter Martha Judkins; son Henry. Ex., son Henry Westbrook. D. March 16, 1786. R. Sept. 13, 1787. Wit. John Simmons Sr., Samuel Drewry, William Rose. Page 233.

ATKINSON, Hardy. Leg.- wife Ann; son Elias; son Elisha. Ex. friend Benjamin Blunt. D. Oct. 25, 1783. R. Dec. 13, 1783. Wit. William Whitehead, Richard Deloach, Samuel Atkinson. Page 234.

WILLIAMS, Benjamin. Leg.- son Ethelbert Carr Williams at eighteen; wife Mary; son Richard Egbert Williams; daughter Marian when sixteen. Exs., Josiah Wick and wife Mary Williams. D. June 9, 1787. R. Sept. 13, 1787. Wit. James Moore, Hardy Johnson, Rebecca Johnson. Page 234.

ELLIS, Jeremiah. Leg.- wife Ann; son Jeremiah; son Henry Ellis. Exs., wife and sons Jeremiah and Henry Ellis. D. April 7, 1786. R. Sept. 13, 1787. Wit. William Thomas, Joel Newsum, Sally Newsum. Page 236.

BARNES, Burwell. Account current. Signed, Nathan Barnes, Adm. Audited by Thomas Edmunds, Samuel Edmunds, James Wilkinson. R. Sept. 13, 1787. Page 237.

WESTBROOK, Miday. Leg.- sister Ann Westbrook; sister Rebecca Westbrook. D. July 23, 1786. R. Oct. 11, 1787. Wit. John Blake, Hannah Westbrook. Page 237.

MORGAN, Foster. Leg.- brother Jarrett Morgan; refers to land sold Thomas Turner; James R. Morgan, son of brother Jarrett Morgan. Ex. brother Jarrett Morgan. D. Feb. 4, 1786. R. Oct. 11, 1787. Wit. Thomas Turner, Simon Harris, Richard

Harrison. Page 238.

JACKSON, Kindred. Leg.- brother William; Jean Brewer; brother Isham Jackson. Exs., uncle John Jackson and friend Newit Edwards. D. Feb. 23, 1787. R. Oct. 11, 1787. Wit. Patience Jackson, Mathew Williamson, Charles Joyner. Page 239.

UNDERWOOD, John. Leg.- son Mathew land patented in Feb. 14, 1761; son John; daughter Sarah Williams; daughter Elizabeth Pope; to all my grandchildren. Exs., friends Thomas Edmunds and Thomas Vaughan. D. June 29, 1787. R. Oct. 11, 1787. Wit. Robert Carr, Patience Pedin, James Pedin. Page 240.

TURNER, Sampson. Account current. Signed, Clear Turner. Audited by Benjamin Ruffin and Thomas Edmunds. R. Oct. 11, 1787. Page 241.

GEORGE, William. Signed, Benjamin Spratley, Ex. Audited by Thomas Holliday and Edmund Tyler. R. Oct. 11, 1787 Page 242.

JACKSON, Kindred. Estate appraised by Micajah Edwards, Charles Birdsong, Bartur (?) Taylor. R. Dec. 13, 1787. Page 243.

JOHNSON, Simon Jr. Signed, Simon Johnson, Adm. Account current. Balance due widow and orphans. Audited by James Clark and Henry Jones. D. 1785. R. Dec. 13, 1787. Page 243.

CRUMPLER, Benjamin. Leg.- son John land adjoining John Mercer and West Tynes; son Benjamin land adjoining Benjamin Cocke, Mathew Boykin and Valentine Jenkins; son William; son Arthur land adjoining Thomas Turner; wife Elizabeth. Ex., son John Crumpler. D. March 23, 1785. R. Dec. 13, 1787. Wit. John Pursell, Joseph Wright, John Wright. Page 244.

APPLEWHITE, Thomas. Leg.- Arthur Applewhite, son of Arthur Applewhite; Henry Wills Applewhite, son of John Applewhite; Mary Jean Carr, daughter of Joshua Carr; George Thomas Williams, son of Absalom Williams. Ex. Absalom Williams. D. June 26, 1787. R. Dec. 13, 1787. Wit. James Williams. Page 245.

POPE, Joseph. Account estate. Signed, William Pope, Ex. Audited by Thomas Edmunds, Nathan Barnes and Samuel Edmunds. R. Dec. 13, 1787. Page 246.

WESTBROOK, Mrs. Helen. Inventory. Signed, Henry Westbrook. R. Jan. 10, 1788. Page 247.

PORCH, James. Leg.- wife Ann and my six children, Peggy, Thomas, Peterson, James, Pennington. Exs., Jesse Cooper, Jesse Wrenn and wife Anna. D. May 3, 1787. R. Jan. 10, 1788. Wit. Patience Bass, Lucy Johnson, John Smith, Arthur Matthews. Exs., refused to qualify, administration granted Moses McKenny. Page 248.

VASSER, Joseph. Of Parish of Nottoway. Leg.- son Etheldred, land adjoining James Calthorpe and Thomas Lane; son Benjamin; son Joseph; daughter Mary Underwood; son William Vasser. Ex., son Etheldred Vasser. D. Oct. 30, 1786. R. Jan. 10, 1788. Wit. John Pond, John H. Pond, Stephenson Pond. Page 249.

JOYNER, Jonas. Inventory. Signed, Elisha Darden. Adm. D. Jan. 8, 1788. R. Feb. 14, 1788. Page 250.

POWERS, Charles. Signed, Moses Johnson. Adm. Audited by
Arthur Bowin and Lemuel Jones. R. Feb. 14, 1788. Page 250.

WILLIAMS, Henry. Moses Johnson. Adm. D. Jan. 21, 1788.
Balance due the orphans. Audited by E. Herring, Lemuel Jones,
Sampson Pitman. R. April --, 1788. Page 251.

BARRETT, William. Leg.- son William; son Willis my plantation
in Nansemond; rest of my estate among all my children. Exs.,
wife and friend Jordan Denson. D. Dec. --, 1787. R. Feb.
14, 1788. Wit. Giles Joyner, William Joyner, Henry Jones.
Page 252.

VASSER, Joseph. Inventory. R. Feb. 14, 1788. Page 253.

HOLT, Thomas. Leg.- son Charles; son Thomas; daughter Amy
Martin; daughter Sarah Land; granddaughters Rebecca and Ann
Rawlings; granddaughter Nancy Rawlings; to Polly Rawling's
daughter Nancy Rawlings at eighteen; granddaughter Mason
Kirby Holt; son Frederick Holt; my security on a bond to
Burrel Bell to be taken out of son Thomas' portion. Exs.,
son Thomas Holt. D. Dec. 29, 1786. R. April 11, 1788.
Wit. Thomas Gilliam, Jr., William Barnes, Joseph Fort.
Thomas Holt, refused extx., and Nathan Holt qualified. Page
253.

UNDERWOOD, John. Estate appraised by John T. Blow, William
Thomas and Samuel Francis. R. April 11, 1788. Page 254.

RUFFIN, Benjamin. Inventory. R. May 8, 1788. Page 256.

SUTER, John, Sr. Leg.- son John; son Henry; daughter Elizabeth;
son William (not twenty one) son Arthur (not twenty one);
daughter Rebecca at eighteen; if either should die without
issue, estate given them to be divided between the two
brothers or brother and sister, that I had by the same woman.
Exs., son John Suter and Henry Smith. D. March 31, 1786.
R. June 12, 1788. Wit. James Vaughan, Ph<u>obe</u> Vaughan, John
Hollcome (?). Page 257.

DAUGHTRY, Elizabeth. Leg.- friend James Gardner, Jr., all my
part of John Daughtry's estate due from David Wright and
bonds from David Edwards and William Tallaugh; friend Peter
Hines, if he continues at the place called Littletown; friend
Elizabeth Boyt; sister Mary Wright. Ex., friend James
Gardner, Jr. D. May 25, 1785. R. June 12, 1788. Wit.
James Gardner, Sr., Mathew Garner, Elisha Darden. Page 259.

BAILEY, Mary. Inventory. Signed, Jordan Judkins. R. July
10, 1788. Page 260.

APPLEWHITE, Thomas. Estate appraised by John Whitehead, John
Bishop and Thomas Oberry. R. July 10, 1788. Page 261.

WILLIAMSON, William. D. Dec. 30, 1785. Estate appraised by
William Stephenson, Sr., Arthur Boykin, Solomon Holmes. R.
July 10, 1788. Page 260.

STEPHENSON, Thomas. Leg.- wife Mary; son Robert; son Willis;
son John; daughter Charlotte; son Charles; son Stephen; pro-
vision for unborn child; daughter Elizabeth; son Edmund; son
Thomas Stephenson. D. Feb. 15, 1788. R. July 10, 1788.
Wit. Samuel Brister, Stephen Summerell, James Summerell.
Exs., sons Edmund and Thomas Stephenson. Page 262.

DAUGHTRY, Elizabeth. Estate appraised by William Fowler, Holland Darden, Joshua Gardner. R. Sept. 11, 1788. Page 263.

WESTBROOK, Mary. Leg.- granddaughter Beck Westbrook, daughter of Patty Newsum; daughter Patty Newsum. Ex., brother Arthur Foster. D. April 22, 1788. R. Sept. 11, 1788. Wit. William Claud, John Claud, Jr. Page 265.

DREW, Newit. Account current. Ex., Jeremiah Drew. 1775. Signed, William Myrick and Randolph Newsum, Exs. of Jeremiah Drew. Audited by John Wright, John Simmons, Sr. Mark Nicholson. R. May 11, 1788. Page 265.

TURNER, Thomas. Leg.- wife Ann; son Thomas; son Amies; to all my children, Thomas, Amos, Chacy, Holland, Nanny and Charlotte. D. Oct. 20, 1785. R. Sept. 11, 1788. Exs., wife and son Thomas Turner. Wit. Benjamin Crumpler, Arthur Turner, Arthur Crumpler. Page 267.

WILLIAMSON, Robert. Of the Parish of Nottoway. Leg.- wife Selah; John, son of Jacob Williamson; Joshua, son of Jacob Williamson; rest of estate to John and Joshua Williamson and Valentine Jenkins. D. Feb. 27, 1787. R. Sept. 11, 1791. Wit. John Crumpler, Benjamin Crumpler, Arthur Crumpler. Exs. wife Selah and friend John Crumpler. Page 268.

BOYKIN, Simon. Leg.- son Arthur land bought of James Baisden; son Simon, land bought of Rand's Exs.; daughter Martha Bridger; grandchildren James, William, Patsy and John children of Martha Bridger; granddaughters, Sally Williams Boykin and Charlotte,- daughters of Simon Boykin. Exs., sons, Arthur and Simon Boykin. D. June 16, 1787. R. Sept. 11, 1788. Wit. Elizabeth Williams, John Summerell, Daniel Herring. Page 268.

JENKINS, Spencer. Leg.- wife Ann; son Jesse; son William; daughter Sally Britt; daughter Molly Williford; daughter Betsey Jenkins. Exs., wife and sons Jesse and William Jenkins. D. March 29, 1788. R. Sept. 11, 1788. Wit. Hartwell Cocke, John Andrews. Page 270.

CRUMPLER, Benjamin. Inventory. Signed, John Crumpler. R. Nov. --, 1788. Page 272.

BARNES, Burwell. Account current. Signed, Nathan Barnes. Adm. Audited by J. Wilkinson, Samuel Edmunds, Thomas Edmunds. R. Sept. 11, 1788. Page 272.

SCOTT, James Jordan. Account current. Signed, Jordan Denson, Ex. 1780. Among items, Joseph Scott, paid in full his share of the estate; paid Miriam Scott her share and as guardian of the orphans. Audited by Shadrack Lewis, A. Jones and Jos (or Jas. ?) Vick. R. Sept. 11, 1788. Page 273.

BROOKS, William. Of the Parish of St. Luke. Leg.- daughter Ann Dunkin; to Hannah Swett, wife reversion to my son William Swett; Etheldred Brantley. Exs., friends, Etheldred Brantley, Henry Bittle, Michael Warren. D. May 9, 1788. R. Oct. 9, 1788. Wit. John Powell, William Bittle, Joseph Gurley. Page 276.

PORTER, Thomas, Sr. Leg.- wife Julan (written later Julia); son Thomas; son Henry the plantation on which Britton Porter now lives; son Newit, land on which Richard Demory now lives;

grandson Drury Porter when twenty one the land on which my son Solomon Porter formerly lived. Exs., wife and son Thomas Porter. D. Aug. 7, 1785. R. Oct. 9, 1788. Wit. Nathan Bryant, Etheldred Brantley. Page 276.

JOYNER, Jethro. Leg.- wife Martha; to all my children. Exs., wife and friend Arthur Bowing. D. July 6, 1788. R. Oct. 9, 1788. Wit. Joseph Bradshaw, Mathew Charles, Jethro Charles. Page 278.

WORRELL, Richard. Leg.- son Shadrack land bought of Henry Pope; son Richard; son William; son Mathew; son-in-law Charles Council; daughter Molly; sons-in-law John Lankford and Joseph Brewer or their heirs are to have no part of my estate; granddaughter Cherry Worrell; friend Jethro Charles. Exs., son-in-law Charles Council and son Shadrack. D. Sept. 19, 1788. R. Oct. 9, 1788. Wit. Benjamin Bradshaw, Richard Pope, Mathew Charles. Page 279.

BARRETT, William, Jr. D. May 1788. Estate appraised by Henry Jones, John Bowers and Tamer Joyner. R. Oct. 9, 1788. Page 280.

WILLIAMSON, Thomas. Estate appraised by John Andrews, John Clayton and Timothy Atkinson. Signed, John Taylor, Ex. R. Oct. 9, 1788. Page 282.

EDWARDS, William. Account current. 1783. Signed, Thomas Holladay and John Taylor. R. Oct. 9, 1788. Page 284.

VICK, Mathew, Sr. Leg.- son Simmons; son Kirby; wife Sarah; daughters Milly Porter, Winny Porter, Lydia Vaughan and Isabell Vick; son Council; son Mathew; son Joseph; son Knowell, land bought of Hardy Johnson; son Joel Vick. Exs., friends Jesse Vick and Shad Lewis. D. Sept. 26, 1788. R. Oct. 9, 1788. Wit. Joseph Vick, Hardy Johnson, Martha Doyel. Exs., refused and Josiah Vick, qualified. Page 284.

WORRELL, Richard. Estate appraised by William Joyner, Jethro Charles and <u>Martha</u> Charles. D. Dec. 11, 1788. Page 286.

NORFLEET, Cordall. Leg.- Cordall N. Bynum a tract, formerly belonging to James Fason in Northampton County, N. C.; reversion to my children, Elizabeth, John (not of age) and Sarah Norfleet; wife Mary Norfleet. Exs., wife and friends John and James Wilkinson. D. March 21, 1788. R. Dec. 11, 1788. Wit. Moses Johnson, John Williford, James Wilkinson. Page 288.

MERCER, Robert. Account Current. 1775. Paid Robert Mercer a portion of his legacy. Signed, Joseph Holliman, Ex. of Joseph Holleman, who was ex. of Robert Mercer. Audited by M. Holleman, William Urquhart and Burwell Williamson. R. Dec. 11, 1788. Page 290.

BLUNT, Colonel William. Estate appraised by <u>Chs</u> Ross, Jos. (or Jas ?), Turner, Henry Smith. R. Feb. 12, 1789. Page 291.

JOYNER, Jethro. Estate appraised by Hardy Pope, John Carstarphen, Joseph Bradshaw, Charles Council. R. Feb. 12, 1789. Page 293.

POPE, William. Of the Parish of St. Luke. Leg.- sister Mourning Pope; wife Prudence Pope. Exs., wife and friend

Simon Harris. D. 1772. R. Feb. 12, 1789. Wit. Henry Pope, Rebecah Harris, William Mackey. Page 294.

LUTER, John. (Listed in Torrence as Suter). Estate appraised by John Blunt, Lazarus Cook and James Turner. R. Feb. 12, 1789. Page 294.

BLAKE, Thomas. Leg.- son Samuel; son John; son Etheldred; son James; son Benjamin; son Thomas Blake. Exs., sons, Samuel, John and Benjamin Blake. D. Oct. 5, 1784. R. Feb. 12, 1789. Wit. Howell Edmunds, William Vaughan, John Claud, Burwell Westbrook. Page 296.

CLEMENTS, Thomas, Jr. Inventory. Signed by William Urquhart and Hartwell Cock. D. Feb. 2, 1785. R. Feb. 14, 1788. Page 298.

POPE, Patience. Account current. Signed, Nathan Barnes. Ex. Audited by Samuel Edmunds and Jesse Cooper. D. 1779. R. Feb. 12, 1789. Page 298.

PARKER, Drury. Of the Parish of St. Luke. Leg.- wife Milly and her child begotten by me; son Howell; son Richard; son William; son Thomas land I bought of Benjamin Cooper; son Edwin; son Frederick; daughter Lewcy; daughter Patty; daughter Nanny; daughter Luky (or Suky); daughter Tempy; daughter Judith; daughter Betsey; daughter Polly; son Mathew. Exs., brother Richard Parker, Jeremiah Drew and Randolph Newsum. D. June 13, 1783. R. Feb. 12, 1789. Will signed Drewry Parker. Page 299.

COBB, Samuel. Leg.- son Mathew; son Kinchen, land adjoining Demsey Cowper, Will Greswitt's orphans and Dr. Samuel Browne; son Samuel; son Burgwin, land adjoining Simon Murfee and Henry Cobb; my brother Henry Cobb and Simon Vaughan to divide my land; wife Mary Cobb. D. April 4, 1785. R. Feb. 12, 1789. Exs., sons Mathew and Kinchen Cobb. Wit. Demsey Cooper, Thomas Pope, Nicholas Cobb. Page 301.

HINES, David. Leg.- to James Bowing, natural son of Lucy Bowing; to my sister Mary Hines' child. D. Dec. 14, 1788. R. Feb. 12, 1789. Wit. Richard Hallcome, John Arrington, Lemuel Stewart, Mary Bowing. John Simmons, qualified as Ex. Page 303.

BOYKIN, William, Sr. Leg.- daughter Patience Whitehead; daughter Catherine Harris; son William, residue of estate to my following children, Brittain, William, Shadrack, Sarah Williamson, widow and Martha Hough. Exs., sons William and Shadrack Boykin. D. Oct. 26, 1786. R. Feb. 12, 1789. Wit. Edward Neal, Stephen Summerell, James Hough. Page 304.

SUMMERELL, John. Account current. Signed, Jacob Turner and Henry B----, trustees. Audited by William Urquhart and H. Holleman. R. Feb. 12, 1789. Page 305.

TUNNELL, Mary. Estate appraised by James Lundy, Richard Harrison and Benjamin Harrison. D. Feb. 1, 1787. R. April 9, 1789. Page 307.

STANTON, James. Leg.- wife Christian; son Sampson; to my three sons and five daughters, Silvanus, James, Sampson, Elizabeth, Sarah, Lucy, Mary and Faith Stanton. Ex., son Sampson Stanton. D. July 29, 1762. R. April 9, 1789. Wit. Benjamin Bayley, Joseph Watkins, Nathaniel Briggs, Stephen

Hamlin, William Hamlin. Page 307.

GRAY, Ann. Leg.- Lyda Ramsey, with reversion of bequest to brother John Gray; sisters Honour Sharp, Lyda Ramsey and Mary Blake; Catron Ramsey; Mary Morgan; Thomas Turner and Mary Smith. Exs., Henry Ramsey and brother John Gray. D. Feb. 21, 1784. R. April 9, 1789. Wit. Martha Morgan, Mary Morrell, Priscilla LeMore, Susanna Turner. Page 308.

BROWNE, Benjamin. Estate at "Round Hill" appraised by Arthur Exum, John H. Pond and Thomas Wood. D. April 5, 1788. R. April 10, 1789. Page 309.

THORPE, Timothy. Of St. Luke's Parish. Leg.- nephew John T. Richardson; nephew John, son of William Person, land on Angelica Swamp; neice Peggy Ridley; neice Patsey Thorpe; nephew John, son of Phillip Person; mother and the bequest at her death to be equally divided between John T. Richardson; John son of Phillip Person; Dorothy Atherton; Peggy Ridley and Patsey Thorpe. Exs., Peterson Thorpe and Phillip Person. D. Jan. 27, 1776. R. April 9, 1789. Wit. William Moore, Sarah Atkinson. Jordan Richardson, qualified as Executor. Page 310.

EVERITT, John. At a Court held for Nansemond County, John Lawrence and Etheldred Everitt gave bond for administration on his estate, Jan. 14, 1782. Appraised by Elisha Darden, Etheldred Warren and William Hart. Examined by Richard Baker, Etheldred Warren and William Hart. D. Sept. 9, 1782. R. April 9, 1789. Copy produced by <u>Ethel</u> and John Everitt of Nansemond County to be put on the records of Southampton County. Page 311.

JOHNSON, Giles. Of Nottoway Parish. Leg.- son Stephen; daughters, Sarah, Mary and Penelope, when twenty one; wife Mary Johnson. Exs., friends David Barrow and John Johnson. D. Feb. 19, 1789. R. June 11, 1789. Wit. James Clark, Simon Johnson, <u>Pettaway</u> Johnson, Elizabeth Johnson. Page 313.

HOLLEMAN, Josiah John. Account current. Signed, John Clayton, Ex. Paid Solomon Holmes estate, proportion for clothing for soldiers; paid for Mrs. Holleman's funeral sermon; paid for hiring a soldier. Audited by William Urquhart, Solomon Holmes. R. June 11, 1789. Page 314.

JOHNSON, Charity. Estate appraised by Isaac Williams, William Crichlow and James Butts. Signed, Joseph Vick, Ex. R. June 11, 1789. Page 316.

HINES, Richard. Estate appraised by Benjamin Stewart, Micajah Ellis and John Kirby. R. July 9, 1789. Page 317.

STANTON, James. Account estate. Signed, Sampson Stanton. Audited by Thomas Edmunds and Jacob Randolph. R. July 11, 1789. Page 318.

DARDEN, Elisha. Leg.- wife Pheribe; son Jacob; son Jones (not fourteen), lots in Murfreesborough on the Meherrin River; daughter Salley Barnes, with reversion to her children; daughter Esther; daughter Betsey; daughter Clotilda; daughter Milly Darden. Exs., son Jacob and friends John Bowers and David Barrow. D. Dec. 3, 1788. R. July 9, 1789. Wit. James Scoggins, Charles Hedgpeth, Polly Glover. Page 319.

HINES, David. Estate appraised by Jesse Arrington, John Simmons, Jr., and Micaj Ellis. Signed, John Simmons. R. July 9, 1789. Page 321.

VICK, Richard. Of Nottoway Parish. Leg.- wife Elizabeth; brothers Joshua, Giles and Silas; sister Sarah; sister Piety Vick. Exs., brothers, Joshua and Giles Vick. D. May 1, 1789. R. July 9, 1789. Wit. Jesse Arrington, Martha Arrington, Lucy Arrington. Page 321.

JOYNER, Henry. Estate appraised by Thad Lewis, Benjamin Beale and Joshua Beale. R. July 9, 1789. Page 322.

BULLS, Jesse. Estate appraised by Edmond Johnson, Etheldred Pitman and Benjamin Bradshaw. D. Sept. 25, 1788. R. July 9, 1789. Page 324.

JOYNER, Ann. Account current. Signed, Arthur Bowin. Audited by Daniel Simmons and David Barrow. R. July 9, 1789. Page 324.

WORRELL, Richard. Account current. Paid Mary Worrell, paid Shadrack Worrell, paid Charles Council, paid William Worrell's guardian, paid Mathew Charles, guardian of Richard paid John Carstarphan, guardian of Mathew Worrell. Audited by James Clark, John Johnson, Arthur Bowing. R. July 9, 1789. Page 325.

HARRIS, Amos. Of the Parish of St. Luke. Leg.- son William; son West,- friends Joshua Thorpe, John Applewhite and Arthur Applewhite to divide the land between them; younger sons Amos and Henry, the land on which I and James Wentworth now live; four daughters, Mary McKenny, Salley, Rebecca and Patience Harris; my three youngest children, Amos, Patience and Henry; daughter Ann Horn. Exs., friend Joshua Thorp, son William Harris and nephew Arthur Applewhite. D. July 15, 1785. R. Sept. 10, 1789. Wit. Thomas Peete, Joshua Thorpe, William Johnson. Page 325.

VICK, Shadrack. Estate appraised by John Rochelle, Jeremiah Drake and Drewry Beal. D. Nov. 28, 1788. R. Sept. 11, 1789. Page 327.

TURNER, Benjamin. Signed, John Barrow, Thomas Turner and Nathan Harris. Audited by Thomas Edmunds and Richard Blow. R. Sept. 11, 1789. Page 328.

VICK, Jacob. Leg.- daughter Mourning Jordan, land granted me by patent in Nov. 3, 1750; wife Patience; son Jacob; daughter Lydda Vick. Exs., wife and son Jesse Vick. D. Oct. 20, 1784. R. Nov. 11, 1789. Wit. Benjamin Whitfield, Trial Bailey, Martha Bailey. Page 329.

NICHOLSON, Joshua. Account current of Howell Edmunds, one of his Ex. Cash paid Mary Nicolson, one third part of the estate. Audited by Ben. Blunt, Mich^l. Warren and Thomas Edmunds. R. Oct. 8, 1789. Account current with John Kirby, one of his Ex. Audited by Thomas Edmunds and Michael Warren. Page 332.

HARRIS, James. Leg.- nephew Joel, son of brother Drewry Harris, reversion to nephew James, son of brother Moses Harris; then to Nancy, daughter of brother Drewry Harris. Exs., friends John Rogers and James Lundy. D. June 16, 1789. R. Oct. 8, 1789. Wit. John Rogers, John Tunnell, Martha Britt,

Priscilla McMore. Page 333.

JOHNSON, Abraham. Account current. Signed, Josiah Johnson, Ex. Audited by Thomas Turner and John Barrow. R. Oct. 8, 1789. Page 334.

GRAY, John. Estate appraised by James Lundy, Samuel Francis and Benjamin Blunt, Jr. D. March 14, 1789. R. Oct. 8, 1789. Page 334.

NEGRO, Tom. (formerly the property of Lemuel Jones). Leg.- wife Fanney. Ex., Edmund Johnson. D. Oct. 26, 1787. R. Oct. 8, 1789. Wit. Lemuel Jones. Page 336.

MERCER, John. Estate appraised by John Crumpler and Arthur Boykin. D. Dec. 1788. R. Oct. 8, 1789. Page 336.

BOWDEN, Robert. Estate appraised by John Britt, Joseph Wright and Lighborn Lowe. R. Oct. 8, 1789. Page 339.

COKER, Jonathan. Estate appraised by John Hart, Joseph Hart and Jesse Washington. Signed, Thomas Clary. D. Feb. 23, 1787. R. Oct. 8, 1789. Page 339.

BROOKS, William. Estate appraised by Benj Kindred, John Powell and William Bittle. Signed, Henry Bittle and Michael Warren. R. Oct. 8, 1789. Page 341.

VICK, Robert. Leg.- son Jordan; to all my children. Ex., son Jordan Vick. D. Aug. 21, 1788. R. Oct. 8, 1789. Wit. James Bryant, Jesse Vick, John Vick. Page 342.

IVY, John, Sr. Leg.- wife Mary; son Benjamin; son Phillips; daughter Becky Bass. Exs., sons Benjamin and Phillips Ivy. D. Jan. 16, 1787. R. Dec. 10, 1789. Wit. John Williamson, Richard Gilliam, John Reese, Jr. Page 343.

LUNDY, John. Leg.- son Peyton; son John; wife Edith; daughter Nancy Rivers; daughter Elizabeth; daughter Pattey; daughter Clarimon Holt Lundy. Exs., friends Buckner Wittemore, John Rogers and wife Edith Lundy. D. July 28, 1789. R. Dec. 10, 1789. Wit. John Rogers, John Berryman, Jr., David Johnson. Page 344.

TYLER, Jeremiah. Of St. Luke's Parish. Leg.- (refers to land bought of William Jarrell, which he is to give him a title to at twenty one); wife Elizabeth; son William Jarrell Tyler, when of age; daughter Martha Kinchen Tyler; provision for unborn child. Exs., wife and father Edmund Tyler. D. Feb. 4, 1789. R. Dec. 10, 1789. Wit. John T. Blow, Sr., Robert Wellons, William Blow. Page 345.

EDWARDS, John. Leg.- son Micajah; son Newit, land adjoining William Simmons, Emslus Derring, William Jackson and Mathew Williamson; son Joel land adjoining John Wood, Benjamin Whitfield, Robert Furgunson, Apaphroditus Williams and Ephraim Williams; son James, land adjoining James Barnes and Jordan Vick; son West, land adjoining Newit Edwards; daughter Mary Whitfield; grandson George Whitfield; daughter Elizabeth Everit; daughter Sally Birdsong; wife Ann Edwards. Exs. sons Micajah and Newit Edwards. D. June 30, 1789. R. Dec. 10, 1789. Wit. James Foster, William Simmons, John Cook. Page 346.

HINES, Howell. Leg.- wife Ann; children Dolly C.; Sarah
Elizabeth C. Hines. Exs., Captain Josiah Vick and Mr. James
Chappell. D. Nov. 4, 1789. R. Dec. 10, 1789. Wit. Nath[1]
Davis, Bolding Hines, Ann Derby. Page 349.

JENKINS, Spencer. Estate appraised by Timothy Atkinson, Jacob
Turner and John Andrews. R. Dec. 10, 1789. Page 350.

BRITT, Thomas. D. July 1789. Estate appraised by John Andrews,
Simon Boykin and John Pursell. D. Dec. 10, 1789. Page 352.

VICK, Robert. D. 1789. Estate appraised by Nathan Barnes,
Jacob Williams and Charles Birdsong. R. Dec. 11, 1789.
Page 352.

WILLIAMS, Elias. Leg.- nephew Mathew Peirce; nephew Nicholas
Williams; nephew Elias Williams; brother John Williams, rest
of estate to all my brothers and sisters. Ex., friend Rice
B. Peirce. D. Jan. 10, 1781. Wit. Nicholas Williams,
Benjamin Williams. Page 353.

MURFEE, Richard, Sr. Leg.- wife Lucy; son Simon; son William;
daughter Molly; daughter Lucy Daughtrey; daughters Celia,
Sally and Nancy; grandson Francis Murfee; daughter Elizabeth
Williams. Exs., sons Simon and William Murfee. D. Nov. 21,
1788. R. Dec. 11, 1789. Wit. Josiah Vick, Wilson Davis.
Page 354.

KELLO, Richard. Leg.- daughter Mary Cocke; son Samuel; son
Richard Kello. Ex., son Samuel Kello. D. May 25, 1789. R.
Jan. 14, 1790. Wit. Benjamin Parker, Richard Cocke, Jr.
Page 355.

BROWN, Jean. Leg.- sister Elizabeth Day; Benjamin son of Joshua
Hines and his wife Lucy; Henry Hines son of aforesaid; to
William Foster the grandfather of Benjamin and Henry Hines;
Lucy Hines, daughter of William Foster. Ex., Col. Samuel
Kello. D. Sept. 5, 1789. R. Jan. 14, 1790. Wit. Thomas
Lain, Micah Ellis. Page 356.

DREWRY, Samuel. Leg.- son Samuel, land adjoining Joel Woods
and William Crichlow; daughter Mary Salter; granddaughter
Katherine Johnson when eighteen; daughter Ann Simmons; wife
Elizabeth; son James; son Humphrey; son Joseph when twenty
one. Exs., son Samuel and son-in-law Spratley Simmons. D.
Feb. 4, 1789. R. Jan. 10, 1790. Wit. Edwin Gray, Joel
Wood, Humphrey Drewry. Page 357.

POPE, Henry. Estate appraised by John T. Blow, Richard Blow and
Benjamin Edwards. R. Feb. 11, 1790. Page 359.

DARDEN, Elisha. Inventory. Signed, Jacob Darden, Jr. R.
April 8, 1790. Page 360.

CARR, John. Account current. D. 1786. Signed, Elisha Darden,
Ex. Audited by Jacob Darden, Sr., Holland Darden and Henry
Gardner. R. Feb. 8, 1790. Page 362.

JOYNER, Jonas. Account current. Signed, Elisha Darden Adm.
D. 1788. Audited by Jacob Darden, Sr., Holland Darden and
Henry Gardner. R. Feb. 8, 1790. Page 364.

COBB, Samuel. Estate appraised by Abraham Mitchel, Mathew Wills
and Thomas Lawrence. Signed, Mathew Cobb and Kinchen Cobb,
Exs. R. April 8, 1790. Page 365.

THORPE, Moses. Leg.- wife; son John, with reversion to his son
Aaron; daughter Elizabeth Harris; daughter Sarah Briggs Thorpe,
with reversion of bequest to Moses Harris' two sons; son John
my land in N. C. and a negro bought of Benjamin Barham; to
Jordin son of Tabitha Bass. Exs., son John, Lewis Thorpe and
John Williamson. D. Dec. 1, 1786. R. June 10, 1790. Wit.
Wike Ivey, John Williamson. Codicil witnessed by John
Williamson and Charles Southward. Page 366.

JOHNSON, Ralls. D. Feb. 16, 1789. Estate appraised by James
Johnson, Arthur Bowing, Joseph Bradshaw. R. June 10, 1789.
Page 369.

BRADSHAW, Arthur. Account current. Signed, Thomas Bradshaw.
Among items- paid his quota for clothing for a soldier.
Audited by D^d Barrow, Hardy Pope. D. April 14, 1790. R.
June 10, 1790. Page 370.

DREWRY, Samuel, Sr. Inventory. R. July 8, 1790. Page 371.

BRITT, Edward, Sr. Leg.- son Edward; son Johnson; daughter
Patience Williams; son-in-law Arthur Holleman; daughter Mary
Allen; wife Sarah; daughter Sarah Summerell; daughter Caty;
daughter Betsey Britt. Exs., sons Edward and Johnson Britt.
D. July 26, 1789. R. July 8, 1790. Wit. A. Holleman,
John Williamson, John Clayton. Page 372.

JOHNSON, Giles. Estate appraised by James Clark, Henry Jones
and Hardy Pope. R. July 8, 1790. Page 373.

WILLIAMS, Benjamin. Inventory. Signed, J^o. Vick and Mary
Williams, Exs. R. July 9, 1790. Page 375.

CALVERT, Christopher. Estate appraised by Joseph Scott, Jr.
William Edwards and Joshua Beal. D. July 11, 1789. R.
Sept. 9, 1790. Page 377.

COKER, Henry. Leg.- daughter-in-law Mary, now the widow of my
son Jonathan, with reversion to my grandson Jonathan; grandson
James, son of Jonathan; wife Sarah; grandson Wilson Coker;
daughter Holland; daughter Mary Coker. Exs., Jordan Judkins
and Joshua Bailey. D. Aug. 14, 1789. R. Oct. 14, 1790.
Wit. Thomas Phillips, Absolum Bailey, Thomas Hart. Page 379.

GRAY, Edwin. Leg.- son Joseph, land adjoining Charles Briggs
and John Cobb; son Thomas the land I bought of Anthony
Calthorpe; son Edwin; son Henry land adjoining Benjamin Ruffin;
daughter Mary; brother James Gray the land we purchased to-
gether of Wills Cowper in Nansemond Co.; wife. Exs., brother
James; sons Joseph, Thomas and Edwin and friend Daniel Simmons.
Provision for education of young son Henry. D. Sept. 3, 1788.
R. June 1790. Wit. Benjamin Ruffin, Benjamin Ruffin, Jr.,
Samuel Kello. Page 380.

LEWIS, Benjamin. Parish of St. Luke. Leg.- wife Mary son
Zebulon land adjoining Joshua Thorp; son Benjamin land bought
of Mial Harris; daughter Elizabeth Butts; daughter Fanny Butts;
daughter Nanny Turner with reversion to her children Elizabeth
and Edwin Turner; daughter Sally Rochell with reversion to her
children; daughter Becky; daughter Jenny Lewis. Exs., wife,
son Zebulon and son-in-law Benjamin Butts. D. Aug. 13, 1788.
R. Oct. 14, 1790. Wit. Etheldred Taylor, James McNiel, Henry
Westbrooke, John Simmons, Sr. Page 383.

MOORE, Thomas. Account current. Signed, Sarah and James Moore and Richard Blow. D. Jan. 1773. Audited by Joseph Vick, John T. Blow and George Gurley. R. Oct. 14, 1790. Page 385.

SLADE, Samuel. Leg.- wife Mary; son William; son Jethro; son Joshua; rest of my estate to my seven youngest children. Ex., Samuel Slade. D. Nov. 21, 1789. R. Oct. 14, 1790. Wit. Henry Lane, William Slade, Jethro Slade. Page 389.

WILLIAMSON, Robert. Estate appraised by Leighborn Lowe, (Love ?); Joseph Wright and Jacob Turner. R. Oct. 14, 1790. Page 391.

COUNCIL, James. Leg.- wife Elizabeth; daughter Elizabeth Turner, land adjoining Richard Worrel, Joshua Turner and John Turner; son Charles; daughter Anne Sandiford. Exs., son Charles Council and Hardy Pope. D. Oct. 8, 1785. R. Oct. 15, 1790. Wit. Lawrence Joyner, Rebeckah Joyner and Mary Bowing. Page 391.

COUNCIL, James. Inventory. D. Nov. 13, 1790. Page 392.

WELLENS, John. Leg.- son William; son Benjamin; wife Mary; daughter Rebecca Exum and her husband Robert Exum. Exs., sons William and Benjamin Wellens. D. July 16, 1784. R. Dec. 10, 1790. Wit. Thomas Lain, John Wellens, Lucretia Wellens. Page 393.

STEPHENSON, Thomas, Sr. Estate appraised by Arthur Boykin, John Clayton, Sr. and Arthur Doles. Signed, Thomas Stephenson. D. Dec. 10, 1790. Page 394.

READ, John. Leg.- daughter Patience Swet; son Cordall; wife Sarah; children, - Tabitha Byrd, Priscilla Byrd; Mason Read; Sally Read. Exs., friend Willie Francis and James Swet. D. Aug. 23, 1790. R. Dec. 10, 1790. Wit. Cordall Francis, Hardy Hunt. Page 395.

GRIFFIN, Benjamin. Account current. Signed, Micajah Griffin, Ex. Audited by D. C. Barrow, Hardy Pope, Edmund Tyler, Lem. Jones, S. Kello. Page 396.

HART, Drewry. Leg.- brother John Hart; to John Webb son of Nathaniel Land; to Elizabeth Daughtrey Carr, daughter of Lawrence Carr. Exs., brother John Hart and Nathaniel Land. D. Oct. 4, 1790. R. Jan. 10, 1791. Wit. Nanney Ireland, James Foster. Page 397.

EDWARDS, John. Inventory. Signed, Micajah and Newit Edwards. R. Jan. 10, 1791. Page 398.

TAYLOR, James. Account current. Audited by John Wright, James McNeil and Mark Nicholson. R. Jan. 10, 1791. Page 401.

WELLENS, John. Inventory. Signed, William and Benjamin Wellens. R. Feb. 10, 1791. Page 402.

WILLIAMSON, Celah. Inventory. Signed, John Crumpler, Adm. D. Dec. 16, 1790. R. Feb. 10, 1791. Page 402.

TURNER, Thomas. Estate appraised by Ledbetter Lowe. Levi Lane and Joseph Wright. Signed, Ann Turner Extx. R. Feb. 10, 1791. Page 403.

UNDERWOOD, John. Account current. Signed, Thomas Edmunds and Thomas Vaughan, Exs. Among items, paid Mathew Underwood his part of estate; paid the two children their part of their grandfather's estate; paid John Underwood his part of the estate, paid his eight children their part of their grandfather's estate; paid Sally Williams her part of the estate, paid her five children their part of their grandfather's estate; paid Thomas Pope his part of estate; paid Thomas Pope, Sally Pope's part of her grandfather's estate; paid Henson Pope his part of his grandfather's estate; paid William Pope, guardian of John Pope. Audited by Arthur Foster and John T. Blow. R. Feb. 10, 1791. Page 404.

JOHNSON, Giles. Account current. Signed, David Barrow and John Johnson, Exs. Paid the widow her proportion; paid Benjamin Johnson, ditto; Sarah Johnson, same; reserved money for schooling the orphan Penelope Johnson. Audited by Edmund Tyler, David Barrow and Arthur Foster. R. Feb. 10, 1791. Page 405.

BLOW, Richard. Estate appraised by Arthur Foster, Thomas Edmunds and Samuel Edmunds. D. March 15, 1786. R. Feb. 10, 1791. Page 406.

PERSON, Philip. Estate appraised by Richard Harrison, Richard Clifton and Benjamin Harrison. R. Feb. 10, 1791. Page 409.

EVANS, Hannah. Of St. Luke's Parish. Leg.- grandson William Evans; granddaughter Hannah Thompson Evans; grandson Benjamin Moseley Evans; daughter Mary Pope; daughter Martha Pope. Ex., John T. Blow. D. June 27, 1785. R. Feb. 10, 1791. Wit. George Blow, Henry Briggs. Page 410.

BRADSHAW, Martha. Leg.- daughter Penelipa Griffin; daughter Rody; to Joseph Bradshaw. Ex., Edward Griffin. D. Oct. 8, 1786. R. Feb. 11, 1791. Wit. Arthur Turner, Joshua Whitney, Chasey Bradshaw. Page 411.

HOWELL, Hartwell. Account current. Signed, Elizabeth Howell, Admtx. Audited by Thomas Vaughan and Thomas Edmunds. R. Feb. 11, 1791. Page 412.

WILLIAMS, Nicholas. Leg.- son Cowper; son John; daughter Lucy Joyner's negro not to be liable for debts of Lewis Joyner or any man she might hereafter marry; daughter Mary Parker; daughter Martha Buxton; daughter Ann Pitt, profits of my land in N. C., with reversion to her eldest son; daughter Elizabeth Peirce. Exs., sons Cowper and John Williams. D. March 4, 1791. R. April 14, 1791. Wit. J. Vick, John Davis, William Williams. Page 413.

IVEY, Henry. Leg.- wife Winney; son Adam when twenty one land adjoining Joshua Thorpe; son Peterson; son Wyke; daughter Charlotte Knight; daughter Elizabeth Newsum; daughter Sally; daughter Rhode Ivey. Exs., sons Peterson and Adam Ivey and John Williamson. D. Jan. 26, 1791. R. April 14, 1791. Wit. Howell Harris, Joseph T. Thorpe, John Williamson. Page 416.

LUNDY, John. Estate appraised by Fran^s Branch, Richard Gilliam and James Lundy. R. April 15, 1791. Page 418.

HART, Drewry. Estate appraised by Samuel Maget, Andrew Cheatham and John Gilliam. R. April 15, 1791. Page 419.

MANN, Sarah. Leg.- Ephraim Bryant; brother Jonas ----. Ex., brother James Bryant. D. March 8, 1791. R. April 15, 1791. Wit. Thomas Channell, Polly Pope, <u>Winee</u> Pope. Page 420.

WILLIAMS, Isaac. Estate appraised by Jo. Vick, Demcy Cotton and Lewis Joyner. D. Dec. 22, 1788. R. April 15, 1791. Page 421.

THORPE, Captain Timothy. Account current with Timothy Thorpe, Jr. decd. Paid William Andrews in right of his wife Maney; paid John Simmons in right of his wife Lucy; paid Dr. Annanias Randal in right of his wife Temperance; paid Martha Ridley; paid Jordan Richardson in right of his wife Silvia. Signed, Jordan Richardson. Audited by A. <u>Madele</u> and John Goodwyn. R. April 15, 1791. Page 423.

POPE, Hardy. Leg.- wife Mary, items bought of Joseph Scott; Molly Pope; widow of my son Henry Pope; son Hardy, when twenty one; granddaughter Nancy Pope; friend David Barrow; trustees of will, Daniel Simmons, Shadrack Lewis, John Johnson and James Clark. Exs., wife and David Barrow. D. Nov. 30, 1789. Wit. Alex Sanders, Joseph Harris, James Clark. Codicil: If son Hardy or granddaughter Nancy Pope die without issue, reversion to my near kinsman, John son of Joseph Pope and David Barrow to be used toward the support of the Gospel of Christ. D. Nov. 30, 1789. R. April 15, 1791. Wit. Joseph Harris, James Clark. Page 425.

JONES, Martha. Account current with Jordin Richardson, Adm. of the estate of Timothy Thorpe, Ex. of said Martha. D. 1781. Audited by Alex Madele (or Madell), John Goodwyn. R. May 15, 1792. Page 426.

TAYLOR, Charlotte. Leg.- my mother Temperance all my portion of my father's estate. Extx., mother Temperance Taylor. D. Nov. 30, 1790. R. April 15, 1791. Wit. Robert Taylor, John Taylor. Page 427.

HARRIS, Henry. Of the Parish of St. Luke. Leg.- daughter Nancy with reversion to the children of my four brothers, Benjamin, Abraham, Meshaland and Hardy Harris. Exs., friends Lawrence and Henry Smith. D. Feb. 6, 1791. R. June 9, 1791. Wit. William Drewry, Elizabeth Harris, Cealia Council. Page 428.

PARKER, Drewry. Estate appraised by William Chambless, William Myrick and Joel Newsum. D. March 3, 1789. R. June 9, 1791. Account current. Signed, Randolph Newsum, Ex. Audited by Edward Fisher and John Taylor, Jr. R. June 9, 1791. Page 430.

TURNER, Pass. Leg.- wife Ann; all my children, Polly, Nathan, Rebekah, John, James and Josiah. Exs., friends David Barrow and John Johnston. D. March 23, 1791. R. June 9, 1791. Wit. Samuel Johnson, Samuel Corbett, John Luter, Pettaway Johnson. Page 431.

BARHAM, Charles. Leg.- son Robert; granddaughter Milley Barham; daughter Mary Harris; daughter Lucy Deloach; Drewry Parker with reversion to all the children he had by my daughter Elizabeth; grandson Joel Newsum; grandson Barham Newsum; son James Barham. Exs., son James and grandson Joel Barham. D. Sept. 17, 1783. R. June 9, 1791. Wit. James Battle, Moses Foster, Elizabeth Holding, John Simmons, Sr. Edward Fisher qualified as Ex. James Barham being dead and the other refusing. Page 432.

BARHAM, James. Of the Parish of St. Luke. Leg.- son Joel; daughter Martha Harris; daughter Sarah Fisher; daughter Rebecca Holleman; son James; daughter Mary; daughter Susanna Macom; son Judkins; son Samuel; son Timothy Thorpe Barham; son John; granddaughter Phebey Barham, daughter of Judkins. Exs., sons Joel, James and Samuel Barham and sons-in-law Edward Fisher and William Holleman. D. Feb. 26, 1791. R. June 9, 1792. Wit. John Simmons, Jr., William Butts, Edward Fisher qualified as Ex. Page 434.

FORT, John. Estate appraised by John Taylor and Mark Nicholson. R. June 9, 1791. Page 435.

TAYLOR, Etheldred. Leg.- wife Elizabeth; daughter Elizabeth when eighteen. Exs., brother John Taylor and my relative Mr. Charles Taylor. D. Feb. 20, 1791. Wit. Edward Fisher, William Ellis, Henry Taylor. Codicil; to Ann Milton, alias Ann Bowser, with reversion of bequest to Patsey Milton, so called daughter of Ann Milton, Jr. Wit. Thomas Ridley, William Wright, William Newsum. R. July 14, 1791. Exs., refused to qualify and executorship was granted John Taylor, Jr. Page 437.

WRIGHT, David. Estate appraised by Joseph Scott, Jr., Richard Beal and Joshua Beal. D. Feb. 19, 1791. R. July 14, 1791. Page 439.

PORCH, James. Estate appraised by Jesse Cooper, William Harris and Lewis Harris. D. Feb. 6, 1788. R. July 14, 1791. Page 441.

POPE, Henry. Account current. Signed, Mary Pope, Admtx. Audited by John Thomas Blow and William Crichlow. R. July 14, 1791. Page 442.

FOSTER, William. Leg.- wife Edith; son John; son William; daughter Nancey; daughter Rebecca; unborn child. Exs., Robert Goodwyn, Micajah Ellis and John Simmons, Sr. D. Jan. 20, 1791. R. July 15, 1791. Wit. John Simmons, Jr., Miles Cary, Jesse Arrington, Thomas Hollcome, Micajah Ellis. Robert Goodwyn qualified. Page 443.

HARRIS, Hardy. Estate appraised by John Blunt, James Turner and Edmund Turner. D. Dec. 21, 1790. R. Sept. 8, 1791. Page 444.

FORGUSON, Robert. Estate appraised by James Maget, Micajah Edwards and Saml. Maget. D. Sept. 1790. R. Sept. 8, 1791. Page 446.

THORP, Moses. Estate appraised by J. Harris and George Ivey. R. Sept. 8, 1791. Page 447.

PORCH, James. Account current. Signed, Moses McKenny. Audited by Jesse Cooper and Arthur Applewhite. R. Oct. 13, 1791. Page 447.

IVEY, John. Estate appraised by Moses Thorp, Rich'd Gilliam and James Lundy. D. Jan. 8, 1790. R. Oct. 13, 1791. Page 450.

CALTHORP, John. Leg.- son John; son James; son Henry; son Nowell. D. April 14, 1783. R. Oct. 13, 1791. Wit. Patience Turner, Thomas Turner, Jordan Bass. Page 451.

DAVIS, Thomas. Leg.- uncle Henry Davis, Sr., two negro girls in Northampton County, N. J., if he will bring them to Virginia and manumit them at age of twenty one; brothers Etheldred and James Davis. Ex. uncle Henry Davis. Wit. Joel Davis, Philip Davis. D. R. Oct. 13, 1791. Page 452.

SPEED, Robert. Estate appraised by James Edwards, Henry Briggs and Richard Johnson. D. Dec. 14, 1790. R. Oct. 13, 1791. Page 453.

TURNER, Henry. Parish of St. Luke. Leg.- son Jacob; land adjoining Capt. Nicholas Maget and Arthur Whitehead; daughter Mary Parker; granddaughter Patience Turner; son Jacob and his children now living, Henry, Etheldred, Rebecca, Patience, Milly, Susannah and William Turner. Ex., son Jacob Turner. D. Dec. 15, 1789. Proved Sept. 9, 1790. R. Oct. 13, 1791. Wit. John Whitehead, James Maget, Elizabeth Turner. Page 454.

BENNETT, John. Leg.- daughter Mary Rose; daughter Martha; daughter Holland Screws; son William; son Samuel; son Moses; son Lemuel and son Elias; daughter Rebeccah. D. March 21, 1788. Oct. 13, 1791. Wit. Richard Doyel, Henry Bools; Lem'l. Jones. Exs., son William and friend Edmund Johnson. Page 455.

POPE, Hardy. Estate appraised by Henry Jones, Mathew Charles and John Johnson. Signed, Mary Pope Extx. D. Sept. 20, 1791. R. Oct. 13, 1791. Page 456.

WILLIAMS, Epaphroditus. Leg.- son Ephraim land adjoining part of Robert Bryant's patent, adjoining Jacob Williams, Joel Edwards, Robert Fargason and Edmond Barret, Sr.; son Jacob; daughter Sarah Bryant; daughter Elizabeth Worrell. Exs., sons Ephraim and Jacob Williams. D. April 8, 1791. R. Dec. 8, 1791. Wit. Lewis Bryant, Joel Edwards. Page 459.

MARTIN, James. Leg.- wife Amey; son Kinchen; daughter Lucy Gurley. Exs., wife and son-in-law George Gurley. D. Oct. 18, 1791. R. Dec. 8, 1791. Wit. George Gurley, Thomas Newsum, Jr., John Newsum. Page 460.

BRADSHAW, Benjamin. Estate appraised by Arthur Bowing, Richard Doyel and John Worrell. Signed, Jacob Bradshaw and Benjamin Bradshaw. R. Feb. 9, 1792. Page 461.

THORPE, Joshua. Leg.- nephew Lewis, son of John Thorpe; sister Elizabeth Pritchard; neice Lucy, sister of aforesaid Lewis Thorpe. Ex., nephew Lewis Thorpe. D. Jan. 22, 1792. R. Feb. 9, 1792. Wit. Charles Maclemore, Adam Ivey, L. Mason, Fred'k Horn. Page 462.

SIMMONS, John. Estate appraised by Jos. Vick, Benj. Korby and Rice B. Pierce. R. Feb. 9, 1792. Page 463.

RICKS, Ann. Estate appraised by John Davis, Jos. Vick, and Leml. Hart. D. Nov. 19, 1791. R. Feb. 9, 1792. Page 464.

SIMMONS, John. Account current. Signed, Daniel Simmons. Audited by Robert Taylor and Daniel Butts. D. Nov. 9, 1792. R. Feb. 9, 1792. Page 467.

BRITT, John. Leg.- son William; daughter Tamer; four youngest sons Benjamin, Joseph, Beasent and Arianton; wife Priscilla; my seven children - Sarah Johnson, Mary and above named sons.

Exs., Benjamin Britt and John Crumpler. D. Feb. 8, 1786.
P. Jan. 8, 1791. R. Feb. 9, 1792. Wit. John Pursell,
Edmund Crumpler, William Crumpler, Brittain Britt qualified,
Exs., refusing. Page 468.

DRAPER, Thomas. Leg.- daughter Mourning; son Jesse; son
Jeremiah, land bought of John Worrel; son Ephraim; son William;
son Thomas; daughter Sarah Jordan. D. 19th of 4 mo. 1788.
Ex., son Jesse Draper. Wit. Thomas Ricks, Robert Ricks and
Richard Ricks. Codicil. - son Ephraim Draper also to be an
Ex. D. 11th of 2 mo. Wit. Lemuel Jones. R. Feb. 9,
1792. Page 470.

TURNER, Henry. Of the Parish of St. Luke. Leg.- son John;
daughter Elizabeth Bittle Turner when twenty one or married;
son Benjamin; unborn child; my store in Northampton N. C.,
known as William and Henry Turner and Company, to be con-
tinued if he choses, with my son John living with him and my
son to inherit my part; son Benjamin my lot in Princetown.
Exs., friend William Turner and Will Turner the son of
Benjamin to manage the store in this place. D. Dec. 13,
1791. R. March 8, 1792. Wit. Nicholas Warren, Nathaniel
Edwards, William Bittle. Page 472.

DARDEN, Holland. Leg.- wife Pheribe; son Jacob; son Jonathan;
son James; son John; wife to have all of the estate that fell
to her from her first husband; son John, land adjoining
Robert Fisher; son Holland; daughter Anne; daughter Edith;
son Jonah; daughter Julia; my mother to have my part of my
father's estate. Exs., sons Jacob, Jonathan and James Darden
and friend John McCabe. D. Feb. 22, 1792. R. March 8,
1792. W. James Carr, John Birdsong, Robert H. Disher. Son
Jonathan land adjoining Joshua Gardner. Page 474.

THOMAS, Henry. Estate appraised by Benjamin Blunt, Jr., Henry
Harrison and Cordey Clifton. D. April 17, 1789. R. March
13, 1792. Page 477.

GRAY, Anna. Estate appraised by Thomas Turner, John Mundell
and Benjamin Blunt, Jr. D. April 20, 1789. R. March 13,
1792. Page 478.

HILL, Reubin. Estate appraised by Samuel Maget, Newit Edwards
and Etheldred Everett. D. 1789. R. May 10, 1792. Page
479.

HOLT, Thomas. Account current. Signed, Nathan Holt. Audited
by John Judkins and Robert Andrews. R. May 10, 1792.
Page 480.

VICK, William. Account current. Signed, Lewis and Pilgrim
Vick, Exs. Audited by John T. Blow and Thomas Edmunds. D.
1784. R. May 10, 1792. Page 481.

DAVIS, Thomas. Inventory. Signed, Henry Davis, Ex. D. May
28, 1792. R. June 14, 1792. Page 482.

DRAPER, Thomas. Signed, Ephraim Draper, Ex. Appraised by
Micajah Griffin, Charles Council and William Wills. D.
June 14, 1792. Page 483.

ELLIS, Hezekiah. Estate appraised by Randolph Newsum, R.
Clements and Joel Newsum. D. Jan. 20, 1791. R. June 14,
1792. Page 484.

HART, John. Of the Parish of Nottoway. Leg.- wife Jane; son
Samuel; daughter Rebecca; son John; son Charles; son Lemuel;
son Henry Hart. Exs., sons Henry and Samuel Hart. D.
March 12, 1792. R. June 14, 1792. Wit. Jesse Womble,
Thomas Washington, Jesse Washington. Page 485.

BARNES, Peninah. Estate appraised by Lemuel Hart, George
Washington and David Washington. Signed, Jacob Barnes, Adm.
D. March 3, 1791. R. June 14, 1792. Page 486.

BENNETT, William. Estate appraised by John T. Blow, William
Cricklow, Benjamin Edwards. R. June 14, 1792. Page 487.

TYLER, Jeremiah. Estate appraised by John T. Blow, Benjamin
Edwards and Amos Stephenson. D. Dec. 16, 1789. R. June
14, 1792. Page 489.

DAVIS, Thomas. Account current. Signed, Henry Davis. Audited
by Thomas Edmunds and John Taylor. R. June 14, 1792. Page
491.

TAYLOR, Etheldred. Estate appraised. (not signed). D.
Aug. 10, 1791. R. June 14, 1792. Page 492.

VICK, Mathew, Sr. Estate appraised by John Johnson, William
Cricklow and James Butts. Signed, Joseph Vick. D. Dec. 6,
1788. R. June 15, 1792. Page 494.

HINES, Howell. Estate appraised by Abraham Mitchell, William
Edwards and Mathew Wills. Signed, Josiah Vick, Ex. R.
June 15, 1792. Page 496.

HUTCHINGS, Daniel. Of Norfolk Borough. Leg.- wife Elizabeth;
provision for unborn child, with reversion to brother Robert
Moseley, alias Hancock. Exs., wife and brother-in-law
Thomas Wilson. D. May 27, 1756. Wit. Joseph Holt, Ann
Miller. Codicil: The house bought of Capt. Pulloyal to be
disposed of and divided as in above will. March -, 1766.
Wit. William Godfrey, John Livingston. Proved by Alenader
Guthrie, who testified that the said Hutchings was a Captain
of a Packet from Norfolk to Burwell's Ferry. William James
qualified as Elizabeth Hutchings was deceased. R. July 12,
1792. Page 498.

HELLWIG, John. Leg.- wife Mary; children George and Polly, land
purchased of Charles Hancock Birdsong; now in possession of
Miriam Birdsong; reversion to wife at death of said Miriam
Birdsong; Neice Lucy Lane. D. May 29, 1791. R. July 12,
1792. Exs., friends Benjamin Ruffin, Thomas Gray, Joseph
Ruffin. Wit. John Cobb, Sarah Ruffin, Benjamin Ruffin, Jr.
Page 500.

THORPE, Joshua. Estate appraised by Thomas Peete, Arthur
Applewhite and John Reese. R. July 12, 1792. Page 501.

PHILLIPS, Moses. Leg.- Mary Cocke, the wife of William Cocke
of Surry County; to friend Samuel Kello. Ex., Samuel Kello.
D. Sept. 30, 1789. Wit. Benjamin Drew, Francis Young, Jr.
Codicil. Mary Cocke is deceased and her child, above bequest
to Samuel Kello. D. Nov. 1, 1791. Wit. John Hausmann,
Edward Griffin. R. July 13, 1792. Page 503.

DARDEN, Holland. Estate appraised by Joshua Gardner, John Lee,
Henry Gardner. R. July 13, 1792. Page 504.

VICK, Samuel. Account current. Signed, George Gurley. Audited, George Gurley, Jr. and Nathan Barnes. R. Aug. 9, 1792. Page 509.

TURNER, William. Audited by John Blunt and John Wilkinson. R. Aug. 9, 1792. Page 507.

TURNER, Pass. June 1791. Estate appraised by Simon Johnson, John Luter and Henry Jones. R. June 13, 1792. Page 509.

HARRIS, Nathan. Inventory. Signed, Mary Harris. R. Sept. 13, 1792. Page 509.

BLAKE, Thomas. Account current. Signed, John and Benjamin Blake. D. March 25, 1789. Audited by John Barrow and Jesse Cooper. R. Sept. 13, 1792. Page 510.

MURFEE, Richard, Sr. D. Dec. 15, 1789. Appraised by David Edwards, William Edwards and James Edwards. R. Sept. 13, 1792. Account estate. Signed, William Murfee, Ex. Matt Murfee named as one of the family. Audited by Henry Briggs and James Edwards. R. Sept. 13, 1792. Page 514.

WILLIAMS, Nicholas. 1791. Inventory. Signed, John Williams. R. Sept. 13, 1792. Page 516.

ARRINGTON, Jesse. Estate appraised by John Simmons, Micah Ellis and Lewis Knight. D. July 19, 1792. R. Sept. 13, 1792. Page 517.

GRIZZARD, (Grizard) William. Account current dated July 15, 1779. Signed, Moses Johnson. Bills paid for Huling Grizard, Tabitha Grizard and Jeremiah Grizard. Audited by John Wilkinson and Cordall Bynum. R. Oct. 11, 1792. Page 518.

CRENSHAW, John. Estate appraised by Samuel Maget, James Maget, Howell Whittington. R. Oct. 11, 1792. Page 518.

COKER, Nathaniel. Sept. 1781. Account estate. Signed, Richard Kello. Paid for schooling for Salley Coker; paid Wison Coker one seventh part of the slaves. Audited by Beverley Boothe, Edmund Tyler. R. Oct. 11, 1792. Page 519.

DAY, Edmund. Account current. Signed, William Whitehead, Ex. D. Jan. 22, 1783. Audited by Nicholas Maget and Thomas Ridley. R. Oct. 11, 1792. Page 522.

MURRAY, Mary. Leg.- daughter Elizabeth Smith, land bought of Benjamin Barham; bequest to daughters (not named) son William Alexander Smith; residue of estate to be divided between Mary Harwood and Sarah Maget. Exs., John Harwood, William Maget and Elizabeth Smith. D. Jan. 17, 1791. R. Oct. 11, 1797. Wit. Edward Fisher, Benjamin Barham, William Holliman. Page 529.

WILLIAMSON, Burwell. Leg.- wife Lucy; daughter Wilmouth Jordan; daughter Nancy Williamson. Exs., wife, son-in-law Joseph Jordan, daughter Nancy and friend Samuel Kello. D. May 22, 1792. R. Nov. 8, 1792. Wit. Micajah Holleman, John Nelms, George Summerell. Page 530.

COBB, John. Parish of Nottoway. Leg.- son Exum; son Michael; son Jeremiah; son Benjamin; son Thomas and son George Blow Cobb; daughter Rebecca Mecome, if she does not live with Samuel Mecome; grandson Mathew Mecome when twenty one; granddaughter Polly Mecome; Captain Charles Briggs to be paid 90 ₺ to maintain my four youngest sons, Jeremiah, Benjamin, Thomas and George until they are fifteen; daughter Elizabeth Wootten; granddaughter Jane Exum Wootten at twenty one. Exs., William Hines (Sheriff), son Michael Cobb and Thomas Gray. D. Oct. 1, 1792. R. Nov. 8, 1792. Wit. Lucy Lane, Richard Pond, Sr., Drewry Pond. Page 531.

BRADSHAW, Benjamin. Leg.- son Jacob, the plantation bought of Joseph Jones; son Benjamin, tract bought of Arthur Williams, adjoining Joseph Bradshaw and Ephraim Spivey; son Philip, land bought of Moses Joyner, adjoining Sampson Pitman, Charles Cosby and Charles Powers; son William; son Richard; daughter Gelina; daughter Ridley; daughter Lucy Stephens; wife Mary Bradshaw. Exs., sons Jacob and Benjamin Bradshaw. D. March 20, 1790. R. Feb. 10, 1791. Wit. Francis Young, Jr., William Bradshaw, Philip Bradshaw. Page 536.

WESTBROOK, John. D. Dec. 21, 1785. Estate appraised by James Lundy and William Claud. R. Nov. 9, 1792. Page 538.

IVEY, Henry. D. May 27, 1791. Appraised by John Williamson and John Reese, Sr. R. Page 540.

LAWRENCE, Thomas. Leg.- daughter Rhoda; daughter Susannah; son William; wife Margaret; children of my deceased daughter Elizabeth. Exs., wife and son William Lawrence. D. Feb. 12, 1790. R. Feb. 14, 1793. Wit. Josiah Murfee, Francis Murfee, William Edwards. Page 541.

JONES, James. Leg.- son James; wife Lucy; son Jordan; son Anselm; daughter Lucy West; daughter Molly Kitchen and Rebecca Sebrell. Exs., sons Anselm, James and Jordan Jones. D. Aug. 15, 1787. R. March 13, 1793. Wit. Charles Briggs, Jr., Allen Rogers. Page 543.

TAYLOR, Colonel Henry. Account current. Signed, Etheldred Taylor. Paid John Taylor's legacy; paid board for Charlotte and Henry Taylor; paid for linens for my mother; paid for Elizabeth Taylor's wedding clothes; paid James Taylor for William Taylor's estate; paid Col. Gray for Lucy Taylor's estate; paid my mother for H. Taylor and the three girls in 1782; paid Mary, Martha and Charlotte Taylor; paid William Taylor's legatees. Etheldred Taylor, deceased. Audited by John Wright, Thomas Ridley, Thomas Peete. R. Feb. 14, 1793. Page 543.

BARHAM, James. Inventory. R. Jan. 10, 1793. Page 547.

BARHAM, Charles. Appraisal. (not signed). R. Jan. 10, 1793. Page 549.

HAISTY, Moses. Inventory. D. Feb. 6, 1792. R. Jan. 10, 1793. Page 550.

COCKE, Hartwell. Leg.- wife Sarah; William Urquhart my case of bottles presented me by Redmond Hackett, Esq.; John Clements; four sons of Edward Archer,- John, William, Richard and Samuel Archer; Thomas Fearn, John Fearn and Drewry Andrews. Exs., wife Sarah, brother Robert Cocke, Col. Richard Cocke, Sr., Col. Samuel Kello and friend William Urquhart. D. Oct. 28, 1792. R. Jan. 10, 1793. Wit. Thomas Fearn, Thomas Gray, Francis Clements, John Andrews, Solo. Holmes, John Fearn. Page 551.

JOYNER, Arthur. Leg.- son Robert; son Kemp; son Theophilus; daughter Mary Green Joyner. Exs., friends John Davis and Burwell Rawlings. D. Sept. 20, 1792. R. Jan. 11, 1793. Wit. Lewis Joyner, Thomas W. Clements, John Smith. Page 553.

COUNCIL, John. Of the Parish of Nottoway. Leg.- son Amos land adjoining John Worrell, Giles Johnson and William Mackey; son Jesse; daughter Lydda; daughter Tabitha; daughter Sarah; daughter Temperance; son John Council. Exs., sons Amos and Jesse Council. D. Jan. 2, 1785. R. April 11, 1793. Wit. David Barrow, Giles Johnson, Stephen Johnson. Page 554.

SPEED, Robert. Leg.- son Edwin; son George; son Robert; daughter Milly; wife Ann Speed. Exs., friends John Johnson and Josiah Vick. D. Sept. 14, 1790. R. Dec. 10, 1790. Wit. Jo. Vick, Hardy Doyel, Lucy Pledger. Page 556.

JOHNSON, Josiah. Of St. Luke's Parish. Leg.- wife Hannah, with reversion to all my children. D. R. June 13, 1793. Wit. Newit Claud, Nancy Johnson, Nancy Harrison. Page 558.

THORPE, Jeremiah. Of Parish of St. Luke. Leg.- wife Martha; son Timothy land in N. C.; son Hardy; son Willie; daughter Olive Thorpe; son Joshua; son Harry; daughter Sarah Check; grandchildren, the orphans of my deceased daughter Mary Spence; daughter Lucy Long; daughter Polly Long; granddaughters Martha and Polly Long. Ex., son Joshua Thorpe. D. Dec. 18, 1792. R. June 13, 1793. Wit. John Atkinson, Aron Smith, Lewis Harris, Lucy D. Duprea. Page 558.

GILLIAM, Robert. Leg.- son John; daughter-in-law Penelope Gilliam; grandson John, son of Joseph Gilliam when he is eighteen. Exs., son John and Jacob Turner. D. March 11, 1787. R. June 13, 1793. Wit. Jacob Barrett, Exum Everitt, Nathan Britt. Page 561.

COUNCIL, John. Estate appraised by Arthur Bowing, John Carstarphen, Jacob Bradshaw. Signed, Amos Council and Jesse Council, Exs. R. June 13, 1793. Page 562.

HELVEY, John. Estate appraised by William Mellone and William Spivy. R. May 11, 1793. Page 564.

JONES, Mathew. Parish of Nottoway. Leg.- son Albridgton land left me by my father; daughter Sarah; daughter Ann; daughter Elizabeth; sister Mary Jarrell. Ex. brother Albridgton, also to be guardian of my children. D. July 26, 1793. R. Wit. Lewis Joiner, George Camp, Joshua Joiner, Jr. Page 566.

LAWRENCE, Robert. Leg.- wife Priscilla, land formerly in Nansemond, but now in Southampton; son Josiah; son Jesse; son Jacob land adjoining Nicholas Maget; daughter Sarah Williams, negroes in possession of Isaac Williams, daughter Mary Foreman negroes in possession of John Foreman; son-in-law Benjamin Ellis; daughter Priscilla Allen, negroes in possession of Richard Allen; to Lawrence Ellis. Exs., sons Josiah and Jacob Lawrence. D. Dec. 29, 1791. R. Sept. 12, 1793. Wit. Samuel Maget, John Bishop, Nath'l Land, Lawrence Williams. Page 566.

JONES, William. Leg.- Nancy Simmons, daughter of Mason Simmons; Henry J. P. Westbrooke, son of Parson Westbrooke, deceased; Mason Simmons Westbrooke, daughter of aforesaid; Richard H. Simmons, son of William Simmons; mother with reversion to my brother Edwin Simmons and to his children; brother William

Simmons. Exs., brothers William and Edwin Simmons. D. July 22, 1793. R. Sept. 12, 1793. Wit. James Butts, Jo. Vick, Robert H. Fisher, Edwin Simmons. Page 568.

HART, Henry. Leg.- son Benjamin; daughter Elizabeth; daughter Ann; wife Lucy Hart. Exs., Joseph Hart, Sr., Benjamin Hart. D. Aug. 17, 1792. R. Sept. 12, 1793. Wit. Jesse Womble, Robert Hart, John Hart. Page 569.

HART, Samuel. Leg.- brother Henry; sister Rebecca my plantation, if she will pay Richard Andrews for the said land; brother John; brother Charles Hart. Exs., brother Henry Hart and Thomas Washington. D. Aug. 2, 1793. R. Sept. 12, 1793. Wit. Benjamin Bailey, William Atkinson, John Andrews. Page 569.

MOODY, Philip. Estate appraised by Lewis Joyner, Jr., Benjamin Williams and George Washington. Ex., John Andrews. D. March 26, 1783. R. Sept. 12, 1793. Account current, audited by William Urquhart and Arthur Boykin. Page 570.

COCKE, Hartwell. Estate appraised by Sol. Holmes, John Andrews, Timothy Atkinson. R. Oct. 10, 1793. Appraisal in Brunswick by Benjamin Johnson, William Thomas Pennington and William Johnson. Page 573.

CROCKER, Arthur. Estate appraised by William Bailey, Thomas Brock and Harmon Harris. D. Jan. 10, 1793. R. Oct. 10, 1793. Page 574.

DREW, Dolphin. Account current. Signed, S. Kello, Adm. Audited by Will Hines and Thomas Ridley. R. Oct. 10, 1793. Page 575.

WHITEHEAD, John. Leg.- wife Meriam, the plantation on which I live bought by my grandfather of William Powers, adjoining Arthur Whitehead, after death of my mother; sons (all under age) Maximillan, Lewis Augustus, Jack Anthony, Arher Meade, Adolphus and Lemuel Murder Whitehead; my land in Gates County, N. C.; which I bought of James Parke and Benjamin Harrell to be sold, also the land patented by my father in July 1774; daughter Sally, daughter Mitildy; daughter Lucindy; daughter Harriet. Exs., wife, Robert Jordan, Sr., Hansel Bailey of Surry Co., John Maget, Samuel Maget. D. July 8, 1791. R. Dec. 8, 1791. Wit. Jacob Lawrence, Samuel Maget. Page 576.

REESE, Olive. Leg.- son John; son Joseph; son Edwin; son Lewis; daughter Rebeccah; daughter Silvia Reese. Ex., Benjamin Blunt, Jr. D. May 15, 1793. R. Oct. 10, 1793. Wit. Benjamin Williamson, Edwin Bass, John Williamson. Page 578.

BARNES, Nathan. Leg.- wife Martha; son John; son Britain; son Cordall; daughter Jeansy; sister Mary Barnes. Exs., wife, son John Barnes and David Barrow. D. June 15, 1790. R. Oct. 10, 1793. Will proven by James Wilkinson, Benjamin Drew and William Vick, Jr. Page 578.

TAYLOR, Robert. Leg.- neice Patsy Woodlief, daughter of Thomas and Martha Woodlief; reversion to my five relations, William Browne and Ann Browne, descendants of William and Ann Browne decd.; Samuel Browne, Martha Browne and Mary Browne, children of Benjamin Edwards and Mary Mason Browne; sister Mary Mason Browne, the plantation on which William Gilbert is overseer; Aunt Temperance Taylor a mare I had of Mr. John Taylor. Exs., brother-in-law Benjamin Edwards Browne and cousin Etheldred

Taylor. D. Jan. 3, 1789. R. Nov. 14, 1793. Wit.
Etheldred Taylor, Thomas Blow, John Taylor. Page 579.

LAWRENCE, Thomas. Estate appraised by A. Mitchell, Simon
Murfee, James Edwards. R. Nov. 14, 1793. Paid legacies to
William and Susanna Lawrence. Page 580.

EXUM, Benjamin. Account current. Signed, John and Exum Cobb,
Exs. D. 1785. Paid John Elvin, who married the widow, paid
Ann Salter for her legacy from John Cobb's estate; paid John
Cobb a legacy. Audited by Benjamin Ruffin, Benjamin Kirby
and Thomas Butts. R. Nov. 14, 1793. Page 582.

BRITT, John. Estate appraised by Arthur Boykin, West Tynes and
John Pursel. R. Dec. 12, 1793. Page 583.

GILLIAM, Thomas. Leg.- wife Cala; daughter Lucy Johnson; son
Thomas; daughter Mary Tucker; Jemimah Sorsberry to live on my
plantation during her single life, or as long as my wife lives
or her brother Henry. D. Sept. 27, 1793. Proved by Robert
Tucker, John Rochell, William Butts and Thomas Gilliam. Wit.
John Simmons, Sr., Levy Rochell, Peter Simmons. Cala
Gilliam's refusal to accept the will, witnessed by Mary
Sorsberry, Henry Sorsberry. Thomas Gilliam, Jr., qualified.
R. Dec. 12, 1793. Page 584.

GARDNER, Joshua. Leg.- wife Ann; my surviving children,- Henry,
John, James, Jesse, Ann, Betsey, Rhoda, Polly and Peggy; son
Henry the tract bought of Moses Darden; son Jesse land bought
of Mathew Jones, adjoining John McCabe; daughter Ann Jones;
daughter Betsey Carr; daughter Polly Darden Gardner. Exs.,
wife and son Henry Gardner. D. Feb. 4, 1793. R. Dec. 12,
1793. Wit. Jacob Darden, Sr., Jacob Darden, Jr., Jonathan
Darden. Page 586.

PRETLOW, Mary. Leg.- Ann Ricks, wife of Robert Ricks; Rebecca
Hunnicutt, widow of James Hunnicutt; Sarah Bailey, wife of
Lemuel Bailey; Barnaby Nixon of Prince George; Peter Peebles,
Jr.; James Peebles; remainder of estate to Thomas, Robert,
Richard, Joseph, Mary and Milicent Ann Ricks, the children of
my brother Robert Ricks; Elizabeth and Sarah Bailey, daughters
of my sister Elizabeth Scott, deceased. Ex., nephew Robert
Ricks. D. July 28, 1792. R. Dec. 12, 1793. Wit. Thomas
Pretlow, Ann Pretlow, Thomas Taylor. Page 587.

GARDNER, James. Leg.- son James, land adjoining James James
Daughtrey, Col. Benjamin Baker, Mathew Gardner and John
Daughtrey; to three of my grandchildren, sons of my son John
Gardner, deceased, viz.- Jesse, David and John the land bought
of Thomas Sharp, adjoining Nicholas Cobb; son Jesse, land ad-
joining Robert Darden Sharpe, the land granted Robert Bryant;
son Joseph; daughter Juda, wife of Thomas Holland; daughter
Mary, wife of James Vaughan; daughter Sarah, wife of William
Fowler; daughter Margaret, wife of Josiah Vick; daughter
Martha, wife of Abenezer Buxton, reversion of bequest to her
son Joseph Buxton; daughter Penelope; daughter Honour; wife
Sarah, land purchased of John Lawrence. Exs., wife Sarah,
brother Joshua and son Jesse Gardner. Joshua Gardner, John
Carr and Henry Gardner to divide my estate. D. Aug. 23,
1784. R. Dec. 12, 1793. Wit. Joshua Gardner, Mathew
Gardner, Henry Gardner, John Carr. Page 598.

CALTHORPE, James. Leg.- Aggy Cursey; Mary Black; Joshua Cursey,
son of Aggy Cursey; provision for unborn child of Aggy Cursey.
Ex., Joshua Claud. D. Jan. 31, 1793. R. Dec. 12, 1793.

Wit. John Claud, Turner Person, Sterling Francis. Page 600.

BARNES, Peninah. Account estate. Signed, Jacob Barnes, Adm. William Barnes, guardian. Audited by Jo. Vick and Lem. Hart. R. Dec. 13, 1793. Page 601.

MOUNTFORD, Thomas. Account estate. Signed, Wade Mountford, Adm. Audited by Daniel Simmons and Henry Jones. R. Jan. 9, 1794. Page 601.

SIMMONS, Benjamin. Account estate. Signed, John Simmons, Adm. Audited by Zebulon Lewis, John Wright and Mark Nicholson. R. Jan. 9, 1794. Page 602.

BRANTLEY, James. Estate appraised by James Wilkinson, Howell Edmunds, Jr. and Nath'l. Edwards. R. Jan. 9, 1794. Page 604.

THOMAS, Henry. Account estate. Signed, Mary Thomas, Admtx. D. 1789. Audited by Robert Mabry, Thomas Turner, John Williamson and James Lundy. R. Feb. 13, 1794. Page 604.

BAILEY, Mary. Account current. Signed, Jordan Judkins, Adm. D. 1787. Paid Celia Barlow; paid the children of Ann Coker, deceased a legacy left them by Barnaby Bailey; paid Elizabeth Hay her legacy; paid J. Harrison his one third part of the sale of the land. Audited by Sam. Kello and John Haussman. R. Feb. 13, 1794. Page 605.

LAWRENCE, Robert. Inventory. Signed, Jacob Lawrence. R. Feb. 13, 1794. Page 606.

REESE, Olive. Estate appraised by James Lundy, George Ivey and John Thorpe. D. Dec. 17, 1793. R. Feb. 13, 1794. Page 606.

GARDNER, James, Sr. Estate appraised by Jacob Darden, Sr., Mathew Gardner and William Edwards. Signed, Jesse Gardner. D. Dec. 21, 1793. R. Feb. 13, 1794. Page 607.

CLAUD, John. Leg.- wife Sally to have the north side of the land adjoining Hailey Foster, Dunn's Branch and Walden Kersey; daughter Polly Claud Francis; daughter Lucy; daughter Fanny Claud Francis. Exs., John Barrow and Henry Barrow. D. April 3, 1793. R. Feb. 13, 1794. Wit. Aaron Smith, Benjamin Miller, Philip Claud, Joshua Westbrooke. Page 608.

KELLO, Richard. Account current. D. 1789. Signed, S. Kello, Ex. Among items, - account as guardian of Presly Barrett and of John Mecom. Paid John Kerby his proportional part of the estate of John Mecom, deceased. Account as administrator of Nathaniel Coker. Audited by William Urquhart and M. Holleman. R. Feb. 13, 1794. Page 610.

RIDLEY, Jack Edwards. Leg.- wife Jane and my brother by law William Wright. Exs., wife and William Wright. D. Feb. 26, 1793. R. Feb. 13, 1794. Wit. Matt Figures, Mary Figures, L. Mason, Fil. Washington. Page 611.

POPE, Jesse. Leg.- son Nathaniel and adjoining Nathan Barnes, Amos Joyner and Evans Pope; daughter Jinny; daughter Mary; son David; daughter Hannah Beal; remainder of estate to be divided between John, Zedekiah, Jesse, Hannah, Jinny and Mary Pope. Exs., son Nathaniel Pope and Asa Beal. D. Oct. 22, 1791. R.

Feb. 13, 1794. Wit. Nathan Barnes, Amos Joyner, Evans Pope. Page 612.

THORPE, John, Jr.; Account current. Signed, Martha Thorpe and Hardy Harris. Paid Hardy Harris his wife's proportional part of the estate of John Thorpe, Sr. D. Aug. 6, 1793. R. Feb. 13, 1794. Audited by Robert Mabry, John Williamson and James Lundy. Page 612.

THORPE, John, Sr. Account current. Signed, Martha Thorpe and Hardy Harris, Exs. of John Thorpe, Jr., decd., who was the Ex. of John Thorpe, Sr. The following were paid equal sums of their father's estate:- Mildred Spence; Aaron Thorpe; Moses Thorpe; Jeremiah Thorpe; Olive Reese; Mary Reese; Sarah Harris; Drucilla Thompson; John Thorpe, Jr. Audited by Robert Mabry, John Williamson and James Lundy. R. Feb. 13, 1794. Page 614.

KINDRED, Benjamin. Leg.- mother Ann Kindred; brother John; brother Elisha; sister Mary Edwards. Ex., friend George Blunt. D. Feb. 9, 1793. R. Feb. 13, 1794. Wit. Drew Powell, Hosea Newton, William Newton. Page 614.

COOPER, Jesse. Estate appraised by A. M. Neil, Henry Adams and William Crichlow. D. Feb. 4, 1794. Account current. Signed, Robert Speed and John Johnson, Exs. D. 1790. Audited by Jo. Vick and Joseph Scott. R. Feb. 14, 1794. Page 616.

CLAUD, John. Estate appraised by Aaron Smith, Jesse Holt and Burwell Westbrooke. R. March 13, 1794. Page 617.

MOORE, Mrs. Sarah. Account current. Signed, John Simmons. D. 1785. Audited by Thomas Ridley and Joseph Wright. R. March 13, 1794. Page 618.

MERCER, John. D. 1776. Signed, John Pursell, surviving Ex. Paid funeral expenses of Patience Mercer; paid Betsey Mercer's legacy; paid Grace Mercer's legacy; a receipt from Henry Levy for a legacy from Robert Mercer's estate. Audited by Solomon Holmes and William Urquhart. R. March 17, 1794. Page 619.

DRAPER, Thomas. Account current. Signed, Ephraim Draper, Ex. D. 1792. Paid legacies to the following, Thomas, William, Jesse and Jeremiah Draper; Edmond Jordan his wife's legacy and my own. Audited by Lemuel Jones and J. Denson. R. April 10, 1794. Signed, Ephraim Draper, Ex. Page 619.

SPIVEY, William. Appraised by John Adams, William Wellons and Benjamin Andrews. Signed, Charles B. Briggs. D. April 29, 1793. R. April 10, 1794. Page 620.

SPIVEY, John. Estate appraised by John Spratley and Henry Simmons. Signed, Charles Briggs, Adm. S. Dec. 14, 1793. R. April 10, 1794. Page 621.

ROCHELLE, John. Of the Parish of St. Luke. Leg.- wife Judeth; all my children, land and property in North Carolina. Exs. brother Levi Rochelle and friend James Butts. D. Feb. 30, 1794. R. April 10, 1794. Wit. George Gurley, Jeremiah Drake, Stephen Handcocke. Page 621.

JOHNSON, Josiah. Inventory. Signed, Hannah Johnson. R. April 10, 1794. Page 622.

EVANS, Hannah. Inventory. Signed, John Thomas Blow, Sr. D. Feb. 26, 1791. R. April 10, 1794. Page 623.

HELVEY, John. Signed, Mary Helvey, Adm. Audited by Benjamin Ruffin and Charles Briggs. R. April 10, 1794. Page 623.

JONES, Mary. Parish of Nottoway. Leg.- cousin Mary Williams. Ex., Elisha Whitney. D. June 1, 1783. R. April 10, 1794. Wit. Joshua Whitney, Jemima Hatfield, Ann Whitney. Page 623.

HARRIS, West. Leg.- wife Julia, land adjoining William Harris; son Hardy when twenty one. Exs., friends Henry Thorpe, Arthur Applewhite, John Richardson. D. Feb. 14, 1794. R. April 10, 1794. Wit. Morris Dunn, Mabel Dupree, John T. Richardson. Page 624.

WILLIAMS, Isaac. Signed, John Davis, Adm. D. 1789. Account current. - paid Jordan Denson for maintaining Edwin and Elizabeth Williams; paid Joseph Denson for maintaining Sally and Joseph Williams; paid Josiah Vick his account as Ex., of Benjamin Williams decd. Audited by Samuel Calvert and James Bennet. R. May 8, 1794. Page 626.

HINES, Richard. Signed, Charles Briggs, Adm. Paid the widow Hines. Audited by Samson Stanton and Benjamin Ruffin. D. 1789. R. June 11, 1794. Page 627.

COUNCIL, John. Signed, Amos Council and J. Council Exs. Paid seven legatees. D. Jan. 24, 1794. R. June 12, 1794. Page 627.

POPE, John. Account current. Paid legacy to Henson Pope; bonds delivered to the orphans. Audited by Thomas Edmunds and Samuel Edmunds. D. Feb. 11, 1793. R. June 12, 1794. Page 628.

IVEY, Henry. Signed, Peterson Ivey. Paid Winna Ivey, widow of Henry Ivey decd., by virtue of a marriage contract. D. 1791. R. June 12, 1794. Audited by Kin Turner, Solomon Cooper and Benjamin Blunt, Jr. Page 629.

CLAUD, Joshua. In account with Byrd Lundy, decd. 1777, by clothes sold at Harrisburg. Signed, Lewis Thorpe. Ex. of Byrd Lundy. Paid Henry Tiller for orphans of Byrd Lundy decd. Audited Robert Mabry and James Lundy. R. July 10, 1794. Page 630.

LUNDY, Byrd. Account estate dated 1778. Signed, Lewis Thorpe, Ex. Paid Phebe Lundy, part of her legacy; Paid Mary Lundy, part of her legacy. Paid each of following the same amount, - Mary Lundy, Henry Tiller, Phebe Lundy, Edwin Lundy, Byrd Lundy, Joshua and James Lundy, when they come of age and Jabez Morris; paid Francis Branch and wife as per decree; to Henry Morris the balance of his wife's legacy. Audited by Robert Mabry and James Lundy. Signed, Lewis Thorpe, Ex. R. July 10, 1794. Page 631.

BRYANT, Lewis. Account current. Audited by Simon Everett and Charles Birdsong. R. July 10, 1794. Page 631.

SPIVY, William. Leg.- daughter Sarah; son Benjamin; son Britain; daughter Mary Powers; daughter Martha Kitchen; to John and Mary Spivy, children of William Spivy, one share of estate. Exs., sons Benjamin and Britain Spivy. D. June 21,

1793. R. July 10, 1794. Wit. Thomas Lain, Joseph Lain.
Page 632.

DREW, Jeremiah. Account current. Signed, William Myrick and
Randolph Newsum, Exs. D. 1785. Paid Thomas Fitzhugh's
legacy; paid Ansalemn Harris' legacy; paid Newit Edwards for
the Drew orphans; to Henry Thorpe his wife's legacy; Newit
Drew's legacy. R. July 10, 1794. Audited by John Wright,
John Simmons and Edward Fisher. Page 633.

HOLLEMAN, Micajah. Of Nottoway Parish. Leg.- wife Mary; son
Arthur at twenty one; son Exum at twenty one. Exs., friends
Jesse Williamson, Samuel Kello and William Urquhart. D.
Dec. 24, 1788. R. June 12, 1794. Wit. Benjamin White, Jr.,
Absalom Williamson. Page 635.

JONES, James. Account estate. Signed, Anne Harris, Extx.
Paid Theophilus Scott a judgement obtained by him and Mary
his wife in the Court of Southampton County versus the Exs.
Audited by William Thomas, Thomas Fitzhugh and John Gurley.
R. July 10, 1794. Page 636.

JONES, William. Account current. Legacies paid to Nancy
Simmons, Mason L. Westbrook, Henry J. P. Westbrook, Richard
H. Simmons, Mary Jones, Loisa Simmons, Edwin Simmons, by
James Edwards, Ar Mitchell and James Butts, Auditors. D.
Nov. 27, 1793. R. Aug. 14, 1794. Page 637.

MARTIN, James. Inventory. Signed, George Gurley, Jr. R.
Sept. 11, 1794. Page 638.

POPE, Jesse. Inventory. Signed Nathaniel Pope, Ex. R.
Sept. 11, 1794. Page 638.

BEAL, Benjamin, Sr. Account current. Signed, William Williams,
Adm. Audited by A. Jones, Wm. H. Baker. D. Feb. 17, 1787.
R. Sept. 11, 1794. Page 639.

TILLAR, John. Of the Parish of St. Luke. Leg.- wife Rebecca,
with reversion to son Jack Tillar Westbrook, alias Tillar
when twenty one; sister Polly Tillar and sister-in-law Sally
Westbrook. Exs., friends Thomas Westbrook and Ben. Avent.
D. Feb. 11, 1794. R. Sept. 11, 1794. Wit. John Atkinson,
William Holleman, John Mecom. Page 640.

THORP, Martha. Leg.- John Harris son of Edward Harris until
my son Joseph Thorp is twenty one; to my four youngest
children, Pamelia, Fanny, Sally and Joseph Thorp. Exs.,
friends John Harris and James Harris. D. April 21, 1794.
R. Sept. 11, 1794. Wit. Aaron Smith, Newit Claud, James
Smith, Lucy Long. Page 640.

CLEMENTS, Benjamin, Jr. Account current. Signed by Thomas
Peete, the surviving Ex. D. 1788. Paid Thomas Gilliam, Jr.
guardian of Thomas C. Gilliam as by decree of the Southampton
Court; to John Rochelle as per decree; to William Urquhart,
Ex. of Thomas Clements, Jr. R. Sept. 11, 1794. Page 641.

VAUGHAN, William. Leg,- wife Ann; son William; son Thomas; son
James land bought of Samuel Nicholson; son John; son Howell;
son Henry. Exs., brother Thomas Vaughan and friends Thomas
Turner and Thomas Ridley. D. Dec. 10, 1793. R. Oct. 9,
1794. Wit. William Edmunds, Etheldred Brantley. Page 643.

PEIRCE, Elizabeth. Parish of Nottoway. Leg.- daughter
Elizabeth; daughter Martha Cobb; son Peter; son Bolton; son
Spencer; son Nathaniel. Exs., Robert Goodwyn and Joseph
Vick. D. R. April 28, 1794. Wit. Jo. Vick, Josiah
Cashiel (?), Benjamin Andrews. Page 644.

JONES, Mary. Estate appraised by Joseph Denson, Henry Jones
and Toomer Joyner. Signed, Elisha Whitney. D. April 1794.
R. Oct. 9, 1794. Page 645.

BOOTH, Moses. Parish of Nottoway. Leg.- wife Diana; son
Peter land purchased of Benjamin Phillips, Phillips Booth and
Henry Blow; son John land bought of Moses Booth; daughter
Martha Warren. Exs., sons Peter and John Booth. D. Aug. 5,
1794. R. Oct. 9, 1794. Wit. Peter Bailey, H. John Burgess,
Charles Bailey. Page 645.

TAYLOR, Robert. Estate appraised by Mark Nicholson, John
Taylor, Sr., Miles Cary, James Miller. R. Oct. 9, 1794.
Page 646.

LUNDY, Edward, Sr. Account current. Signed, William Lundy,
Ex. of Edward Lundy, Jr., decd. Audited by Robert Mabry,
Thomas Turner and John Williamson. R. Nov. 13, 1794.
Page 648.

REESE, John, Sr. Parish of St. Luke. Leg.- wife Mary; son
Randolph; son Rogers; son Rivers; son Reuben; son Rowell;
son John; son Joseph; daughter Patty, wife of Mathew Morgan;
daughter Mary, wife of John Thorpe; daughter Selah, wife of
Benjamin Adams, Jr.; daughter Lucy Johnson; daughter Sally,
wife of Benjamin Ivey; daughter Sucky, wife of Philip Ivey.
Exs., son Randolph and Roger Reese and friend Henry Thorp.
D. Dec. 1, 1792. R. Nov. 13, 1794. Wit. William
Grizzard, Randolph Millton, Thomas Pete. Page 649.

GARDNER, James, Sr. Account current. Signed, Jesse Gardner,
Ex. Audited by Henry Gardner, James Darden and Jacob
Darden, Jr. R. Dec. 11, 1794. Page 650.

COBB, John. Account current. Signed, William Hines and M.
Cobb, Exs. Audited by Charles Briggs, J. Vick and John H.
Pond. D. 1792. R. Dec. 11, 1794. Page 650.

ANDREWS, Ann. Inventory. D. Oct. 24, 1793. R. Dec. 11,
1794. Page 651.

ANDREWS, William, Sr. Account current. Signed, William
Andrews and John Andrews. Paid legacies to John, Thomas and
Drury Andrews. Audited by William Urquhart and John Urquhart.
D. 1772. R. Dec. 11, 1794. Page 652.

ANDREWS, Ann. Account current. Signed, John Andrews, Adm.
Audited by William Urquhart and John Urquhart. R. Dec. 11,
1794. Page 653.

PORTER, James. Leg.- wife Ann; son Jacob; son James; son
Nathan; daughter Edith Vick; daughter Priscilla Vick; daughter
Penina Parten; daughter Leddice; daughter Lucy; daughter
Polly when eighteen. Exs., sons Jacob and Nathan Porter. D.
Oct. 6, 1791. R. Dec. 11, 1794. Wit. Benjamin Blunt,
Benjamin Faircloth, Ephraim Faircloth. Page 654.

RICKS, Ann. Account current. Signed, William Crichlow, Adm.
Audited by Alexander M. Neil, John T. Blow, Henry Adams. D.

1792. R. Dec. 11, 1794. Page 655.

VICK, William, Sr. Leg.- son Thomas, who has removed to Georgia; daughter Sarah wife of Howell Dugger; granddaughter Patsey Dugger; granddaughter Polly Dugger; daughter Rachele, wife of James Pennington; daughter Dorcas, wife of John Boykin; son Newit; daughter Patience, wife of Daniel Browne; son Burwell; son William, land on which Holloway Denson formerly lived, adjoining William Whitehead and Mary Pope; daughter Charlotte; wife Martha. Exs., wife and sons William and Newit Vick. D. Aug. 8, 1794. R. Dec. 11, 1794. Wit. Jo. Vick, Ann Barnes, John Fennel. Page 656.

LAND, Bird. Leg.- son Littleberry; son Lieuallen; daughter Lucretia, wife of Britton Bowers; son Lewis Land. Ex., son Littleberry Land. D. Aug. 22, 1794. R. Dec. 11, 1794. Wit. Mathew Gardner, Jr., William Fowler, Edwin Beal. Page 657.

THORP, Susanna. Leg.- George Edwards my nephew by marriage. Ex., George Edwards. D. Nov. 6, 1791. R. Dec. 11, 1794. Wit. Richard Wren, William Wren. Page 658.

IVEY, John. Account current. Signed, Phillip Ivey. Audited by John Williamson, James Lundy, John Thorpe. D. Jan. 1790. R. Jan. 8, 1795. Page 658.

WESTBROOK, John. Leg.- son Jarret; son Zachariah; daughter Betsey; daughter Dolly Westbrook. Exs., Howell Scarbrough and Robert Murrel (Preacher). D. Dec. 22, 1794. R. Jan. 8, 1795. Wit. Henry Warren, William Marks, Ann Westbrook. Page 659.

TURNER, Benjamin. Leg.- wife; son Walter; son Mathew; daughter Sally; daughter Elizabeth Turner. Exs., friends William Boykin, Joel Boykin, John Urquhart. D. Nov. 6, 1794. R. Jan. 8, 1795. Wit. Britain Britt, Mathew Shereman. Page 661.

JOHNSON, John, Sr. Of Parish of St. Luke. Leg.- son John land adjoining John T. Blow, Benjamin Williams and Thomas Williams; wife Ann and my five children. Exs., son John Johnson and son-in-law William Pope. D. Jan. 30, 1779. R. Dec. 11, 1794. Wit. John Thomas Blow, Mary Blow, Sally Jarrell. Page 662.

PETERSON, Gomer. Estate appraised by Samuel Maget and James Barnes. D. Oct. 1791. R. Jan. 8, 1795. Page 663.

VICK, Jacob. Estate appraised by John Jackson, Jacob Bailey and Giles Vick. D. 1st of 2 mo. 1790. R. Jan. 8, 1795. Page 664.

THORP, Susanna. Inventory. Signed, George Edwards. R. Jan. 8, 1795. Page 665.

DARDEN, James. Leg.- wife Ann; son Elisha, with reversion to my sister Julia Darden and Jacob Darden's children. Exs., Jacob Darden, Sr. and Jacob Darden, Jr. D. Dec. 5, 1794. R. Jan. 8, 1795. Wit. Robert H. Fisher, Stephan Pope, Zerobabell Stakes. Page 665.

DARDEN, James. Inventory. R. Jan. 15, 1795. Page 669.

BOOTH, Moses, Sr. Inventory. Signed, Peter Booth. R. Feb. 12, 1795. Page 669.

THOMAS, William. Of Parish of St. Luke. Leg.- son Henry the land adjoining my land called Sarah Carter's; son William twenty one; son John when twenty one; daughter Lucy; my sister Elizabeth; son John land known as Betty Edwards'; granddaughter Charlotte Pretlow; son George Gurley Thomas when twenty one. Exs., son Henry Thomas and George Gurley, Jr. D. Dec. 29, 1794. R. Feb. 12, 1795. Wit. William Newsum, John Gurley, John T. Blow, Sr. Page 670.

VICK, Robert. Account current. Audited by Charles Birdsong, William Vick and Newit Vick. D. May 15, 1794. R. Feb. 12, 1795. Page 672.

BLUNT, Elizabeth. Leg.- daughter Frances Briggs Lucas, land bought of Lewis Griggs in the County of Greensville; son Benjamin William Blunt, with reversion to friends William Lucas of Mecklenburg County and Rebecca Raines, wife of Hartwell Raines. Ex., husband, Samuel Blunt. D. Sept. 26, 1794. R. Feb. 12, 1795. Wit. Benjamin Blunt, George Blunt. Page 672.

BLUNT, George. Leg.- father Benjamin Blunt. Ex., father Benjamin Blunt. D. Dec. 2, 1794. R. Feb. 12, 1795. Wit. Sam. Blunt, Ben Edwards, William Blow. Page 673.

APPLEWHITE, Ann. Leg.- son William; son Thomas when twenty one; daughter Mary Barham; son John; son Hardy; to the four children of Jesse Cooper; to my eleven children; son Benjamin; daughter Sally Desheil (?); daughter Priscilla Jordan; daughter Joan; daughter Rebecca; daughter Nancy Applewhite. Ex., son John Applewhite. D. Feb. 3, 1795. R. Feb. 12, 1795. Wit. Josiah Dashiele, Thomas Peete, Lucy Waller. Page 674.

CHARLES, Mathew. Of the Parish of Nottoway. Leg.- wife Mary; granddaughter Margaret Joyner; son Jethro; grandson William Charles. Exs., son Jethro and wife Mary. D. Feb. 21, 1794. R. Feb. 12, 1795. Wit. Joshua Miniard, Robert Council, James Clark. Page 673.

POWELL, James L. Estate appraised by Henry Adams, Richard Ricks and William Crichlow. D. June 28, 1794. R. Feb. 12, 1795. Page 675.

ADAMS, Benjamin. Leg.- daughter Sally Ivy; daughter Priscilla Prince; wife Margaret; daughter Charlotte; daughter Nancy; son Arthur; daughter Betsey; granddaughter Sally Adams. Exs., wife and son-in-law Joseph Prince. D. Oct. 30, 1794. R. March 12, 1795. Wit. Herbert Pate, Jordan Pate, Richard Mason. Page 676.

BITTLE, Robert. Leg.- to my --- Henry Bittle; son Kirby; daughter Mary Lanier; grandson Henry Barham the negroes now in possession of his father Benjamin Barham; son John; daughter Mildred Turner; grandson Benjamin Turner; grandson Benjamin Bittle; granddaughter Elizabeth Bittle; to daughter of Mildred Turner; son William Bittle. Exs., sons Henry and William Bittle. D. Feb. 14, 1795. R. April 9, 1795. Wit. Will Edmunds, Jacob Summerell, Thomas Holladay. Page 677.

JARROTT, Fortunatus. Leg.- brother John Jarrott; my clothes to be divided between brother John and William Peoples; to Susanna, daughter of William Peoples; to Henry Bell, son of George Bell, the land I had of Benjamin Wheeler; sister Nancy Jarrott. Ex., John Jarrott. D. Dec. 13, 1795(?). R. March 5, 1795. Wit. William Peebles, Wiley Hopkins, Joseph Hopkins. Joel Lane, Judge of the Court of Wake County, N. Car. to take the oath of Wiley Hopkins and Joseph Hopkins, that above signatures are their own. Page 678.

BOYKIN, John, Sr. Of Nottoway Parish. Leg.- daughter Cherry, wife of Robert Eley; son Mathew; son John; son Joel; son Daniel; daughter Patience, wife of Jacob Turner; daughter Elizabeth; daughter Martha, wife of Thomas Vick; daughter Ava, wife of William Branch; daughter Keziah; daughter Sarah, wife of Arthur Sherod; son Ely Boykin. Exs., son Ely Boykin and Jacob Turner. D. Oct. 8, 1794. R. April 9, 1795. Wit. Britton Britt, John Cook, Frederick Boykin. Page 680.

WOMMACK, Thomas. Leg.- son Carter, said son to take care of his mother Elizabeth Wommack; to John Memore (?) children, namely James, Elizabeth, Polly and John; to Harris Thomson, son of Lodowick Thomson; balance of my estate to be sold and divided between my surviving children. Ex., son Carter Wommack. D. Jan. 26, 1794. R. April 9, 1795. Wit. William Wright, Byrd Lundy. Page 681.

KELLO, Richard. Estate appraised by A. Exum, R. Exum, J. ------. R. April 9, 1795. Page 682.

Account current. Signed. Sam Kello Ex. Audited by Will Hines, Charles Briggs and J. Denson. R. April 9, 1795. Page 683.

REESE, Olive. Account current. Signed, John Reese, Sr. (deceased) Adm. Audited by Robert Mabry and John Williamson. R. May 14, 1795. Page 684.

CALTHORPE, James Butts. Estate appraised by Thomas Gray, Richard Pond and John H. Pond. D. April 25, 1795. R. May 14, 1795. Page 684.

WESTER, William, Jr. Estate appraised by James Edwards and Mathew Wills. D. Dec. 13, 1794. R. May 14, 1795. Page 685.

HARRIS, Landon. Estate appraised by Thomas Fitzhugh, John Taylor, Sr. and Sterling Capel. D. Jan. 22, 1793. R. June 11, 1795. Page 686.

MCNEIL, JAMES. Leg.- freedom to negro slave Molly; to nephew Alexander McNeil. Exs., nephew Alexander McNeil, Thomas Edmunds and Charles Taylor. D. Oct. 9, 1794. R. June 11, 1795. Wit. John T. Blow, Jr., John Taylor, Sr., John Chrichlow and John Fort. Page 687.

BRISTER, Samuel. Leg.- wife Ann; to my five last children, namely John, Benjamin, James, Hannah and Willis. My other children having been provided for. Ex., wife Ann Brister. D. Oct. 2, 1794. R. June 11, 1795. Wit. James Summerell, Thomas Travis, Arthur Doles. Page 688.

RIDLEY, Mathew. Of the Parish of St. Luke. Leg.- to mother Sarah Drew; friend Henry Blunt, son of John Blunt; to Francis Ridley, son of Thomas Ridley, Sr.; to Thomas Holladay, son of

John Holladay, decd. Exs., uncle James Ridley and Henry Blunt. D. April 13, 1795. R. June 11, 1795. Wit. Thomas Ridley, Stephenson Blake, Amey Ridley, Maney Blake. Page 689.

ATKINSON, Ann. Leg.- daughter Ann; son Elisha; son Elias; daughter Rachel Williams; daughter Elizabeth Delk. D. Feb. 12, 1794. R. June 11, 1795. Wit. Jesse Johnson, Phebe Atkinson. Page 689.

HALLCOME, Richard. Estate appraised by Thomas Turner, Arthur Turner & Thomas Fitzhugh. Signed, Charles Briggs. D. Dec. 19, 1794. R. June 11, 1795. Page 690.

SPIVEY, William. Account current. Signed, Charles Briggs, Adm. Audited by Benjamin Ruffin, Samson Stanton. Among items, bond due the father William Spivey's estate. D. April 28, 1795. R. June 11, 1795. Page 691.

RAMSEY, Catherine. Estate appraised by Etheldred Brantley, Henry Blunt, Willie Francis. D. Feb. 26, 1795. R. June 11, 1795. Page 692.

STEWART, Benjamin. Leg.- wife Lyddia the use of my plantation and personal estate, at her death plantation to son Henry, rest of estate to all my children then living and to my grandson Charles Stewart. Exs., wife and friend Robert Goodwyn. D. March 5, 1794. R. June 11, 1795. Wit. Daniel Butts, Robert Goodwyn, John Scott. Page 693.

TURNER, Benjamin. Estate appraised by Sol Holmes, Arthur Doles, Timothy Atkinson. D. April 4, 1795. R. July 9, 1795. Page 693.

WOMMACK, Thomas. Estate appraised by Francis Branch, Carter Wommack, John Berryman and Henry Tillar. D. April 16, 1795. R. July 9, 1795. Page 696.

PORTER, James. Estate appraised by Littleton Fort, James Turner, Benjamin Turner. D. Jan. 31, 1795. R. July 9, 1795. Page 697.

SUTER, William. Leg.- sister Rebecca; brother Henry; brother John; brother Arthur Suter. Exs., brother Arthur and Nathaniel Edwards. D. April 28, 1795. R. July 9, 1795. Wit. Aaron Smith Jeremiah Inman, Nathaniel Edwards. Page 698.

STEWART, Samuel. Inventory. Signed, Humphrey Drewry, Adm. D. Dec. 22, 1792. R. July 9, 1795. Page 699.

MYRICK, Henry. Estate appraised by William Chambliss, Thomas Peete and Hardy Applewhite. Signed, William Myrick, Adm. D. Feb. 23, 1795. R. Sept. 10, 1795. Page 700.

WHITEHEAD, Mary. Leg.- daughter Elizabeth Newby; daughter Mary Bentel (?); daughter Polly Cotton, slave Jesse Cotton has now in his possession; granddaughter Peggie Bridger; grandson Alexander Whitehead; grandson Nathaniel Newby; granddaughter Sally Newby. Exs., Joseph Bentel and Jesse Cotton. D. July 19, 1795. R. Sept. 10, 1795. Wit. Jacob Turner, Elizabeth Everett, Mary Jacobs, Etheldred Turner. Page 701.

THORP, John. Leg.- wife Polly; refers to hogs on Charles Bass' pond; son Aaron; daughter Elizabeth Reese; daughter Susanna; son Moses; son John; daughter Polly; provision for an unborn child; the legacy due by the will of John Reese for my wife to be sold and invested in a slave. Exs., John Harris, Sr., Randolph Reese, Rivers Reese and Roger Reese. D. July 7, 1795. R. Sept. 10, 1795. Wit. John Williamson, Nathaniel Smith, Rowell Reese. Page 702.

SUMMERRELL, Jacob. Leg.- daughter Barbary DeLoach; daughter Margaret; son Hartwell; son Sam Manning Summerrell when twenty one; daughter Lucy; daughter Sally Caul (?). Ex., William Bittle. D. R. Sept. 10, 1795. Wit. William Edmunds, Thomas Holladay, John Turner. Page 703.

HUNT, Miles. Estate appraised by Roger Reese, Thomas Pate, Jr., John Reese. D. May 22, 1795. R. Sept. 11, 1795. Page 704.

FORT, Olive. Estate appraised by Joel Turner, Mark Nicholson, Arthur Foster. D. Oct. 1794. R. Sept. 11, 1795. Page 704.

BRISTER, Samuel. Estate appraised by James Summerell, Thomas Summerell, Thomas Stephenson. D. Aug. 1795. R. Oct. 8, 1795. Page 706.

JARRETT, Fortunatus. Estate appraised by Richard Drewry, Thomas Newsum, Abel Ezell. Signed by John Jarrett, Ex., of Sussex County. D. April 18, 1795. R. Oct. 8, 1795. Page 707.

HART, Samuel. Estate appraised by Robert Hart, Jesse Womble and Richard Hart. D. Dec. 1793. R. Oct. 8, 1795. Page 707.

WILLIAMSON, Calia. Account current, signed John Crumpler, Adm. Paid Sally Fly her part of the estate, paid Winnie Fly, ditto. Audited by Solomon Holmes and Jacob Turner. D. Dec. 1791. R. Oct. 8, 1795. Page 708.

BEAL, Ephraim. Estate appraised by Joseph Scott, Shad Lewis and Hardy Johnson. D. Sept. 27, 1794. R. Oct. 8, 1795. Page 708.

LAND, Bird. Estate appraised by William Beale, Richard Beale, Richard Beale, Jr. D. Dec. 20, 1794. R. Oct. 8, 1795. Page 709.

ANDREWS, Faithy. Leg.- Britain Britt, son of Britain and Pamelia Britt, my part of my father's estate, sister Pamelia Britt. Ex., Britain Britt, Sr. D. May 20, 1795. R. Oct. 8, 1795. Wit. Rebecca Turner, Patsey Britt. Page 710.

NICHOLSON, Mary. Leg.- son Charles Briggs Nicholson; rest of estate between all my children, with an equal part to Polly and Nancy Barham. Exs., son Charles and Bird Lundy. D. Sept. 23, 1795. R. Oct. 8, 1795. Wit. John Mecom, James Mecom, Janny Myrick. Page 710.

COBB, Michael. Leg.- money after just debts are paid to be used for the education of my brothers, Benjamin, Thomas and George until they are fifteen, agreeable to my father's will; wife and all my children until my youngest child Jack Cobb is twenty one. Exs., brother Exum Cobb, Spencer Pierce and Charles Briggs, Jr. D. Nov. 10, 1795. R. Dec. 10, 1795. Wit. Will Hines, George Clements, Rebecca Mecom. Page 711.

BROWNE, Olive. Leg.- friend Thomas Lain; to Lucy Hines, daughter of William Foster; to Polly and Joseph Lain, children of Thomas Lain. Exs., friend Thomas Lain and his son Joseph when of age. D. Oct. 9, 1794. R. Dec. 11, 1795. Wit. Micajah Ellis, Bolin Ellis. Page 712.

TURNER, Willie. Leg.- mother Lucy Turner, with reversion to John Westray Turner; if he should die under age to Lucy and John Little. Ex., friend Lewis Dupree. D. April 1, 1794. R. Sept. 11, 1794. Wit. Cordal Francis, John Winddom. Page 713.

PURSELL, Martha. Of Parish of Nottoway. Leg.- son John; to Arthur Crumpler. Ex., Arthur Crumpler. D. Feb. 18, 1795. R. Dec. 10, 1795. Wit. John Crumpler, Amos Turner. Page 714.

COBB, Henry. Of Parish of Nottoway. Leg.- to my five grandchildren, Amey, Robert, Ann, Betsey and Henry Grimmer; daughter Milla Grimmer; son-in-law Seymour Vaughan my land; granddaughter Chlotella Cobb; granddaughter Betsey Vaughan at death of son-in-law Seymour Vaughan and daughter Amy Vaughan to my grandchildren Henry and Ann Vaughan. Ex., son-in-law Seymour Vaughan. D. Jan. 5, 1791. R. Dec. 10, 1795. Wit. Asa Beale, Josiah Murfee, Francis Murfee. Page 714.

LOWE, Levi. Leg.- wife Sally; son Elias; son Micajah; son Spencer; daughter Sally; daughter Betsey; daughter Cherry; daughter Nancy Lowe. Ex., son Elias Lowe. D. March 12, 1795. R. Dec. 10, 1795. Wit. John Pursell, Mathew Crumpler, John Wright. Page 715.

WESTBROOK, John. Account current. Signed, Lucy Turner, Adtx. Paid Turner Person for Mary Person's share of a negro. Audited by Robert Mabry and James Lundy. D. Aug. 27, 1786. R. Sept. 11, 1795. Page 716.

FISHER, Mary. Inventory. Signed, Robert H. Fisher, Adm. D. June 23, 1795. R. Dec. 10, 1795. Page 717.

HART, Henry. Estate appraised by William Atkinson, Richard Hart and Jesse Womble. D. Dec. 10, 1795. Signed, Joseph and Benjamin Hart, Exs. Page 717.

Account current. Paid Elizabeth Hart her legacy; paid Ann Hart ditto; paid Benjamin Hart ditto. R. Feb. 11, 1796. Page 718.

APPLEWHITE, Ann. Inventory. Signed, John Applewhite, Ex. R. Feb. 11, 1796. Page 720.

MURFEE, Simon. Leg.- son Richard, my plantation at death or marriage of my wife; son Simon; son Josiah; son Francis; son Burwell; son Drewry; son Wills Murfee. Exs., friends Josiah Vick, Samuel Calvert and son Josiah Murfee. D. March 28, 1795. R. Feb. 11, 1796. Wit. James Edwards, William Edwards, Giles Wester. Page 720.

FORT, John. Of the Parish of St. Luke. Leg.- mother; sister Rebecca Barnes' children; sister Temperance; brother Edwin Fort. Exs., friends William Chambless and Joseph Thorpe. D. Sept. 13, 1795. R. Feb. 11, 1796. Wit. William Capele, Kinchen Jelke, Charles Nicholson. Page 721.

ANDREWS, John. Leg.- daughter Elizabeth; daughter Sally; wife Lucy; son James; daughter Nancy Boykin. Exs., William Urquhart, John Urquhart, wife Lucy Andrews. D. June 9, 1795. R. Feb. 11, 1796. Proved by depositions of William Urquhart, Jacob Turner, Daniel Butts. Page 722.

BARNES, Jacob. Leg.- son Benjamin, land adjoining James Barnes; son Jacob land on J. Whitehead, James Barnes and Nathan Barnes; daughter Ann; daughter Selah Vick; wife Elizabeth, reversion to sons Josiah and Thomas Barnes; sons Joshua and Thomas Barnes land in Pitt County, N. Car. and son James land in Edgecomb County, N. Car. Exs., wife Elizabeth and son Josiah Barnes. D. Sept. 15, 1790. R. Feb. 11, 1796. Wit. Edmund Barrett, James Barnes, Jesse Vick, Jesse Barrett. Page 723.

VAUGHAN, Lydia. Nuncupative will, made in the home of Noel Vick, in presence of Milly Porter and Patty Vick. Dec. 29, 1795. "What I have to be divided between Lydia Porter, Polly Vaughan, Fanny Vick and Betsey Vick. I desire that Milly Porter will see it done according to my desire." Signed, Jo. Vick, William Johnson. R. Feb. 11, 1796. Page 723.

HART, Jesse. Leg.- son Richard with reversion to my son Moses; son William with reversion to son Samuel; son Moses land bought of Jesse Womble; daughter Mary; daughter Mildred; daughter Jane; daughter Charity; wife Nancy with reversion of the bequest to the following children:- Richard, Olive, Sarah, Mary, Moses, Mildred, William, Jane, Charity and Samuel Hart. Exs., son Richard Hart and Jesse Womble. D. Dec. 31, 1790. R. Feb. 11, 1796. Wit. Joseph Hart, Benjamin Hart, Jesse Hart. Page 724.

MYRICK, Ann. Leg.- son William; son John; son Howell; grandson Howell Jones. Exs., son William Myrick and grandson Howell Jones. D. Feb. 18, 1795. R. Feb. 11, 1796. Wit. H. Arrington, John Marks, John Myrick. Page 725.

VICK, William. Inventory. Signed, Newit Vick. D. Dec. 1794. R. Feb. 11, 1796. Page 726.

COBB, Henry. Estate appraised by A. Jones, Joseph Scott and James Edwards. D. Feb. 1, 1796. R. Feb. 11, 1796. Page 726.

NICHOLSON, Joshua. Additional account current. Signed, Howell Edmunds one of the Exs. Among items, paid Edward Lundy, Ex. Audited by John Wilkinson and James Gee. R. Feb. 11, 1796. Page 727.

BRITT, John. Account estate. Brittain Britt, Ex. Among items:- paid Tamer Britt's legacy; paid Benjamin Britt his part of the land sold, paid Joseph Britt ditto; paid Beasant Britt ditto; paid Arrington ditto; paid the following their part of the personal estate: Sarah Johnson, Tamor Britt, and Polly Britt; paid the widow's dower. Audited by William Urquhart and Sol Holmes. D. 1791. R. Feb. 11, 1796. Page 728.

CHARLES, Mathew. Estate appraised by Arthur Bowing, Henry Jones and James Clark. D. March 18, 1795. R. Feb. 12, 1796. Page 729.

DARDEN, Holland. Account current. Signed, Jacob Darden, Ex. Among items:- paid the Doctor's account for the illness of Jonah and Holland Darden, decd.; paid Ann Darden her share of

the estate; paid Holland, Jr., ditto; paid John ditto; paid
Jonah ditto; paid Ann and Edith Darden, ditto; for schooling
the orphans of Elisha Darden. Audited by Henry Gardner and
Jesse Carr. D. 1792. R. Feb. 12, 1796. Page 730.

GARDNER, John. Estate appraised by J. Vick, Josh. Slade and
Jacob Joyner, Jr. D. Dec. 21, 1795. R. Feb. 12, 1796.
Page 731.

COCKE, Hartwell. Account estate, Signed by William Urquhart.
Audited by Sol Holmes and John D. Haussman. D. Nov. 1792.
R. Feb. 15, 1796. Page 731.

URQUHART, William. Estate appraised by Kinchen Jelks, William
Chambliss and Richard P. Clements. D. Feb. 28, 1795. R.
April 15, 1796. Page 733.

TURNER, Willie. Estate appraised John Blunt, Henry Smith and
John Person. D. Oct. 11, 1794. R. April 15, 1796. Page
734.

BEALE, Benjamin, Jr. Leg.- wife Elizabeth a tract in Roger's
Neck; friend Jordan Denson to dispose of certain parts of my
estate and pay the debts I owe Jordan Denson & Co. and
Pretlow and Randolph; son Jeremiah; son-in-law Solomon Gobb;
son Shadrack; my daughters Elizabeth Williams, Charlotte
Carr, Polly Williams, Silvia Beale and Peggy Beale; the
children of my wife by her former husband a right to what
belonged to their father's estate. Ex., wife Elizabeth Beale.
D. Feb. 16, 1793. R. April 15, 1796. Wit. Joseph Scott,
James Scott, J. Denson. Page 736.

HARRIS, John Dawson. Leg.- John Edmunds Dawson; Edmond Turner;
Polly Dawson; William Phillips; John and Bowling Barnes,
sons of Bailey Barnes. Exs., Edmund Turner and John E.
Dawson. D. April 6, 1796. R. April 15, 1796. Wit. Henry
Smith, William Sturgeaon, Henry Brantley. Page 737.

VICK, James. Leg.- wife Sarah Nicholson, land bought of Lewis
Joiner, adjoining Arthur Arrington, William Crumpler, Thomas
Williams and Nathaniel Jones; son Parks N. Vick; son Richard
tract bought of Benjamin Andrews adjoining Samuel Drewet,
Charles Briggs; daughter May Worrell; daughter Tabitha Vasser,
with reversion to her children; son Joseph; son James; to my
---- Sarah Vick, with reversion to my children Parks
Nicholson, Richard and Rebecca Vick. Exs., friend Micajah
Holliman and wife Sarah Vick. D. Sept. 13, 1795. R. April
15, 1796. Wit. Noel Waddell, Josiah Murfee, Thomas W.
Clements. Page 739.

DRAKE, Cordal. Leg.- wife Polly, daughter Polly with reversion
of bequest to brothers Silas and Arthur Drake. Ex. wife
Polly Drake. D. Sept. 5, 1795. R. June 9, 1796. Wit.
Bailey Oberry, Eaton Joyner, Elizabeth Lowe. Page 739.

WHITFIELD, Benjamin. Leg.- son Benjamin; son Reuben; son John;
daughters, Elizabeth Crenshaw, Mary Hargraves and Sarah
Revell. Exs., sons Benjamin, Reuben and John Whitfield. D.
Jan. 26, 1787. Wit. Mary Whitfield, Reuben Whitfield, Jesse
Vick. Codicil: Mary Hargrave now a widow to have a home on
John Whitfield's land. D. June 8, 1796. Wit. Jesse Vick,
Elisha Whitfield, Stephen Hancock. R. June 9, 1796. Page
740.

COCKER, Henry. Account current. Signed, Joshua Bailey, Jordan Judkins, Mark Judkins and John Brittle. D. Nov. 14, 1790. R. June 9, 1796. Page 742.

WILLIAMS, Richard. Estate appraised by William Hart, Henry Gardner and John Lee. R. June 9, 1796. Page 742.

PIERCE, Rice B. Account current. Michel Cobbs, decd. Adm. Account versus Elizabeth Pierce, decd. Account versus Elizabeth Pierce, Jr. Account versus Spencer Pierce. Audited by Samuel Calvert and J. Vick. R. June 9, 1796. Page 743.

BLUNT, George. Inventory. Signed, Ben. Blunt. R. June 9, 1796. Page 744.

KINDRED, Benjamin. Estate appraised by Thomas Holladay, Samuel Edmunds, John Powell. Signed, Benjamin Blunt, Ex. D. May 10, 1794. R. June 9, 1796. Page 745.

COKER, Henry. Further appraisal by Peter Bailey, Benjamin Branch and Newsum Branch. D. Nov. 2, 1790. R. June 9, 1796. Page 746.

FULGHAM, Mary. Leg.- daughter Martha Joiner; daughter Ann Turner. Exs., sons-in-law Thomas Joiner and Pass Turner. D. March 21, 1786. R. Feb. 12, 1796.

BROWNE, Jesse. Account estate with administrators of Samuel Ridley Browne. Among items, paid Martha Jack's representatives; paid Elizabeth R. Kelle's children; paid Robert Dickens and wife; paid John Atkinson's representatives; paid representatives of Peter Pelham and wife Parthenia; paid Jesse Browne; paid William Wilkinson and wife Jane; paid John Faulcon and wife Lucretia; paid Samuel Browne. decd. his representatives. All paid the same amount. D. Nov. 7, 1795. Jesse Browne, Anthony Browne, Albridgton Browne, James Browne and John Browne, heirs of Samuel Browne, decd. Ex. of Jesse Browne. Audited by Naack Williams, Samuel Maget, Miles Everett. R. July 14, 1796. Page 748.

JONES, Richard. Account current. Signed, Jacob Barnes, Ex. D. Sept. 1780. Received of John Simmons, Ex. of James Jones, being part of Richard Jones' share of his father's estate. Audited by Alexander McNeil and Mark Nicholson. R. July 14, 1796. Page 749.

MURFEE, Simon. Estate appraised by James Edwards, Semour Vaughan and William Lawrence. D. Feb. 25, 1796. R. July 14, 1796. Page 750.

SCARBROUGH, Mary. Estate appraised by James Bennett, Thomas W. C. Clements, J. Bell and Moody Collier. D. Feb. 29, 1796. R. July 14, 1796. Page 752.

WILLIAMS, Mathew. Estate appraised by Absalom Joyner, John Williams and David Washington. Signed, Lewis Williams, Adm. D. June 27, 1795. R. July 14, 1796. Page 752.

WHITEHEAD, Mary. Inventory. D. Aug. 8, 1796. R. Sept. 8, 1796. Page 753.

REESE, John, Sr. Estate appraised by Joseph Fort, Newit Claud and Thomas Peete. R. Dec. 8, 1796. Page 754.

ADAMS, Benjamin. Estate appraised by Zebulon Lewis, John

Applewhite and William Applewhite. D. March 19, 1795. R. Sept. 8, 1796. Page 756.

ELLISON, Gerard R. Leg.- wife Sarah; son Caleb, land adjoining Jesse and Etheldred Washington; son Edwin; son James when twenty one; my three other children, Dorcas, Gutie and Zachariah Ellison. Exs., Gideon Ellison and Samuel Cornwell. D. July 1, 1795. R. Sept. 8, 1796. Wit. Joshua Bailey, Absalom Bailey, Thomas Washington, Charles Sadler. Page 757.

THOMAS, Nathan. Estate appraised by Benjamin Blunt, Jr., James B. Womack and Etheldred Turner. D. July 11, 1796. R. Oct. 13, 1796. Page 759.

CALTHORPE, James Butts. Account current. Signed, James Pond, Adm. Audited by Exum Cobb and William Wellons. R. Oct. 13, 1796. Page 760.

CALTHORPE, James. Estate appraised by Robert Mabry, Benjamin Blunt and Thomas Turner. D. April 15, 1795. R. Oct. 13, 1796. Page 761.

THORPE, John. Estate appraised by John Williamson and George Ivey. Signed, Benjamin Blunt, Jr. D. Oct. 29, 1795 and Dec. 15, 1795. R. Oct. 13, 1796. Page 762.

LANCASTER, James. Leg.- wife Rebeckah; refers to mill built with Lemuel Bailey; daughters Mildred and Jerusha one half of the mill built in Isle of Wight County with Lemuel Bailey; daughters Polly and Zilla; granddaughter Elizabeth Champion Bell; friend John Gwaltney to be guardian for my daughter Jerusha; wife Rebecca to be guardian for daughters Polly and Zilla, son-in-law James P. Bell to be guardian for grand- daughter Elizabeth C. Bell. Ex. friend John Gwaltney. D. March 12, 1796. R. Oct. 13, 1796. Wit. Herbert Sledge, John Bryant, David Davis, James Delk. Page 763.

HOLLAMAN, William. Leg.- son John land adjoining Joseph Hart and William Bailey; son William, land adjoining Micajah Holleman; wife Lucy; son Thomas Holleman. Exs., wife and sons John and William Holleman. Wit. Exum Harris, Joseph Hart, Charles Sadler. D. Jan. 19, 1795. R. Oct. 13, 1796. Page 765.

POND, Richard. Leg.- son Drewry; son William; wife Mary; daughter Nancy Megee; daughter Dianah; son Samuel, daughter Mary; son Daniel Pond. Exs., wife Mary and sons Drewry and William Pond. D. March 5, 1794. R. Oct. 13, 1796. Wit. John Pond, Tabitha Bond, Dianna Pond. Page 766.

BLOW, Henry. Leg.- wife Sally, until my two children, Sally and William Blow come to lawful age. Exs., brothers Micajah and Thomas R. Blow, brother-in-law Owen Myrick. D. May 27, 1796. R. Oct. 13, 1796. Wit. William Chambliss, Michael Blow, Janney Myrick. Page 768.

POPE, Simon. Estate appraised. Not signed. D. Jan. 7, 1796. R. Jan. 13, 1796. Page 768.

COBB, Michael. Estate appraised. Not signed. Signed, William Wellons and John H. Pond. R. Oct. 13, 1796. Page 769.

MYRICK, Henry. Account current. Signed, William Myrick, Adm. Among items;- cash paid William Chambliss, guardian of Owen Myrick; cash paid for Fanny Myrick to guardian Henry Myrick;

by cash received in the house of Howell Myrick, decd. D.
Feb. 7, 1796. R. Oct. 13, 1796. Audited by Richard Clements
and John Taylor, Jr. D. Feb. 7, 1796. R. Oct. 13, 1796.
Page 772.

BEALE, Benjamin. Estate appraised by Shad Lewis, Joseph Scott
and Stephen Johnson. D. May 14, 1796. R. Oct. 13, 1796.
Page 772.

LUNDY, Elizabeth. Estate appraised by Robert Mabry, James
Harris and James Lundy. Signed, Lunsford Lundy. D. Nov. 17,
1795. R. Nov. 11, 1796. Page 774.

TURNER, Pass. Account current. Signed, James Clark, Adm. Paid
widow according to will. Audited by Daniel Simmons and
Pettaway Johnson. R. Oct. 13, 1796. Page 775.

STEWARD, Lemuel. Account current. Supplies the widow and
children. Audited by John Taylor, Jr., and Newit Drew. D.
June 22, 1793. R. Oct. 13, 1796. Page 776.

JOHNSTON, Stephen. Of Nottoway Parish. Leg.- wife Sarah all
the remains of her estate that she brought into my estate;
son John; son William; daughter Polly; son Johnson; daughter
Sally; son Stephen Johnston. Exs., sons Benjamin and Mathew
Johnston. (Name written interchangably Johnson and Johnston.)
D. Sept. 27, 1796. R. April 17, 1797. Wit. David
Washington, Thomas Camp, Joseph Vick. Page 776.

TURNER, James. Leg.- son Edmund at twenty one, reversion to
son Benjamin, when of age; reversion to son Edmund when of
age; daughter Nancy Turner. Exs., Henry Blunt, William Blunt,
Edmund Turner, Richard Blunt. D. Feb. 14, 1797. April 17,
1797. Wit. William Blunt, Newit Harris, Edmund Turner,
Henry Blunt, Richard Blunt. Page 778.

HARRIS, Edmund. Leg.- wife Elizabeth; to Penny Carr Harris and
Jinny Harris at twenty one, daughters of Landon Harris; to my
five children, Sterling, John, Peyton, James and Charlotte
Turner. Exs., sons Peyton and James Harris. D. May 20,
1795. R. Aug. 21, 1797. Wit. Francis Branch, Peyton Lundy,
John Williamson. Page 779.

DELOACH, Solomon. Leg.- wife Lucy; to Solomon, son of Richard
Deloach decd.; Allen DeLoach Dunn; Thomas DeLoach Dunn;
Williamson Parker; Frederick, son of Drewry Parker, decd.
Ex., Colonel Samuel Kello. D. Nov. 14, 1795. R. May 16,
1797. Wit. Burwell Long, Lucy Myrick, John Meglamore.
Page 780.

JONES, Lenuel. Leg.- son Joseph; son Samuel; daughters, Peggy,
Elizabeth, Martha and Ann. Exs., brothers-in-law Jordan and
Joseph Denson. D. Nov. 23, 1796. R. May 15, 1797. Wit.
Henry Butts, Edmund Johnson, Zachariah Doyel. Page 781.

BISHOP, Joseph. Parish of Nottoway. Leg.- wife Ann, son Mark,
son Daniel; daughter Martha Bishop; daughter Rebecca Wells;
daughter Mary Holt, son William Bishop. Exs., wife Ann and
son William Bishop. D. Sept. 15, 1795. R. May 15, 1797.
Wit. Henry Davis, Joel Davis. Exs., refused and Edmund
Marks qualified. Page 782.

EDWARDS, Benjamin. Leg.- nephew Benjamin Blunt; remainder of my
estate to be divided between the children of my brothers
William and Richard Edwards; the children of my sisters

Elizabeth Edmunds and Ann Blunt. Exs., brothers William and Richard Edwards. D. Dec. 17, 1796. R. May 15, 1797. Wit. Richard Blow, John T. Blow, Jr., William Blow. Page 783.

DRAKE, Barnaby, Sr. Leg.- son Exum; daughter Sarah, wife of John Powell; daughter Martha; to Albuin (?) son of Jacob Jenkins; son Simmons; wife Mary; son Burwell, when of age; youngest daughters, Milbra and Penny; daughters Mourning and Martha land adjoining that Samuel Hart bought of Exum Drake; wife Mary. Ex., son Simmons Drake. D. Dec. 26, 1791. R. May 15, 1797. Wit. Jesse Willeford, Thomas Carlile, John Beaton. Page 783.

JOYNER, Joshua. Parish of Nottoway. Leg.- son John; son Joshua; son Drewry; son Nelson; son Elisha; daughter Fereby; daughter Edith; wife Martha. (Refers to eight children only seven named.) D. Sept. 14, 1783. R. May 15, 1797. Exs., sons John and Joshua Joyner. Wit. Joseph Scott, Jr., Joseph Mountfortt, Joshua Joyner. Page 785.

HARRIS, William. Account current. Signed, Jo. Vick, Sheriff. D. April 13, 1797. R. May 15, 1798. Page 787.

DENNING, John. Estate appraised by John D. Hausmann, John Clayton, Thomas Lane. D. Oct. 8, 1796. R. May 15, 1798 (?) Page 787.

BAILEY, Captain Hartwell. Estate appraised by Mark Judkins, Peter Booth, James Booth. D. Jan. 16, 1796. R. May 15, 1797. Page 788.

HICKS, William. Estate appraised. (not signed) D. Nov. 1796. R. May 15, 1797. Page 790.

THORPE, Moses. Account current. Signed, John Thorpe, Ex. Audited by Robert Mabry and John Williamson. D. 1790. R. May 15, 1797. Page 792.

LITTLE, William. Estate appraised by James Lundy, James Harris, Lunsford Lundy. D. May 29, 1794. R. May 15, 1797. Page 791.

WESTBROOKE, Samuel. Account current. Signed, Burwell Westbrook, Ex. D. 1785. Among items, paid Hannah Westbrook guardian to Turner, David, Joel, Samuel and Pheby Westbrook; paid Sheriff, copy of execution Ann and Rebecca Westbrook, decd., by the amount of that part of the estate sent Mary Westbrook during her life. Audited by Robert Mabry and James Lundy. D. Dec. 23, 1786. D. May 15, 1797. Page 793.

HART, Robert. Leg.- son John; son Robert; son Drewry; wife Sarah; daughters, Avereler, Silvier and Sarah. Wit. Richard Hart. D. Dec. 22, 1789. R. May 15, 1797. Wit. Joseph Hart, Joseph Hart, Jr., Jesse Hart. Ex. refused and John Hart qualified. Page 794.

BLUNT, Elizabeth. Estate appraised by J. Kindred; Drew Powell and William Newton. D. Aug. 29, 1796. R. May 15, 1797. Page 795.

HART, Jesse. Estate appraised by William Adkinson, Charles Sadler and Joseph Hart. D. Feb. 23, 1796. R. May 15, 1797. Page 795.

APPLEWHITE, Henry. Account current, signed by John Applewhite, Ex. Audited by Zebulon Lewis and Thomas Peete, Jr. R. May 15, 1797. Page 796.

HARRIS, Amos. Account current. Signed, Arthur Applewhite the surviving Ex. Audited by Robert Mabry, John Williamson and L. Mason. D. March 12, 1790. R. May 15, 1797. Page 799.

EDWARDS, William. Leg.- son James land bought of Speed and that of Mills Applewhite, adjoining Jonah Edwards; son Elias; refers to land which he has sold to Simon Murfee; son Albridgeton; daughter Sally Wester; daughter Elizabeth Williams; daughter Lyddy Lawrence; daughter Mary; wife Priscilla; son William. Exs., sons James, William and Elias Edwards. D. March 21, 1794. R. Sept.   , 1795 (?). Wit. (not given). Page 800.

HARRIS, William. Account current. Adm. Arthur Applewhite, being deceased, presented by John Applewhite his Adm. Audited by Robert Mabry, John Williamson and L. Mason. D. July 19, 1794. R. May 15, 1797. Page 801.

APPLEWHITE, Ann. Account current. Signed, John Applewhite, Ex. Among items; interest on money advanced to Sarah Moore and Henry Applewhite. Audited by Thomas Peete and Thomas Peete, Jr. R. May 15, 1797. Page 802.

POWELL, James. Account current. Signed, Samuel Calvert, Adm. Audited by James Bennett, T. W. Clements. R. May 15, 1797. Page 803.

BARHAM, Robert. Of the Parish of St. Luke. Leg.- wife Hannah; daughter Peggy; daughter Charlot; daughter Sally; son Howel; daughter Mary Cooper; to all my children- Milly Hutchings, Patsey Gilliam; Betsey Gilliam; Peggy; Charlot; Sally and Howel. Exs., friend John Simmons and Joel Barham. D. March 20, 1792. R. May 15, 1797. Wit. John Simmons, Sr., Levy Rochell, Joel Barham and Peter Mannery. Page 803.

DAUGHTERY, Elizabeth. Account current. Signed, James Gardner, Ex. D. 1790. Audited by James Edwards, William Fowler and William Edwards. R. May 16, 1797. Page 804.

KIRBY, John. Estate appraised by John Simmons, Micah Ellis, Moody Collier. D. Jan. 30, 1797. R. July 17, 1797. Page 805.

FLETCHER, Benjamin. Estate appraised by Sol Homes. Timothy Atkinson, Britten Britt. D. Aug. 19, 1796. R. July 17, 1797. Page 807.

JOYNER, Joshua, Jr. Estate appraised by J. Scott, John Bowers, Willis Bowers. D. Feb. 1, 1797. R. July 17, 1797. Page 808.

HALCOME, Richard. Account current. D. 1797. Audited by Benjamin Ruffin and Philips Davis. R. July 17, 1797. Page 809.

WILLIAMS, Richard. Leg.- wife Rachel; son George; daughter Elizabeth Williams. Ex., Charles Birdsong. D. June 29, 1795. R. July 17, 1797. Wit. Charles Birdsong, Giles Joiner, Mathew Bryant. Page 811.

153

HURST, William. Leg.- wife Nancy; son William; my eight children, Amy, Abraham, Charles, Cate, Easter, Oliver, Delitha and Write. Ex., Charles Birdsong. D. June 20, 1795. R. July 17, 1797. Wit. Charles Birdsong, Giles Joyner, Mathew Bryant. Page 812.

JONES, James, Sr. Estate appraised. Signed, James, Anselm and Jordan Jones. Appraisers not named. D. March 3, 1793. R. July 17, 1797. Page 814.

GRAY, John. Account current. Signed, Hannah Gray, Admtx. Audited by Thomas Turner and Benjamin Blunt, Jr. R. July 17, 1797. Page 815.

POND, Mason. Estate appraisal. Appraised by John Collier, William Wellons and John Davis. D. June 5, 1797. R. July 17, 1797. Page 816.

BEALE, Richard. Leg.- daughter Millia; son Asa the plantation bought of Hardy Pope; son Abia; daughter Eady; son Silah, tract bought of William Ward; son Elijah; son Dickey; son Jacob; daughter Nancy; daughter Alice. Exs., sons, Asa, Abia and Silah Beale. D. Jan. 9, 1797. R. July 17, 1797. Wit. Kinchen Edwards, William Fowler, Margaret Joiner. Page 817.

DELOACH, Solomon. Estate appraisal. Signed, Fred'k. Parker, Adm. Appraised by William Chambless, Richard Clements, Joel Barham. D. June 15, 1797. R. July 17, 1797. Page 318.

TRAVIS, Pyland. Leg.- wife Lucy; daughters, Tabitha and Patey Travis. Exs., brother Charles Travis and Drury Lane. D. Nov. 16, 1795. R. July 17, 1797. Wit. Richard Hargrave, Samuel Hargrave, Catherine Travis. Page 820.

BISHOP, Joseph. Estate appraisal. Appraisers, Mark Judkins, James Booth, Britain Travis. D. April 5, 1797. R. July 17, 1797. Page 820.

THOMAS, William. Appraisal. Not signed. R. July 17, 1797. Page 822.

WILLIAMS, Richard. Account current. Signed, Jordan Williams, Ex. Audited by Jacob Darden, Sr., and Jacob Darden, Jr. D. 1794. R. July 17, 1797. Page 824.

COOPER, Jesse. Account current. Signed, Cordal Barnes. Among items, to paid the balance of his wife's guardian's accounts. Audited by Jo. Vick and A. M. Neil. D. Jan. 19, 1794. R. July 17, 1797. Page 824.

BELL, Richard. Estate appraised by William Fowler, Kincheon Edwards, Willis Johnson. D. Feb. 19, 1797. R. July 17, 1797. Page 827.

CHARLES, Jethro. Estate appraised by James Clark, Charles Council, Arthur B --ing. D. Nov. 19, 1796. July 17, 1797. Page 829.

GARDNER, James. Account current. Signed, Jesse Gardner, Adm. Audited by J. Denson and John Davis. R. July 17, 1797. Page 831.

LUNDY, Edith. Leg.- son Peyton; daughter Nancy Rivers; daughter Patsey Nicholson; granddaughter Charlotte and grandson Byrd, children of son Peyton; son John Lundy. Exs., son John and friend Robert Mabry. D. July 30, 1797. R. Aug. 21, 1797. Wit. Moses Johnson, Robert Mabry. Page 833.

DREWRY, Humphry. Leg.- daughter Rebecca; daughter Mary Pond; daughter Hannah Simmons; daughter Elizabeth; daughter Rhody Andrews' children. Exs., friend Samuel Drewry and John Pond, Jr. D. Aug. 15, 1796. R. July 17, 1797. Wit. J. Vick, Thomas Hallcome, Charles Sandiford. Page 835.

TURNER, Arthur. Estate appraised by John Crumpler, John Pursell and Arthur Crumpler. D. Sept. 1795. R. Aug. 21, 1797. Page 836.

EDWARDS, William. Estate appraised by William Fowler, Kinchen Edwards and Seymore Vaughan. Signed by William Edwards and Janes Edwards. D. May 27, 1797. R. Aug. 21, 1797. Page 837.

APPLEWHITE, Thomas. Estate appraisal. Appraisers not recorded. R. July 10, 1788. Page 839.

SOUTHAMPTON COUNTY

WILL BOOK V

HARRIS, West. Account current. Signed, Henry Thorpe, surviving Ex. Audited by James Lundy and John Williamson. D. March 1797. R. Aug. 21, 1797. Page 1.

MILTON, Elisha. Leg.- granddaughter Patsey Milton, daughter of Ann Milton, the deed to be made her by Mr. Eth^d Taylor; to my three children, Leah, Randolph and Ann Milton. Exs., friends Arthur Turner and Benjamin Barham, Jr. D. Dec. 1, 1788. R. Aug. 21, 1797. Wit. Eth^d. Taylor, William Rose, William Jarrell. Page 2.

ADAMS, Benjamin. Account current. Signed, Joseph Prince, Ex. Audited by Thomas Peete and John Applewhite. D. 1795. R. Aug. 21, 1797. Page 3.

EDMUNDS, Ann. Leg.- Mary Edmunds Dawson; Rebekah Turner; my three granddaughters Sall Simmons, Jane Edmunds Dawson, (3 ?); great granddaughter Ann Northington Turner; said Ann dies without issue reversion to the children of Edmund Turner; reversion of Jane Edmund's request to Sally Simmons' children. Ex. Edmund Turner. D. Oct. 31, 1791. R. Aug. 21, 1797. Wit. Willie Francis, John Francis, Mary Smith. Page 3.

DREWRY, William. Of the Parish of St. Luke. Leg.- wife Lucy; son John; son Charles; son Edmunds; daughter to Sally; to Polly Grizzard, daughter of Phebe Grizzard; son John to my brother Richard Drewry to raise; son Edmund to be bound to Humphry Drewry. Ex., brother Richard Drewry. D. May 16, 1791. R. Aug. 21, 1797. Wit. Henry Smith, Aaron Smith, Nathan Turner. Page 4.

RAY, John. Leg.- son William; wife Celah; my children John, Mary, Elizabeth, William and Howell Ray. Exs., wife and Jacob Barrett. D. Aug. 22, 1796. R. Aug. 21, 1797. Wit. William Chitty, William Sandifur, Elizabeth Ray, Isham Jackson. Page 5.

HART, Robert. Estate appraised by Jos. Hart, Jesse Womble and William Bailey. Signed, John Hart. R. Aug. 21, 1797. Page 6.

LOWE, Lighborn. Leg.- my five sons, Jeremiah, Samuel (or Lemuel ?), Cajah, Willias and Wiley; daughter Milly; daughter Patsy. D. Nov. 16, 1796. R. Aug. 21, 1797. Exs., Britain Boykin and John Crumpler. Wit. Micajah Lowe, John Crumpler, Jr., Benjamin Britt. Page 8.

COBB, Michael. Account current. Signed, Exum Cobb, Ex. Paid legacy due Jeremiah Cobb, son of John Cobb deceased; paid board and schooling for Benjamin and Thomas; ditto for George B. Cobb. Audited by Charles Bailey, Sr., Robert Goodwyn, Charles Briggs, Jr., Edwin Gray. R. Aug. 21, 1797. Page 10.

HOWELL, Goodrich. Leg.- brother Alfred Howell after mother's death. Ex., brother Alfred Howell. D. Jan. 3, 1797. R.

Aug. 21, 1797. Wit. James Irwin, Aaron Smith, Thomas Vaughan. Page 12.

ELLIS, Henry. Nuncupative will. Estate to be divided between his four sisters' children: Miles Everett; Benjamin Ellis, Polly C. Ellis and Susan Hatfield. He desired his sister Martha to have his house. D. April 14, 1797. R. Aug. 21, 1797. Proved by Mary Vick, Ann Rowland and Dorcy Drake, having died at the house of Jacob Vick. Page 12.

ELLISON, Gerrard. Estate appraised by William Bailey, Jesse Womble, Rich. Hart. D. Dec. 3, 1796. R. Aug. 21, 1797. Page 13.

SUTER (or Luter), John. Account current. Signed, Henry Smith, Ex. Audited by Henry Blunt and Nathaniel Edwards. D. July 19, 1788. R. Aug. 21, 1797. Page 14.

HARRIS, Landon. Signed, Ann Harris, Admtx. Audited by John Taylor, Jr., Rand. Newsum. D. 1795. R. Aug. 21, 1797. Page 16.

BAILEY, Captain Hartwell. Account current. Signed, Jordan Judkins, Peter Bailey. Among items, paid Jesse Carrell for taking care of two orphans; articles bought for the widow. Audited by James Gray and John Brittle. R. Aug. 21, 1797. Page 16.

BURGESS, Henry John. Leg.- wife Sarah; daughter Elizabeth Matilda when eighteen; son Albridgton Samuel Hardy Burgess when twenty one. Exs., Captain James Gray, Col. Albridgton Jones, Gen. Lawrence Baker, Dr. Simmons J. Baker. I appoint Gen. Baker, guardian to my daughter if her mother should die and Dr. S. Baker, guardian to my son. D. Feb. 14, 1797. Wit. William Kello, Thomas Ridley, William D. Hines. Codicil: My exs. to repair my house. Wit. Elizabeth Baker, Willis Wilkinson, Emily Briggs. R. March 28, 1797. Page 17.

LANCASTER, James. Estate appraised by Edward Bailey, Harmon Harris and John Williamson. R. Oct. 16, 1797. Page 18.

TRAVIS, Pyland. Estate appraised by Burrell Barrett, John Jones and Anselm Jones. Signed, Drewry Lane, Ex. R. Oct. 16, 1797. Page 20.

CLAUD, Edwin. Leg.- all my children, when son Joseph is twenty one. Ex., wife Elizabeth and friend Henry Barrow. D. July 11, 1797. R. Oct. 16, 1797. Wit. John Barrow, William Fitzhugh, Jr., Joseph Mundell. Page 21.

EVANS, Hannah. Signed, John T. Blow, Sr., Ex. Account current. Among items, paid heirs to the estate of Martha Pope, Nathaniel Pope and Ben C. M. Evans. Audited by Thomas Edmunds and Henry Thomas. R. Oct. 16, 1797. Page 22.

JOHNSTON, Elijah. Estate appraised by Thomas Wood, John Morris, Joel Davis. Signed, John Jones. D. Oct. 16, 1797. Page 22.

REESE, John. Account current. Signed, Roger and Randolph Reese. Audited by Zebulon Lewis and Thomas Peete. D. Dec. 1794. R. Oct. 16, 1797. Page 23.

POND, Richard, Sr. Estate appraised by Thomas Gray, Thomas Wood and Thomas Laine. D. Nov. 12, 1796. R. Dec. 18, 1797. Page 24.

MAGET, Nicholas. Leg.- son John; son James land purchased of
William Bryant; son Samuel, plantation adjoining Arthur
Whitehead and said son; son William, land in Northampton Co.,
N. Car., son Nicholas; to Sally Everett daughter of Etheldred
and Elizabeth Everett; negroes given to John Edmunds, decd.,
to be considered his part of my estate; negroes put in the
possession of Etheldred Everett decd., may be considered his
part of my estate. Exs., sons, John and Samuel Maget. D.
Dec. 10, 1795. R. Dec. 18, 1897. Wit. William Bryant, Sr.,
Exum Everett, Jacob Gilliam. Page 25.

VICK, James. Estate appraised by John Davis, James Bell,
Spencer Pierce. D. Oct. 3, 1796. R. Dec. 18, 1797. Page 27.

CLARKE, William. Leg.- wife Sarah, the land left me in Surry
County by my grandfather Clarke's will. Extx., wife Sarah.
D. Sept. 8, 1797. R. Dec. 18, 1797. Wit. Humphry Drewry,
Harris Johnston, John Blake. Page 28.

HART, John. Estate appraised by Jesse Carrel, John Brittle
and Newsum Branch. R. Dec. 18, 1797. Page 28.

MERCER, John. Account estate.- paid John Crumpler for schooling two children. Audited by William Urquhart and Solo.
Holmes. R. Dec. 18, 1797. Page 30.

GARDNER, Joshua. Estate appraised by William Fowler, Jonah
Edwards, Robert Pebworth. Signed, Martha Gardner. D. Oct.
28, 1797. R. Dec. 18, 1797. Page 30.

ATKINSON, Ann. Estate appraised by J. Kindred, Henry Porter
and Thomas Taylor. Signed, Elias Atkinson. D. Dec. 2, 1796.
R. Dec. 18, 1797. Page 31.

WESTBROOK, William. Estate appraisal. (not signed) D. Nov.
5, 1796. R. Jan. 15, 1798. Page 32.

DAVIS, Henry. Leg.- son Archibald; son Henry after his mother's
death; daughter Hannah Ray; daughter Jeany; my negro Samuel
a tract of land adjoining Richard Blunt. Exs., wife Lucy,
son Henry and Phillip Davis. D. Oct. 12, 1797. R. April 16,
1798. Wit. Nathaniel Davis, Sarah Mitchel, Charles Briggs,
Sr. Page 33.

WHITEHEAD, William. Appraisal. (not signed) D. Sept. 20,
1796. R. June 15, 17--. Page 34.

BROCK, Thomas. Leg.- wife Lucy with reversion of bequest to my
three children, John; Thomas Ellis and Polly McKenny Brock;
to Belah Williford's four children, Josiah; Samuel; Susanna
and William when twenty one; son William; son Benjamin; granddaughter Susanna Williford. Exs., Edward Bailey and Solomon
Holmes and son William. D. Feb. 8, 1795. P. Aug. 21, 1797.
R. Jan. 15, 1798. Wit. Sarah Bailey, William Bailey, James
Butts. Page 38.

WESTBROOK, Henry. Parish of Nottoway. Leg.- brother William
Person Westbrook; mother Priscilla Westbrook. Ex., brother
William Person Westbrook. D. Oct. 3, 1793. R. Jan. 15, 1798.
Wit. John Simmons, Sr., Sally Westbrook. Page 40.

HOLLEMAN, Will. Estate appraised by Edward Bailey, William
Atkinson, Joseph Hart. D. Dec. 19, 1796. R. Jan. 15, 1798.
Page 40.

WILLIAMS, Jacob. Estate appraised by Henry Branch, Drew Branch and John Warren. D. Nov. 23, 1797. R. Jan. 15, 1798. Page 42.

BLAKE, Ben. Estate appraised by John Barnes, Harris Johnson and Joseph Turner. D. Nov. 30, 1797. R. Jan. 15, 1798. Page 43.

CRUMPLER, Beasant. Parish of Nottoway. Leg.- son William; Allen Johnson; son Beasant; Allen Little; Eley Johnson; wife Sarah; daughter Molly Jones; daughter Betsey Crumpler; daughter Sally Crumpler. Exs., son Beasant and friend John Crumpler. D. Oct. 1, 1795. R. Jan. 15, 1798. Wit. William Crumpler, Benjamin Crumpler, West Tyus, Jr. Page 45.

CHARLES, Eleanor. Leg.- son William; son Charles; daughter Elizabeth. Exs., friend Josiah Johnson and Joseph Denson. D. Oct. 2, 1797. R. Jan. 15, 1798. Wit. Thomas Chappell, Joseph Denson, Jr., Caty Joiner. Page 46.

LOWE, Lighborn. Estate appraised by Arthur Crumpler, Jacob Turner, James Johnson. D. Oct. 26, 1797. R. Jan. 16, 1798. Page 47.

BENNETT, John. Inventory. Signed, William Bennett, Ex. R. Jan. 16, 1798. Page 48.

DELOACH, Sarah. Parish of St. Luke. Leg.- daughter Lucy; daughter Polly; son Richard Deloach. Ex., son Richard Deloach. D. Aug. 20, 1797. R. Jan. 16, 1798. Wit. Will Barnes, Joshua Johnson. Page 49.

POPE, Nancy. Orphan of Henry Pope in account with Samuel Roe. D. 1796. Page 50.

NEWSUM, Sampson. Account current. Signed, Robert Andrews, Ex. Audited by William Chambless and Richard P. Clements. D. 1779. R. April 17, 1798. Page 50.

MYRICK, Henry. Account current. Signed, William Chambless. Among items: paid Fanny Myrick balance due her from her guardian Henry Myrick; paid Henry Myrick ditto; paid Owen Myrick ditto; paid John Myrick ditto; each paid the same amount of his estate,- Sally Blow; Nancy Fort; Fanny Myrick and Owen Myrick; cash paid Owen Myrick, guardian of Lucy Myrick, cash paid myself as guardian of John Myrick. Audited by Richard P. Clements and John Taylor, Jr. R. April 17, 1798. Henry Myrick, grandson of Henry Myrick. Page 51.

BRANTLEY, Etheldred. Estate appraised by William Edmunds, William Blunt and John Moore. D. Dec. 22, 1797. R. April 17, 1798. Page 53.

WARREN, Benjamin. Estate appraised by Boaz G. Summerell, Henry Branch, Henry Summerell. D. Dec. 8, 1797. R. Page 54.

KIRBY, Ann. Leg.- my land to be equally divided between Moody Kirby, Gideon Bell and Lewis Kirby; rest of estate to be divided between my brothers and sisters,- William Kirby, Moody Kirby, Zelby Drake, Gideon Bell, Pamelia Bell and Elizabeth Bell. Ex., Moody Cotton.(?). D. R. May 21, 1798. Wit. Nicholas Williams Gilas (?) Kirby, James Bell. Page 55.

DAWSON, Tuke. Parish of Nottoway. Leg.- wife Ann; three daughters, Rebecca, Elizabeth and Catherine Denson; son

Joseph Dawson. Exs., wife Ann and Peter Denson. D. Jan. 14, 1789. R. May 21, 1798. Wit. Joseph Hill, Mills Denson, Rebecca Denson. Page 56.

DREWRY, Humphry. Estate appraised by William Wellons, Arthur Bowing and Jesse Gardner. R. May 21, 1798. Page 56.

DREWRY, William. Estate appraised by William Blunt, John Blunt and Henry Blunt. Signed, Robert Mabry. D. Jan. 8, 1798. R. Page 57.

BARHAM, Charles. Estate account. Signed, Edward Fisher, Adm. Audited by John Simmons, Sr., Thomas Turner and Mark Nicholson. D. Feb. --, 1796. R. May 21, 1798. Page 58.

BROCK, James. Leg.- wife Hannah; grandson John Chavos, commonly called John Brock, son of my daughter Elizabeth Brock; daughter Sarah Read. Extx., daughter Sarah Reas. D. Feb. 5, 1798. R. May 21, 1798. Wit. John Day, John Kindred. Page 58.

HASTY, Moses. Account current. Signed, Edward Fisher. Audited by John Simmons, Jr., Thomas Turner, Mark Nicholson. D. Feb. 25, 1792. R. May 21, 1798. Page 59.

GILLIAM, Arthur. Estate appraised by Moses Foster, Robert Nicholson and William Butts. Signed, Robert Goodwyn. R. May 21, 1798. Page 60.

BARHAM, James. Account current. Legacies paid Joel Barham, James Barham, Judkins Barham, Samuel Barham, Timothy Barham, John Barham, Joel Harris, William Holleman, Bailey Barnes, John Meacome and Edward Fisher. Audited by John Simmons, Jr., Thomas Turner and Mark Nicholson. R. May 21, 1798. Page 61.

ALLEN, Arthur. Account estate. Signed, William Boykin, Adm. D. 1777. Legacies paid James Allen, Benjamin Allen, Ann Allen, Polly Allen, Holland Allen. Audited by Sol. Holmes, Timothy Atkinson. R. May 21, 1798. Page 62.

RANDOLPH, Temperance. Account current. Signed, William Brown, Adm. Audited by William Blunt and Richard Harrison. D. 1796. R. July 16, 1798. Page 62.

TURNER, Henry. Account current. Signed, William Turner, Ex. Paid Will Turner his legacy; paid widow's dower. Henry Turner in account with William Turner; refers to his orphans and expenses paid for John Turner, Elizabeth Turner and Benjamin Turner. D. 1792. R. July --, 1798. Page 63.

SMITH, Aaron. Of St. Luke's Parish. Leg.- estate to be used for the education of my children until son Thomas becomes twenty one; wife Rebecca; children, William Turner Smith; Thomas and Polly Smith. Exs., friends Thomas Holladay, Jr., and Benjamin Blunt. D. Feb. 4, 1798. R. May 21, 1798. Wit. James B. Womack, Burwell Westbrook, David Westbrook. Page 65.

CHARLES, Elenor. Estate appraised by Arthur Bowing, Henry Jones and Mills Daniel. R. July 16, 1798. Page 67.

SPIVEY, William. Appraisal. Signed, Britain Spivey and Benjamin Spivey. D. March 1794. R. July 16, 1798. Page 68.

BROCK, James. H. Cl. Servents(?), Thomas Jones, Drew Powell and John Woodward, Appraisers. D. July 14, 1798. R. July 16, 1798. Page 68.

BRYANT, William. Leg.- wife Sally, with reversion to son Cordal Bryant the land adjoining Edmund Barrett and Jacob Williams; another tract adjoining James Vick, Lewis Worrell, Giles Joyner and Jordan Vick; to Lewis Worrell. Exs., wife Sally and Drewry Bryant. D. Sept. 20, 1797. R. July 16, 1798. Wit. Lewis Worrell, Nathan Williams, Jacob Williams. Page 69.

WADE, Wilson. Estate appraised by Cordial Row, Mills Daniel and Jacob Corbett. D. Nov. 9, 1797. R. July 16, 1798. Page 70.

CRUMPLER, Beasant. Estate appraised by Britain Boykin, James Johnson and Arthur Crumpler. R. Aug. 20, 1798. Page 71.

BRADSHAW, Thomas. Leg.- wife Susannah; son William; my three children, William, Martha and Edia Bradshaw. Exs., wife Susannah and son William Bradshaw. D. Sept. 16, 1796. R. Aug. 20, 1798. Wit. Elizabeth Hedgepeth, Micajah Griffin, Jr., Elizabeth Griffin. Page 72.

ROGERS, Collins. Estate appraised by Thomas Gilliam, Robert Nicholson and Henry Simmons. Signed, James Guy (?). D. Jan. 28, 1797. R. Aug. 20, 1798. Page 73.

WILLIAMS, Henry. Account current. Signed, Arthur Bowen, Adm. D. 1788. Paid William Boykin, guardian of Sally and Elizabeth Williams; paid Shadrack Corbett for his wife; paid Elisha Whitney for his wife. Audited by Sam. Kello and Saml. Kello, Jr. R. Aug. 20, 1798. Page 74.

NEWTON, Alice. Estate appraised by Nathan Bryant, J. Kindred, Drew Powell. Signed, William Newton. D. April 1793. R. Aug. 20, 1798. Page 74.

CLIFTON, Cordey. Estate appraised by Henry Harrison, James Lundy and Richard Harrison. D. May 25, 1798. R. Aug. 26, 1798. Page 75.

SUTER, Arthur. Inventory. Signed, John Suter. D. Oct. 20, 1796. R. Aug. 20, 1798. Page 76.

TAYLOR, Temperance. Inventory. Signed, John Taylor. R. Oct. 15, 1798. Page 77.

JONES, Sarah. Leg.- mother-in-law my estate received from my deceased husband, Charles B. Jones; reversion to Ann Jones and Elizabeth B. Jones, daughters of the said Elizabeth, Hannah B. Jones, daughter of Thomas Jones, Rebecca W. Jones, daughter of aforesaid Thomas; Susannah Drew, Sarah Norfleet Blunt, daughter of William Blunt; my mother Mary Gee; Lavinia Norfleet Gee, daughter of my father-in-law James Gee, all the land I am entitled to in Southampton and Northampton, N. Car., at the death of my brother to my mother Mary Gee; uncle John Wilkinson. Exs., uncle John Wilkinson and father-in-law James Gee. D. Sept. 21, 1798. R. Oct. 15, 1798. Wit. Martha Williamson, Henry Coker, James Wilkinson. Page 77.

BITTLE, Robert. Inventory. Signed, William Bittle, Ex. D. Aug. 19, 1795. R. Oct. 15, 1798. Page 79.

NEWSUM, Patience. Parish of St. Luke. Leg.- Isham Newsum and Sally his wife; to my said daughter Sally Newsum with reversion to Martha Gilliam and Elizabeth Newsum; Martha Taylor with reversion to my five granddaughters, Nancy, Sally N., Betsey, Mary and Lucy Taylor; Patsey G. Newsum; two daughters, Martha Taylor and Sally Newsum's children. Ex., friend Thomas Jones. D. June 1, 1798. R. Oct. 15, 1798. Wit. Thomas Pope, John Barrow, Lucy Barrow. Page 80.

BUTTS, Elizabeth. Parish of St. Luke. Leg.- son Benjamin; daughter Jenny; my four children, namely Benjamin, Robert, Jenny and Polly Nicholson. Exs., friends Zeblon Lewis and Benjamin Lewis. D. July 2, 1798. R. Oct. 15, 1798. Wit. Zebulon Lewis, Richard P. Clements, James Simmons. Page 81.

BYRD, James. Estate appraised by John Blunt and William Blunt. D. Oct. 28, 1790. R. Oct. 15, 1798. Page 82.

DELOACH, Richard. Estate appraised by Thomas Edmunds, Eth'd Edmunds and Nathan Pope. D. Jan. 26, 1798. R. Oct. 15, 1709. Page 82.

DELOACH, Sarah. Estate appraised by Thomas Edmunds, Eth'd Edmunds and Nathan Pope. D. Jan. 26, 1798. R. Oct. 15, 1798. Page 82.

VICK, Joshua. Appraisal of estate remaining in the hands of Elizabeth Wilson, the relict of said Joshua at the time of her death. Signed, William Vick. Appraisers:- William Murfee, Richard Blow and Amos Stephens. Signed, Jeremiah Drake as to the negroes. R. Oct. 15, 1798. Page 83.

COBB, Exum. Parish of Nottoway. Leg.- surviving brothers and sisters; sister Rebecca Mecom; my negro man to be hired during the life of Mrs. Mary Norseworthy and the money to be divided as above. Ex., Charles Briggs, Jr. D. Jan. 26, 1798. R. Oct. 15, 1798. Wit. James Irwin, Ann Salter, Will Hines. Page 85.

BRADSHAW, Thomas. Estate appraised by Arthur Bowing, Miles Griffin and John Worrell. D. Sept. 6, 1798. R. Oct. 15, 1798. Page 86.

BRISTER, Samuel. Leg.- wife Mary; daughter Polly; daughter Frances Brister. Ex., John Urquhart. D. Jan. 29, 1798. R. Oct. 15, 1798. Wit. William Urquhart, Samuel Johnson. Page 86.

VICK, Joshua. Account current of the estate lent to his wife Elizabeth with William Vick, Adm. and to which is added the estate of Elizabeth Wilson, formerly Elizabeth Vick, decd. Audited by George Gurley, Richard Blow and Drewry Beal. R. Sept. 17, 1798. Page 87.

REESE, Mary. Account current. Signed, Randolph Reese. Audited by Zebulon Lewis and Thomas Peete. D. Feb. 1796. R. Oct. 15, 1798. Page 88.

BIRD, James. Account current. Signed, John Wilkinson, Adm. Audited by William Blunt and Willie Francis. D. Oct. 29, 1791. R. Oct. 15, 1798. Page 88.

BROCK, Thomas. Estate appraised by William Atkinson, Joseph Hart and Richard Hart. D. 1797. R. Dec. 17, 1798. Page 89.

LANCASTER, Rebecca. Estate appraised by Edward Bailey, John Womble, David Davis. D. Jan. 1798. R. Dec. 17, 1798. Page 91.

JOHNSON, Sarah. Parish of St. Luke. Leg.- son Harris; grandson Jordan Johnson the land on which Hannah Johnson now lives; granddaughter Rebecca Harrison; Nancy Johnson; to all my granddaughters, Rebecca Harrison, Nancy Johnson, Sally Johnson, Martha Johnson and Molly Johnson. Exs., son Harris Johnson and Joel Johnson. D. Feb. 2, 1795. R. Dec. 17, 1798. Wit. Stephenson Blake, Lucy Blake, Spratley Stevenson. Page 92.

WORRELL, Josiah. Estate appraised by James Barnes, Newit Vick and Micajah Edwards. D. March 1795. R. Dec. 17, 1798. Page 93.

MAGET, Nicholas. Estate appraised by William Bryant, Sr., William Bryant, Jr., and Exum Everett. D. Nov. 1797. R. Dec. 17, 1798. Page 94.

MYRICK, Ann. Estate appraised by Howell Jones, Richard Blunt, John Barham and Benjamin Barham. D. Feb. 16, 1796. R. Dec. 17, 1798. Page 95.

NICHOLSON, Charles. Leg.- father, after emancipation of slaves. Exs., father Harris Nicholson and Dr. Anselm Bailey, Jr. D. Aug. 27, 1798. R. Dec. 17, 1798. Wit. Benjamin Hines, John Foster. Page 97.

CLAUD, Edwin. Estate appraised by Burwell Whitfield, David Westbrook and John Blake. D. April 19, 1798. R. Dec. 17, 1798. Page 97.

JOHNSON, Stephen. Estate appraised by Jo. Scott, Lem . Hart and Absalom Joyner. D. March 29, 1797. R. Dec. 17, 1798. Page 99.

SPEED, Charles. Leg.- grandchildren, Suckey, Dickey and Milly Speed, children of my son Henry Speed, decd.; son William; wife Jenny; son Thomas; grandchildren Charles, Rhoda and Patience, the children of my son William. Exs., friends, Charles Briggs and Henry Briggs. D. Sept. 20, 1798. R. Dec. 17, 1798. Wit. Joseph Vick, Silas Pledger, Lucy Pledger. Page 100.

MYRICK, Howell. Manumits slaves. Leg.- estate to my children, Evans; William M.; Howell; William and Benjamin; sister Sarah Evans to live with my children. Exs., brother Etheldred Evans and Sally Evans. D. May 15, 1798. R. Dec. 17, 1798. Will proved by Anthony Evans and John Applewhite. Page 101.

WARREN, Benjamin. Leg.- wife Mary Warren. Extx., wife Mary Warren. D. Dec. 16, 1794. R. Wit. Edm. Tyler, Sally Warren. Page 102.

RAWLINGS, Edwin. Estate appraised by Clait Clifton, John Rives and John Lundy. D. Sept. 1, 1798. R. Nov. 19, 1798. Page 102.

CRAFFORD, John. Account current. William Hines, Adm. Paid Mary Crafford for the benefit of the children, proportional part paid to the following:- Mary Crafford's dower, Henry Crafford, Elizabeth Crafford and Lucy Crafford. Audited by Robert Goodwyn and Charles Briggs. R. Nov. 20, 1798. Page 103.

WILLIAMS, Benjamin. Account current. Signed, Josiah Vick, Ex. and Mary Williams Extx. Paid expenses of Polly and Egbert Williams. States the widow had married John Williams. (large estate, covering fourteen pages.) D. 1787. R. Aug. 21, 1798. Page 104.

JUDKINS, Jordan. Estate appraised by Edward Bailey, Thomas Pretlow and John Womble. D. Oct. 1798. R. Jan. 22, 1799. Page 118.

CALVERT, Christopher. Account current. Signed, Samuel Calvert, Adm. Paid taxes in the Borough of Norfolk; the heirs of the estate paid their proportional part; paid Albridgeton Jones in right of his wife Frances; Mathew Calvert; Ann Holt Calvert; Cornelius B. Calvert; Samuel Calvert; Spencer Pierce in right of his wife Mary; heirs of intestate the proportional part of the estate of Cornelius B. Calvert's estate; paid Peggy Calvert, widow. Audited by J. Vick and Thomas W. Clements. D. 1789. R. Jan. 22, 1799. Page 120.

SPIVEY, John. Account current. Signed, Charles Briggs, Adm. Paid bond to the estate of his father William Spivey. Audited by Benjamin Ruffin and Sampson Stanton. D. 1794. R. Jan. 22, 1799. Page 126.

JOYNER, Mary. Leg.- James Joyner; Ely Joyner, son of Joshua Joyner; Baker Joyner; Elizabeth Joyner of Jonas Joyner; Elisha Joyner of John Joyner; Shadrack Cobb; Joshua Joyner of John Joyner. D. Oct. 22, 1798. R. Jan. 22, 1799. Wit. Baker Joyner, Elizabeth Joyner, Shadrack Cobb. Page 127.

VICK, Simon. Leg.- Andrew Mack Mial; granddaughter Mason Vick; grandson Littleberry Vick; grandson John Vick; granddaughter Lucy Vick; grandson Peterson Vick; son Jacob; son Jesse; son John Vick. Ex., son Jacob Vick. D. Sept. 26, 1798. R. Jan. 22, 1799. Wit. Thomas Pope, Ben Gray, John Barrow, Jonas Bryant. Page 128.

PERSON, Anthony. Leg.- wife Elizabeth; provision for unborn child; brother John Person with reversion to the children of Henry Person's present wife. Exs., John Person and Richard Blunt. D. Aug. 20, 1798. R. Feb. 18, 1799. Wit. William Sturgeon, Henry Harrison, Henry Hayley (?). Page 128.

POND, Richard. Account current. Signed, Mary Pond and Drewry Pond. Paid Daniel Pond, son of Daniel Pond; Mathew Pond son of Daniel Pond his proportional part of his grandfather's estate. Audited by Edwin Gray and John H. Pond. R. Feb. 18, 1799. Page 129.

GRAY, Colonel Edwin. Account current. Signed, Edwin Gray Ex. Paid Edmund Blunt his portion of the estate. Audited by Benjamin Ruffin, Charles Briggs, Jr., and Charles Briggs, Sr. R. Feb. 18, 1799. Page 130.

WILLIAMS, Sion. Leg.- wife Mary; son Drewry; son John; daughter Frances Bun (?); son Burwell; son Jordan; son Jeremiah; daughter Polly; son Eley land adjoining Burwell Williams, Amos Council and Hardy Johnson; son Sion land adjoining John Williams, Titus Fowler and Burwell Williams. Friends Joseph Scott, Absalom Joyner and Samuel Rowe to partition land; rest of my estate to my children, Jordan, Silas, Benjamin and Lucy; the reversion of my bequest to my wife to my son George Williams. Exs., sons Drewry and Burwell Williams. D. Jan. 16, 1799. R. Feb. 18, 1799. Wit. Absalom Joyner, Cordall

Rowe, R. Johnson. Page 131.

BRITT, Benjamin. Estate appraised by Joel Edwards, Thomas Everett, George Edwards. D. Jan. 23, 1797. R. Feb. 18, 1799. Page 133.

TURNER, Arthur. Account current. Signed, Everett Turner. Audited by Joel Boykin, John Crumpler, Jacob Turner. D. Aug. 1797. R. Feb. 18, 1799. Page 134.

THORP, Jeremiah. Account current, with the Ex. Administrator. Paid Willey Thorp's legacy; paid Hardy Thorp; paid Lucy Long for her daughter Polly. Ex., Joshua Thorpe decd. Balance due the orphan of Mary Spencer, agreeable to will. Audited by John Williamson and James Lundy. R. Feb. 18, 1799. Page 134.

GARDNER, Joshua. Inventory. Signed, Henry Gardner and Ann Gardner. D. Dec. 16, 1793. R. April 15, 1799. Page 135.

CARR, Jesse. Estate appraised by Jacob Darden, Jordan Williams and Semour Vaughan. D. Jan. 28, 1797. R. April 15, 1799. Page 136.

PERSON, John. To be buried agreeable to the form established by the Ancient Freemasons. Leg.- nephew John Anthony Person at twenty one, reversion to surviving children of Henry and Polly Person, namely Rebecca, Elizabeth and Polly Person; neice Marianna Person at twenty one with reversion to Rebecca, Elizabeth, Polly and John Anthony Person; neice Elizabeth Person. Ex., Henry Person. D. Dec. 1, 1798. R. April 15, 1799. Wit. Thomas Holladay, William Sturgeon, Peter Blow. Page 137.

POND, Mary. (The elder). Leg,- daughter Mary Wood; Mary Pond, the wife of my grandson John Pond, Jr.; son John; children of my deceased son Richard Pond. Exs. John H. Pond and William Wellons. D. May 19, 1798. R. April 15, 1799. Wit. Dianna Pond, Samuel Pond, Benjamin Oney. Page 138.

TURNER, Ann. Estate appraised by John Suter, Pettway Johnson and Sam. Corbett. D. Jan. 18, 1799. R. April 15, 1799.

JONES, Lem[l]. Appraisal. (not signed). R. April 16, 1799. Signed, Joseph Jones, Ex. Page 140.

JONES, Lemuel. Account current. Signed, Joseph Jones. Audited by Edm. Tyler and John Clayton, Jr. R. April 16, 1799. Page 141.

GARDNER, Joshua. Account current. Signed, Ann Gardner and Henry Gardner, Exs. To cash paid Daniel Webb a legacy left his wife. Audited by Jacob Darden, Sr., and Jacob Darden, Jr. D. 1793. R. April 16, 1799. Page 142.

DARDEN, Ann. Estate appraised by Jacob Darden, Semour Vaughan, Jordan Williams. D. April 20, 1799. R. May 20, 1799. Page 143.

SIMMONS, Henry. Signed, Charles Briggs, Adm. Estate appraised by Micajah Ellis, John James and John Applewhite. D. Dec. 19, 1798. R. May 20, 1799. Page 143.

BLOW, Benjamin. Account current. Signed, James Blow. Audited
by James Millar and Jo. G. Blunt. D. 1797. R. May 20, 1799.
Page 145.

JOINER, Jesse. Parish of Nottoway. Leg.- wife Priscilla land
left me by Joseph Vick; son Lewis; son Amos land given me by
my father, on which Thomas Lowe now lives by rent; son Lemuel;
daughter Margaret; daughter Sally; daughter Elizabeth;
daughter Martha; daughter Levina Joyner. Ex., son Lewis
Joyner. D. Sept. 25, 1789. Wit. William Ingram, Lucy Joyner,
Lewis Joyner. Codicil leaving further bequest to son Lemuel
Joyner. 1798. Wit. Jos. Scott, Job Wright, George Camp.
R. May 20, 1799. Page 145.

MORRIS, Nicholas, Sr. Leg.- daughter Dizey Booth; daughter
Mary Pond; Elizabeth Nash, my housekeeper; son John. Ex.,
son John Morris. D. June 21, 1797. R. May 20, 1799. Wit.
William Briggs, Charles Briggs, Sr., Goodrich Wills. Page
147.

TURNER, John. Leg.- uncle Benjamin Turner; cousin Joseph
Turner. Ex., Thomas Holladay, Jr. D. April 2, 1799. R. May
20, 1799. Wit. Turner Newsum, Nathan Turner, Eliza Turner.
Page 147.

STEPHENSON, Sally. Widow. Parish of Nottoway. Leg.- son
William; daughter Sally; daughter Dizey; son Charles; son
Lemuel Stephenson. Ex., son Charles Stephenson. D. 1799.
R. May 20, 1799. Wit. Arthur Holleman, Benjamin White.
Page 148.

JARROTT, Fortunatus. Account current. Signed, John Jarrott,
Ex. Legacy paid John Jarrott; legacy paid Nancy Jarrott.
Audited by John Applewhite and Hardy Applewhite. R. June 15,
1799. Page 149.

RIDLEY, John E. Account current. Signed, William Wright, Ex.
Audited by Robert Mabry, Nathaniel Wyche and Lewis Thorpe.
D. 1794. R. July 15, 1799. Page 149.

THORP, Joshua, Jr. Inventory. Signed, Hardy Thorp, Adm. D.
Oct. 25, 1794. R. July 5, 1799. Page 151.

SMITH, Aaron. Estate appraised by Benjamin Blunt, Jr., Henry
Barrow and Jesse Holt. D. Aug. 1, 1798. R. July 15, 1799.
Page 151.

THORP, Joshua, Jr. Account current. Signed, Hardy Thorp, Adm.
Audited by Benjamin Blunt, Jr. and James Lundy. R. July 15,
1799. Page 152.

POND, Mary. Estate appraised by Richard Pond, Sr., Drewry Pond
and John Morris. D. May 1, 1799. R. Aug. 19, 1799. Page
152.

MYRICK, Ann. Account current. Signed, Howell Myrick, Ex.
Audited by Rand. Newsum and John Wall. D. 1796. R. Aug. 19,
1799. Page 153.

JOYNER, Jesse. Estate appraised by Kinchen Edwards, William
Beal, John Bryant. D. June 1, 1799. R. Aug. 19, 1799.
Page 154.

JOHNSON, Stephen. Account current. Signed, Benjamin Johnson,
Ex. Audited by William Crichlow and W. Evans. D. 1797. R.

Aug. 19, 1799. Page 154.

ATKINSON, Ann. Account current. Signed, Elias Atkinson, Ex. Paid legacies as follows: to Rachel Williams, Elisha Atkinson, Benjamin Delk, Ann Atkinson. Audited by Lazarus Cook and Drew Powell. D. 1795. R. Aug. 19, 1799. Page 155.

PAYN, Thomas. Estate appraised by Michael Warren and LtN (?) Fort. D. Dec. 4, 1796. R. Oct. 21, 1799. Page 156.

GARDNER, Ann. Leg.- son James; son Amos Gardner. Exs., friends Capt. Joseph Vick and Arthur Bowing. D. Aug. 22, 1799. R. Oct. 21, 1799. Wit. Benjamin Vick, John Adams. Page 157.

TAYLOR, John, Jr. Leg.- sons William and Henry at twenty one; wife; my children, William, Nancy, Elizabeth, Hannah and Henry Taylor. Exs., Robert Goodwyn, Ellis G. Blake. D. Feb. 10, 1799. R. Nov. 19, 1799. Wit. Ellis Gray Blake, Thomas Peete. Page 157.

HANCOCK, Samuel. Estate appraised by Benjamin Branch, Joseph Washington and James Johnson. R. Dec. 16, 1799. Page 158.

BRIGGS, Samuel. Leg.- half brother Henry Briggs, the plantation purchased of Richard Blow and Capt. Thomas Chappell, which was given me by my father, my wife to be allowed her right of dower; sister Martha Edmunds; half brother William Briggs; nephew David Edmunds; nephew George Edmunds, rest of estate to wife with reversion to my sister Edmund's children, namely Susan, Davy and George and my brother Charles Briggs' two cons, namely Samuel and Duncan. Ex., father Charles Briggs. D. Nov. 7, 1799. R. Dec. 16, 1799. Wit. Charles Briggs, Jr., Henry Davis, John Pitmon. Page 159.

PURSELL, John. Parish of Nottoway. Leg.- son Arthur land adjoining Valentine Jenkins and my father's line; son Peter; daughter Mary Pursell. Exs., sons Arthur and Peter Pursell. D. Sept. 5, 1799. R. Dec. 16, 1799. Wit. Valentine Jenkins, William Jenkins, Wilton F. L. Jenkins. Page 160.

CARSTARPHEN, John. Leg.- my estate to be equally divided between my wife Margaret; son John; David and Margaret Carstarphen. Exs., wife Margaret, Arthur Bowing, Mical Griffin. D. Nov. 26, 1799. R. Dec. 16, 1799. Wit. Jacob Turner, Jr., John Worrell, Jr., John Worrell. Page 161.

WORRELL, Richard. Leg.- wife Tabitha, reversion of bequest to son Richard then to Shadrack and William Worrell; Edith Council. Exs., Arthur Bowing and Mical Griffin, Jr. D. Oct. 12, 1799. R. Dec. 16, 1799. Wit. Temperance Council, Edwin Council, Robert Council. Page 161.

LUNDY, John. Leg.- to John Rivers. Exs., friend John Rivers and Henry Smith. Wit. Benjamin Blunt, Jr., James Wilkinson, John McLemore. D. Oct. 18, 1799. R. Dec. 16, 1799. Page 162.

WILLIAMS, George. Leg.- son Absalom, land adjoining my son Charles in Hertford Co., N. Car.; son Solomon; rest of my estate to my following children, Absalom, Elisosha Grantham, Janet Story, Elizabeth Darden & Nancy Sandefur. Ex. son Absalom Williams. D. Aug. 24, 1797. R. Dec. 16, 1799. Wit. Isaac Williams, Josiah Williams, Daniel William, Arthur Carr. Page 162.

BOWDEN, Robert. Account current. Signed, Thomas Bowden, Ex. Legacies paid the following, - widow, Betsey Bowden, Sally Bowden, Milly Bowden and William Bowden. Audited by John Crumpler and John Pursell. R. Dec. 16, 1799. Page 163.

WILLIAMS, Robert. Parish of St. Luke. Leg.- wife Rebecca, with reversion to grandson Elisha Williams, son Robert Williams. D. July 14, 1783. R. Jan. 20, 1800. Wit. George Gurley, William Thomas, George Gurley, Jr. Probation granted Robert Williams. Page 164.

JOINER, Jacob, the younger. Leg.- wife Martha; son Charles; son Jacob, the land bought of Dr. Thomas Peete to the line of land conveyed by me to Jesse W. Moore; son Charles the land devised me by my uncle Bridgman Joiner; son William land devised me by my father and lands purchased of Silas Lowe; daughters, Polly, Sally and Martha Joiner; provision for unborn child. Exs., wife and brother Jordan Joiner. D. Sept. 20, 1799. R. Jan. 20, 1800. Wit. Samuel Slade, Peggy Powers, Martha Vitching, J. Denson. Page 164.

VICK, William. Leg.- wife Elizabeth until my daughter Polly Boykin arrives to age of eighteen or marries; daughter Polly. My land in Raleigh, N. Car. to be sold and the proceeds to be divided between my daughters. Exs., wife, friend Benjamin Blunt, Burwell Vick, James Gee. D. June 15, 1799. R. Jan. 20, 1800. Wit. Lazarus Cook, George Gurley, Jr., Holladay Revell. Page 166.

REESE, Olive. Account current. Signed, Robert Mabry Adm. Paid Nathan Felts his wife's portion of her father's estate; Olive Reese, Admtx. Paid each the same amount, Edwin Bass, John McLemore and Kinchen Turner the guardian of Lewis, orphan of Edward Reese. Bond received of Roger Reese Administrator of John Reese, who was the former Adm. of Olive Reese. Audited by Benjamin Blunt, Jr. and John Williamson. D. April 3, 1795. R. Jan. 20, 1800. Page 167.

LITTLE, William. Account current. Signed, Robert Mabry, Adm. Audited by Benjamin Blunt, Jr., John Williamson. D. May 29, 1794. R. Jan. 20, 1800. Page 168.

VAUGHAN, William. Appraisal. Etheldred Brantley one of the appraisers died before the return was made. Appraised by Jesse Holt and Henry Bittle. Signed, Thomas Vaughan and Thomas Turner, Exs. R. Jan. 20, 1800. D. Nov. 7, 1794. Page 170.

MEGLAMORE, John. Leg.- wife Letty, with reversion to son John; daughter Sally Whitehorn with reversion to her children; daughter Betty Baley; daughter Hetty; granddaughter Nancy Lunday. Ex., son John Meglamore. D. May 15, 1797. R. Jan. 20, 1800. Wit. William Newsum, Peter Simmons, Robert Myrick. Page 171.

ADAMS, Henry. Leg.- wife Mary; daughter Martha Tyler; daughter Julia Adams. Ex., son-in-law Edward W. Tyler and friend Robert Goodwyn. D. Jan. 7, 1800. R. Feb. 17, 1800. Wit. Jeremiah Cobb, Samuel Kello, Robert Exum. Page 172.

JOYNER, Jacob. Estate appraised by John Davis, J. Vick and Burwell Williams. D. Jan. 29, 1800. R. Feb. 17, 1800. Page 173.

MITCHELL, Abraham. Estate appraised by Marthew Wills, James Edwards and Jacob Darden, Jr. D. Oct. 26, 1798. R. Feb. 17, 1800. Page 174.

WOMMACK, Thomas. Account current. Signed, Carter Wommack, Ex. Paid to John McLemore, guardian to Betsey, James, Polly and John McLemore, the legacies left them by the decedent. Audited by Byrd Lundy and James Lundy. D. 1795. R. Feb. 17, 1800. Page 176.

LUNDY, Elizabeth. Account current. Signed, Lunsford Lundy, Adm. Audited by Robert Mabry and James Harris. D. 1795. R. Feb. 17, 1800. Page 177.

BRYANT, Jonas. Leg.- son Ephrim and his wife the land adjoining Richard Williams, Lewis Bryant, with reversion to my son Bennet William Bryant; wife Sarah land adjoining the line of Lewis Bryant and James Bryant; daughters, Lyddy and Pherebah Bryant. Exs., brother Lewis Bryant and friend James Maget. D. Nov. 7, 1799. R. Feb. 17, 1800. Wit. James Bryant, Winna Cook, Elizabeth Stricklin. Page 177.

BRACY, Ann. Leg.- brother Francis Bracy; sister Mary Wright; sister Elizabeth Beal; sister Petiance Johnson; sister Miriam Edwards. Ex. friend Kinchen Edwards. D. Jan. 22, 1800. R. Feb. 17, 1800. Wit. John Fowler, William Fowler, Polly Beal. Page 179.

TURNER, Pass. Account current. Signed, Henry Jones, Adm. Audited by Joseph Denson, Arthur Bowing and Presley Barrett. D. Dec. 1797. R. Feb. 17, 1800. Page 179.

CHARLES, Jethro. Account current. Signed, Eleanor Charles, Extx. Audited by Daniel Simmons and Arthur Bowing. D. 1797. R. Feb. 17, 1800. Page 180.

JONES, James. Account current. Signed, Hanselm Jones, James Jones and Jordan Jones. Audited by Charles Briggs and Burwell Barrett. D. 1798. R. Feb. 17, 1800. Page 181.

NEWSUM, Benjamin. Leg.- daughter Elizabeth, reversion to granddaughter Dysa Newsum and grandson Crafford Newsum. Ex. Charles Briggs Nicholson. D. Dec. 14, 1799. R. Feb. 17, 1800. Wit. Charles B. Nicholson, Crafford Newsum, Hamlin Harris, William Applewhite. Page 181.

POND, Drewry. Leg.- My land adjoining John Pond and John Morris to be sold. Beloved wife with reversion to all my children. Exs., brother Samuel Pond, William Wellons and Thomas Wood. D. Feb. 15, 1800. R. Feb. 17, 1800. Wit. Robert Magee, Diana Pond, Nancy Magee. Page 182.

SIMMONS, Henry. Account current. Signed, C. Briggs, Adm. Audited by Benja. Ruffin and Phillip Davis. D. Dec. 19, 1799. R. April 21, 1800. Page 182.

BRACY, Ann. Estate appraised by William Edwards, William Beal. Signed, Kinchen Edwards, Ex. R. April 21, 1800. Page 183.

IVY, Henry. Leg.- wife Charlotte; son William; provision for unborn child. Ex., father George Ivy. D. Feb. 2, 1800. R. April 21, 1800. Wit. Lunsford Lundy, Edward Bass, Robert Murrell (copied by clerk when will was proven, Robert Murry) Page 184.

SEWARD, Edwin. Leg.- nephew Coufield Seward; mother Sarah Thorpe, with reversion to sister Mary Harris then to her surviving children. Exs., nephew Coufield Seward and kinsman Byrd Lundy. D. Jan. 27, 1796. R. April 26, 1800. Wit. Henry Ivy, Joel McLemore, John McLemore. Page 185.

LUNDY, Priscilla. Estate appraised by James Harris and Peyton Lundy. (Peyton Harris died before signing). D. Feb. 9, 1799. R. April 21, 1800. Page 186.

WILKINSON, John. Leg.- son Nathaniel when twenty one land on the Meherrin River and two lots in Murfreesboro; son John Lewis Wilkinson land partly in Virginia and N. Car. with reversion of bequests to my brother James Wilkinson. Exs., brother James Wilkinson, brother-in-law Benjamin Weldon Williamson, friend Ely Eley and Cordall N. Bynum. D. June 11, 1799. R. April 21, 1800. Will proved by James Gee, S. Kello, William Blunt, John Bynum and Benjamin W. Williamson and Simon Everett. James Wilkinson and Benjamin W. Williamson. Page 186.

BROWNE, John. Nuncupative will. Proved by Albridgton Browne, Margaret Browne, John McLemore and Richard Harrison. Leg.- wife and her heirs. Brothers, Jesse and James Browne to manage his affairs. D. Jan. 21, 1800. P. Jan. 28, 1800. R. April 21, 1800. Page 188.

M. NEIL, James. Estate appraised by Lem^1. Hart, William Crichlow and Robert Ricks. D. Aug. 22, 1795. R. April 21, 1800. Page 188.

HARRIS, Ruth. Parish of St. Luke. Leg.- grandson Anthony Harris, son of Simon Harris; granddaughter Sally Harris, daughter of Mary Barrom; grandson William Turner, son of Thomas Turner. Ex. John Bynum. D. June 10, 1799. R. Oct. 21, 1799. Wit. Sally Phillips, Rebkah Williams, Henry Turner. Page 189.

CLAUD, Sally. Leg.- son-in-law Hartwell Felts, he to take my son Nuet Newson to raise; daughter Dority Claud; estate to be divided among Dority Claud and Sally Claud and son Nuet Newsom. Exs., Humphrey Drewry and Harris Johnson. D. Feb. 15, 1800. R. March 18, 1800. Wit. Isaac Sullivan, Dorcas Tanner, Sally Felts. Page 190.

BRANTLEY, Etheldred. Appraisal (not signed). D. May 22, 1797. R. June --, 1800. Page 190.

MCLAMRE, John. Estate appraised William Champless, Frederick Parker and Richard P. Clements. D. March 7, 1800. R. May 19, 1800. Page 192.

DREWRY, Humphrey. Account current. Signed, Samuel Drewry. Legacies paid Rebecca Drewry, Joseph Drewry, Charles Simmons in the right of his wife Hannah and the children of Robert Andrews. Audited by Samuel Calvert and Charles Briggs, Jr. D. Dec. 1796. R. July 21, 1800. Page 194.

JONES, Thomas. Leg.- wife Sally if she educates my children, Hannah Briggs Jones and Rebecca Williamson Jones; nephew William Henry Gee, son of James Gee. Exs., wife and friends James Gee and Sam^1. Edmunds. D. May 20, 1799. R. July 21, 1800. Wit. Henry Blunt. Nathl. Edwards, John Whitehead. Page 195.

SUMMERELL, James. Leg.- son Sikes, land adjoining the line of Lucy Williamson and Thomas Summerell; wife Anna with reversion to son Lemuel Butts Summerell; daughter Lucretia Branch; my three daughters, Diana, Sally and Eleanor Summerell; son James Summerell. Exs., William Boykin and Silas Summerell. D. Feb. 24, 1800. R. July 21, 1800. Wit. Benjamin Brister, William Holden, Shadrack Boykin. Page 197.

WHITEHEAD, Arthur. Estate appraised by Jacob Darden, Jr., James Maget and Holliday Revell. D. Dec. 28, 1799. R. July 21, 1800. Page 198.

WHITEHEAD, William. Account current. Signed, John Whitehead, Adm. (A merchant) Audited by James Wilkinson, James Gee, Will Edmunds (Edmund Turner was also appointed an auditor, but did not serve). D. Dec. 1, 1796. R. July 21, 1800. Page 200.

DAVIS, Henry. Inventory. D. Sept. 12, 1798. Page 202.

Account current. Signed, Henry Davis, Ex. Audited by Charles Briggs, Sr., Phillip Davis. R. July 21, 1800. Page 203.

JOINER, Molly. Estate appraised by Lewis Joyner and Amos Joyner. D. Feb. 8, 1799. R. Aug. 18, 1800. Page 204.

BRITT, Benjamin. Account current. Among items, paid to the widow. Audited by Joel Edwards and Thomas Everett. R. Aug. 18, 1800. Page 204.

POPE, Josiah. Estate appraised by Sam. Edmunds, Etheldred Edmunds and John Kindred. D. Jan. 24, 1800. R. Aug. 18, 1800. Page 205.

ELLIS, Henry. Estate appraised by George Edwards, Edmond Barrett, Jacob Barrett. R. Aug. 18, 1800. Page 207.

CORBITT, Jacob. Estate appraised by Thomas Camp, Lemuel Rowe; Joseph Turner. D. May 1, 1800. R. Aug. 18, 1800. Page 207.

CARTER, Joseph. Inventory. Signed, George Gurley and Richard Blow. R. Aug. 18, 1800. Page 208.

STEVENSON, Thomas. Parish of Nottoway. Leg.- wife Nancy with reversion to my three sons, Josiah, Martin and Bennett; daughter Elizabeth Stevenson. D. Aug. 29, 1800. R. Oct. 20, 1900. Wit. Arthur Doles, Edward Hatfield, Mary Stevenson. Page 208.

SUMMERELL, Boaz Guin. Leg.- wife Elizabeth; son Thomas; son William; daughter Nancy Bools if her husband will pay twenty pounds to my daughter Milly; son Herod; after sale of my estate the money to be divided among all my children or their representatives. I desire that John Clayton, Jr., Joseph Jones, William Boykin and Henry Branch, or any three of them to divide my land. Exs., sons William and Thomas Summerell. D. Feb. 1, 1797. R. Oct. 10, 1800. Wit. John D. Houssman, Joseph Jones, Elizabeth Jones. (Joseph Jones was a Quaker). Page 209.

SEWARD, Edwin. Estate appraised by John Williamson, James Lundy and George Ivy. R. Oct. 20, 1800. Page 211.

WILLIAMS, George. Estate appraised by James Harrison, Jesse Battle and William Hart. D. Dec. 23, 1799. R. Oct. 20, 1800. Page 211.

BROWNE, Olive. Inventory. Signed, Thomas Lane, Ex. D. Oct. 20, 1800. Page 213.

WASHINGTON, George. Of Nottoway Parish. Leg.- son William; wife Easter; grandson Henry Johnson, son of Mathew Johnson and Sally his wife; remainder of estate to be sold and divided among all my children then living. Ex., son William Washington and David Washington. D. Oct. 2, 1800. R. Oct. 20, 1800. Wit. Joseph Bracy, Arthur Drake, James Whitehead. Page 213.

STEWARD, Liddia and Benjamin Steward. Account current. Signed, James Hosea. Audited by John Simmons, Jr. and Micah Ellis. D. 1799. R. Oct. 20, 1800. Page 214.

CARSTARPHAN, John. Estate appraised by Pressley Barrett, Benjamin Bradshaw, Charles Councill and Jeremiah Joyner. D. Jan. 2, 1800. R. Dec. --, 1800. Page 215.

WORRELL, Richard. Estate appraised by Shadrack Worrell, Charles Council and Joseph Turner. R. Dec. --, 1800. Page 216.

COBB, Lazarus, Sr. Leg,- son Josiah, land adjoining William Harcum and the land which was my brother William Cobb's; son Nicholas; son Lazarus, land adjoining my brother Henry Cobb and David Edwards; son Frederick; daughter Mildred Cobb. Exs., sons Frederick and Nicholas Cobb. D. Oct. 3, 1800. R. Dec. --, 1800. Wit. Jacob Darden, Jr., William Harcum, Victor Eley. Page 127.

FORT, Joshua. Account current. Signed, Lewis Thorp, Ex. Paid Selah Fort one third of the money from Thorp's estate; the following paid the same amount,- Priscilla Fort, Joshua Fort, William Barnes, Elizabeth Fort, Joseph Fort, John Fort, Edwin Fort, Temperance Fort. Credited Joshua Fort's proportional part of the estate of Joseph Thorp. Audited by James Lundy, Robert Mabry and Nathaniel Wyche. D. Aug. 1, 1800. R. Dec. 15, 1800. Page 218.

ELLIS, Henry. Account current. Audited by Jesse Barrett and Jacob Barrett. R. Dec. --, 1800. Page 219.

PERSON, Anthony. Estate appraised by John Moore, John Blunt and Richard Harrison. Signed, Richard A. Blunt. R. Jan. --, 1801. Page 220.

INDEX

N.B. Parenthesis indicates number of times name appears on the page.

(?), Absalom 34
(?), Arthur 25
(?), Ben 74
(?), Faithy 109
(?), George 31
(?), J. 142
(?), John 30
(?), Jonas 125
(?), Lewis 21
(?), Thomas 30
-ort, John 79
Abraham, John 22
   Martha 22
   Sarah 22
Adams, Arthur 141
   Benjamin 141 (will), 148, 155
   Benjamin Jr. 139
   Betsey 141
   Charlotte 141
   Collen 83
   Darling 83
   David 1
   Edwin 83
   Elizabeth 45
   Henry 45 (will)(3), 46, 56, 72, 83, 136, 139, 141, 167 (will)
   Howell 84
   John 1 (2), 45, 61, 136, 166
   Julia 167
   Margaret 141
   Martha 45
   Mary 1, 45, 63, 74, 83, 167
   Nancy 141
   Priscilla 57
   Reuben 45
   Robert 79
   Sally 141
   Tamer 94
   Thomas 74, 94 (will) (3)
   Thomas Jr. 84
Adkins, Howell 23
   Mial 23
Adkinson, William 151
Allen, Ann 159
   Anne 104
   Arthur 33, 45, 57 (2), 61, 79, 104, 108, 159
   Benjamin 159
   Holland 159
   James 33, 104, 159
   Martha 33
   Mary 33, 122
   Polly 159
   Priscilla 132
   Richard 132
Alsobrook, Selah 62
Ammon, Thomas 4
Andrews, Ann 56, 139 (2)
   Benjamin 136, 139, 147
   David 45, 54
   Drewry 131
   Drury 56, 139
   Elizabeth 146

Andrews (cont.)
   Elizabeth Bryan 56
   Faithy 144 (will)
   Henry 45, 47
   James 64, 146
   Jane 54
   John 56 (2), 89, 91, 96, 115, 116, 121 (2), 131, 133 (3), 139 (3), 146 (will)
   Lucy 35, 89, 107, 146 (2)
   Maney 125
   Mary 108
   Rhody 154
   Richard 45, 47, 133
   Robert 21, 30, 39, 56, 61, 77, 78, 128, 158, 169
   Sally 146
   Sarah 56
   Stephen 108
   Thomas 56, 139
   W. 37
   Will 43
   William 18, 20, 56 (will) (2), 58, 61, 90, 93, 98, 125, 139
   William Sr. 139
Applewhaite, Henry (H'y) 12, 59, 90
Applewhite, Ann 97, 141 (will), 145, 152
   Anne 84
   Arthur 7, 97 (2), 106, 107, 109, 113 (2), 119, 126, 129, 137, 152 (2)
   Beckey 97
   Benjamin 97, 141
   Hardy 97, 141, 143, 165
   Henry 33, 55 (2), 97 (will) (2), 100, 152 (2)
   Henry Wills 113
   Janey 97
   Joan 141
   John 97 (2), 102, 113, 119, 141 (2), 145, 148-149, 152 (3), 155, 162, 164, 165
   Mills 152
   Nancy 97, 141
   Priscilla 97
   Rebecca 141
   Salley 97
   Sally 103
   Thomas 97, 113 (will), 114, 141, 154
   William 97, 141, 149, 168
Archer, Edward 92, 131
   John 92, 131
   Richard 131
   Samuel 131
   William 131
Arlington, Ann 20

Arlington (cont.)
   Benjamin 20
   John 20 (will)
Armistead, Anthony 111
   Frances 24
Armstrong, Mary 77
Arrington, (?) 146
   Ann 21
   Arthur 11, 21, 147
   Benjamin 20, 22, 32
   Elizabeth 21, 24
   H. 146
   Jesse 20, 21, 56, 59, 76, 119 (2), 126, 130
   John 1, 4, 20, 21 (will) (3), 22, 24, 32, 117
   Lucy 119
   Martha 119
   Patience 21, 24
   William 49
Artice, John 19
Artis (Artiss), Abraham 55, 59
Ashley, Edmund 105
Atherton, Betty 31
   Dorothy 118
   Temperance 84
Atkins, James 24
   Mial 90
   Savory 94
   widow 10 (lame son)
Atkinson, (?) 105
   Amy 23
   Ann 49, 112, 143 (will) (2), 157, 166 (2)
   Betty 69
   Burwell 34
   Celia 49
   Easter 49
   Elias 112, 143, 157, 166
   Elisha 112, 143, 166
   Elizabeth 62, 69, 76
   Hardy 23 (2), 45, 102, 112 (will)
   Holland 69
   Isham (Isam) 105 (2), 107
   James 49, 76, 85
   Jesse 105
   Joel 67
   John 48, 76, 83, 132, 138, 148
   Joseph 83 (2), 104
   Lucy 49, 83
   Martha 105
   Mary 69, 83
   Mial 83 (will)
   Michael 49
   Nancy 84
   Nathan 49
   Olive 4
   Patience 49 (2)
   Patty 69
   Phebe 105, 143
   Priscilla 49

Atkinson (cont.)
  Robert 47
  Sally 69
  Samuel 8, 105 (will)
    (2), 107, 112
  Sarah 49, 118
  Thomas 14, 24, 49
    (will) (3)
  Thomas Sr. 60
  Timothy 14, 15, 69
    (will) (3), 91, 116,
    121, 133, 143, 152,
    159
  William 83, 133, 145,
    157, 161
Austin, Charles 72
  John 72
  Molly 72
  Richard 72
  Ruth 72 (2), 76
  William 72 (will), 76
Avent, Ben. 138
Avery, Edward 66
  Elizabeth 66
  Etheldred 66
  Fortune 66, 80 (will)
  Joel (Joell) 56, 66, 90
  Martha 66
  Richard 28, 34 (2), 66
    (will), 99
  Thomas 66
Avory, Richard 70
(?), Henry 117
B--ing, Arthur 153
Bage, Rebecca 81
  Thomas 81 (2)
Bailey, (?) 101
  Abidan (Abidian) 98
    (2), 103 (3)
  Absalom (Absolum) 98
    (2), 103, 122, 149
  Amey 82, 96
  Anselm Jr. (Dr.) 162
  B. 62, 105
  Barbary 63
  Barnaby (Barnabey) 17,
    31, 32, 46, 49 (2),
    51, 52 (2), 57 (2),
    60, 62, 63, 72, 73,
    77, 99 (will), 101,
    135
  Barnaby Jr. 31
  Barnaby Sr. 31
  Benjamin 17, 22, 35,
    38, 51, 63, 64, 80,
    103 (will), 110, 133
  Charles 57, 63, 72,
    139
  Charles Sr. 155
  Edmund 98 (2), 103 (2)
  Edward 156, 157 (2),
    162, 163
  Elijah 98, 103
  Elizabeth 63, 134
  Exum 98
  Hansel 133
  Hartwell 63
  Hartwell (Capt.) 151,
    156
  Jacob 96, 140
  James 99
  John 13, 14, 31 (3),
    33, 40, 47, 50, 52,
    54 (2), 56, 57 (2),
    60, 62, 63, 64
  John Sr. 51
  Joseph 98, 103

Bailey (cont.)
  Joshua 64, 80, 98 (3),
    101, 103 (2), 122,
    148, 149
  Lemuel 134, 149 (2)
  Lucy 46, 65, 99
  Martha 98, 103, 119
  Mary 46, 99 (2), 101,
    114, 135
  Peter 57, 139, 148, 156
  Richard 46, 72, 77, 93,
    99 (2), 103, 104
  Robert 65 (will) (2),
    67, 72, 89, 106
  Sally 81
  Samuel 19, 93, 110
  Sarah 63 (will) (2),
    64, 65, 103, 134
    (2), 157
  Sharah 57
  Trial 35, 103, 119
  Tryal 98 (2)
  Walter 65
  William 13, 14, 31,
    57 (will), 60, 62,
    98, 133, 149, 155,
    156, 157
Bailey (?), Benjamin 111
Bailey (?), Hannah 109
Baisden, James 115
  Mary 17
Baker, Benjamin (Col.)
    134
  Elizabeth 156
  James 4
  Lawrence (Gen.) 156
    (2)
  Richard 118
  Simmons J. (Dr.) 156
    (2)
  Wm. H. 138
Baley, Betty 167
Ballard, Elisha 28
Barcroft, William 2
Barden, William 72
Baret, Martha 74
  Simon 74 (2)
Barham, Benjamin 7, 11,
    17, 43, 46 (2), 64,
    78 (will) (2), 122,
    130 (2), 141, 162
  Benjamin Jr. 155
  Charles 2, 7, 10, 11,
    13, 14, 17 (2), 19
    (2), 22, 44, 125
    (will), 131, 159
  Charlot 152 (2)
  Elizabeth 17 (2), 78,
    108, 125
  Fanny 78
  Hannah 152
  Henry 141
  Howel 152 (2)
  James 10, 11, 41, 44,
    46, 59, 125 (3), 126
    (will) (3), 131, 159
    (2)
  Joel 125 (2), 126 (2),
    152 (2), 153, 159
  John 78 (2), 97, 99,
    108, 126, 159, 162
  Johnson 17
  Judkins 126 (2), 159
  Lucy 78
  Martha 17
  Mary 4, 17, 78, 97,
    126, 141

Barham (cont.)
  Milley 125
  Nancy 144
  Peggy 152 (2)
  Phebey 126
  Polly 144
  Robert 17 (will) (3),
    19, 125, 152 (will)
  Sally 152 (2)
  Samuel 126 (2), 159
  Sarah 10, 17
  Thomas 17, 108
  Timothy 159
  Timothy Thorpe 126
  William 77, 78 (2)
Barker, Lucy 87
  Mary 68, 87
  Nancy 87
  River 45
  William 87 (will), 98
Barlow, Celia 99, 135
  Samuel 20
  Tamer 52
Barly, Hannah 109
Barmer, William 67
Barnes, Ann 140, 146
  Bailey 28, 147, 159
  Benjamin 20, 28 (2),
    33, 37, 41, 79
    (will), 80 (will),
    87, 94, 146
  Bowling 147
  Britain (Britian,
    Britten, Britten)
    28 (2), 33, 49, 133
  Burwell 23, 28, 71,
    90, 112, 115
  Buxton 28
  Chastity 28
  Cordall (Cordal) 133,
    153
  Edee 28
  Edward 13, 19, 23
    (will), 30
  Elizabeth 13, 23 (2),
    51, 54, 146 (2)
  Ferebo 58
  Henry 9
  Jacob 19 (2), 21, 23
    (2), 30, 32, 33, 38,
    41, 49, 72, 77, 79,
    80, 87, 88, 93,
    100, 112, 129, 135,
    146 (will) (2), 148
  James 23, 72, 120,
    140, 146 (4), 162
  Jeansy 133
  John 19, 79, 96, 133
    (2), 147, 158
  Johnson 74
  Joshua 23, 28 (will),
    29, 33, 42, 146
  Josiah 49, 146 (2)
  Katherine 91
  Lucy 28
  Martha 23, 46, 133
  Mary 46, 79 (2), 87
    (2), 88, 94 (2),
    133
  Milly 79, 80, 87
  Nathan 38, 46 (2), 49,
    70, 75, 77, 79, 80,
    83, 96, 98, 112,
    113, 115, 117, 121,
    130, 133 (will),
    135, 136, 146

175

Barnes (cont.)
  Peninah 79, 87, 129, 135
  Pening 80
  Phereby 28
  Priscilla 23
  Rebecca 145
  Sally (Salley) 28, 118
  Sarah 4, 33, 77
  Thomas 35 (2), 45 (will), 48, 146 (2)
  Will 158
  William 45, 79 (2), 80, 87 (3), 94 (2), 96 (2), 104, 114, 135, 171
Barram, Benjamin 76
  Charles 48
Barredell, Robert 84
Barret, Edmond Sr. 127
  Jacob 41
  Mary 38 (2)
  Sarah 38
Barrett, Burrell 156
  Burwell 168
  Charles 89
  Edmond 9 (will) (4), 170
  Edmund 71, 72, 96, 104, 146, 160
  Hancock 89
  Jacob 9, 20, 49 (2), 87, 132, 155, 170, 171
  Jesse 146, 171
  Mary 23
  Presley (Presly, (Pressley) 89, 110, 135, 168, 171
  Rawleigh 92
  Rolley 89 (2)
  Sarah 9 (2)
  Simon 9
  William 82, 89 (2), 92, 107, 108, 114 (will) (2)
  William Jr. 116
  William Sr. 89 (will), 92
  Willis 114
Barrom, Mary 169
Barron, D. 106
Barron (?), John 106
Barrow, D. C. 123
  Daniel 21, 68
  David (D^d.) 88, 100 (2), 110, 118 (2), 119, 122, 124 (2), 125 (4), 132, 133
  Edith 41, 63
  Elizabeth 28 (3), 34
  Fortune 28
  Henry 135, 156, 165
  Hosea 34
  Jane 28
  Jean 34
  John 28, 34, 36, 41, 62, 66, 68 (will)(3), 71, 83, 85, 89, 93, 94, 98, 99 (2), 101, 107, 110, 119, 120, 130, 135, 156, 161, 163
  John Jr. 36, 50, 63
  Joseph 48
  Lucy 161
  Penelope 48

Barrow (cont.)
  Phebea Hill 68
  Phoeby H. 83
  Sarah 28, 85
  Simon 28 (2), 34
  Thomas 28 (will) (3), 29, 34 (2), 51
  William 68
Barrow (?), D. 106
Basden, Hugh 29
  James 22, 29
  James Jr. 17, 47
Bass, Ann 82
  Arthur 79 (2), 82, 83
  Becky 120
  Burges 79
  Charles 52 (2), 82 (will) (4), 100, 143
  Charles Jr. 100
  Creasy 83
  Dixon 82
  Edward 168
  Edwin 82, 133, 167
  Hardiman 82
  Hardy 79, 100
  Henry 79, 82 (2)
  Howell 82
  James 13, 34, 52
  Jordan (Jordin) 82, 122, 126
  Joshua 79 (will), 80
  Mary 13
  Middy 13
  Newit 82
  Patience 113
  Roger 82
  Selah 79
  Tabitha 82, 122
  Thomas 79
Bassett, John 58, 59
Battle, James 90, 125
  Jesse 171
  Martha 48
  William 38, 48
Bavion (?), John 2
Baxter, David 6, 7
Bayley, Benjamin 117
  John 29
  Mary 29
Beal, Abigail 58
  Asa 135
  Benjamin 43, 59, 91, 100, 106, 109, 110, 112
  Benjamin Sr. 110(will), 138
  Drewry 101 (2), 103, 104, 105, 108, 119, 161
  Drury 75 (2), 86
  Edwin 140
  Elizabeth 168
  Ephraim 144
  Hannah 135
  Isbel 110
  John 27, 30, 31, 32 (2), 34, 35 (2), 37, 40, 41, 42, 43, 54, 58, 59, 60, 75 (2), 82, 102, 110 (2)
  Joshua 31, 54, 58 (2), 86, 100, 107, 109, 122, 126
  Lillia 75
  Peter 58
  Polly 168
  Priscilla 97

Beal (cont.)
  Rachel 110
  Richard 30, 108, 112, 126
  Richard Jr. 59
  Sarah 100
  William 97, 165, 168
Beale, Abia 153 (2)
  Alice 153
  Asa 145, 153 (2)
  Benjamin 76, 102, 119, 150
  Benjamin Jr. 147 (will)
  Burwell 75, 76, 100
  Dickey 153
  Drewry 97, 104
  Eady 153
  Elijah 153
  Elizabeth 147 (2)
  Hardy 75 (will)
  Jacob 67 (2), 153
  Jeremiah 147
  John 58, 76, 100
  Joshua 119
  Martha 78
  Millia 153
  Nancy 153
  Patty 76
  Peggy 147
  Priscilla 76, 100
  Richard 144, 153 (will)
  Richard Jr. 144
  Sarah 75
  Shadrack 147
  Silah 153 (2)
  Silvia 147
  William 76 (will) (3), 78 (4), 100 (2), 144
Beall, Burwell 71
  Drury 71
  John 71 (2)
  Lillia 71
Beaton, John 97, 151
Beel, Abigail 43
  Benjamin Jr. 24
  Benjamin Sr. 24
  Burwell 94
  John 30, 43 (will)(2)
  Joshua 43 (2)
  Lydia 38, 43
  Martha 30 (2)
  Mary 30
  Richard 30 (2), 43, 54 (2)
  Richard Jr. 30 (2)
  Sallie 94
  Sarah 94 (will)
  Thomas 30 (will)
Beel (?), George 74
Beele, Martha 30
  Thomas 30
Bell, Burrel 114
  Elizabeth 158
  Elizabeth Champion (Elizabeth C.) 149 (2)
  George 74, 142
  Gideon 158 (2)
  Henry 142
  J. 148
  James 74, 157, 158
  James P. 149
  Pamelia 158
  Richard 153
Benet, Mary 12

Bennet, Constance 37
  James 137
  John 37 (will) (3)
  Lucy 43
  William 37
Bennett, Betha 16
  Constant 8
  Elias 127
  James 148, 152
  John 127 (will), 158
  Lucy 21 (2)
  Lemuel 127
  Martha 127
  Mary Rose 127
  Moses 21, 127
  Rebeccah 127
  Samuel 127
  Sarah 16
  William 16 (2), 19, 27, 30, 127 (2), 129, 158
Bentel, Joseph 143
Bentel (?), Mary 143
Berryman, John 143
  John Jr. 120
Best, James 35
Bidgood, John 73, 76
Binns, Charles 109
Birchett, James 91
Bird, James 161
  John 77
Birdsong, Charles 100, 113, 121, 137, 141, 152 (2), 153
  Charles Hancock 129
  John 128
  Miriam 129 (2)
  Sally 120
Bishop, Ann 150 (2)
  Daniel 150
  John 110, 111, 114, 132
  Joseph 150 (will), 153
  Mark 150
  Martha 150
  William 150 (2)
Bittle, Benjamin 141
  Drewry 33
  Drury 92
  Elizabeth 33, 141
  Henry 85, 101, 104, 108, 115, 120, 141 (2), 167
  John 18 (will), 87, 141
  Judith 20
  Kirby 141
  Lucy 18, 88
  Mary 68
  Robert 26, 32, 41, 45, 57 (2), 59, 64, 92, 141 (will), 160
  Sarah 18, 23
  William 18, 33 (will) (3), 35, 38, 115, 120, 128, 141 (2), 144, 160
  William Sr. 18
Black, James 96
  Mary 134
Blair, John 5
Blake, Ben. 158
  Benjamin 117 (2), 130
  Ellis Gray (Ellis G.) 166 (2)
  Etheldred 117
  James 117
  John 66, 68, 104, 112, 117 (2), 130, 157, 162

Blake (cont.)
  Lucy 162
  Maney 143
  Mary 118
  Samuel 93, 97, 117 (2)
  Stephenson 143, 162
  Thomas 97, 117 (will) (2), 130
Bland, Mary 28
Blayley, Benjamin 111
Blow, Ann 109 (2)
  Benjamin 109, 165
  Henry 139, 149 (will)
  James 109, 165
  John 32, 38 (2), 62
  John T. 94, 104, 111 (2), 114, 121, 123, 124 (2), 128, 129 (2), 139, 140
  John T. Jr. 142, 151
  John T. Sr. 120, 141, 156
  John Thomas 44, 45 (2), 47, 50 (2), 52, 53, 58, 66, 67, 77 (2), 79, 84, 89, 90, 91, 99, 126, 140
  John Thomas Sr. 109, 137
  Lucy 37, 57
  Maray 54
  Martha 37 (2), 44
  Mary 37, 49, 84, 140
  Micajah 149
  Michael 149
  Peter 109, 164
  Richard 37 (3), 44 (2), 46, 54, 61, 68 (2), 72, 93, 109 (will), 119, 121, 123, 124, 151, 161 (2), 166, 170
  Richard Jr. 44 (2)
  Samuel 13, 15, 16, 24 (2), 37 (will), 39, 60
  Thomas 76, 109, 134
  Thomas R. 149
  Sally 149 (2), 158
  William 120, 141, 149, 151
Blunt, Ann 50, 73 (2), 109, 151
  Ben. 119, 148
  Benjamin 5 (will) (3), 7, 11, 45, 47, 48, 52, 61, 64, 68 (2), 69, 71, 73, 77 (2), 86, 90, 99, 104, 112 (2), 139, 141, 148, 149, 150, 159, 167
  Benjamin Jr. 86, 120, 128 (2), 133, 137, 149 (2), 153, 165 (2), 166, 167 (2)
  Benjamin William 141
  Edmund 68, 73, 104, 163
  Elizabeth 11, 73, 141 (will), 151
  George 136, 141 (will) (4), 148
  Henry 5, 6, 9, 11, 12, 15 (will), 17, 73, 142, 143 (2), 150(2), 156, 159, 169

Blunt (cont.)
  James 73
  Jo. G. 165
  John 5, 11, 32, 40, 41, 42, 43, 44, 50, 51, 52, 56, 60, 61 (2), 62 (2), 64 (2), 65, 76, 77 (2), 78, 80, 86 (3), 93 (2), 94 (3), 97, 103, 106, 110, 112 (2), 117, 126, 130, 142, 147, 159, 161, 171
  Mary 11, 15, 85, 112 (2)
  Priscilla 5, 11 (2), 60, 93 (will)
  Richard 150 (2), 157, 162, 163
  Richard A. 171
  Samuel (Sam) 141 (2)
  Sarah 11, 15 (2), 73
  Sarah Norfleet 160
  Thomas 15 (2), 17, 18, 40, 46, 53, 55, 56, 73 (will) (3), 104, 108, 109 (2)
  William 5, 11, 26, 32, 34 (3), 36, 40, 42 (2), 43, 44 (2), 48, 50, 52, 56, 59, 60, 62 (3), 64, 69, 73, 77 (2), 81, 83, 94, 103, 110, 112 (2), 150 (2), 158, 159 (2), 160, 161 (2), 169
  William (Col.) 116
  William Sr. 60 (2), 105, 112
Boasman, Mary 19
Bock (?), William 3
Bond, Tabitha 149
Bools, Henry 127
  Nancy 170
Boon, Eday 14
  John 81
  Thomas 14, 39
  William 14, 39
Boone, Mary 73
  Thomas 14
Booth, Arthur 17, 32, 47 (will) (2), 49, 51, 56, 57, 62
  Benjamin 57
  Beverley (Beverly) 17, 70 (2), 77 (2), 94
  David 70
  Diana 139
  Dizey 165
  Elizabeth 70 (2), 77
  Faith 17
  Faitha 51 (2)
  James 17, 47 (2), 51, 56, 57, 62, 151, 153
  John 17, 51 (2), 139 (2)
  Lucy 47
  Martha 47, 99
  Mary 62
  Maze 70
  Michael 47, 57, 62
  Moses 17 (3), 32, 47 (2), 51 (2), 60, 70 (3), 77, 139 (will) (2),
  Moses Sr. 141

Booth (cont.)
  Patience 17, 51
  Patty 57, 63
  Peter 139 (2), 141, 151
  Phillip (Phillips) 51, 139
  Robert 17 (will)(3), 32, 62, 70 (will) (3), 72, 77
  Sarah 17, 47, 51, 57 (2), 62
  Sary 17
  Shelly 17, 51 (will), 52, 57
  William 51, 57, 62
  William G. 47
Boothe, Beverley 130
Bosman, Howell 53
Bowden, Betsey 167
  Bille 111
  Elias 111
  Elizabeth 111
  Mary 111
  Milly (Milley) 111, 167
  Rady 111
  Robert 111 (will), 120, 167
  Sally (Salley) 111, 167
  Thomas 167
  William 167
Bowdin, Thomas 111
Bowen, Arthur 27, 107, 160
  Benjamin 27
  Charles Butts 64
  John 12, 27 (will), 28, 76
  Jonathan 27
  Martha 27
  Mary 27 (2)
  Rebecca 27
Bowers, Britain 68
  Britton 140
  John 116, 118, 152
  Lucretia 140
  Mary 5
  Middey 68
  Randolph 68 (2)
  William 5, 50, 68 (will), 81
  Willis 152
Bowin, Arthur 16, 98, 114, 119
  John 7, 16 (will) (6), 18, 19 (2)
  William 49
Bowing, Arthur 75, 108, 116, 119, 122, 127, 132, 146, 159 (2), 161, 166 (3), 168 (2)
  James 117
  Lucy 117
  Mary 117, 123
Bowser, Ann 126
Boykin, Arthur 89, 93, 100, 114, 115 (2), 120, 123, 133, 134
  Britain (Brittain) 117, 155, 160
  Charlotte 115
  Cherry 15
  Daniel 142
  Dorcas 140
  Elizabeth 15, 142
  Ely 142

Boykin (cont.)
  Frederick 142
  Jesse 62
  Joel 140, 142, 164
  John 7, 10, 15 (3), 16, 17, 24, 40, 42, 82 (2), 87, 140, 142
  John Sr. 142 (will)
  Keziah 142
  Mathew 65, 113, 142
  Mrs. 98
  Nancy 146
  Polly 167 (2)
  Sally Williams 115
  Sarah 82
  Shadrack 117 (2), 170
  Simon 40, 42, 66, 115 (will) (4), 121
  William 19, 48, 100, 106, 117 (3), 140, 159, 160, 170 (2)
  William Jr. 83
  William Sr. 117 (will)
Boyle, Edward 18
Boyt, Elizabeth 114
Bracey, Frances 94
  Francis 33, 43, 94
  Sarah 30
Bracy, Ann 94, 168 (will) (2)
  Francis 91, 168
  Joseph 171
  Mary 94
  Meriam 94
  Patience 94
  Sarah 95
Braddy, Margaret 3 (will)
Bradsha, Elizabeth 16
Bradshaw, (?) 37
  Ann 25
  Arthur 25, 91, 122
  Avey 73
  Benjamin 15, 18, 27 (2), 35, 39, 43, 53, 116, 119, 127 (2), 131 (will) (3), 171
  Chasey 124
  Diana 24
  Edia 160
  Elias 73 (2)
  Elizabeth 25, 73 (2), 103
  Gelina 131
  Honour 25, 73
  Jacob 111, 127, 131 (2), 132
  Joseph 24 (2), 25 (will) (2), 27 (2), 34, 37, 39, 57, 73 (will) (3), 75, 91, 98, 116 (2), 122, 124, 131
  Martha 25, 103, 124 (will), 160
  Mary 25, 53, 131
  Philip 131 (2)
  Richard 131
  Ridley 131
  Rody 124
  Semor 73 (2)
  Susannah 160 (2)
  Thomas 25, 73, 91, 92, 122, 160 (will), 161
  William 73 (2), 131 (2), 160 (3)
Branch, Arthur 105
  Ava 142

Branch (cont.)
  Bailey 44, 47 (2), 50, 52, 86 (2), 108
  Benjamin 3 (3), 47, 54 (2), 58, 86, 105, 148, 166
  Drew 158
  Drewry 86
  Dunn's (?) 135
  Edmund 47
  Elizabeth 3 (will)(2), 73, 86
  Francis (Fran[s]) 124, 137, 143, 150
  George 3, 29, 30 (3), 47 (will), 50, 52 (2)
  Henry 47, 86, 158 (2), 170
  Howell (Howel) 47, 73, 86 (will), 89, 105
  Jesse 86
  Lidia 3
  Lucretia 170
  Lucy 47
  Martha 47, 54 (will), 57, 58, 86
  Mary 16, 47
  Mary Deloach 54, 58
  Moses 105 (2), 107
  Newsom 47 (2), 50, 89
  Newsum 148, 157
  Ogborne 105 (will), 107
  Olif 108
  Peter 86
  Ruth 43 (2)
  Sarah 36, 105
  William 43 (will), 44, 68, 105, 142
Brantley, Britain 66
  Etheldred 103 (2), 115 (2), 116, 138, 143, 158, 167, 169
  Henry 147
  James 135
  John 6, 9, 20, 31
  Joshua 93, 99, 101
  Phillip 2, 3, 6 (2), 9, 12 (2)
  Thomas 31
Braswell, Jacob 71
  Jesse 23, 48
  Sarah 3
Brewer, Ann 80 (2)
  Elizabeth 80
  Frances 80
  George 28
  Hardy 80 (3)
  Henry 80
  Isham 113
  Jacob 80
  Jean 113
  Jesse 80
  John 37, 80 (will)(2)
  Joseph 116
  Mial 37
  Pacience 80
  Reace 80
Brewter, Mary 3
Brewton, Sarah 3
Briant, Alse 19
  William 19
Bridger, James 36, 115
  John 115
  Martha 115 (2)

Bridger (cont.)
    Peggie 143
    William 76, 115
Bridgers, Patsy 115
Briggs, Ann 84
    C. 168
    Charles 8, 21, 24, 32,
        37 (2), 39, 44, 47,
        51, 63, 68, 71, 72,
        74, 84 (2), 89, 91,
        105, 109, 111 (2),
        122, 131, 136, 137
        (2), 139, 142, 143
        (2), 147, 157, 162
        (2), 163, 164, 166
        (2), 168
    Charles B. 136
    Charles Jr. 131, 144,
        155, 161, 163, 166,
        169
    Charles Sr. 163, 165,
        170
    Duncan 166
    Elizabeth 37
    Emily 156
    Henry 43, 47, 48, 50,
        51 (2), 52 (2), 62,
        69 (2), 81, 84 (will)
        (2), 86, 91, 99, 111
        (2), 124, 127, 130,
        162, 166
    Nathaniel 117
    Samuel 166 (will) (2)
    Sarah 111
    William 165, 166
Briount, John 106 (will)
    (2)
    Mary 106
    Sarah 106
Brister, Ann 142 (2)
    Benjamin 142, 170
    Frances 161
    Hannah 142
    James 142
    John 142
    Mary 161
    Polly 161
    Samuel 114, 142 (will),
        144, 161 (will)
    Willis 142
Bristol, Samuel 93
Britain, Elisha 81
    John 35
    see also Brittain
Britt, Arianton 127
    Benjamin 155
    Breasant 146
    Benjamin 4, 13, 15, 69,
        91, 104 (will) (2),
        127, 128, 146, 164,
        170
    Betsey 122
    Britain (Brittain,
        Britten, Britton) 61,
        104, 128, 140, 142,
        144 (2), 146, 152
    Britain Sr. 144
    Caty 122
    Edward 47, 88, 122 (2)
    Edward Sr. 122 (will)
    Henry 76
    Holland 104
    James 76
    Jesse 76 (2)
    John 30, 66, 76 (2),
        87, 120, 127 (will),
        134, 146

Britt (cont.)
    John Sr. 76 (will)
    Johnson 122 (2)
    Jordan 104
    Joseph 104 (2), 127,
        146
    Martha 119
    Marthat 76
    Mary 127
    Mathew 61, 104
    Nathan 132
    Pamelia 144 (2)
    Patsey 144
    Polly 146
    Priscilla 127
    Sally 104, 115
    Sarah 122
    Tamer (Tamor) 127, 146
        (2)
    Thomas 121
    William 76, 127
Brittain, John 18
    see also Britain
Brittle, John 148, 156,
    157
    Kirby 69
Brock, Benjamin 103, 157
    Burwell 98
    Dorothy 51
    Elizabeth 159
    Hannah 159
    James 159 (will), 160
    John 157, 159
    Lucy 157
    Polly McKenny 157
    Sarah 98 (2), 103
    Thomas 45, 47, 58, 101,
        103, 110, 133, 157
        (will), 161
    Thomas Ellis 157
    William 157 (2)
Bromadge, Christopher 96
Brooks, Thomas 62
    William 84, 115 (will),
        120
Broom, William 9 (2)
Brown, Ann 67
    Charles 1
    Jane 39
    Jean 121 (will)
    Jesse 6, 12 (2), 14,
        17
    John 21, 22, 39 (will)
        (2), 42, 44, 53, 58
        (2), 73, 76, 85
        (will)
    Michael 59
    Olive 39, 58, 85 (2)
    Samuel 15, 52
    William 67, 159
Browne, Albridgton 148,
    169
    Ann 133 (2)
    Anthony 148
    Atkinson 48
    Benjamin 118
    Benjamin Edwards 133
    Daniel 140
    Dickins 48
    Dr. 71, 111
    Esther 45, 86
    Henry 72, 73, 86
    Holland 33
    Jack 48
    James 148, 169
    Jenny 48

Browne (cont.)
    Jesse 29 (2), 33 (2),
        41, 45, 47 (will)
        (2), 51, 86 (will),
        89, 148 (4), 169
    John 94, 148, 169
        (will)
    Margaret 169
    Martha 133
    Mary 133
    Mary Mason 133 (2)
    Mourning 33
    Nancy 56
    Olive 145 (will), 171
    Parsons 48
    Parthenia 48
    Patience 140
    Sally 86
    Samuel 47, 48, 133,
        148 (2)
    Samuel (Dr.) 117
    Samuel Ridley 148
    Tabitha 41
    Thomas 33 (will), 35,
        37, 86
    William 133 (2)
Browning, John 4
Bruce, James 4
Bryan, Alice 2
    Ann 2 (2)
    Elizabeth 2
    Guil (?) 2
    John 2
    Lewis 2
    Morning 2
    Rebecca 2
    Robert 2 (will) (2)
    Sarah 2
    Thomas 2 (2)
    William 2 (2)
Bryant, Alce 19
    Benjamin 49
    Bennet William 168
    Celia 94
    Colia 60
    Cordal 160
    Davis 74
    Drewry 160
    Elizabeth 22, 24
    Ephraim (Ephrim) 125,
        168
    James 65, 75, 104, 120,
        125, 168 (2)
    John 11, 20, 24 (2),
        26, 30, 106 (will)
        (3), 108 (2), 110
        (3), 149, 165
    Jonas 100, 104 (3),
        163, 168 (will)
    Lewis 24 (will) (2),
        55, 65, 74, 104
        (will) (3), 105,
        127, 137, 168 (3)
    Lewis Jr. 26
    Lyddy 168
    Mary 5, 23 (will), 26,
        106 (2), 110
    Mathew 152, 153
    Nathan 61, 82, 94,
        104, 107, 116, 160
    Pherebah 168
    Polly 61
    Robert 4, 5, 127, 134
    Sally 160 (2)
    Sarah 104, 106, 127,
        168
    Seley 104

Bryant (cont.)
  William 20, 24, 28, 49,
    61, 157, 160 (will)
  William Jr. 162
  William Sr. 157, 162
Buffkin, John 79
Bull, Lindy 44
Bullock, Priscilla 95
Bulls, Benjamin 39
  Jesse 39 (2), 119
  John 39
  Martha 39
  Patty 39
  William 5, 28, 39
    (will) (3)
Bun (?), Frances 163
Bunn, Ann 9
  Olive 91
  Patience 9
  Sarah 9
Burgess, Albridgton
    Samuel Hardy 156
  Elizabeth Matilda 156
  H. John 139
  Henry John 156 (will)
  Sarah 156
  Thomas 12
Burn, Ann 80
  David 79 (will) (2),
    80
  Dorcas 25
  Hardy 25, 80
  Jacob 88
  Patience 80 (3)
  Sampson 79
Burnell, Charity 61
    (will), 62
  Nanny 61
Buskin, John 51, 71
Butler, Henry 93
Butt, Peter 4
Butts, Benjamin 73, 81
    (2), 90, 122, 161
  Betty 81
  Daniel 73, 81, 127,
    143, 146
  Elizabeth 73 (2), 81,
    122, 161 (will)
  Fanny 122
  Henry 150
  James 73, 81, 101, 118,
    129, 133, 136, 138,
    157
  Jenny 161
  Jesse 73
  John 73, 81, 97
  Lucy 73, 81
  Mary 47, 73, 99
  Molly 81
  Peter 1 (2), 2 (3), 6,
    10, 16, 47, 53, 61,
    72, 73, 81 (will),
    90
  Sarah 52 (2), 73
  Thomas 56, 65, 72, 73,
    74, 78, 81 (4), 86,
    90, 134
  Thomas Clement
    (Clements) 73, 81
  William 72, 73, 81,
    126, 134, 159
Buxton, Abenezer 134
  Joseph 134
  Martha 124, 134
Bygrave, Robert 1, 7, 11
Bynum, Ann 62
  Benja. 73

Bynum (cont.)
  Benjamin 20 (2), 24,
    25, 26, 29, 30, 46,
    60, 61 (2), 73
  Benne 22
  Bennett 60
  Betsey 73
  Bryant 73
  Colen Whitehead 73
  Collin 61
  Cordall 107, 130
  Cordall Norfleet
    (Cordall N.) 60, 61,
    116, 169
  Ea. 46
  Eliby 73
  Elizabeth 5, 60 (will),
    62, 66 (3)
  Elizabeth Sugars 61
  Jennett 22
  John 62, 169 (2)
  Lewcy 20
  Lucy 54
  Martha 51, 62
  Michael 52, 60 (2), 61
    (will), 73 (2)
  Mille 22
  Milly 60
  Nathan 73
  Selah 61
  Sugars 22
  Turner 22 (2), 61, 73
  William 3 (2), 5, 8
    (2), 13, 19, 32, 46,
    58, 60 (2), 61 (2),
    62 (will) (4), 66,
    110
Byrd, Arthur 84 (3)
  Charles 84
  James 84, 161
  John 84 (will) (2)
  Moses 84
  Natah 84
  Philip 84
  Priscilla 123
  Susannah 84
  Tabitha 123
Calthorp, A. 60
  Charles 51
  Ellenmere 73
  Henry 126
  James 126
  John 126 (will) (2)
  Joseph Phillips
    Charles 9
  Nowell 126
Calthorpe, Anne 29
  Anthony 29, 51, 64 (2),
    122
  Charles 12, 29 (will),
    31, 32, 34
  Diana (Dianah) 51, 64
  Edward 29 (2), 64 (2)
  Elener 64 (will)
  Elener Clifton 64
  Elizabeth 29
  James 113, 134 (will),
    149
  James Butts 29, 142,
    149
  Lucy 99
  Martha 29
  Mary Bailey 99
  Sarah 29 (2)
Calvert, Ann Holt 163
  Christopher 122, 163
  Cornelius B. 163 (2)

Calvert (cont.)
  Mathew 109, 163
  Peggy 163
  Samuel 109, 137, 145,
    148, 152, 163 (2),
    169
Camp, George 132, 165
  Thomas 150, 170
Campbell, Betty 17
Camps, Thomas 110
Capel, Sterling 85, 142
Capele, William 145
Caple, Thomas 14
Care, Robert 109
Carle (?), Joseph 2
Carlile, Thomas 151
Carr, Abigail 109
  Arthur 166
  Betsey 134
  Charlotte 147
  Dickinson 109
  Elizabeth 45
  Elizabeth Daughtrey
    123
  Grace 31
  James 128
  Jesse 109, 147, 164
  John 31 (2), 32, 35,
    37, 109 (will) (2),
    111, 121, 134 (2)
  Joshua 113
  Lawrence 109, 123
  Mary 2
  Mary Jean 113
  Rebecca 31
  Robert 8, 24, 27, 31
    (will) (3), 32 (2),
    35 (2), 45, 67, 83,
    109, 113
  Sarah 31
Carrel, Jesse 111, 157
  Thomas 108
Carrell, Jesse 54, 60,
    63, 156
  Mary 19
  Sarah 54
  Thomas 44, 49, 50
Carroll, Charity 64
  Elizabeth 64
  Lucy 64
  Patty 64
  Priscilla 64 (3)
  Samuel 64
  Thomas 64 (will) (2)
Carstaphen, John 91
Carstaphney, John 86
Carstarphan, John 119,
    171
Carstarphen, David 166
  John 116, 132, 166
    (will) (2)
  Margaret 166 (3)
Carter, Joseph 170
  Ralph 82
  Sarah 141
Cary, Ann 111
  Elizabeth 11, 36 (2),
    58
  James 1
  James Jr. 1
  Miles 11, 22, 28, 29,
    36, 38 (will) (2),
    72, 85, 104, 126,
    139
  Nathaniel 38
  Richard 38
  William 42

Cashell, John 59
Cashiel (?), Josiah 139
Cathan, John 69
Cathen, Josiah West 103
Caul (?), Sally 144
Cell (?), John 68
Chalmers, David 97
Chambless, William 125, 145, 153, 158 (2)
Chambliss, William 143, 147, 149 (2)
Champless, William 169
Chanel, James 83
Channel, James 109
  John 41
  Joseph 43
  Judith 22
  Mary 109
Channell, James 83, 103
  John 55
  Thomas 125
Chapman, John 5
Chappel, Thomas 15, 39
Chappell, James 69, 121
  Thomas 16, 31, 158
  Thomas (Capt.) 166
Chapple, James 83 (2), 107
Charity, Joseph 99
Charles, Charles 158
  Eleanor (Elenor) 158 (will), 159, 168
  Elizabeth 158
  Jethro 116 (3), 141, 153, 168
  Martha 116
  Mary 141 (2)
  Mathew 18 (2), 26 (3), 30, 70, 71, 97, 116 (2), 119, 127, 141 (will), 146
  Rebecca 18 (will), 21
  William 158
Chavos, John 159
Cheatham, Andrew 124
Cheaves (?), Winney 90
Check, Sarah 132
Childs, Joseph 64
Chitty, Edward 15, 18
  John 87
  John Sr. 91, 102
  Ruth 18
  William 155
Chrichlow, John 142
  see also Crichlow
Clack, William Jr. 89
Clanton, John 24
Clark, Anne 98
  Carter 5
  Frances 5 (2)
  Franklin 104
  James 5, 98 (2), 113, 118, 119, 122, 125 (3), 141, 146, 150, 153
  Jesse 5, 32
  John 5, 62, 98 (will)
  Jordan Thomas 5
  Mary 98
  Rebecca 98 (2)
  Sarah 5 (2)
  Thomas 5 (will), 6
  Warner 98
  William 98
Clarke, (?) 157
  Judity 98
  Mathew 97

Clarke (cont.)
  Peter 20
  Sa-ly 98
  Sarah 157 (2)
  William 157 (will)
Clary, Ann 63
  James 63 (2)
  Martha 67
  Thomas 120
Claud, Charlotte 62
  Dority 169 (2)
  Edwin 156 (will), 162
  Elizabeth 60, 156
  John 56, 61, 66 (2), 71, 86, 108, 110, 112, 117, 135 (will) (2), 136
  John Jr. 115
  Joseph 9, 46, 51, 156
  Joshua 6, 8, 10, 11, 21 (2), 32, 39, 56, 58, 60, 66 (will)(5), 68 (will), 134, 137
  Lucy 135
  Lydia 66
  Newit (Newitt) 60, 132, 138, 148
  Philip 60 (will), 61, 66, 86, 135
  Sally 135, 169 (will) (2)
  William 56, 66 (2), 71, 74, 93, 110, 112, 115, 131
Clayton, John 18, 19 (2), 20, 24, 35, 49, 57, 58, 60, 64, 66, 69, 116, 118, 122, 151
  John Jr. 164, 170
  John Sr. 123
  Mary 25, 35
Clements, Anna 73
  Ben 40
  Benjamin 2, 14, 16, 22, 73 (will) (3), 79, 81 (will) (2), 86, 89
  Benjamin Jr. 18, 34, 43, 47, 56, 61, 89, 138
  Benjamin Sr. 39
  Elizabeth 73, 81 (2), 111 (2)
  Francis 81, 111, 131
  George 73 (2), 144
  Jane 85
  John 81, 111, 112, 131
  Lucy 73
  Martha 106
  R. 128
  Richard 73, 150, 153
  Richard P. 147, 158 (2), 161, 169
  Sally Williamson 106
  Sarah 81
  T. W. 152
  Thomas 60, 73 (3), 81 (2)
  Thomas Jr. 106 (will), 117, 138
  Thomas W. 132, 147, 163
  Thomas W. C. 148
Clemons, Thomas 34
Cleveland, John 89
  Patsey 89
  William 89 (will)

Clifton, Benjamin 6, 17, 29, 56 (will) (2), 58, 82 (2), 100
Claibourn 82
Clait 162
Cordey 82, 128, 160
Dorcas 91
Jesse 56, 65
John 56 (2), 66
Maria 82
Mary 82
Richard 56 (2), 90, 124
Samuel 56, 81
Sarah 82 (2)
Susannah 83
Thomas 5, 6, 9, 22, 56, 72, 79, 82 (will)
William 56
Clother (?), Mary 23
Cloud, Joshua 54
Cloyd, Joshua 41
Cobb, Anne 30, 31
  Benjamin 130, 131, 144, 155
  Burgwin 117
  Catrin 3
  Chlotella 145
  Croker (Crocker ?) 72
  Deborah 12
  Elizabeth 94, 98
  Exum 105, 130, 134, 144, 149, 155, 161 (will)
  Frederick 171 (2)
  George 131, 144
  George Blow (George B.) 130, 155
  Hardy 89, 98
  Henry 12 (2), 33, 71, 72, 78, 101, 117 (2), 145 (will), 146, 171
  Jack 144
  Jeremiah 130, 131, 155, 167
  John 30, 37, 46, 68, 72, 74, 97, 105 (2), 107, 122, 129, 130 (will), 134 (3), 139, 155
  Joseph 4 (2), 8, 9 (2), 10 (2), 11 (2), 12 (2), 13, 14, 16 (2), 18 (2), 23, 25, 27, 29, 32, 72
  Joseph Jr. 14
  Josiah 171
  Kinchen 117 (2), 121
  Lazarus 12 (2), 72, 171
  Lazarus Sr. 171 (will)
  M. 139
  Martha 139
  Mary 48, 105, 117
  Mathew 117 (2), 121
  Michael 12 (2), 14, 29, 31 (will) (3), 37, 105, 130, 131, 144 (will), 149, 155
  Mildred 171
  Nicholas 12 (will)(3), 13, 117, 134, 171 (2)

181

Cobb (cont.)
  Samuel 12 (2), 48, 72, 117 (will) (2), 121
  Sarah 12, 31
  Shadrack 163 (2)
  Thomas 130, 131, 144, 155
  William 12 (will) (3), 13, 14, 71, 72, 78, 79, 171
Cobbs, Michel 148
Cock, Hartwell 117
  William 1
Cocke, Benjamin 113
  Hartwell 106 (2), 115, 131 (will), 133, 147
  John Hartwell (Col.) 106
  Mary 121, 129 (2)
  Pleasant 81
  Richard 106
  Richard Jr. 121
  Richard Sr. (Col.) 131
  Robert 131
  Sarah 111, 131 (2)
  William 129
Cocker, Henry 148
Cockerell, Selah 41
Coffield, Pamelia 67
  Thomas 54, 66
Coggan, Ann 80
  John 38
  Mary 80
Coggin, John 48
Coging, Anne 104
  John 104
Coker, Ann 99, 135
  Henry 73, 122 (will), 148, 160
  James 122
  Holland 122
  Jonathan 120, 122 (2)
  Mary 122 (2)
  Nathaniel 49, 76, 87, 130, 135
  Salley 130
  Sarah 122
  Wilson 122
  Wison 130
Coleman, James 6
Colliar, Ann 33
  George 33 (will)
  Jane 33 (2)
  Rebeccah 33
  Sarah 33
Collier, George 34, 37
  John 153
  Moody 148, 152
Collins, Samuel Bridger 72
Connor, Martha 71
Cook, John 120, 142
  Lazarus 75, 87, 88, 100, 117, 166, 167
  Winna 168
Cooke, Lazarus 83
Cooper, Benjamin 26, 117
  Demsey 26, 43, 117
  James 21, 26
  Jesse 26, 76, 86 (2), 94, 106, 107, 113, 117, 126 (2), 130, 136, 141, 153
  John 26, 54 (2), 63, 75, 101
  Mary 26, 152
  Samuel 68

Cooper (cont.)
  Solomon 70, 75, 137
  Susannah 112
  William 12, 13, 23 (2), 26 (will), 27, 43
  Winifred 54
Corbett, Jacob 160
  Samuel (Sam.) 125, 164
  Shadrack 160
Corbitt, Jacob 170
Cord, Ann 3
  Elizabeth 3
Cornett, Joseph 78
Cornwell, Samuel 149
Cosby, Averiller 25
  Charles 8 (2), 17, 18 (3), 25 (4), 26, 29, 31, 32 (2), 34, 35 (4), 44, 51, 52 (2), 53, 58, 60, 131
Cotis (?), Mary 23
Cotton, Demcy 125
  Drury 89
  Jesse 143 (2)
  Polly 143
Cotton (?), Moody 158
Council, Amos 132 (3), 137, 163
  Cealia 125
  Celah 34
  Charles 69, 108, 116 (3), 119, 123 (2), 128, 153, 171
  Cutchins 80
  Edith 80, 166
  Edwin 166
  Elizabeth 37, 123
  Hodges 15, 18, 37, 38
  Hodges Jr. 27, 34
  J. 137
  James 37, 123 (will) (2)
  Jesse 66, 67, 132 (3)
  John 21, 37, 38, 43, 58, 60, 63, 78, 132 (will) (3), 137
  Lydda 132
  Mary 79
  Robert 141, 166
  Sarah 34, 37, 80, 132
  Tabitha 132
  Temperance 132, 166
Councill, Charles 171
  Joshua 97
Cowper, Demsey 117
  Wills 122
Crafford, Arthur 3
  Elizabeth 51, 162
  Henry 3 (2), 4, 5, 18, 21, 33, 51 (will), 52, 162
  John 51 (2), 62, 66, 77, 88, 162
  Lucy 162
  Mary 3, 162 (2)
Craven, James 45
Crenshaw, Amey 64
  Ann 82
  Anne 96 (will)
  Elijah 111 (2)
  Elizabeth 111, 147
  John 48, 64, 67, 75, 82 (2), 111 (will), 130
  Joseph 65
  Polly 111
  Samuel Maget 82

Crenshaw (cont.)
  Thomas 4, 7, 10, 12, 13, 16, 18, 20 (2), 25, 26, 38, 47, 48, 49, 59, 82 (will), 91
Crichlow, William 118, 121, 126, 136, 139, 141, 165, 169
  see also Chrichlow
Cricklow, William 129 (2)
Crizard, Newit 49
Crocker, Arthur 3, 133
  Benjamin 3 (2), 4, 8, 19, 20 (3), 21, 28, 48
  Elijah 100
  Elisha 3, 20 (will), 21, 28
  Elizabeth 85
  Hartwell 86, 91, 98
  Mary 20 (3)
  Moses 3, 20 (will)
  Robert 3 (will) (2)
  Sarah 20, 28 (2), 34, 86 (will), 87, 104
Croker, Ann 73
Croney (?), John 21
Crumpler, Arthur 113, 115 (2), 145 (2), 154, 158, 160
  Beasant (Bessant) 51 (2), 72, 158 (will) (2), 160
  Benjamin 51, 66, 72 (2), 92, 107, 113 (will) (2), 115 (3), 158
  Betsey 158
  Cherry 51
  Edmund 65, 128
  Elizabeth 51, 113
  John 3, 66, 113 (2), 115 (3), 120, 123, 128, 144, 145, 154, 155, 157, 158, 164, 167
  John Jr. 155
  Lucy 51
  Mary 51
  Mathew 145
  Sally 158
  Sarah 51, 158
  William 3 (will) (5), 5, 51 (will) (2), 57, 113, 128, 147, 158 (2)
Curl, Joseph 17
  Thomas 79 (will)
Curle, Thomas 105
Curney, Thomas 76
Cursey, Aggy 134 (3)
  Joshua 134
Daniel, Mills 159, 160
Darden, Ann 140, 146, 147, 164
  Anne 128
  Benjamin 111
  Betsey 118
  Carr 9
  Clotilda 118
  Edith 128, 147
  Elemuel 111
  Elisha 109, 111, 113, 114, 118 (will) (2), 121 (3), 140, 147

Darden (cont.)
  Elizabeth 166
  Esther 118
  Henry 4, 13
  Holland 115, 121 (2), 128 (will) (2), 129, 146 (2)
  Holland Jr. 147
  Jacob 111, 118 (2), 128 (2), 140, 146, 164 (2)
  Jacob Jr. 121, 134, 139, 140, 153, 164, 168, 170, 171
  Jacob Sr. 121 (2), 134, 135, 140, 164
  James 128 (2), 139, 140 (will) (2)
  Jeb. 111
  John 109, 128 (2), 147
  Jonah 128, 146, 147
  Jonathan 128 (3), 134
  Jones 118
  Julia 128, 140
  Martha 109
  Mary 4
  Milly 118
  Moses 134
  Pheribe 118, 128
Dashiele, Joshiah 141
Daughtery, Elizabeth 152
Daughtrey, Elizabeth 2
  James 134
  John 134
  Lucy 121
  Robert 111
Daughtry, Elizabeth 114 (will), 115
  James 37, 42, 82
  Mary 77
  Robert 27, 29
David, Martha 7
Davis, Anne 67
  Archibald 157
  Charles 24
  David 35, 93, 149, 162
  Drury 74 (2)
  Edwin 24, 67, 77
  Elizabeth 49, 67
  Etheldred 24, 74, 127
  Gideon 17, 26
  Hannah 16, 67, 74 (2), 75
  Hannah Ray 157
  Henry 61, 67, 74 (2), 77, 127, 128, 129, 150, 157 (will) (2), 166, 170 (2)
  Henry Sr. 127
  Isham 97
  James 74, 127
  Jeane 74
  Jeany 157
  Joel 24, 67, 74, 107, 127, 150, 156
  John 11 (will) (2), 13, 14, 15, 16, 19 (will) 25, 49, 62, 70, 79, 80, 82, 97, 124, 127, 132, 137, 153 (2), 157, 167
  Josiah 103
  Judah D. 19
  Lewis 19, 49 (will), 53
  Lucy 157

Davis (cont.)
  Martha 11, 19 (will) (2), 20
  Mary 19
  Nathan 61
  Nathaniel (Nath¹.) 24 (will) (2), 37, 121, 157
  Phillip (Philip, Philips) 67 (2), 74, 75, 107, 127, 152, 157, 168, 170
  Rachel 19, 49
  Samuel 5, 9, 42, 48
  Sarah 11, 24 (2), 37, 61
  Thomas 9, 11, 16, 24 (2), 37, 61, 74 (will) (3), 77, 127 (will), 128, 129
  Thomas Jr. 16 (2), 67 (will), 68
  William 11
  Wilson 121
  Winnefred 51
Dawson, Ann 58, 158, 159
  Britain 59
  David 58, 59 (2)
  Demse 11
  Dorcas 59
  Elizabeth 58, 59, 158
  Henry 3 (2), 4, 14, 59 (will), 101
  Iavid 101
  Jane Edmunds 155 (2)
  John 11 (will) (2), 16, 42, 59, 82
  John Edmunds (John E.) 147 (2)
  Joseph 159
  Joshua 3, 8, 11, 101
  Mary 11, 40, 81
  Mary Edmunds 155
  Polly 147
  Rebecca 158
  Solomon 11, 59
  Tuke 158 (will)
Day, (?) 39
  Abner 96
  Ann 50
  Charlotte 50
  Edmund 67, 96 (will) (2), 130
  Edmund Jr. 46
  Edward 88
  Elizabeth 39, 50, 94, 121
  Elizabeth Brown 50
  Hill 71
  John 96, 159
  Mary 50, 64, 71
  Patty 100
  Phebe 50
  Priscilla 50
  Rebecca 50 (2)
  Susanna 96
  Thomas 10, 21, 28, 35, 41 (3), 46, 50 (will) (2), 54, 61, 64, 94
  Thomas Jr. 71
Dean, William 10
Dean (?), Betty 10
Deane, Robert 5
Delk, Benjamin 166
  Elizabeth 143
  Hannah 19 (2)

Delk (cont.)
  Jacob 19
  James 149
  John 19
  Joseph 14, 15, 19 (will), 20, 23, 33, 46, 53, 68
  Joseph Jr. 18
Deloach, Allen 103
  Ann 103 (4)
  Averilla 103
  Barbary 144
  Benjamin 103 (will), 104
  Benjamin C. 58, 73, 76, 78, 93
  Elizabeth 103
  John 43, 73
  John Hudson 73
  Lucy 125, 150, 158
  Martha 103
  Mary 103
  Polly 158
  Richard 96, 112, 150, 158, 161
  Sarah 158 (will), 161
  Solomon 19, 59, 150 (will) (2), 153
  Thomas 103
  William 29, 30 (2), 32, 73 (will), 76
Demmery, Collin 87
  David 87
  Day 87
  Frederick 87 (will)
  Micajah 87
  Richard 87
  Tempy 87
Demory, Richard 115, 116
Denning, John 151
Denson, Ann 49 (2), 50
  Benjamin 17, 18, 21 (4), 22, 34, 37 (3), 38
  Catherine 158
  David 49, 108
  Dority 49
  Elizabeth 49 (3), 50 (will), 50
  Francis 11, 31, 49 (will), 50
  Holloway 140
  Hollowell 21, 37
  J. 67, 71, 78, 87 (2), 94, 99, 101, 102 (2), 136, 142, 147, 153, 167
  Ja. 107
  James 49, 61
  Jethro 21, 37, 59
  John 17, 21 (will) (2), 23, 37, 83, 97
  Jordan 42, 43, 66, 79 (2), 81, 96 (3), 97, 114, 115, 137, 147, 150
  Jordan, & Co. 147
  Joseph 18, 21, 21 (2), 22, 34, 37, 39, 47, 137, 139, 150, 158, 168
  Joseph Jr. 96, 158
  Mills 159
  Peter 159
  Rebecca 159
  Sarah 49 (2), 50, 102
  Thomas 49
  Tooke (Took) 31, 49

Denson (cont.)
  Tuke 79
  W. 83
  William 31, 32, 49, 108
Derby, Ann 121
Derring, Emslus 120
Desheil (?), Sally 141
Dickens, Robert 148
Dickenson, Joel 61
  Mary 61
Dickson, James 51
Disher, Robert H. 128
Disto, David Edloe 12 (2)
Doles, Arthur 89, 105, 106, 108, 123, 142, 143, 170
  Benjamin 44, 61, 108 (2)
  Elizabeth 102
  Henry 94 (2)
  Jesse 108
  Joseph 10, 108 (will)
  Sarah 108
Donson, J. 65
Dortch, John 63
  Ruth 63
Dowles, Joseph 2
Doyel, Daniel 41
  Edmund 44
  Edward 1, 51
  Hardy 44, 57, 66, 132
  Josiah 65
  Kinchen 111
  Marget 53
  Martha 116
  Patty 65
  Richard 127 (2)
  Sarah 65
  Shadrack 65
  William 47, 53
  Zachariah 150
Doyell, William 99
Doyels, Mary 57
Doyle, Carr 25, 88, 91
  Daniel 25, 27 (2), 34, 39
  Dorcas 25
  Edmund 25 (2)
  Edward 15, 25 (will), 26, 43
  Elizabeth 25 (2)
  Hardy 25 (2), 39 (2), 43 (2), 91
  Hary 86
  Jacob 25
  Josiah 25
  Lydda 25
  Mary 70
  William 25, 34, 64, 70, 86
Drake, Ann 7, 59, 65 (will), 66
  Anne 14, 60
  Arthur 147, 171
  Baldy 65
  Barnaby (Barneby) 7, 19, 29
  Barnaby Jr. 65 (3)
  Barnaby Sr. 151 (will)
  Britten 14, 16
  Burwell 151
  Cordal (Cordial) 65, 147 (will)
  Dorcy 156
  Edmond 16 (2)
  Elizabeth 16, 107

Drake (cont.)
  Etheldred 68
  Exum 151 (2)
  Francis 16
  Honor 48
  Isaac 48
  Jeremiah 104 (2), 108, 119, 136, 161
  Jesse 26 (3), 33, 45, 48, 49, 59 (will) (2), 60
  Joel 48
  John 7 (will), 10, 14, 24 (2), 26 (2), 33, 48 (will) (3), 52, 59, 66, 76
  John Sr. 7
  Jonah 48
  Joshua 7
  Jurden 48
  Lazarus 14
  Margaret 16 (2)
  Martha 16, 48, 151 (2)
  Mary 7 (2), 14, 65 (2), 96, 151 (2)
  Mathew 16 (2)
  Milbra 151
  Molly 48
  Mourning 151
  Nathaniel 16
  Penelope 48
  Penny 151
  Polly 147 (3)
  Richard 16 (will) (4), 18
  Ridley 65
  Sarah 96 (2)
  Silas 147
  Simmons 151 (2)
  Thomas 7 (2), 14 (will) (3), 16, 48, 96 (will), 97
  Timothy 7, 27, 65, 96
  Tristrom 16
  William 14 (2), 16, 48, 50
  Zelby 158
  Zellah 48
Draper, Ephraim 128 (3), 136 (2)
  Jeremiah 128, 136
  Jesse 49, 128 (2), 136
  Mourning 128
  Patience 49
  Thomas 49, 66, 128 (will) (2), 128, 136 (2)
  William 128, 136
Dreaper, Thomas 11, 21
Drew, (?) 138
  Anne 106
  Benjamin 129, 133
  Dolphin 106, 133
  Edward 2 (will) (2), 4, 33, 65, 72, 92
  Frances 2
  James 106 (2)
  Jeremiah 10, 41, 60, 61, 62, 64, 65 (2), 67, 70, 86, 90, 93, 94, 98, 106 (will), 110, 115 (2), 117, 138
  Jesse 65 (2), 75, 86, 93 (will), 98, 100, 112
  John 17

Drew (cont.)
  Mary 41, 106 (3)
  Milly 57, 59, 63
  Newit (Newitt) 2 (3), 6, 9, 13 (2), 24, 41, 61, 65 (will), 98, 106, 115, 138, 150
  Priscilla 106
  Sarah 106, 142
  Susanna (Susannah) 106, 160
  Thomas 2
Drewet, Samuel 147
Drewry, Charles 155
  Edmund (Edmunds) 155 (2)
  Elizabeth 62, 70, 121, 154
  Humphrey 121 (2), 143, 169 (2)
  Humphry 154 (will), 155, 156, 159
  James 86 (2), 121
  John 111, 155 (2)
  Joseph 169
  Lucy 155
  Nicholas 86 (2)
  Rachel 86 (2)
  Rebecca 154, 169
  Joseph 121
  Richard 86 (2), 144, 155 (2)
  Sally 155
  Samuel 39, 72, 78, 112, 121 (will) (3), 154, 169
  Samuel Jr. 62
  Samuel Sr. 122
  Sarah 86
  Thomas 70 (will)
  William 11, 86 (will) (3), 91, 125, 155 (will), 159
  William Jr. 91, 106
  William Sr. 106
  see also Drury
Drewy, Elizabeth 70
Driver, Martha 16
Drury, Elizabeth 70
  Thomas 70
  Will 36
  William 31, 97
  see also Drewry
Dugger, Howell 140
  Patsey 140
  Polly 140
  Sarah 140
Dunford, Thomas 55 (will)
Dunkin, Ann 115
Dunkley, Catherine 1 (3), 2, 7, 18
  John 1 (will) (2), 2
  Katherine 15 (will), 16
  Moses 15 (2)
  Ralph 15
Dunn, Ann 36, 73
  Morris 137
  Thomas Deloach 150
  William 17, 25, 29
  William Jr. 30
Duprea, Lucy D. 132
Dupree, Elizabeth 85
  Frances 50
  Haley 49

Dupree (cont.)
  Lewis 145
  Mabel 137
  Susannah 49
Duprey, Elizabeth 71
  Faith 71
  Robert 64
Durdan, Robert 11
Ealey, William 97
Edmunds, Ann 36, 45, 52
    (will), 55, 81, 82,
    155 (will)
  Anne 58
  Charles 45, 58, 70, 77
  David 10 (2), 18, 20,
    21, 22 (2), 24, 28,
    31, 32, 35, 36 (2),
    38, 46, 48, 49, 51,
    54, 57, 59, 70, 80,
    81 (will), 85, 86,
    166
  David Jr. 66
  David Sr. 66
  Davis 39
  Davy 166
  Elizabeth 151
  Etheldred (Eth'd) 70,
    77, 161 (2), 170
  George 166 (2)
  H. 15, 29, 46
  Henry 45 (2), 70
  Howell (Howel) 1, 2, 4,
    5 (2), 6, 18, 24, 28,
    44 (2), 45 (will)
    (3), 46, 51 (2), 66,
    70 (2), 77, 81, 82,
    85, 86, 90, 91, 92,
    94, 97 (2), 106, 111,
    117, 119, 146
  Howell (Capt.)10, 35
  Howell (Col.) 58, 102
  Howell Jr. 10, 135
  Howell Sr. 10
  Jeremiah 22 (will), 24
  John 45 (2), 70, 77,
    157
  Jonas 22
  Lucy 35, 45 (2), 58,
    70, 102 (2)
  Martha 45 (2), 58, 166
  Mary 22, 45 (3), 52
    (2), 55, 58, 70
    (will), 71, 77
  Samuel (Sam., Saml.)
    45 (2), 58, 69, 70
    (2), 77 (2), 79, 80,
    83, 85, 96 (2), 101,
    105, 108, 110, 111,
    112, 113, 115, 117,
    124, 137, 148, 169,
    170
  Sarah 45, 58, 70 (3),
    77, 102
  Susan 166
  Thomas 20, 45 (4), 52,
    55, 57, 58, 61, 64,
    68, 69, 70, 77 (3),
    82, 90, 94, 96 (2),
    98, 100, 101, 105,
    106, 110, 111 (3),
    112, 113 (3), 115,
    118, 119 (3), 124
    (3), 128, 129, 137,
    142, 156, 161 (2)
  Will 141, 170

Edmunds (cont.)
  William 10, 45 (2),
    58, 70 (2), 77 (2),
    81, 82, 92, 97, 99,
    138, 144, 158
Edward, Sarah 75
Edwards, Albridgeton 152
  Alice 11, 36
  Ann 22, 48, 84, 85 (3),
    90, 99, 100 (2), 120
  Anne 47, 91
  Arthur 6, 9, 11, 53
    (2)
  Ben 141
  Benjamin 22, 25 (will)
    (2), 47, 84, 85 (2),
    90, 99, 100 (2),
    121, 129 (2), 133,
    150 (will)
  Betty 141
  Charlotte 87
  David 89, 109, 114,
    130, 171
  Elias 152 (2)
  Elizabeth 3 (2), 15,
    22 (will), 24, 29,
    47 (3), 56, 74, 84,
    85, 90 (will) (2),
    98, 99 (2), 100 (2)
  George 48, 87 (2), 92,
    101, 140 (3), 164,
    170
  Jacob 23
  James 120, 127, 130
    (2), 134, 138, 142,
    145, 146, 148, 152
    (3), 168
  Janes 154
  Jesse 36
  Joel 120, 127 (2), 164,
    170
  John 3, 5, 9, 14, 18,
    19, 21, 23 (will),
    25 (3), 29, 30, 32,
    35, 39, 41, 44, 46,
    49, 52, 59 (2), 62,
    75, 88, 92, 96, 120
    (will), 123
  Jonah 59, 70, 78, 152,
    157
  Jonas 69, 97
  Jordan 85
  Joseph 22
  Kinchen (Kincheon) 153
    (2), 154, 165, 168
    (2)
  Lucy 47, 85, 99, 111
  M. 10, 11, 13, 21, 23,
    30, 47
  Martha 22, 79, 99
  Mary 85, 136, 152
  Micah 22
  Micajah 7, 8, 9 (2),
    10, 11, 12, 14, 16,
    25, 28, 29 (2), 38,
    43, 47 (will) (2),
    56, 82, 83, 84
    (will), 92, 98, 99,
    100 (3), 113, 120
    (2), 123, 126, 162
  Micajah (Capt.) 99
  Michael 50
  Miriam 168
  Nathaniel (Nath'l)
    128, 135, 143 (2),
    156, 169

Edwards (cont.)
  Newit 85, 91, 113,
    120 (3), 123, 128,
    138
  Patience 22, 23
  Patty 22
  Priscilla 19, 152
  Richard 47, 84 (2),
    90, 92, 99, 100,
    104, 105, 150, 151
  Sally 87
  Sarah 51, 52, 111
  Susannah 84
  Thomas 3, 13, 22, 23
    (2), 24 (2), 25
    (2), 36, 41, 48
    (2), 71, 85 (will),
    87
  W. 71
  West 120
  William 3 (will) (2),
    4, 19-20, 22 (2),
    23, 25, 47, 67, 71,
    84 (2), 87 (will),
    90 (2), 91, 99, 100
    (3), 106, 108, 116,
    122, 129, 130, 131,
    135, 145, 150, 151,
    152 (will) (4), 154
    (2), 168
Eldridge, William 10
Eley, Cherry 142
Ely (Eley) 107, 169
  Robert 81, 142
  Samuel 31, 92-93
  Victor 171
  William 107
Ellis, Ann 112
  Benjamin 132, 156
  Bolin 145
  Edwin 75
  Elizabeth 74
  Faithy 75
  Hannah 110
  Henry 112 (2), 156
    (will), 170, 171
  Hezekiah 128
  Jeremiah 38, 45, 112
    (will) (3)
  Lawrence 132
  Martha 156
  Micah 121, 130, 152,
    171
  Micaj 119
  Micajah 118, 126 (2),
    145, 164
  Polly C. 156
  Samuel 110
  William 126
Ellison, Caleb 149
  Dorcas 149
  Edwin 149
  Gerard R. 149 (will)
  Gerrard 156
  Gideon 149
  Gutie 149
  James 149
  Sarah 149
  Zachariah 149
Ellzey, John 65
  see also Elzey
Elvin, John 134
Elzey, John 57 (will)
  Kezia 57
  William 57
  see also Ellzey

Emmory, Frederick 97
English, Nathan 105, 108
Ennis, Raman 5, 6, 8, 45
Eppes, Edward 40 (2), 71
  George 26, 40
  Mary 40
  William 40
Evans, Anthony 162
  Ben C. M. 156
  Benjamin 23, 28, 44, 47, 49 (2), 55, 67
  Benjamin Moseley 124
  Elizabeth 4 (will) (2)
  Etheldred 162
  Frances 49
  Hannah 28, 49, 124 (will), 137, 156
  Hannah Thompson 124
  James 4 (2)
  Jesse 4
  Mathew Womble 4
  Patience 4
  Sally 162
  Sarah 4, 162
  W. 165
  William 124
Everet, Keton 49
Everett, Elizabeth 143, 157
  Etheldred 110, 128, 157 (2)
  Exum 157, 162
  Jenett 58
  John 102
  Joseph 5, 19, 20, 24, 26, 32, 49, 58 (will), 59
  Miles 148, 156
  Sally 157
  Sarah 58
  Simon 4, 5 (will), 17, 19, 45, 101, 137, 169
  Thomas 164, 170
Everit, Elizabeth 120
Everitt, Ann 87
  Elizabeth 87 (2)
  Ethel 118
  Etheldred 118
  Exum 87, 132
  Femby 87
  John 118 (2)
  Keton 87
  Mary 87
  Thomas 87, 88 (2)
  Thomas Sr. 87 (will)
Exum, A. 142
  Ann 53
  Arthur 12, 40, 76, 102, 118
  Barneby 12
  Benjamin 31, 72, 105 (will), 106, 134
  Elizabeth 62
  Elijah 12
  Francis 7 (will), 9, 22
  James 53
  Joseph 12
  Martha 33
  Mary 12, 105
  Michael 12
  Moses 12
  Parnel Robert Pursell (?) 12 (2)
  Patience 12, 65
  R. 142

Exum (cont.)
  Rebecca 123
  Robert 123, 167
  Sarah 12, 40
  Tabitha 33
  William 2, 12 (will) (3), 30
Ezell, Abel 144
Fagon, Peter 111
Faircloth, (?) 96
  Ann 25
  Anne 13
  Benjamin 26, 139
  Ephraim 139
Fanning, Mary 50
Fargason, Robert 127
Farrer (?), Ralph 61
Farrow, Betty 10
Fason, James 116
Faulcon, Jacob 106
  John 148
  Lucretia 148
Fearn, George 35
  John 131 (2)
  Mathew 35
  Thomas 131 (2)
Felts, Hartwell 169
  Nathan 167
  Sally 169
Fennel, John 140
Ferguson, John 91
  see also Fogerson, Forgason, Forgueson, Forguson, Furgunson
Figures, Bartholomew 81
  Elizabeth Lucy 81
  Joseph 81 (will), 96, 105
  Mary 135
  Matt 135
  Richard 81
  Selah 65
  Thomas 81 (3), 96
  William 81
Fisher, D. 31, 36, 71, 84
  Daniel 37, 43, 83 (2), 84
  Edward 125 (2), 126 (3), 130, 138, 159 (3)
  Mary 145
  Robert 128
  Robert H. 133, 140, 145
  Sarah 126
Fitzhugh, Priscilla 65
  Thomas 63, 90, 93(2), 106, 138 (2), 142, 143
  William Jr. 156
Fletcher, Benjamin 152
Flugunion (?), Daniel 5
Fly, Sally 144
  Saphera 71
  Winnie 144
Fogerson (?), Ann 75
  John 75 (will)
  Josiah 75
  William 75
  see also Ferguson, Forgason, Forgueson, Forguson, Furgunson
Foord (?), Denham 56
Ford, Ann 75
Foreman, John 132

Foreman (cont.)
  Mary 132
Forgason, Ann 32
  John 32
  See also Ferguson, Forgerson, Forgueson, Forguson, Furgunson
Forgueson, John 17
  See also Ferguson, Fogerson, Forgason, Forguson, Furgunson
Forguson, Robert 126
  See also Ferguson, Fogerson, Forgason, Forgueson, Furgunson
Forster, Arthur 6
  John 6
  Richard 50
  William 59
Fort, Ann 70 (will), 80
  Arthur 6, 34 (will), 35, 40
  Betty 6, 34
  Edwin 86, 145, 171
  Elias 6, 26, 57, 63, 64, 92
  Elizabeth 171
  Henry 6, 34, 40 (2)
  Howell 70
  Jesse 100
  John 6 (will) (2), 7, 21, 39, 40, 70, 72, 77, 78, 81, 86, 93, 126, 142, 145 (will), 171
  Joseph 86, 114, 148, 171
  Joshua 6, 18, 34 (3), 40 (2), 41, 44, 58, 68, 86 (will) (2), 87, 171 (3)
  Littleton 70, 143
  LtN (?) 166
  Nancy 158
  Olive 144
  Priscilla 34, 171
  Rebecca 6, 34 (2), 40 (will) (2), 41
  Selah 171
  Temperance 145, 171
  Turner 70
Foster, (?) 39
  Alice 39
  Alis 58 (will)
  Alse 12, 60
  Amey 34, 58, 68
  Amy 12, 39
  Anthony 40 (2)
  Arthur (Arhthur) 14, 39, 46, 53, 58, 61, 67, 71, 77, 78, 80, 81, 89, 90, 94, 97, 104, 107, 110, 112, 115, 124 (3), 144
  Christopher 12, 39 (will), 44
  Dolly 40
  Edith 126
  Elias 5, 19, 29, 39
  Fanny 23
  Haley (Hailey) 96 (2), 135
  Henry Collier 107
  James 107, 120, 123
  John 39 (2), 96(will), 97, 126, 162

Foster (cont.)
  Lucy 39
  Mary 39
  Moses 39 (2), 40, 58 (2), 60, 68 (2), 86, 125, 159
  Nancey 126
  Newit 12, 39 (2), 40 (will)
  Rebecca 126
  Richard 39 (2), 71, 96
  Sarah 39
  Sterling 107
  William 53, 79, 82 (2), 85, 121 (2), 126 (will) (2), 145
Fowler, Ann 71
  Arthur 4
  Benjamin 71
  Charles 71
  Edmund 4
  James 8, 20, 67, 69 (will) (2), 70
  John 168
  Sarah 22, 53, 69, 134
  Titus 163
  William 9, 43, 69 (2), 71 (will)(2), 72, 74, 106, 115, 134, 140, 152, 153 (2), 154, 157, 168
Francis, Ann 36
  Benjamin 36
  Charlotte 86
  Cordall (Cordal) 123, 145
  Drury 49
  Elizabeth 86
  Elizabeth Briggs 50, 86
  Fanny Claud 135
  Frederick 36
  Jane Briggs 86
  John 36, 49, 85, 86, 155
  Milly Colliar 86
  Molley 86
  Polly Claud 135
  Sally 86
  Samuel 114, 120
  Sarah 50
  Sterling 36, 81, 85, 135
  Thomas 36 (will), 38, 44, 86 (will), 90
  William 8, 18, 36, 49, 53, 67, 97, 98
  Willie (Wilie) 86, 123, 143, 155, 161
Freeman, James 57, 92
  John 88
  Lucy 36
  Olive 92
  Robert 36
  Thomas 36
Frizzell, Martha 68
Fulgham, Mary 148 (will)
Furgunson, Robert 120
  see also Ferguson, Fogerson, Forgason, Forgueson, Ferguson
Gardiner, James 37
  John 43
Gardner, Amos 88, 166
  Ann 88 (2), 134 (2), 164 (2), 166 (will)
  Betsey 134
  David 134

Gardner (cont.)
  Henry 121 (2), 129, 134 (5), 139, 147, 148, 164 (2)
  Honour 134
  James 3, 10, 12, 13, 42, 88, 134 (will) (2), 152, 153, 166
  James Jr. 114 (2)
  James Sr. 114, 135, 139
  Jesse 88 (2), 134 (5), 135, 139, 153, 159
  John 21, 69, 70, 88 (will) (3), 89, 114, 134 (2), 147
  Joseph 134
  Joshua 10, 115, 128, 129, 134 (will)(4), 157, 164 (2)
  Juda 134
  Martha 157
  Mary 88
  Mathew 134 (2), 135
  Mathew Jr. 140
  Mitty 88
  Peggy 134
  Penelope 134
  Pheby 88
  Polly 134
  Polly Darden 134
  Rhoda 134
  Sarah 134 (2)
Garner, Elizabeth 2
  James 9 (will)(3)
  John 9 (2)
  Joshua 9 (2)
  Juda 9
  Mathew 114
  Mary 2
  Penelope 9
Garner (?), James 10
Garris, Amos 5, 49 (will) (2), 50, 56
  Benjamin 49
  Hannah 49 (2)
  John 49 (2)
  Joshua 49 (2)
  Lidea 49
  William 49
Gathon, John 49
Gatling, Rebecca 13
Gay, Charles 68
  Edmund 68 (will)(2), 104
  John 68
  Jonathan 68
  Mary 102
  Thomas 68, 104
  William 68
Gee, James 146, 160 (2), 167, 169 (2), 170
  Lavinia Norfleet 160
  Mary 160 (2)
  William Henry 169
George, Ann 88 (2)
  Anne 93
  John 88
  William 88 (will), 93, 113
Gibbons, John 42
Gilbert, William 133
Gilliam, Anselm 75
  Arthur 14 (2), 34, 159
  Betsey 152
  Burrell 14
  Cala 134 (2)

Gilliam (cont.)
  Charles 73
  Drury 14
  Ephraim 14
  Isham 75
  Jacob 157
  Jeremiah 34
  Jesse 88 (will)
  John 22 (2), 34 (will), 37, 44, 49, 87, 88 (2), 124, 132 (3)
  Joseph 49, 88, 132
  Judith 73
  Judy 34
  Lucy 34 (2)
  Martha 161
  Mary 34
  Patsey 152
  Penelope 132
  Penelopy 88
  Richard (Rich^d.) 120, 124, 126
  Robert 2, 20, 87, 92, 132 (will)
  Sarah 14 (2)
  Thomas 34, 57, 134 (will) (3), 160
  Thomas Clements (Thomas C.) 73, 138
  Thomas Jr. 60, 94, 114, 134, 138
  Walter 14 (will), 22
Glover, George 64 (will), 67
  Jonathan 64
  Margarett 64
  Polly 118
  Samuel 64
  William 82
Gobb, Solomon 147
Godfrey, William 129
Godwin, Jacob 30
  Jonathan 20
  Joseph 30
  Mary 38
Goodwyn, John 125 (2)
  Robert 126 (2), 139, 143 (2), 155, 159, 162, 166, 167
Grantham, Elisosha 166
Gray, Ann 1, 118 (will)
  Anna 128
  Ben 163
  Benjamin 38 (will)(3), 40
  Catherine 38
  Col. 131
  Edmund 54
  Edward 51
  Edwin 32, 33, 36, 37, 39, 46, 47, 49, 50 (2), 54, 63, 71, 72, 73 (2), 74, 81, 97, 108, 109, 121, 122 (will) (3), 155, 163 (2)
  Edwin (Col.) 163
  Hannah 153
  Henry 122 (2)
  J. 3, 7, 10, 17, 21, 29 (2), 34, 43, 54 (2), 56, 57, 60 (2), 62, 63, 111
  James 38, 50 (2), 54, 56, 99, 111, 122 (2), 156

Gray (cont.)
  James (Capt.) 156
  Jesse 38 (2)
  John 97, 118 (2), 120,
    153
  Joseph 2, 12, 14, 36,
    37, 50 (will), 54,
    73, 122 (2)
  Lucy 50
  Mansfill 21
  Martha 21
  Mary 21, 38, 122
  Richard 38
  Sarah 3, 50
  Thomas 16, 18, 31, 37,
    122 (2), 129, 131
    (2), 142, 156
  Thomas Jr. 50
  William 88
  William Watson 41
Greamer, William 23
Gregory, Francis 17
  Patience 17
Gresswit, Mathew 88
  Sarah 88
  William 88 (will)
  see also Gresswitt,
    Greswitt, Griswitt
Gresswitt, William 72,
    93
  see also Gresswit,
    Greswitt, Griswitt
Greswitt, Thomas 50
  Will 117
  see also Gresswit,
    Gresswitt, Griswitt
Griffen, Benjamin 57
Griffin, Andrew 4 (2), 8
    (2)
  Beck 16
  Benjamin 64, 66, 86
    (will)(2), 92, 123
  Catherine 4
  Edward 124, 129
  Elizabeth 160
  Epenetus 8
  Jack 86
  James 86
  Jones 4, 15
  Lemuel 4
  Lot 4
  Martha 4, 8
  Mary 4, 8 (will)
  Mathew 4 (will), 5 (2),
    6
  Micajah 69, 78, 86, 92,
    105, 106, 112, 123,
    128
  Micajah Jr. 160
  Mica¹. 166 (2)
  Miles 161
  Olive 86
  Penelipa 124
  Rebecca 4
  Richard 87
  Roche (?) 16
  Sarah 4
  Thomas 54
  Wiley 86
Griffing, Sarah 38
Griggs, Lewis 141
Grimer, Mary 48
Grimmer, Amey 145
  Ann 145
  Betsey 145
  Henry 145
  John 59

Grimmer (cont.)
  Mary 48
  Milla 145
  Robert 48, 145
  William 23
Grisard, Lucy 6
Griswitt, Anthony 48
  Elizabeth 48 (2)
  George 48
  James 48
  Martha 48
  Thomas 48 (will)(2),
    60
  William 48 (2)
  see also Gresswit,
    Gresswitt, Greswitt
Grizard, Ambrose 65
    (will)(2)
  Betty 65
  Celia 78
  Charlotte 78
  Dorcas 78
  Elizabeth 78, 80
  Hardy 65 (2)
  Hulin (Huling) 77, 130
  Isum 78
  Jeremiah 130
  Jerry 78
  John 65
  Mary 77
  Mille 65
  Pheba 78
  Priscilla 65
  Sarah 65
  Tabitha 78, 130
  Thomas 77
  William 77 (will)(2),
    80, 130
Grizzard, Ambrose 95
  Hardy 82
  Jeremiah 82
  Milly 51
  Phebe 155
  Polly 155
  William 130, 139
Groce, Francis 42
  Priscilla 42
Gurley, Ann 23
  Benjamin 23, 24, 25
  Elizabeth 26
  George 4, 7, 10 (2),
    12, 13 (2), 14, 15,
    48 (2), 50, 57, 58,
    59, 67, 71, 82, 85,
    87 (2), 94, 97, 101,
    103, 104, 123, 127
    (2), 130, 136, 161,
    167, 170
  George Jr. 3, 7, 13
    (2), 14, 15, 16, 22,
    23, 25 (3), 29, 32,
    36, 45 (2), 48, 130,
    138, 141, 167 (2)
  George Sr. 13, 23, 48
    (will)
  John 3, 48, 138, 141
  Joseph 115
  Lucy 127
  Martha 71, 85
  Mary 22, 25, 71
  Mary Jr. 23
  Nicholas 23 (will)(2),
    24, 30, 67
  Nicholas Jr. 30
  Priscilla 75
  William 23
Guthrie, Alenader 129

Guthrie (cont.)
  Daniel 1
Guy (?), James 160
Gwaltney, John 149 (2)
  Michael 75
  W. 69
  William 59, 75, 82
Gwi, William 76
Gwin, Thomas 39
  William 76
Hackett, Redmond 131
Hail, Joseph 87
  Obadiah 87
Haile, Elizabeth 73
  Joseph 73
Haisty, Benjamin 42, 88
  Elizabeth 42 (2)
  Isabel 42
  James 42 (will)(3),
    43 (2)
  John 42 (2), 88
  Joshua 42
  Mathew 42
  Moses 42, 131
  Robert 42
  Samuel 100
  Sarah 42
  see also Hastey,
    Hasty
Halcome, Richard 152
Hale, Elizabeth 69
  Joseph 69
Hall, Elizabeth 88
  George 87 (will)(2),
    88, 92 (2)
  James 87, 88, 92
Hallcome, Richard 117,
    143
  Thomas 154
Hamlin, Richard 40, 54
  Stephen 117-118
  Will 50
  William 104, 118
Hancock, Lucy 89
  Robert 129
  Samuel 166
  Stephen 147
  Thomas 42
Handcock, Henry 92
  Lewis 42
  Thomas 42
  William 42 (will), 44
Handcocke, Stephen 136
Harcum, William 171 (2)
Hardin, (?) 97
Hargrave, Mary 47, 147
  Michael 69
  Miriam 98, 103
  Richard 153
  Samuel 153
Hargraves, Mary 147
  Michael 64
Harper, John 40
Harrell, Benjamin 133
  Jesse 73
Harris, Abraham 125
  Absalom 62 (3)
  Amos 20, 26, 29, 36,
    61 (2), 62, 66, 84
    (2), 91, 102, 119
    (will)(3), 152
  Ann 2, 4, 33, 156
  Anne 138
  Ansalemn 138
  Anthony 169
  Avis 57

Harris (cont.)
  Benjamin 57, 62 (will)
    (2), 65, 98, 101, 125
  Carter 108 (will)
  Catherine 117
  Charlotte 107
  Drew 2, 33
  Drewry 90, 94, 107, 119
    (2)
  Drury 29, 83, 92, 99
  Edmund 150 (will)
  Edward 2, 4, 16, 17 (2),
    45, 46, 53, 68, 72,
    78, 81, 84, 92, 138
  Edward Sr. 92
  Edwin 107
  Elizabeth 57, 59, 108,
    122, 125, 150
  Exum 149
  Faith 13
  George 2
  Hamlin 168
  Hardy 53, 62, 64, 75,
    79, 80, 84 (3), 85,
    86 (3), 90 (2), 93,
    97, 102, 125, 126,
    136 (3), 137
  Harmon 57, 93, 102,
    133, 156
  Henry 2, 6, 15, 16 (2),
    60, 74, 119 (2), 125
    (will)
  Herman 56
  Howell (Howel) 57 (2),
    90, 124
  J. 126
  Jacob 6, 15, 29 (will),
    30, 43 (3)
  James 2 (4), 29, 83,
    90, 108, 119 (will)
    (2), 138, 150 (2),
    151, 168, 169
  Jesse 39, 79
  Jinny 150
  Joel 57, 85, 104, 119,
    159
  John 2 (2), 3, 13, 20,
    33 (will)(3), 55, 57
    (will), 58, 82 (will),
    83, 107 (2), 108,
    138 (2)
  John Dawson 147 (will)
  John Sr. 144
  Joseph 24, 57, 84, 125
    (2)
  Joshua 16, 21, 46, 79,
    108
  Julia 137
  Landon 142, 150, 156
  Lewis 52, 61, 84, 126,
    132
  Lucy 57
  Martha 2, 33, 126
  Martin 2 (will)(2), 3
  Mary 2 (3), 4, 29 (2),
    62, 63, 90 (will),
    94, 107, 125, 130,
    169
  Mathew 2, 19 (2), 20
  Meshaland 125
  Mial 122
  Michael 62, 93, 97
  Molly 57
  Moses 67, 94, 119, 122
  Nancy 107, 119, 125

Harris (cont.)
  Nathan 2, 33 (2), 66,
    82 (2), 83, 88, 96,
    99, 101, 102, 107
    (will), 119, 130
  Newit (Newitt) 2, 12,
    33, 41, 82, 107, 150
  Olive 65, 84
  Patience 57, 119 (2)
  Penny Carr 150
  Peyton 150, 169
  Priscilla 84
  Randolph 52
  Rebecca (Rebecah) 57
    (2), 117, 119
  Richard 92, 107
  Robert 2 (3)
  Ruth 43 (2), 169 (will)
  Sally (Salley) 119,
    169
  Sarah 53, 84, 136
  Sathy 62
  Simon 3, 24, 33, 43
    (will)(4), 49, 57
    (will), 59, 63, 69,
    76, 81, 82, 92, 94,
    112, 117, 169
  Susan 52
  Thomas 2, 33, 82
  West 62, 119, 137 (will),
    155
  Will 62
  William 2, 24, 43, 57,
    119 (2), 126, 137,
    151, 152
Harrison, Amima 67
  Amy 107 (will)
  Anne 67
  Anselm 108
  Benjamin 69, 82, 117,
    124
  Charlotte 67
  Daniel 107
  Dorothy 82
  Elizabeth 67
  Harmon 67
  Henry 6, 10, 11, 33,
    36, 69 (3), 81, 128,
    160, 163
  J. 135
  James 171
  Joseph 67 (2)
  Mary 67, 107
  Nancy 132
  Nathaniel 69
  Olive 67
  Rebecca 67, 162 (2)
  Richard 69 (2), 81,
    112-113, 117, 124,
    159, 160, 169, 171
  Samuel 67 (will), 78
  Sarah 110
  Solomon 67, 68, 83, 99
  William 11, 33, 49, 67,
    69 (will), 94
Hart, Ann 133, 145
  Avereler 151
  Benjamin 133 (2), 145
    (2), 146
  Charity 146 (2)
  Charles 129, 133
  Drewry 123 (will),
    124, 151
  Elizabeth 28, 45, 47
    (will)(3), 54, 56,
    133, 145

Hart (cont.)
  Henry 17, 45 (will)
    (2), 54 (3), 129
    (2), 133 (will)(3),
    145
  Henry Sr. 46
  Jane 45, 47, 129, 146
    (2)
  Jesse 47 (3), 56, 62,
    146 (will)(2), 151
    (2)
  John 45, 47 (3), 54
    (2), 110, 120, 123
    (2), 129 (will)(2),
    133 (2), 151 (2),
    155, 157
  Joseph (Jos.) 40, 45
    (2), 47 (3), 54 (3),
    110, 120, 145, 146,
    149 (2), 151 (2),
    155, 157, 161
  Joseph Jr. 151
  Joseph Sr. 133
  Lemuel (Lem., Leml.)
    103, 127, 129 (2),
    135, 162, 169
  Lucy 47, 133
  Mary 28, 47, 56, 146
    (2)
  Mildred 146 (2)
  Moses 146 (3)
  Nancy 146
  Olive 146
  Rebecca 129, 133
  Richard (Rich.) 144,
    145, 146 (3), 151,
    156, 161
  Robert 47 (will)(3),
    50, 56, 133, 144,
    151 (will)(2), 155
  Robert Jr. 28
  Samuel 129 (2), 133
    (will), 144, 146
    (2), 151
  Sarah 45, 47 (2), 56,
    146, 151 (2)
  Silvier 151
  Thomas 47, 122
  William 110, 111, 118
    (2), 146 (2), 148,
    171
Harwood, John 130
  Joseph 12, 51
  Mary 100, 130
Hase, Mary 17
Hastey, John 53
  see also Haisty, Hasty
Hasty, Benjamin 34
  Moses 159
  Robert 70
  Sarah 84
  William 17
  see also Haisty,
    Hastey
Hatfield, Charity 77
  Charles 88 (2), 90,
    105
  David 10
  Edward 170
  Elizabeth 77
  Jemima 88, 137
  Jemimy 77
  John 10, 26
  Josiah 77 (will), 105
  Mary 10 (2), 77
  Mildred 77
  Mills 105

Hatfield (cont.)
  Philemon 10 (2), 13, 14, 64, 67, 77
  Sarah 36
  Selah 77
  Susan 156
  Tabitha 77
  Tillaman 10
  William 10 (will)(2), 12, 13, 14, 35-36
Hausmann, John 129
  John D. 151
  see also Haussman, Houssman
Haussman, John 135
  John D. 147
  see also Hausmann, Houssman
Hay, Elizabeth 135
  John 33
  see also Hays
Hayes, Elizabeth 99
Hayley (?), Henry 163
Haynes, Ea. 39
  Herbert 35
  William 7, 11, 15, 18, 23, 27, 33
Hays, Elizabeth 3
  see also Hay
Hazlewood, Richard 19
Head, Sarah 79
Hedgepeth, Elizabeth 160
Hedgpeth, Charles 109, 118
Hellwig, George 129
  John 129 (will)
  Mary 129
  Polly 129
Helvey, John 132, 137
  Mary 137
Herne, Dennis 8
Herring, Daniel 115
  E. 107, 114
  Elias 35 (2), 42, 52, 63, 78, 80
Hickman, Elizabeth 21
  John 21
  Joseph 21, 27
  Martha 21
  Sarah 21
  William 21 (will), 22
Hicks, William 151
Hill, Isham 72 (2), 75
  Joseph 159
  Mary 3
  Reuben (Reubin) 81, 128
Hilliard, Francis 4, 25
  John 10
Hilsman, Bennett 28
Hines, Ann 89, 121
  Barham 82
  Benjamin 121 (2), 162
  Bolding 121
  David 53, 117 (will), 119
  Dolly C. 121
  Elizabeth 53 (2)
  Henry 121 (2)
  Howell 121 (will), 129
  J. Wm. 83
  John 53 (will)(2), 59, 89
  Joshua 53, 76, 80, 121
  Lucy 82, 85, 121 (2), 145
  Mary 53, 117
  Peter 53, 114

Hines (cont.)
  Richard 53, 118, 137
  Sarah Elizabeth C. 121
  Stephen 53
  Thomas 53, 83
  widow 137
  Will 133, 142, 144, 161
  William 53 (2), 103, 131, 139, 162
  William D. 156
Hitchings, James 22
Hix, Milley 75
Hobday, William 82
Hodges, John 15
  Patience 15
Holden, Benjamin 105 (will)(3)
  Janey 105
  John 47
  Joseph 18
  Samuel 47
  William 105, 170
Holding, Elizabeth 125
Holladay, John 143
  Thomas 87, 99 (2), 116, 141, 142, 144, 148, 164
  Thomas Jr. 159, 165
Hollaman, John 149
  Lucy 149
  William 149 (will)(2)
  see also Holleman, Hollemon, Holliman, Holloman
Holland, Thomas 134
Hollcome, Thomas 126
Hollcome (?), John 114
Holleman, A. 122
  Arthur 57, 62, 65 (2), 122, 138, 165
  Benjamin 80
  Exum 138
  H. 117
  John 149
  Joseph 65 (2), 68, 116
  Josiah John 118
  M. 98, 116, 135
  Mary 138
  Micajah 57, 63, 65, 80 (2), 98 (2), 111, 130, 138 (will), 149
  Mrs. 118
  Ned 110
  Rebecca 126
  Thomas 149
  Will. 157
  William 57, 63, 93, 126, 138, 149, 159
  see also Hollaman, Hollemon, Holliman, Holloman
Hollemon, Joseph John 10
  see also Hollaman, Holleman, Holliman, Holloman
Holliday, Ann 67
  Thomas 113
Holliman, Ann 25 (2), 35
  Arthur 25, 40, 46
  Benjamin 25
  Howell 25
  James 15, 16
  Jesse 25
  John 25
  Joseph 116
  Josiah John 35 (will)

Holliman (cont.)
  Josias John 25
  Lucy 25
  M. 98
  Micajah 62, 89 (2), 147
  Nathan 25 (2)
  Thomas 25 (will)(2)
  William 25 (2), 98, 130
  see also Hollaman, Holleman, Hollemon, Holloman
Holloman, Josiah John 14
  see also Hollaman, Holleman, Hollemon, Holliman
Holmes, Solomon (Sol., Solo.) 114, 118 (2), 131, 133, 136, 143, 144, 146, 147, 157 (2), 159
Holt, Ann 10, 20, 34, 109
  Charles 74, 87, 114
  Clerimont 59
  Etheldred 13, 36, 82
  Frederick 57, 114
  Henry 17, 59, 81, 91
  James 59
  Jesse 37, 83, 136, 165, 167
  Joannah 83
  John 109
  Joseph 26, 129
  Mary 109, 150
  Mason 57, 63
  Mason Kirby 114
  Nathan 114, 128
  Thomas 22, 48, 55, 109, 114 (will)(5), 128
  Thomas Sr. 75
Homes, Sol 152
Hoof, Elizabeth 99
Hook, James 12, 53
Hopkins, Joseph 142 (2)
  Wiley 142 (2)
Horn, Ann 119
  Fred'k 127
Hosea, James 171
Hough, James 117
  Martha 35, 117
Houssman, John D. 170
  see also Hausmann, Haussman
Howel, Nathaniel 52
Howell, Alfred 155 (2)
  Edmund 34
  Elizabeth 57, 59, 63, 124
  Goodrich 155 (will)
  Hartwell 40, 72, 124
  Henry 40
  Nathaniel 40
  Olive 34
  William 31 (will), 32, 33
Hubbard, Olive 94
Hunnicutt, James 134
  Rebecca 134
Hunt, Hardy 123
  Joshua 84
  Lucy 69
  Miles 144
Hurst, Abraham 153
  Amy 153

Hurst (cont.)
  Cate 153
  Charles 153
  Delitha 153
  Easter 153
  Nancy 153
  Oliver 153
  William 153 (will)(2)
  Write 153
Hutchings, Daniel 129
    (will)
  Daniel (Capt.) 93, 129
  Elizabeth 129 (2)
  Milly 152
  William 14
Ingles, Mary 37
Ingraham, James 72
  John 14
  Mary 14
  William 14 (will)(2),
    15
Ingram, Elizabeth 20
  John 19
  William 165
Inman, Elizabeth 44, 45
    (3)
  Jeremiah 143
  John Jr. 32
  John Sr. 5
Ireland, Nanney 123
Irwin, James 156, 161
Ivey, Adam 124 (2), 127
  Benjamin 139
  George 126, 135, 149
  Henry 45, 124 (will),
    131, 137 (2)
  Henry Jr. 25
  John 25, 61, 93, 111,
    126, 140
  John Sr. 33
  Peterson 124 (2), 137
  Philip (Phillip) 139,
    140
  Rhode 124
  Sally 124, 139
  Sucky 139
  Wike 122
  Winna 137
  Winney 124
  Wyke 124
Ivy, Benjamin 120 (2)
  Charles 63
  Charlotte 168
  Davy 95
  Elizabeth 95
  George 63, 97, 168,
    170
  Henry 63 (will)(3), 64
    (2), 66 (2), 74 (2),
    80, 90, 101, 168
    (will), 169
  James 95
  John 63, 75,78, 82 (2),
    85, 95 (will)(2)
  John Sr. 120 (will)
  Joseph 33, 35, 63
  Mary 120
  Phebe 63
  Phillips 120 (2)
  Phillis 63
  Rebecca 95
  Robert 63 (2), 64, 66,
    75
  Sally 141
  Sarah 63
  William 168

Jack, Martha 148
  Thomas 48 (2)
Jackson, Elizabeth 91
  Isham 155
  John 102, 113, 140
  Kindred 39, 113 (will)
    (2)
  Nathan 71, 101
  Patience 39, 113
  Sarah 71 (will), 72,
    101
  Silvy 89
  William 39 (will), 40,
    113, 120
Jacobs, Mary 143
Jacquelin, Edward 5
James, Enos 58, 67
  John 51, 164
  Mary 71, 78
  Patience 51
  William 129
Jarrel, Benjamin 46
Jarrell, Benjamin 8, 12,
    37 (2), 93
  Elizabeth 8
  John 8, 12 (will), 13,
    21
  Martha 8, 31, 60
  Mary 132
  Sally 84, 140
  Sarah 101, 103
  Thomas 8 (will)(4), 9,
    10, 11, 14, 54, 68
  Thomas (Capt.) 3
  Thomas (Col.) 9, 11, 12
  William 3, 8, 120, 155
Jarrett, Fortunatus 144
  John 144
  William 10
Jarrott, Fortunatus 142
    (will), 165
  John 142 (2), 165 (2)
  Nancy 142, 165
Jelke, Kinchen 145
Jelks, Anne 45 (2)
  Betty 45
  Kinchen 147
  Lemuel 45 (2)
  Mary 45
  Richard 108
  Tabby 45
  William 45 (will)(2),
    46
Jenkins, Albuin (?) 151
  Ann 115
  Betsey 115
  Edmund (Edmunds) 36
    (2), 57, 81 (will),
    92
  Edward 4
  Jacob 79, 104, 151
  Jean 36
  Jesse 115 (2)
  Sarah 81
  Spencer 115 (will),
    121
  Valentine 36 (will),
    40, 42, 81 (2), 92,
    113, 115, 166 (2)
  William 115 (2), 166
  Wilton F. L. 166
Johnson, Abraham 11, 62,
    65, 104 (will), 106,
    120
  Abram 73
  Alice 97, 109
  Allen 158

Johnson (cont.)
  Ann 19, 57, 70, 97,
    109
  Anne 6 (3), 32 (3),
    106 (2)
  Beal (?) 19
  Benjamin (Bensjamin)
    2, 6 (will)(2), 40,
    42, 106, 124, 133,
    150, 165
  Benjamin Jr. 6
  Betty 104
  Britain 57
  Celah 64
  Charity 19, 65, 104
    (will), 118
  Christian 53, 69
  Clabay 53
  Council 57
  Daniel 5, 8
  David 31, 37, 53, 65,
    120
  Dempsey (Demsey,
    Demsy) 31, 38, 39,
    43, 64, 90
  Edmond 119
  Edmund 92, 120, 127,
    150
  Eley 158
  Elias 104
  Elibey 91
  Elizabeth 6, 31, 53,
    58, 118
  Esmond 57
  Ester 8
  Giles 59, 76 (3), 81,
    106, 118 (will),
    122, 124, 132 (2)
  Hannah 132, 136, 162
  Hardy 79, 112, 116
    (2), 144, 163
  Harris 62, 70, 104
    (2), 158, 162 (2),
    169
  Henry 5 (2), 8, 14,
    32, 46, 171
  Hester 4
  Isaac 4, 44 (4), 62
  Jacob 5, 6, 31 (will)
    (2), 44, 97, 104,
    106 (will), 112
  James 19, 65, 93, 97
    (2), 107, 122, 158,
    160, 166
  Jesse 6, 34, 41, 68,
    76, 97, 105, 143
  Job 58 (will)
  Joel 162
  John 8 (will)(3), 10
    (2), 28, 31, 34 (3),
    38 (2), 57, 65
    (will), 66, 71, 76,
    78, 79, 81, 85, 90,
    97 (will)(2), 98,
    101, 106, 109, 118,
    119, 124, 125, 127,
    129, 132, 136, 140
    (2), 150
  John Sr. 140 (will)
  Johnson 150
  Jordan 109, 162
  Joseph 8, 19, 42, 48,
    71, 79, 84, 90, 97
  Joshua 6, 79, 158
  Josiah 31, 97, 104
    (2), 120, 132 (will),
    136, 158

Johnson (cont.)
  Katherine 121
  Kinchen 57, 64
  Lazarus 8 (3), 53(will)
  Lucy 8, 113, 134, 139
  Lydia (Lidia) 97, 109
  Martha 6, 8, 38, 53, 57 (2), 64, 69, 70, 77, 162
  Mary 6, 12, 21, 31 (2), 37, 76 (3), 79, 105, 106, 118 (2)
  Mathew 32, 79, 150, 171
  Micajah 104
  Milly 77
  Miriam 31
  Molly 162
  Moses 43, 65 (3), 72, 77, 78, 88, 100 (2), 114 (2), 116, 130
  Nancy 74, 132, 162 (2)
  Nathan 44
  Patience 4
  Patty 19
  Penelope 118, 124
  Penelopy 19
  Peninah (Penina) 31, 97, 109
  Petiance 168
  Pettaway (Pettway) 118, 125, 150, 164
  Polly 150
  R. 164
  Ralls 122
  Rawls 65
  Rebecca (Rebeckah) 19, 32, 65, 90, 97, 109, 112
  Richard 9, 19 (will) (3), 20, 29, 31, 41, 76, 79, 109, 127
  Richard Sr. 29, 92
  Robert 32, 34, 39 (2), 43, 57 (will)(3), 58, 64 (2), 91, 102
  Sally 150, 162, 171
  Samuel 4, 76 (will)(2), 78, 125, 161
  Sarah 8, 41, 57, 104 (2), 106, 118, 124, 127, 146, 150, 162 (will)
  Seley 57
  Simmons 105
  Simon 76 (3), 90, 113, 118, 130
  Simon Jr. 106, 113
  Stephen 20, 32 (will) (2), 43, 58, 79, 87, 96, 111, 118, 132, 150 (will)(3), 162, 165
  William 52, 91, 119, 133, 146, 150
  Willis 153
  see also Johnston
Johnson (?), David 112
Johnston, Benjamin 15, 38 (will), 86, 150
  Charity 86
  Elijah 156
  Harris 157
  Henry 38, 46, 86
  Jacob 38
  Jesse 38
  Job 38, 60
  John, 38, 79, 125, 150

Johnston (cont.)
  Johnson 150
  Joseph 38, 40, 86 (will)
  Lucy 38
  Mary 38, 99 (2)
  Mathew 150
  Molly 86
  Olive 86
  Patty 86
  Polly 150
  Richard 34, 68
  Sally 150
  Sarah 34, 150
  Stephen 38 (2), 150 (will)(2)
  William 38, 150
  see also Johnson
Joiner, Amos 165
  Bridgman 167
  Caty 158
  Charles 83, 167 (2)
  Elizabeth 165
  Giles 152
  Jacob 167 (will)(2)
  Jesse 165 (will)
  John 40, 42
  Jordan 167
  Joshua 40
  Joshua Jr. 132
  Lawrence 98
  Lemuel 165
  Lewis 89, 102, 132, 147, 165
  Margaret 153, 165
  Martha 148, 165, 167 (2)
  Molly 170
  Polly 167
  Priscilla 165
  Sally 165, 167
  Thomas 148
  William 41, 167
  see also Joyner
Jones, A. 5, 6, 7, 12, 22 (2), 31, 33 (2), 41, 48, 51, 109 (2), 110, 115, 138, 146
  A. Jr. 92, 93
  Abraham P. 108
  Abram Parham 54
  Albridgton (Albridgeton, Albridghton) 14, 21, 36, 43, 46, 53, 55, 79, 81, 93, 109 (will)(3), 132 (2), 163
  Albridgton (Col.) 156
  Allen 39
  Ann 31, 76, 108 (2), 132, 134, 150, 160
  Anselm 65, 72, 131 (2), 153, 156
  Arthur 4, 6
  Britain (Brittain, Britten, Britian) 3, 12 (2), 40, 75
  Charles B. 160
  David 54, 76
  Elberton 1
  Eleanor 3, 18
  Elizabeth 1, 6, 12, 17, 19, 47, 55, 76, 132, 150, 170
  Elizabeth B. 160 (2)
  Frances 29, 76, 163

Jones (cont.)
  Hannah Briggs (Hannah B.) 160, 169
  Hanselm 168
  Henry 89, 90, 105, 106, 113, 114, 116, 122, 127, 130, 135, 139, 146, 159, 168
  Honor (Honour) 58 (will), 64 (2)
  Howell (Howel) 54, 75, 108, 146 (2), 162
  Isham 3
  James 6 (2), 9, 13 (2), 16, 22, 29, 31 (2), 34 (2), 35, 36 (2), 42 (2), 46, 54 (will) (3), 55, 60, 63, 64, 72, 76, 86, 101, 108 (will)(2), 131 (will)(3), 138, 148, 153, 168 (2)
  James (Capt.) 105
  James Sr. 153
  Jesse 3, 20, 29, 33, 58, 61
  John 3 (will)(3), 4, 18, 58, 156
  Jordan 131 (2), 153, 168
  Joseph 2 (2), 4, 6, 10, 19, 39, 44, 47 (2), 58 (2), 131, 150, 164 (2), 170 (3)
  Joshua 3
  Lemuel (Lem., Leml.) 47 (2), 50, 56, 58, 66, 70 (2), 106, 114 (2), 120 (2), 123, 127, 128, 136, 150 (will), 164 (2)
  Lucaucy 76
  Lucresy 54
  Lucy 131
  Martha 3, 54, 84 (will), 91, 125 (2), 150
  Mary 53, 54, 55, 70 (2), 137 (will), 138, 139
  Mathew 6, 32, 37 (4), 38, 47 (2), 76, 92 (2), 93, 109, 132 (will), 134
  Molly 158
  Nancy 101
  Nathan 70 (will), 72, 108
  Nathaniel 147
  Peggy 150
  Phillip 6
  Rebecca Williamson (Rebecca W.) 160, 169
  Richard 54, 88 (will), 90, 148 (2)
  Robert 46 (2), 54 (2), 63, 64 (2), 76 (will), 98
  Robey 76
  Sally 169
  Samuel 150
  Sarah 3, 8, 12, 37, 51, 92, 132, 160 (will)
  Sely 12

Jones (cont.)
  Simmons 43, 53
  Simon 3 (2)
  Thomas 7, 12, 13, 14,
    27, 32, 36, 39, 43,
    51 (2), 65, 70, 92
    (will), 93, 160 (3),
    161, 169 (will)
  Thomas Jr. 39
  William 1, 2 (2), 12
    (will), 43, 47 (will),
    50, 109, 132 (will),
    138
  Willie 39
Jordan, Edmond 136
  Elizabeth 3
  John 12 (2), 13
  Joseph 130
  Josiah 10, 84
  Mary 8
  Mourning 10, 119
  Priscilla 141
  Robert Sr. 133
  Sarah 128
  William 13
  Wilmouth 130
Joyce, Bridgman 8
Joyner, Absalom (Absolom)
    75, 96 (3), 148,
    162, 163 (2)
  Alexander 7, 15
  Amey 23
  Amos 70, 88, 104, 135,
    136, 170
  Ann 9, 11, 23, 69 (2),
    80, 107 (will)(2),
    108, 119
  Arthur 17, 26, 132
    (will)
  Baker 65, 163 (2)
  Benjamin 6, 15
  Bridget 27 (2), 28
  Bridgman 9 (will)(3),
    11 (2), 20, 30 (2),
    67 (will), 68
  Britain (Brittain) 38,
    93
  Burgess 65
  Catie 107
  Celia 96
  Charles 46, 70 (2),
    113
  David 7, 15
  Drewry 151
  Drusilla 7 (2), 10
  Eaton 65, 147
  Edith 151
  Elenor (Ellinor) 11,
    15
  Elisha 151, 163
  Elizabeth 23, 75, 163
    (2)
  Ely 163
  Fereby 151
  Gethro 107 (3)
  Giles 11, 15 (2), 23,
    27, 28 (2), 30, 34,
    70, 89, 106, 108,
    114, 153, 160
  Henerilear (?) 8
  Henrietta 26 (will),
    27
  Henry 16, 26 (5), 27,
    31, 32, 33, 56, 70,
    80 (2), 90, 119
  Hoopy 42
  Hope 24, 35

Joyner (cont.)
  Israel 15, 18, 42, 46,
    70 (will), 73
  Jacob 9 (2), 11, 67
    (4), 70, 167
  Jacob Jr. 147
  James 163
  Jeremiah 171
  Jesse 9, 67, 75, 165
  Jethro 69 (2), 73, 107,
    116 (will)(2)
  John 10, 11, 15, 23(2),
    26, 27 (will), 28(2),
    33, 35, 38 (2), 39,
    40, 56, 59, 68, 70,
    110, 151 (2), 163
    (2)
  Jonas 38, 65, 113, 121,
    163
  Jonathan 2, 7 (will),
    10, 15 (3)
  Jordan 70
  Joseph 5, 11 (2), 15,
    23 (will)(3), 35, 42,
    70, 96
  Joseph Jr. 26
  Joseph Sr. 26
  Joshua 8, 11, 38 (will),
    151 (will)(4), 163
    (2)
  Joshua Jr. 152
  Josiah 107
  Judith 38
  Kemp 132
  Lawrence 69 (2), 71,
    73, 75, 79, 88, 107,
    123
  Lemuel 165
  Levina 165
  Lewis 11, 15, 22, 23,
    29, 62, 65, 67, 69,
    70, 73, 79, 81, 95,
    96, 101, 107, 124,
    125, 132, 165 (2),
    170
  Lewis Jr. 73, 78, 89,
    96, 97, 133
  Lewis L. 39
  Lewis Sr. 73, 96
  Lucy 124, 165
  Lydia 88
  Margaret 46, 141
  Martha 26, 70, 80, 116,
    151
  Mary 7, 15, 38(2), 67,
    107, 108, 163 (will)
  Mary Green 132
  Mathew 15 (2), 16, 70
  Moses 11, 15, 131
  Mourning 65
  Nanne 107
  Nathan 38
  Nelson 151
  Patience 7, 15
  Peggy 107
  Priscilla 46
  Rebekah (Rebeckah) 73,
    123
  Robert 132
  Sarah 9, 70 (3)
  Tabitha 65
  Tamer 116
  Theophilus 132
  Thomas 7, 15 (4), 16,
    75 (2)
  Toomer 76, 80, 89, 139

Joyner (cont.)
  William 11 (3), 15
    (will)(3), 16, 18,
    27 (2), 28, 30, 34,
    34, 59 (2), 69 (will)
    (3), 70, 99, 105,
    107 (2), 114, 116
  William Jr. 56
  Willis 88
  see also Joiner
Joyner (?), Joyner 93
Judkins, John 128
  Jordan 99, 114, 122,
    135, 148, 156, 163
  Mark 148, 151, 153
  Martha 69, 112
  William 92
Junnicutt, John 52
Kellam, William 34
Kelle, Elizabeth R. 148
Kello, R. 10, 13, 17,
    19, 20, 21, 31, 34,
    35 (2), 36, 43, 47,
    52, 69, 87
  Richard 3, 15, 24, 30,
    37, 53, 103, 109,
    121 (will)(2), 130,
    135, 142
  Richard Jr. 103
  Richard (Major) 35
  S. 123, 133, 135, 169
  Samuel (Sam.) 58, 62,
    64, 103, 112, 121
    (3), 122, 129 (3),
    130, 135, 138, 142,
    160, 167
  Samuel (Col.) 131, 150
  Saml. Jr. 160
  W. R. 86
  William 156
Kemp, Richard 23
Kennebrew, Edwin 83
    (will)
  Henry 83
  Priscilla 83
  Shadrack 83 (2)
  see also Kinnebrew
Kenny, Mathew M. 101
Kerby, John 135
  Lelas 82
  William 55
  see also Kirby, Korby
Kersey, Walden 135
Killegrew, Agnes 45
Kindred, Ann 86, 136
  Anne 104
  Benjamin (Benj.) 83,
    86, 104, 120, 136
    (will), 148
  Elisha 86, 104, 136
  Elizabeth 104
  Faith 5
  Henry 104 (2)
  J. 87, 151, 157, 160
  John 86, 102, 107 (2),
    136, 159, 170
  Mary 5 (will), 6, 20,
    28, 104
  Samuel 5, 20, 26, 44,
    62, 69, 92, 104
    (will), 108
  Sarah 104
King, Katherine 49 (will)
    (2)
  Martha 102
Kinnebrew, Ann 57, 68
    (will), 69, 71

Kinnebrew (cont.)
  Anne 68
  Edith 57, 59, 63, 71, 85
  Edwin 57, 68, 71, 75, 89, 94
  Jacob 57 (2), 58, 64, 71
  Lot 57, 68 (2), 71
  Prissy 68
  Shadrack 57 (2), 58, 71 (2)
  William 18 (2), 26, 35, 38, 57 (will), 58
  see also Kennebrew
Kinnebrough, William 34
Kirby, Ann 158 (will)
  Benjamin 52, 81 (2), 83, 134
  Frances 19 (2)
  John 16, 20 (3), 57(2), 59, 63, 69, 76, 78, 83, 85, 90, 91, 118, 119, 152
  Judith 20
  Lewis 158
  Mary 57, 63 (will), 64
  Miles 83
  Moody 16, 19 (will), 20 (2), 23, 158 (2)
  Nicholas Williams Gilas (?) 158
  Richard 16, 20 (will) (2), 22, 29, 83 (will)(3), 109
  Richard Jr. 6
  Sally 84
  Silas 81, 83, 88
  Thomas 83
  Turner 57, 59, 63, 99
  Will 35
  William 6, 18 (2), 20 (3), 35, 38 (2), 46, 49, 57 (will)(2), 59 (2), 63 (2), 158
  see also Kerby, Korby
Kitchen, Ann 35
  Benjamin 72 (will)(3), 97
  Betsey 72
  Celia 72
  Dickson 40
  Etheldred 72
  Frederick 72 (2)
  James 21, 31, 35, 57
  Jesse 72
  Lucy 72
  Martha 72, 137
  Mary 72 (2)
  Molly 131
  Nathaniel 72
  Rebecca 40 (2)
  Sarah 72, 98
  Silvia 40
  Thomas 40 (will)(2), 42 (2)
  William 97 (2)
Kitching, Ann 23
  Benjamin 23
  Christian 23
  Elizabeth 23 (2)
  James 23 (will)(2), 28, 31
  Joseph 23
  Lydia 23
  Martha (?) 23
  Mary 23

Kitching (cont.)
  Mathew 23
  Melicent 23
  Patience 23
  William 22, 23, 101
Knight, Charlotte 124
  John 73
  Lewis 130
Korby, Benj. 127
  see also Kerby, Kirby
Lain, Ann 2
  Joseph 138, 145 (2)
  Polly 145
  Thomas 101, 103, 121, 123, 138, 145 (3)
Laine, Thomas 62, 156
Lancaster, Etheldred 105 (2), 107
  James 105 (2), 107, 149 (will), 156
  Jerusha 149 (2)
  Joseph 19, 24, 105 (will), 107
  Lawrence 19, 98
  Mary 105
  Mildred 149
  Polly 149 (2)
  Rebecca (Rebeckah) 149 (2), 162
  Robert 9
  Zilla 149 (2)
Land, Bird 140 (will), 144
  Lewis 140
  Lieuallen 140
  Littleberry 140 (2)
  Mary 40
  Nathaniel (Nath'l) 123 (2), 132
  Sarah 114
Lane, Benjamin 2
  Drury 153
  Faith 2, 67
  Fathy 54
  Henry 123
  Jesse 47
  Joel 142
  John 104
  Joseph 2, 47
  Levi 123
  Lucy 57, 129, 131
  Thomas 64, 66, 75, 78, 85, 94, 100, 113, 151, 171
  William 44, 88
Langley, Thomas 8, 72
Lanier, Mary 141
Lankford, Ann 83
  Elisha 82, 83, 107
  Elizabeth 82, 83, 107
  George 33
  Jesse 83, 107
  John 28, 116
  Margaret 83
  Mary 33
  Rebecca 83
  Thomas 28, 33 (2), 37, 78 (2), 80 (2), 82 (will), 84, 107
  Thomas Jr. 33, 66
Larke, Joseph 12
Laugn (?), William 39
Lawrence, Charles 23, 28 (2), 29
  Elizabeth 131
  George 28, 29, 33
  Hardy 33

Lawrence (cont.)
  Jacob 132 (2), 133, 135
  Jesse 132
  John 9, 11, 118, 134
  Josiah 132 (2)
  Lemuel 109
  Lyddy 152
  Margaret 131
  Priscilla 132
  Rhoda 131
  Robert 20, 30, 132 (will), 135
  Susanna (Susannah) 131, 134
  Thomas 21, 27, 48, 71, 78, 88 (2), 101, 121, 131 (will), 134
  William 131 (2), 134, 148
Ledbetter, John 5
Lee, John 129, 148
  Thomas 2
  William 51
  William, Jr. 51
Levy, Henry 136
Lewis, Becky 122
  Benjamin 14, 28, 35, 37, 61, 69, 78, 84, 86, 87, 93, 98, 122 (will)(2), 161
  Bridget 26
  Catherine 18
  Edmond 18
  Eliplas 74
  James 18 (2)
  Jenny 122
  Joanna 18
  John 9, 30, 33
  Joshua 18 (will)(2)
  Lemuel 110
  Martha 18 (2)
  Mary 84, 122
  Mille 18
  Sarah 18, 97
  Shad 86, 100 (2), 101 (2), 102, 107, 116, 144, 150
  Shadrack 43, 66, 78, 80, 83, 105, 107, 115, 125
  Thad 80 (2), 112, 119
  Theo 80
  Zebulon (Zeblon) 122 (2), 135, 148, 152, 156, 161 (3)
Lewter, Hannah 65
  Joh Sr. 77
Linear, Lucy 112
Lisles, Sarah 74
Lithgee, John 9
Little, Allen 158
  Ann 13
  George 80
  John 15, 32 (will)(2), 34, 42, 69, 145
  Lucy 32 (2), 33, 145
  William 32 (2), 69, 151, 167
Livingston, John 129
Lones, Thomas 92
Long, Arthur 3, 4, 10, 33, 40 (will)(2), 43
  Burwell 150
  Davis 40
  Drewry 40 (2)

Long (cont.)
  Drury 39
  Elizabeth 40
  James 25
  John 25, 40 (2)
  Littleton 40
  Lucy 40, 132, 138, 164
  Martha 132
  Mary 10
  Polly 132 (2), 164
  Prudence 26
  Sarah 40, 74
Longworth, John 74
  Joseph 75, 103
Love, Eleanor (Elenor)
    17, 21, 58
  Elias 17 (will)(2), 21,
    22
  Henry 17, 88
  Margaret 73
  Silas 17, 88
  Thomas 17
Love (?), Leighborn 123
Low, Lightborn 87
Lowe, Betsey 145
  Cajah 155
  Cherry 145
  Elias 145 (2)
  Elizabeth 147
  Jeremiah 155
  Ledbetter 71, 123
  Leighborn (Leighbourn,
    Lighborn) 36, 93,
    120, 123, 155 (will),
    158
  Lemuel (?) 155
  Levi 145 (will)
  Martha 21
  Micajah 145, 155
  Milly 155
  Nancy 145
  Patsey 155
  Patty 66
  Sally 145 (2)
  Samuel 155
  Silas 167
  Spencer 145
  Thomas 165
  Wiley 155
  Willias 155
Lubree, Daniel 10
Lucas, Federic 89
  Frances Briggs 141
  Lila 20
  William 141
Lumbley, Elizabeth 23
  Jesse 23
  Richard 23
  Thomas 23 (2ill)(2), 24
Lunday, Nancy 167
Lundy, Byrd (Bird) 59,
    65, 68, 71 (will)(3),
    78, 81, 83, 137 (2),
    142, 144, 153, 168,
    169
  Charles 144
  Charlotte 153
  Christian 71
  Clarimon Holt 120
  Claud 71
  Drewry 59 (2)
  Drury 57, 65, 68, 74,
    81 (2), 83
  Edith 120 (2), 153
    (will)

Lundy (cont.)
  Edward 17, 52, 59(will)
    (3), 61, 67, 68, 72
    (will), 92, 94, 146
  Edward Jr. 46, 91, 139
  Edward Sr. 139
  Edwin 71 (3), 137
  Elizabeth 71, 72, 81,
    99 (2), 120, 150,
    168
  Frances 72 (2)
  Isham 83, 99 (4)
  James 30, 46, 59, 61,
    71, 72, 78, 81 (2),
    83 (will)(5), 88,
    91, 99 (5), 100, 101,
    105 (2), 107, 110,
    112, 117, 119, 120,
    124, 126, 131, 135
    (2), 136 (2), 137
    (2), 140, 145, 150,
    151 (2), 155, 160,
    164, 165, 168, 170,
    171
  James Jr. 67
  John 59, 72, 81, 92
    (2), 120 (will)(2),
    124, 154 (2), 162,
    166 (will)
  Joshua 71, 137
  Lunsford 72, 99, 150,
    151, 168 (2)
  Mary 83, 99, 137 (2)
  Milly 71
  Molly 83
  Pattey 120
  Peyton 120, 150, 153,
    154, 169
  Phoebe (Phebe, Pheeba,
    (Pheeby) 66, 68, 71
    (2), 78, 137 (2)
  Priscilla 169
  Robert 17, 83 (2), 99
    (will), 101
  Sarah 83 (2), 99
  Thomas 99
  William 72 (2), 99 (6),
    101, 139
  Winifred 99
Lutar, John 88
Luter, John 59, 62, 63,
    65 (2), 78, 106,
    109, 117, 125, 130,
    156
  Thomas 59, 62, 63, 64,
    65, 76, 78
Luter (?), John 44
Lutter, John 56
Lyles, John 5
M (?), Silve 105
Mabry, Abel 14
  Robert 135, 136 (2),
    137, 139, 142, 145,
    149, 150, 151 (2),
    152 (2), 154, 159,
    165, 167 (2), 168,
    171
McCabe, John 128, 134
McCroskey, Chanette 58
  Samuel Smith 58 (2)
McKenny, Mary 119
  Moses 113, 126
  see also McKiney
Mackenny, Sarah 4
Mackey, Ann 24
  Daniel 24 (will)

Mackey, Elizabeth 80 (2)
  Hope 24
  John 24, 26
  Joseph 23, 80 (will),
    81
  Mary 23
  Rebecca 53
  Sally 24
  William 24, 53 (3),
    117, 132
Mackie, Daniel 30, 32
  John 60
McKiney, Mathew 55
  see also McKenny
Mackmial, Andrew 2
Mackmiles, John 23
McLamre, John 169
McLemore, Betsey 168
  Charles 127
  Elizabeth 22, 96, 97
    (2)
  James 96, 168
  Joel 96, 168
  John 13, 22, 33, 96
    (will)(2), 166, 167,
    168 (2), 169 (2)
  McKerina 96
  Olive 96
  Polly 168
  Priscilla 97, 118
  Sarah 69
McMial, Andrew 13
McMore, Priscilla 120
McNeil, Alexander 142
    (2), 148
  James 123, 142 (will),
    169
McNiel, James 122
Macom, Susanna 126
Macy, Jane 18
Maddra, James 74
Madele, A. 125
  Alex 125
Madell, Alex 125
Maer, Abraham 49
Magee, Nancy 168
  Robert 168
  see also Megee
Maget, James 77, 105,
    126, 127, 130, 157,
    168, 170
  John 81, 133, 157 (2)
  Micajah 46, 61
  Nicholas (Nich^s.) 17,
    18, 19 (2), 29, 34,
    43, 44, 48 (2), 49,
    53, 55, 81, 82, 91,
    96, 105 (3), 111
    (3), 130, 132, 157
    (will)(2), 162
  Nicholas (Capt.) 49,
    127
  Samuel (Saml.) 19, 82,
    96, 105 (3), 106,
    111, 124, 126, 128,
    130, 132, 133 (2),
    140, 148, 157 (2)
  Samuel Jr. 43
  Sarah 130
  William 104, 111, 130,
    157
Main, John 91
Major, Nicholas 6
Maning, Richard 17
Mann, Sarah 125 (will)
Mannery, Peter 152

Manning, Elizabeth 2
　Jonathan 2
　Lucy 2
　Mary 2
　Richard 2, 48, 57, 65,
　　108
　Samuel 2 (will), 4, 35
　Sarah 2 (2), 4
　Susannah 2
Marks, Edmund 150
　John 146
　Joseph 87 (2), 98
　Richard 87 (3), 98
　Thomas 18 (2), 28, 34,
　　39, 53 (will), 59
　William 140
Martin, Amy (Amey) 114,
　　127
　Celia 85
　James 56, 89, 127
　　(will), 138
　John 85 (will)
　Kinchen 127
　Lucy 102
Mason, Elizabeth 79
　Isaac 17
　L. 127, 135, 152 (2)
　Littleberry 85, 112 (2)
　Rebekah 112 (2)
　Richard 74, 94, 97, 141
　Thomas 19, 99
Massingaile, Daniel 75
Mathews, Arthur 52, 61
　Elizabeth 7
　Mary 7
　Samuel 88
Matthews, Aaron 4
　Abigail 22
　Ann 4 (2)
　Arthur 82, 100, 113
　Benjamin 4
　Edward 4, 20, 26
　Hugh 4 (will), 6 (2)
　Jacob 4
　John 4, 15, 22 (will),
　　26
　Jonas 4
　Joseph 4 (3)
　Lydia 22
　Mary 82
　Pherriby 22
　Ralph 4 (2), 36
　William 4
Meacom, Mathew 53
Meacome, John 159
Meacum, John 72
Mecom, James 144
　John 62, 135 (2), 138,
　　144
　Mary 62
　Mathais 62 (will)
　Rebecca 144, 161
Mecome, Mathew 130
　Polly 131
　Rebecca 130
　Samuel 130
Megee, Nancy 149
　see also Magee
Meglamore, Hetty 167
　John 150, 167 (will)
　　(3)
　Letty 167
Mellone, William 132
Melton, Elisha 65
Memore (?), Elizabeth
　142
　James 142

Memore (?) (cont.)
　John 142 (2)
　Polly 142
Mercer, Betsey 136
　Betty 66
　Grace 66, 136
　James 65, 66
　John 65, 66 (will)(3),
　　113, 120, 136, 157
　John Jr. 65
　Patience 66, 136
　Robert 47, 65 (will),
　　68, 116 (3), 136
Merring, Daniel Jr. 61
Messer, Robert 10
Mial, Andrew Mack 163
　Sarah 33
　Thomas 33
Middleton, Mary 3
Miles, Elizabeth 8
Millar, James 108, 165
　Sarah 96
　William 49, 50, 72, 81,
　　96
Miller, Ann 129
　Benjamin 135
　James 139
　Sarah 86
　William 67, 68 (2)
Millton, Randolph 139
Milton, Ann 126, 155 (2)
　Ann Jr. 126
　Elisha 35
　Leah 155
　Patsey 126, 155
　Randolph 155
Minard, Jesse 56
　Joshua 76
Miniard, Joshua 28, 39,
　　80 (2), 89, 108, 141
Mirick, Fanny 111
　John 78
　Martha 77
　Owen 4
　see also Myrick
Mitchel, Abraham 121
　Abram 88
　John 68, 74
　Sarah 157
Mitchell, A. 134
　Abraham 48, 50, 51 (2),
　　60, 67, 69, 71, 78,
　　80, 89, 91, 101, 129,
　　168
　Abram 69
　Ar 138
　John 24 (2)
　Molly (negro slave) 142
Mongers, Robert 53
Moody, Elizabeth 96
　Philip 91, 94, 96
　　(will), 133
　Samuel 96
　Sarah 35
　West 96
Moore, Betsey 85
　Elizabeth 54, 64, 71,
　　74, 87, 101, 103,
　　107
　James 11, 50 (2), 54,
　　68, 74 (will)(2),
　　78, 87, 112, 123
　Jesse 74
　Jesse Williams (Jesse
　　W.) 50, 167
　John 54, 64, 101, 103,
　　158, 171

Moore (cont.)
　Martha 74
　Rebecca (Rebakah) 54,
　　64, 85, 101, 103
　Richard 74
　Ruth 6
　Sarah 54 (3), 64 (3),
　　74, 85, 101, 103
　　(will), 104, 123,
　　136, 152
　Thomas 54 (will)(2),
　　64 (2), 123
　William 54, 64, 73,
　　84, 91, 101 (will),
　　102, 118
Morgan, Ann 82
　Anne 95
　Celia 85
　Elizabeth 82
　Foster 82, 112 (will)
　James R. 112
　Jarret 82 (2), 112 (2)
　John 56, 61, 82 (will),
　　85 (will)(2), 90, 92
　Martha 97, 118
　Mary 86, 118
　Mathew 85, 139
　Patience 82
　Rebecca 80
　Salia 85
　Sarah 82, 100
　William 25 (will), 60,
　　67, 82, 98
　William Jr. 25
Morrell, Mary 118
　Mathew 60
Morris, Chislin (Chis-
　　lon) 83 (2), 105
　Elizabeth 108
　Henry 137
　Jabez 137
　John 156, 165 (3), 168
　Nicholas 46
　Nicholas Sr. 165(will)
　Suckey 83
　Thomas Jr. 99
Moseley, Robert 129
Mosley, Else 4
　Joice 77
Moss, Henry 94
Mossom, Jane 81 (2)
　Richard 81 (2)
　William 81
Mounger, Henry 6, 30, 78
　Jethro 6
　Joseph 2, 6 (3), 15,
　　16, 30
　Robert 6 (will)(2)
Mountford, Joseph 78,
　　93, 100, 101
　Thomas 135
　Wade 110, 135
Mountfort, Francis 110
　Joseph 95, 107
　Sarah 110
　Susannah 110
　Thomas 110 (will)(2),
　　112
　Wade 110
Mountfortt, Joseph 66,
　　70, 78, 80 (3), 83
　　(2), 84, 99, 105,
　　110, 151
　Thomas 66, 83, 84, 99
　Wade 82
Mundell, Elizabeth 66,
　　110 (2)

Mundell (cont.)
  John 5 (2), 8, 11, 15,
    16, 21, 22, 31, 40,
    41 (2), 44, 50, 58,
    96, 110 (will)(2),
    128
  John Jr. 96
  Joseph 110, 156
  Lidia 110
  Mary 110
  William 110
Munger, Joseph 2, 13
  Mary 78
Murfee, Burwell 145
  Celia 121
  Drewry 145
  Francis 121, 131, 145
    (3)
  Josiah 131, 145 (3),
    147
  Lucy 121
  Matt 130
  Molly 121
  Nancy 121
  Richard 8
  Richard Jr. 93
  Richard Sr. 121 (will),
    130, 145
  Sally 121
  Simon 101, 109, 117,
    121 (2), 134, 145
    (will)(2), 148, 152
  William 121 (2), 130,
    161
  Wills 145
Murfree, Richard 101
  Simon 98
Murphee, James 92 (will),
    96
  Susanna (Susannah) 92,
    96
Murray, Alexander 98, 100
    (will), 101
  Mary 88, 100, 101, 130
    (will)
  Sarah 100
Murrell (Murrel), Robert
    140, 168
Murry, Alexander (Alex.)
    13, 78
  Robert 168
Myrick, Amy 51
  Ann 51, 59, 146 (will),
    162, 165
  Benjamin 162
  Edmunds 70
  Evans 162
  Fanny 102, 108 (2),
    149, 158(2)
  Henry 108, 143, 149
    (2), 158 (5)
  Howell (Howel) 51, 79,
    99, 102, 109, 146,
    150, 162 (will)(2),
    165
  Janny (Janney) 144, 149
  John 51 (will)(2), 52,
    59 (2), 65, 74, 77,
    83, 105, 108, 112,
    146 (2), 158 (2)
  Lucy 108, 150, 158
  Martha 70
  Mary 84 (will)
  Nancy 108

Myrick (cont.)
  Owen 51 (3), 59, 64,
    78, 102, 108 (will)
    92), 110, 111, 149
    (2), 158 (2)
  Robert 167
  Sarah 102, 108
  Susan 70
  William 51 (2), 106,
    109, 115, 125, 138,
    143, 146 (2), 149,
    162
  William M. 162
  see also Mirick
Nash, Elizabeth 165
Neal, Edward 117
Negro, Fanny 120
  Samuel 157
  Tom 120 (will)
Neil, Alexander M.
    (A.M.) 136, 139, 153
Nelms, John 130
Nelson, William 2
Newby, Elizabeth 143
  Nathaniel 143
  Sally 143
  Thomas 38
Newsom, Ann 36
  Bailey V. 52
  Barham 41
  Benjamin 36
  David 6, 13, 41 (will),
    45
  Jacob 13, 36, 46, 90
  James 41
  Jesse 31
  Joel 36, 41
  Joseph 36 (will), 38,
    43, 45
  Lucy 41
  Martha 4
  Mary 41 (2), 54
  Nuet 169
  Patience 36 (3), 40
  Patty 36
  Randolph 41
  Robert 36, 70
  Sally 36
  Tabitha 40
  William 41
Newson, Nuet 169
Newsum, Agness Polly 77
  Amos 10
  Ann 23
  Barham 125
  Benjamin 26, 55, 168
    (will)
  Crafford 168
  David 10 (2), 19
  Dysa 168
  Elizabeth 10 (will),
    11, 13 (2), 124,
    161, 168
  Fanny 82
  Francis 103
  Gilliam 75
  Hartwell 77 (2), 78,
    108
  Isham 75, 161
  Jacam 107
  Jacob 10, 26, 66, 75
    (will)(2)
  James 85
  Jesse 77
  Joel 112, 125 (2), 128
  John 127

Newsum (cont.)
  Joseph 13 (3), 14
  Julian 13
  Littleberry 75
  Lucy 82
  Marget 108
  Martha 82, 105
  Mary 13, 77
  Mildred 102
  Moses 10
  Nathan 10, 22, 29
  Nathaniel 78
  Patience 161 (will)
  Patsey G. 161
  Patty 107, 115 (2)
  Phebe 85
  Priscilla 28 (will)
  Randolph (Rand.) 84,
    106, 110, 115, 117,
    125, 128, 138, 156,
    165
  Robert 13 (will)(4),
    15, 25
  Robert Jr. 102
  Sally 112, 161 (3)
  Sampson 10, 77 (will)
    (2), 78, 158
  Sarah 13
  Solomon 10, 11
  Thomas 10, 13, 85,
    104, 144
  Thomas Jr. 127
  Turner 85, 165
  William 82, 102, 109,
    126, 141, 167
  see also Nowsum
Newton, Alice 69, 160
  Hosea 136
  John 1, 44
  Shadrack 44
  William 20, 24, 136,
    151, 160
Niblett, James 77
Nicholson, Benjamin 161
  Charles 145, 162
    (will)
  Charles Briggs 85, 144
  Fanny 35, 102, 111
  Harris 162
  Henry 89
  Howell 99
  Jenny 161
  John 84, 99
  Joseph 53, 59
  Joshua (Joshuah) 35
    (will)(4), 36 (2),
    37, 50, 55 (2), 57,
    61 (2), 62, 63 (2),
    64, 66 (3), 67, 73,
    74 (2), 75, 78, 79,
    85 (will), 91, 92,
    95, 102, 111, 119,
    146
  Joshua Jr. 51
  Lucy 70, 102, 111
  Mark 88, 93, 95, 96,
    99, 100 (3), 104,
    115, 123, 126, 135,
    139, 144, 148, 159
    (3)
  Mary 57, 59, 63, 70,
    84 (2), 85, 144
    (will)
  Mary Jr. 103
  Matilda 102, 111
  Parks 147

Nicholson (cont.)
  Patsey 153
  Polly 161
  Rebecca 99
  Robert 159, 160, 161
  Samuel 99 (will), 138
  Sarah 35, 36, 63, 99,
    102 (will), 111, 147
  widow 62
Nicolson, Joshua 75, 78,
    80 (2), 82, 84
  Lucy 77
  Mark 76
  Mary 77, 103, 119
  Samuel 82
Nixon, Barnaby 134
Norfleet, Cordall (Cordal)
    18, 24, 28 (2), 33,
    40 (2), 41, 43, 46,
    52, 59, 61, 62, 77,
    80, 81, 82, 85, 116
    (will)
  Elizabeth 116
  John 116
  Mary 116
  Sarah 116
  widow 9
Norman, William 29 (will),
    32
Norseworthy, Mary 161
Norsworthy, Joseph 21
Norton, Joseph 26, 29
  Joseph Jr. 25 (will)
  M. 22
  Sarah 25
Norvill, Mary 97
Nowsum, Joseph 22
  see also Newsum
Oberry, Bailey 147
  Henry 42
  John 38, 42 (2), 43
    (2), 84
  Nathan 42
  Sarah 28
  Thomas 7, 27, 29, 42
    (will), 43, 114
Oney, Barbary 73-74
  Benjamin 31, 46, 73-74,
    76, 164
  Elizabeth 102
  Hannah 76
  John 32, 76, 102 (will),
    103
  Leonard 29, 76 (will)
    (2), 78
  Lucy 76
  Martha 76
  Mary 76
  Rebecca 102
  Sarah 102 (2), 103
  Thomas 76 (2), 78, 93
Oquin, Daniel 17
Owins, William 108
Owlet, Valentine 36
Pain, Basill 110
Parham, Nathaniel 30
Parke, James 133
Parker, Benjamin 121
  Betsey 117
  Drewry 37, 46, 51, 117,
    125 (2), 150
  Drury 117 (will)
  Edwin 117
  Frederick (Fred'k) 117,
    150, 153, 169
  Howell 117

Parker (cont.)
  Jane 85
  Judith 117
  Lewcy 117
  Luky 117
  Mary 124, 127
  Mathew 117
  Milly 117
  Nanny 117
  Patty 117
  Polly 117
  Richard 53, 81, 117
    (2)
  Suky 117
  Tempy 117
  Thomas 117
  William 117
  Williamson 150
Parr, John 76
Parsons, Benjamin 48
Parten, Penina 139
Pate, Ann 12 (2)
  Edward 12 (will)(2),
    95 (2)
  Herbert 141
  Jordan 141
  Milly 12
  Samuel 12
  Thomas 12, 95 (2)
  Thomas Jr. 144
  Travis 12
  William 95
Payn, Thomas 166
Payne, Basel 112
Pearce, John 41
Pebworth, Robert 157
Peden, James 71
  Mary 22, 25
Pedin, James 113
  Patience 113
Peding, James 48
Peebles, James 134
  Peter Jr. 134
  William 142
Peete, Alexander 73
  Benjamin 73
  Elizabeth 73
  Samuel 34, 73
  Thomas 64, 73 (3), 109,
    110, 119, 129, 131,
    138, 141, 143, 148,
    152, 155, 156, 161,
    166
  Thomas (Dr.) 81, 167
  Thomas Jr. 152 (2)
Peirce, Bolton 139
  Elizabeth 124, 139
    (will)(2)
  Mathew 121
  Nathaniel 139
  Peter 139
  Rice B. 94, 121, 127
  Spencer 139
  see also Pierce
Peircy, Suzana 89
Pelham, Parthenia 148
  Peter 148
Pennington, James 140
  Rachele 140
  William Thomas 133
Peoples, Susanna 142
  William 142 (2)
Person, Anthony 42, 163
    (will), 171
  Benjamin 5, 39
  Colin 39, 92

Person (cont.)
  Collier 91 (will)
  Dorcas 5, 22, 39
  Elizabeth 5, 91 (2),
    163, 164 (3)
  Hannah 5
  Henry 5 (2), 16, 163,
    164
  John 5 (will)(6), 6
    (3), 8, 11, 18, 21,
    22 (2), 39 (will),
    41, 42 (2), 50, 60
    (will), 62, 112,
    118 (3), 147, 163
    (2), 164 (will)
  John Anthony 164 (2)
  John Jr. 5 (2)
  John Sr. 5
  Lucy 22
  Marianna 164
  Martha 84
  Mary 5, 16, 31, 42
    (2), 60, 99, 145
  Nancy 91
  Patsey 90
  Philip (Phillip) 39,
    60, 90 (will), 91,
    118 (3), 124
  Polly 84, 164 (3)
  Prescilla 5
  Presley 39
  Rebecca (Rebeccah) 5,
    164 (2)
  Sarah 5
  Temperance 90
  Tempy 60
  Thomas 5, 9, 42, 112
  Timothy 90
  Turner 22, 39, 90,
    135, 145
  Will 32, 34, 36, 42
  William 5, 15 (2),
    21, 31 (2), 32 (3),
    39, 42 (will)(3),
    60, 118
Pete, Thomas 139
Peterson, Ann 36
  Batt 68
  Gomer 140
  John 68
  Kinchen 84
  Mary 36
  Sally 54
Pheasant (Phaesant),
    John 10 (will)(2), 15
Phillips, Aaron 26, 29,
    31, 32, 38, 40, 46,
    50 (2), 51 (will),
    52, 60
  Benjamin 70, 139
  Edwin 51
  Elizabeth 51
  John 75 (will)(3), 78
  John Jr. 31
  Joseph (Jos.) 13, 14,
    24, 25, 28, 30, 31,
    32, 34 (2), 38, 52,
    63, 75, 78
  Joseph Sr. 40
  Joshua 75
  Lemuel 51
  Lucy 74, 75
  Martha 3
  Mary 51

Phillips (cont.)
  Moses 13, 25, 26, 30
    (3), 47, 50, 57, 64,
    65, 87, 129 (will)
  Priscilla 78
  Sally 169
  Sarah 51
  J. 94
  Thomas 75, 122
  William 147
Pierce, Elizabeth 148
  Elizabeth Jr. 148
  John 66
  Mary 163
  Rice B. 148
  Spencer 144, 148, 157,
    163
  see also Peirce
Piles, Vincent 92
Pillar, John 108
Pinner, Jesse 35
  Sarah 10
Pitman, Amy 6
  Anne 17
  Arthur 3, 9, 14, 30
  Etheldred 119
  Hannah 68
  John 9, 35, 75, 82
    (will), 83, 87
  Lucy 52
  Mourning 82
  Priscilla 51, 52
  Sampson (Samson) 2, 6
    (2), 7, 13, 16, 18,
    25, 41, 43 (2), 51,
    65, 75, 87, 88, 114,
    131
  Samuel 25, 30, 58, 101
  Winifred 52
Pitmon, John 166
Pitt, Ann 124
Pleasants, John 8
Pledger, John 84, 111
  Lucy 132, 162
  Silas 162
Pleger, John 89
Pond, Daniel 15, 30, 66,
    108 (will)(2), 109,
    149, 163
  Diana (Dianah, Dianna)
    149 (2), 164, 168
  Drewry 131, 149 (2),
    163, 165, 168 (will)
  Elizabeth 108
  James 71, 149
  John 80, 97, 108 (2),
    109, 113, 149, 164,
    168
  John H. (John Hawkins)
    71 (2), 102, 113,
    118, 139, 142, 149,
    163, 164
  John Jr. 154, 164
  Martha 10, 71 (2), 80
  Mary 71, 108, 149 (3),
    154, 163, 164 (will)
    (2), 165 (2)
  Mason 153
  Patty 83
  Richard 10, 11, 15, 31,
    58, 66, 71 (will)(3),
    72, 74, 80 (2), 94,
    103, 108 (2), 109,
    142, 149 (will), 163,
    164
  Richard Sr. 131, 156,
    165

Pond (cont.)
  Samuel 108, 149, 164,
    168
  Sarah 71, 108
  Stephenson 113
  Thomas 71
  William 149 (2)
Poole, Elizabeth 92
  James 92
  Susannah 92
  William Murphee 92
Pope, Andrew 45, 69 (4),
    79
  Ann 18, 69, 79 (2)
  Arthur 18, 38
  Benjamin 13, 23 (will),
    25
  Brittain 18
  Charity 18, 44, 77
  Christian 69 (2)
  David 135
  Elizabeth 4, 13 (will)
    (2), 23, 74, 113
  Elijah 44, 77
  Ennis 44
  Evans 135, 136
  Fanny 44
  Hannah 135
  Hardy 24, 30, 32, 33,
    37, 39, 57, 69, 76,
    78 (2), 97, 105, 106,
    116, 122 (2), 123
    (2), 125 (will)(3),
    127, 153
  Henry 15 (will)(2), 16,
    18, 38 (will)(3), 41
    (2), 57, 60, 76, 97,
    116, 117, 121, 125,
    126, 158
  Henson 79, 124, 137
  Hezekiah 69
  Isaac 44, 96
  James 38
  Jehu 77, 137
  Jesse 18, 23, 69 (2),
    70, 135 (will)(2),
    138
  Jinny 135 (2)
  Joel 44 (2)
  John 4 (will)(3), 7,
    8, 9, 13, 14, 18, 30
    (2), 33, 37, 41, 44,
    45, 54 (will), 59,
    69 (4), 70, 79 (will)
    (2), 80, 106, 111,
    124, 125, 135
  Jonathan 44, 77
  Joseph 35, 68, 89, 91,
    113, 125
  Josiah 77, 170
  Joshua 44 (will)(4),
    45 (2)
  Lazrus 38
  Martha 18, 20, 49, 69,
    124, 156
  Mary 15 (2), 23, 49,
    74, 124, 125, 126,
    127, 135 (2), 140
  Meley 23 (3)
  Micajah 44
  Molly 125
  Mourning 15, 116
  Nancy 125 (2), 158
  Nathan 4, 44 (will)
    (4), 46, 53, 77,
    161 (2)

Pope (cont.)
  Nathaniel 135 (2),
    138, 156
  Olive 35
  Patience 44 (2), 53,
    58, 77 (will)(2),
    90, 117
  Phoebe (Phebe) 44, 77
  Polly 58, 125
  Priscills 30
  Prudence 116
  Rebecca 74
  Reuben 44
  Richard 15 (2), 18,
    25, 33, 44, 77,
    116
  Sally 79, 124
  Sarah 15, 35, 44
  Savia 44
  Simon 14, 15, 18, 20
    (2), 25, 149
  Stephen (Stephan) 13,
    18 (will), 20, 24,
    140
  Temperance 79
  Thomas 23 (2), 69,
    117, 124 (2), 161,
    163
  William 3, 4 (3), 7,
    13 (2), 18, 21, 23
    (2), 30 (will)(3),
    33, 41, 43, 69
    (will)(5), 79, 97,
    98, 113, 116 (will),
    124, 140
  William Sr. 79
  William (?) Sr. 33
  Winee 125
  Zedekiah 135
Porch, Ann 113
  James 113 (will)(2),
    126(2)
  Peggy 113
  Pennington 113
  Peterson 113
  Thomas 88, 99, 113
Portear (?), Ann 8
Porteous, John 13, 16
Porter, Ann 20, 139
  Betty 21
  Britton 115
  Daniel 107
  Drury 116
  Henry 115, 157
  Jacob 139 (2)
  James 139 (will)(2),
    143
  John 20, 37, 69, 88,
    103
  Julan 115
  Julia 115
  Leddice 139
  Lucy 139
  Lydia 146
  Milly 116, 146 (2)
  Nathan 139 (2)
  Newit 115, 116
  Polly 139
  Solomon 116
  Thomas 85, 115, 116
  Thomas Sr. 115 (will)
  Winny 116
Portis, John 16
Portlock, Charles 71, 72
Poter, Abraham 80
Powel, John 87, 88

Powell, Dred 136, 151,
    160 (2), 166
  Elizabeth 17
  James 41, 61, 152
  James L. 141
  John 26, 33, 62, 69, 70,
    73, 77, 90, 92, 102,
    107, 108, 111, 115,
    120, 148, 151
  Joseph 17, 24, 62
  Lucy 13
  Martha 61
  Sarah 151
  Seymour 42
  William 41
Power, Eleanor 17
Powers, Charles 24, 32,
    59, 75, 88, 111, 114,
    131
  Henry 100
  Mary 137
  Peggy 167
  William 3, 133
Poynter, Elizabeth 36
  Theophilus 36
  Unity 36
Poythress, John 59
Pretlow
  and Randolph 147
  Ann 134
  Benjamin 110
  Charlotte 141
  Jenney 110
  John 110
  Joseph 110 (3)
  Joshua 5, 110 (2)
  Mary 8, 38, 110 (2),
    134 (will)
  Samuel 110 (2)
  Thomas 38, 110 (will)
    (2), 134, 163
  Thomas Jr. 110
Pride, Halcott Briggs 99
Prince, Joseph 141, 155
  Priscilla 141
  William 99
Pritchard, Elizabeth 127
Pritchette, Henry 59
Pulloyal, Capt. 129
Pully, Esther 7
Pursel, John 134
Pursell, Arthur 40, 42,
    44 (will)(2), 47,
    49, 166 (2)
  John 44 (2), 50, 65,
    66, 71, 85, 92, 102,
    111, 113, 121, 128,
    136, 145 (2), 154,
    166 (will), 167
  Martha 145 (will)
  Mary 44, 166
  Peter 44, 166 (2)
  Thomas 2, 4, 11
Pursell (?), Martha 12
Pylent, Thomas 7
Railey, James 11
  Mary 35
  Miles 35
Raines, Hartwell 141
  Rebecca 141
Raley, Susannah 101
Ramsey, Catherine 50 (3),
    77, 143
  Catron 118
  David 50
  Henry 50, 118

Ramsey (cont.)
  James 21 (2), 32, 39,
    50 (will)(2), 51, 77
  John 50
  Lyda (Lidia) 50 (2),
    118 (2)
  Mary 50
  Temppy 50
  William 50
Rand, (?) 115
Randal, Annanias (Dr.)
    125
  Temperance 125
Randall, Ananias 107
Randolph, Annais 94
  Jacob 68, 118
  Temperance 159
Rawl, John 111
  see also Rawls
Rawlings, Ann 114
  Burwell 132
  Edwin 162
  George 40
  Gregory 28, 45
  Isaac 74 (2)
  John 13, 74 (will),
    101
  Mary 74
  Nancy 114 (2)
  Polly 114
  Rebecca 114
  William 57, 63, 74
Rawls (?), John 111
  see also Rawl
Ray, Celah 155
  Elizabeth 155 (2)
  Howell 155
  James 65
  John 155 (will)(2)
  Mary 155
  Reuben 65
  Sally 65
  William 65 (will), 100,
    155 (2)
Read, Cordall 123
  John 123 (will)
  Mason 123
  Sally 123
  Sarah 123, 159
Reas, Sarah 159
Reaves, Priscilla 43
Reece, Joseph Jr. 71
Reed, Alexander 56
Reese, Christian 59
  Edward 75 (3), 77, 80,
    91, 107, 167
  Edwin 133
  Elizabeth 143
  John 75, 80, 95, 97,
    102, 103, 106, 129,
    133, 139, 144 (2),
    167
  John Jr. 120
  John Sr. 131, 139
    (will), 142, 148,
    156
  Joseph 63, 74, 75
    (will)(3), 77, 78,
    103, 106, 133, 139
  Joseph Jr. 81, 92
  Lewis 133, 167
  Mary 52, 53, 75, 84,
    136, 139 (2), 161
  Olive 52, 53, 107,
    133 (will), 135,
    136, 142, 167 (3)

Reese (cont.)
  Patty 139
  Randolph 139 (2), 144,
    156, 161
  Rebeccah 133
  Reuben 139
  Rivers 139, 144
  Roger 139 (2), 144
    (2), 156, 167
  Rowell 139, 144
  Selah 97, 139
  Silvia 133
Reid, John 39
Renn, Richard 74, 109
Revel, Grace 12
  Holliday 45
  Martha 8
  Simon 70
  see also Revil
Revell, Holladay
    (Holliday) 167, 170
  Sarah 147
  see also Revill
Revil, Charlotte 83
  Holliday 83
  Martha 31
  Mourning 83
  Sampson 83 (will)
  see also Revel
Revill, Sampson 85
  see also Revell
Ricgardson, John Thorp
    84
Richardson, Hannah 67
  John 137
  John T. 118 (2), 137
  Jordan (Jordin) 118,
    125 (3)
  Milly 98
  Silvia 125
Rickards, Richard 8
Ricks, Ann 8, 33, 76
    (2), 103, 127, 134,
    139
  Anne 33
  Elizabeth 8 (will)(2)
  John 76
  Joseph 33, 76 (3), 79,
    103, 106, 134
  Mary 33 (3), 76 (2),
    103 (will)(2), 108,
    134
  Milicent Ann 134
  Milisent 76, 103
  Millicent 33
  Richard 8 (2), 11, 12,
    19, 21, 33 (3), 74,
    76 (will)(4), 78,
    79 (3), 87 (2), 90,
    103, 106, 108, 128,
    134, 141
  Robert 8 (2), 33 (will)
    (2), 46, 76 (4),
    79, 103, 108, 110,
    128, 134 (4), 169
  Thomas 8, 33 (3), 42,
    48, 76 (3), 103,
    106, 128, 134
Riddick, Lemuel 48
Ridley, Amey 143
  Ann 9
  Anne 7
  Arthur 85 (3)
  Bromfield (Brumfield)
    10, 85 (3)
  Day 7, 42, 55, 56, 57,
    60(2), 61, 67 (3)

Ridley (cont.)
  Elizabeth 71, 85 (3)
  Frances 85
  Francis 142
  J. 6, 56, 73
  J. D. 85
  Jack Edwards 135 (will)
  James 1, 2, 4, 5, 7
    (2), 11, 16, 29, 31,
    34, 35, 55 (2), 66,
    67, 78, 85 (will),
    86 (2), 143
  James Day (James D.)
    30, 31, 59, 62, 71
    (will), 77, 85 (3)
  James Day (Dr.) 63
  Jane 135
  John 55
  John Edwards (John E.)
    71, 85, 165
  Martha 60, 84, 125
  Mary 71 (3)
  Mathew 67, 142 (will)
  Nathaniel 7 (will)(2),
    9 (2), 55 (3), 67
    (will)(3), 72
  Pamilla 7
  Peggy 84, 118 (2)
  Priscilla 7 (2)
  Rebecca 71, 85 (4)
  Sarah 67 (2), 72, 85
  Thomas 7, 54, 59, 65,
    67, 90, 95, 96, 106,
    126, 130, 131, 133,
    136, 138, 143, 156
  Thomas Sr. 142
  Will 88
  William 85 (2), 100
Riggan, Sally 67
  William 88
Riggin, Richardson 97
Right, James 85
  John 85
  Joseph 85 (3)
  Mary 85 (will)
Rite, Joseph 44
Rivers, Elizabeth 35,
  102, 111
  John 166 (2)
  Nancy 120, 153
Rives, John 162
Roberts, Christian 44
Robins, James Francis 30
Rochell, John 88, 134
  Levy 134, 152
  Sally 122
Rochelle, John 108, 119,
  136 (will), 138
  Judeth 136
  Levi 136
Roe, Samuel 158
Rogers, Allen 131
  Collins 160
  John 76, 78, 83, 91,
    97 (2), 99, 110 (2),
    119 (2), 120 (2)
  Jonathan 61
  Michael 19
  Prudence 38
  Roger 61
Rollings, Ann 45
Rose, Burrell 36 (2)
  Christian 59
  Francis 43, 53, 74
  Mary 36
  Richard 12, 36 (will)
  William 112, 155

Ross, Chrles (Chs) 86,
  116
Rotchell, Ann 8
  George 8
  John 8 (will)(3)
Row, Cordial 160
  Gordial 102
Rowe, Cordall 163-164
  Lemuel 170
  Martha 27
  Samuel 163
  William 27
Rowell, Benjamin 21
Rowland, Ann 156
Ruffin, Ann 1
  Ben 7
  Benja. 168
  Benjamin 1, 10, 24,
    36, 65, 75, 83, 103
    (will)(3), 105, 109,
    113, 114, 122 (2),
    129, 134, 137 (2),
    143, 152, 163 (2)
  Benjamin (Behjamin) Jr.
    32, 36, 37, 39, 43,
    63, 65, 72, 93, 122,
    129
  Edmund 1
  John 103
  Joseph 129
  Lucy 1
  Sarah 129
Russell, Mourning 98,
  103
Sadler, Charles 149 (2),
  151
  John Smith 98
  Rhoda 98 (2), 103
Salls (?), Elizabeth 8
Salter, Ann 105 (2), 106,
  134, 161
  John 80, 94, 106
  Mary 121
  Will (Wil) Jr. 62, 77
  William 105
  William Jr. 70
Sammons, Betty 94
  James 85
Sammons (?), Betty 74
Sandefur, Hill 10
  Mary 10, 11
  Nancy 166
  Samuel 10
  William 10 (will)(2),
    11
  see also Sandifur
Sanders, Alex 125
Sandiford, Anne 123
  Charles 154
  Samuel 69
Sandifur, William 17,
  155
  see also Sandefur
Saul, Benjamin 23
  Elizabeth 9 (will), 10
  John 40
  Mary 18
Sauls, John 35, 40
Savage, Aaron 16
  Joshua 16
  Moses 16 (will)
  Sarah 88
Scarborough, Benjamin
  72, 89
  Betsey 89
  Brittain 89
  John 89 (will)(3)

Scarborough (cont.)
  Mary 89 (2)
  Patty 89
  Robert 89
  Sarah 89
  Sukey 89
Scarbrough, Howell 140
  Mary 148
  Samuel 84
Scoggins, James 118
Scott, Abigail 30
  Anne 66
  Elizabeth 8 (2), 10
    (will)(2), 68, 104,
    134
  Exum 5 (2)
  J. 152
  James 6, 66, 147
  James Jordan (James
    J.) 5, 9, 10 (3),
    11, 15, 20, 23, 24,
    28, 29, 30 (3), 31
    (3), 32 (2), 33 (3),
    34, 35 (2), 37 (3),
    38, 41 (2), 42 (3),
    43 (2), 46, 51, 53,
    58, 65, 66 (will),
    78, 81 (2), 115
  James M. 43
  Jo. 162
  John 5, 15, 22, 36,
    68, 110, 143
  Joseph (Jos.) 66 (2),
    81, 115, 125, 136,
    144, 146, 147, 150,
    163, 165
  Joseph Jr. 109, 110,
    112, 122, 126, 151
  Mary 138
  Miriam 42, 66, 81 (2),
    115
  Robert 66
  Sarah 66
  Theophilus 138
  Thomas 101, 109
  William 5 (will), 6,
    59, 68 (2), 104
Screws, Holland 127
Sebrell, Benjamin 24
  (2), 40
  Daniel 4
  Joshua 62
  Mary 110
  Rebecca 131
  Samuel 59
Sedget, James 71
Selden, Miles (Rev.) 38
Sellers, Arthur 44
  Fathey 48
Servents (?), H. Cl. 160
Seward, Coufield 169 (2)
  Edwin 85, 102, 111,
    169 (will), 170
  Sarah 109
Sharp, Burivel 88
  Francis 5, 6
  Henry 103
  Honour 118
  John 5
  Thomas 9, 134
Sharpe, Hannah 44
  John 61
  Richard 106
  Robert Darden 134
Sheild, Robert 105
  see also Shield
Shepherd, Solomon 87 (2)

Shereman, Mathew 140
Sherod, Arthur 142
  Sarah 142
Sherrard, Sarah 64
Shield, Charles 36
  Robert 89
  see also Sheild
Shields, Robert 57
Sikes, Andrew 4
Simmons, Ann 52, 109, 121
  Benjamin 1 (3), 2 (2), 4, 14, 20, 28, 29, 34 (2), 35, 37, 38, 40, 54 (will)(2), 135
  Catherine 52
  Charles 1 (5), 2, 6, 16, 18, 20 (2), 21, 22, 43, 52 (will), 53 (2), 169
  Daniel 72, 119, 122, 125, 127, 135, 150, 168
  Edwin 132, 133 (2), 138
  Elizabeth 54 (2)
  Frances 2
  Hannah 154, 169
  Henry 1 (2), 54, 136, 160, 164, 168
  James 161
  John 1 (will)(4), 2, 16, 20, 32 (2), 33, 34, 35 (2), 37, 52 (2), 54 (3), 57, 60, 61, 63 (2), 68, 72, 76, 79, 81, 86, 87, 88, 89, 91 (2), 94, 95, 98, 99, 100, 101, 103, 104, 105, 117, 119, 125, 127 (2), 130, 135, 136, 138, 148, 152 (2), 159
  John (Col.) 1, 4
  John Jr. 56, 59, 119, 126, 159, 171
  John Sr. 69, 98, 108, 112, 115, 122, 125, 126, 134, 152, 157, 159
  Joseph 91 (will), 98
  Keziah 54
  Loisa 138
  Lucy 31, 54, 60, 91, 125
  Martha 54
  Mary 1 (2), 52
  Mary Cock 84
  Mason 52, 109, 132
  Milly Taylor 91
  Nancy 132, 138
  Oluf 91
  Peter 134, 167
  Rebecca 84
  Richard H. 132, 138
  Sally 155 (2)
  Sarah 52 (3), 72, 94
  Silviah 91
  Spratley 54, 86, 121
  Stephen 13, 21 (2)
  Susanna (Susannah) 54, 69
  Thomas 72
  Valentine 39
  William 1, 2 (2), 17, 19 (2), 31, 32, 39, 62 (2), 72 (will), 91, 120 (2), 132-133 (3)

Simon, Augustine 19 (will)(2)
  Jacob 19
  John 19
  Sarah 19
Simons, Jacob 24, 29, 32
  John 2
Simpson, Samuel 92, 97
Sinclair, Arthur 106
Slade, Jethro 123 (2)
  Joshua (Josh.) 123, 147
  Mary 123
  Samuel 17 (2), 23, 27, 123 (will)(2), 167
  William 123 (2)
Sledge, Charles 94
  Herbert 149
  John 85
  Sally 85
Smelly, Giles 11 (will), 12
Smith, Aaron 135, 136, 138, 143, 155, 156, 159 (will), 165
  Absalom (Absolom) 13, 32, 42
  Aron 132
  Arthur 7 (3), 31, 106 (2)
  Benjamin 106
  Elizabeth 7, 100, 130 (2)
  Flood 13, 42
  George 1, 5
  Hannah 13, 42, 59
  Henry 93, 103, 106, 109, 114, 116, 125, 147 (2), 155, 156, 166
  Isom 44
  James 9 (will)(2), 138
  Jane 13 (will)(2), 15
  John 9 (2), 10, 80 (will), 83, 113, 132
  Joseph 7, 13 (3), 42 (2), 62 (2), 106
  Lawrence 13, 42, 125
  Martha 7, 80, 98 (will), 101
  Mary 9 (3), 118, 155
  Mathew 43, 85, 106 (will), 107
  Mourning 106
  Nathaniel 144
  Patience 7, 65
  Polly 159
  Rebecca 159
  Sarah 12, 13, 71
  Thomas 159 (2)
  Turner John 12 (will), 13, 14
  Virgus 7 (will)(2), 31, 106
  William 51, 104
  William Alexander 130
  William Turner 159
Sorsberry, Henry 134 (2)
  Jemimah 134
  Mary 134
Sousberry, Mary 74
Southward, Charles 122
Southworth, John 17
  Thomas 17
Speed, (?) 152
  Ann 132
  Benjamin 69

Speed (cont.)
  Charles 51, 101, 162 (will)(2)
  Dickey 162
  Edwin 132
  George 6, 23, 43, 132
  Hellen 69
  Henry 162
  James 69
  Jenny 162
  John 6
  Mary 43, 51, 72 (will), 75
  Milly 132, 162
  Patience 162
  Rebecca 72
  Rhoda 162
  Robert 51, 84, 127, 132 (will)(2), 136
  Sarah 6
  Suckey 162
  Thomas 162
  William 34, 41, 48, 51, 162 (2)
Spence, Charles 7, 12
  Elizabeth 101
  John 13, 58
  Mary 13, 22, 132
  Media 52, 53
  Midda 84
  Mildred 136
  Sarah 55
  William 13 (will), 16
Spencer, David 101
  Edmund 101 (will), 104, 106
  Ezekiel 101
  Jesse 101
  Mary 101, 164
  William 101
Spivey, Benjamin 39, 90, 159
  Britain 159
  Elizabeth 53
  Ephraim 131
  John 136, 143
  Martha 39
  William 36, 39, 94, 136, 143 (2), 159, 163
Spivy, Benjamin 137 (2)
  Britain 137 (2)
  John 137
  Mary 137
  Sarah 137
  William 103, 132, 137 (will) (2)
Spivye, Aaron 53
  Charity 53
  William 53 (2)
Spratley, Benjamin 88, 93, 113
  John 136
Stakes, Zerobabell 140
Standford, William 59
Stanford, William 44
Stanley, James 40
Stanton, Christian 117
  Elizabeth 117
  Faith 117
  James 117 (will)(2), 118
  Lucy 117
  Mary 117
  Sampson (Samson) 117 (3), 118, 137, 143, 163

Stanton (cont.)
  Sarah 117
  Silvanus 117
Stephens, Amos 161
  George 4
  Lucy 131
  Simon 14
  William 54
Stephenson, Amos 129
  Ann 63 (will), 67
  Benjamin 63
  Catherine 8
  Celah 45 (2)
  Charles 114, 165 (2)
  Charlotte 114
  Dizey 165
  Edmund 104, 114 (2)
  Elizabeth 45 (2), 65, 66, 114
  George 7 (2), 62, 93, 104
  Henry 68
  James 45
  John 19, 114
  Katherine 7 (will)
  Lemuel 165
  Lucy 68
  Martha 63
  Mary 114
  Mathew 45
  Patience 86
  Peter 19
  Robert 114
  Sally 165 (will)(2)
  Sarah 7
  Simon 31, 33, 45 (2), 52, 83, 100
  Solomon 4, 7 (2), 8
  Stephen 114
  Thomas 33, 52, 57, 60, 114 (will)(3), 123, 144
  Thomas Jr. 45
  Thomas Sr. 45 (will), 48, 123
  William 7, 31, 45, 66, 86, 89, 106, 165
  William Sr. 114
  Willis 114
Sterling, James 58, 60, 63 (2)
Stevens, Dorcas 82
  H. 60
Stevenson, Bennett 170
  Elizabeth 170
  Josiah 170
  Martin 170
  Mary 170
  Nancy 170
  Rebekah 81
  Simon 17, 86
  Spratley 162
  Thomas 170 (will)
Steward, Benjamin 171
  Hannah 11
  Lemuel 150
  Liddia 171
  Mary 11 (2)
  Sarah 35
Stewart, Benjamin 74, 83, 89, 118, 143 (will)
  Charles 143
  Henry 143
  Lemuel 117
  Lydia (Lyddia) 89, 143
  Samuel 143
Storrs, Thomas 50, 54

Story, Daniel 7, 11, 103, 104
  Elizabeth 103
  James 25, 27, 48, 67, 103 (will)(2), 104
  Janet 166
  John 103
  Lewis 103
  Mary 11
  Nanny 103
  Salah 103
  Sally 103
  Samuel 74, 103 (2)
  Sarah 48
Street, Asa 96
Strickland, Elizabeth 9
  Joseph 47
Stricklin, Elizabeth 168
Stringer, John 69
Sturgeaon, William 147
Sturgeon, Celia 69
  J. 42
  John 34 (2), 42, 49, 56, 64, 69 (2), 77, 81 (will), 94
  John Williams 81
  Saley 81
  William 81, 163, 164
Sueter, Thomas 93
Suiter, John 80
Suitin (?), John 52
Suitor, John 64
Sullivan, Isaac 169
Summerell, Anna 170
  Boaz Gwin (Boaz G.) 104, 105, 158, 170
  Diana 170
  Eleanor 170
  Elizabeth 170
  George 2, 102 (2), 105, 130
  Gwin 28, 31
  Henry 158
  Herod 170
  Jacob 48, 65, 141
  James 64, 83, 86, 89, 100, 102, 105, 114, 144, 170 (will)(2)
  Janey 102
  Jeremiah 102
  John 17, 22, 26, 29, 31, 57, 66, 83, 86, 87, 93, 102 (will) (4), 106, 108, 115, 117
  Lemuel Butts 170
  Lucy 102
  Milly 170
  Nancy 102
  Sally 170
  Samuel 102 (2)
  Sarah 102 (2), 108, 122
  Sikes 170
  Silas 170
  Stephen 89, 93, 102 (2), 114, 117
  Thomas 102, 144, 170 (3)
  Thomas Travis 142
  William 170 (2)
Summerrell, Boaz G. 47
  Elizabeth 45
  George 45
  Hartwell 144
  Jacob 144 (will)
  Jane 45

Summerrell (cont.)
  John 45, 72
  Lucy 144
  Margaret 144
  Sam Manning 144
  Stephen 45
  Thomas 45
Surkett (?), Martha 10
Suter, Arthur 114, 143, 160
  Elizabeth 114
  Henry 114, 143
  John 44, 103, 114 (2), 117, 143, 156, 160, 164
  John Sr. 114 (will)
  Rebecca 114, 143
  William 114, 143 (will)
Sweney, Ruth 10
Sweny, Semour 56
Swet, James 123
  Patience 123
Swett, Hannah 115
  William 115
Sykes, Lucy 70
Tabb, Edward 51
Tallaugh, Absalom 62 (2)
  William 114
Tamer (?), Nathaniel 77
Tanner, Dorcas 169
  Joseph 4
  Samuel 65
  William 10
Tarver, Mary 74
Tatem, Richard 89
Tatum, Elizabeth 64 (2), 73
  John 62, 73
  Joshua 64 (will), 65, 73
  Rebecca 64, 73
  Richard 73
Taylor, Anna 36
  Anne 61
  Bartin 74
  Bartur (?) 113
  Betsey 161
  Charles 36, 37, 45, 55, 56 (3), 58(will) (2), 61, 68, 88, 126, 142
  Charlotte 84, 125 (will), 131 (2)
  Edmund 25, 26, 35 (3)
  Edward 9
  Elizabeth 23, 84, 88, 126 (2), 131, 166
  Etheldred (Eth^d.) 11 (will)(2), 36 (2), 56, 58, 68 (will), 75, 84 (2), 98, 122, 126 (will), 129, 131 (2), 133-134 (2), 155 (2)
  H. 131
  Hannah 9, 166
  Harris 5, 9, 58, 74 (will), 75
  Henry 11, 28, 31 (2), 38, 41, 46, 55 (2), 56 (2), 58, 60, 63 (2), 67 (2), 72, 73, 74 (2), 75, 78, 84 (will)(3), 92, 98, 126, 131, 166 (2)

Taylor, Henry (Col.) 131
  Hermon 9 (2)
  James 9 (2), 11, 36,
    50, 55, 68, 88(will),
    93, 123, 131
  Jamey 41
  Jesse 48
  John 9, 11, 36 (2),
    49, 56, 58 (3), 67,
    68 (3), 81, 84, 88,
    95, 96, 111, 112,
    116 (2), 125, 126
    (2), 129, 131, 133,
    134
  John Jr. 125, 126, 150
    (2), 156, 158, 166
    (will)
  John Sr. 139, 142 (2)
  Katherine 9 (2), 35
    (will)
  Kinchen 11, 26, 31, 48
    (2)
  Lucy 44, 67 (will), 74,
    131, 161
  Margret 9
  Martha 56, 67, 84, 131,
    161 (2)
  Mary 11, 84, 131, 161
  Mary Mason 56, 67, 84
  Molly 82
  Nancy 161, 166
  Olive 9
  Patience 36 (will)
  Richard 11, 36, 81-82
  Richard Jr. 21
  Ridley 31, 48 (2)
  Robert 56, 67, 84, 125,
    127, 133 (will), 139
  Sally N. 161
  Samuel 74
  Sarah 36, 111
  Susanna 82
  Temperance 41, 67, 75,
    78, 125 (2), 133, 160
  Thomas 9 (will)(3), 74,
    75, 85, 134, 157
  William 10, 11 (2), 18,
    22, 28, 47, 52, 55,
    56 (will)(2), 131
    (2), 166 (2)
Tharpe, Ann 24, 25 (2)
  Joseph 25 (will), 26
  see also Thorpe
Thelwell, Edward 19
Thomas, Drucilla 52
  Elizabeth 53, 141
  George Gurley 141
  Henry 4, 5, 6, 7, 8, 9
    (2), 11 (3), 12 (3),
    13, 15, 16, 23, 24,
    29 (2), 30, 33, 38,
    41, 47, 49 (2), 50
    (2), 53 (will), 55,
    128, 135, 141 (2),
    156
  John 9, 14, 44 (will),
    50, 141 (2)
  Jordan 98, 110
  Lucy 141
  Martha 11, 33, 49, 53
  Mary 53, 75, 135
  Nathan 149
  Richard 6, 7
  Sarah 53
  Will 25, 45, 59

Thomas (cont.)
  William 20, 24, 25, 29
    (2), 32, 36, 40 (2),
    41, 47, 48 (3), 49,
    50, 51, 52 (2), 53
    (2), 55 (2), 56, 58,
    59, 62, 63, 68, 69,
    73 (2), 76, 79 (2),
    85, 89, 97, 102, 104,
    108, 109 (2), 111
    (3), 112, 114, 138,
    141 (will)(2), 153,
    167
Thompson, Drucilla 136
  Rebecca 49
Thompson (?), Drucilla
  53
Thomson, Harris 142
  Lodowick 142
Thorp, (?) 171
  Aaron 143
  Ann 84
  Fanny 138
  Hardy 164, 165 (2)
  Henry 102, 106, 139
  Jeremiah 82, 164
  John 4 (2), 24, 82,
    143 (will)(2)
  Joseph 4, 85, 138 (2),
    171
  Joshua 74, 101, 119,
    122
  Joshua Jr. 165 (2)
  Lewis 171
  Margaret 4
  Martha 84, 138 (will)
  Mary 4 (2)
  Moses 75, 82, 126 (2),
    143
  Pamelia 138
  Peterson 42
  Polly 143 (2)
  Sally 138
  Sarah Briggs 102
  Susanna 140 (will)(2),
    143
  Timothy 4 (will)(3),
    5, 6 (2), 7, 84 (2)
  Willey 164
Thorpe, Aaron 52 (2), 53,
    55, 73, 84, 122, 136
  Ann 75
  Anne 52 (2), 53
  Edith 52, 53, 84
  Hardy 132
  Harry 132
  Henry 52, 53, 84, 137,
    138, 155
  Jeremiah 52, 53, 82,
    84, 132 (will), 136
  John 12, 37 (2), 52
    (will)(2), 53 (2),
    74, 84 (will), 90,
    107, 109 (will), 122
    (3), 127, 135, 139,
    140, 149, 151
  John Jr. 136 (3)
  John Sr. 136 (3)
  Joseph 32, 109, 145
  Joseph T. 124
  Joshua 33, 77, 86, 90,
    119 (2), 124, 127
    (will), 129, 132
    (2), 164
  Lewis 71, 78, 79, 81,
    83, 86, 122, 127 (3),
    137 (2), 165

Thorpe (cont.)
  Lucy 109, 127
  Martha 31, 84 (2), 90,
    132, 136 (2)
  Moses 52, 53, 63, 94,
    122 (will), 136, 151
  Olive 37, 109, 132
  Patsey 118 (2)
  Patty 31
  Peterson 31 (2), 46,
    60, 78, 118
  Phebe 52 (2), 53, 84
  Sarah 169
  Sarah Briggs 122
  Silvia (Silva) 31, 60
  Susannah 37, 109 (2)
  Temperance 31
  Thomas 52, 53, 84
  Timothy 13 (2), 16,
    31 (will)(2), 56,
    60 (2), 73, 74, 76,
    78, 91 (2), 93 (2),
    98, 100, 118 (will),
    125, 132
  Timothy (Capt.) 25,
    54, 55, 125
  Timothy Jr. 125
  Willie 132
  see also Tharpe
Thweath, Jean 30
  Peterson 30
Thweatt, James 30 (2)
  Rebecca 30
  William 26, 30 (will)
Tillar, Henry 143
  Jack 138
  John 138 (will)
  Polly 138
  Rebecca 138
Tiller, Henry 137
Tines, Mary 26
West 85
Tompkins, Bennet 51
Toney (?), Lucresly 89
Tooke, Joseph 57
Travers, Charles 18
Traverse, Charles 17
Travis, Britain
    (Brittain) 93, 153
  Catherine 153
  Charles 10 (2), 153
  Lucy 153
  Patey 153
  Pyland 153 (will),
    156
  Tabitha 153
Tucker, Benjamin 75
    (will)(2), 101
  Elizabeth 75
  Henry 75 (3)
  Henry Crafford 101
  John 75 (2), 101
  Mary 134
  Phebe 75
  Robert 134
  William 75, 105
  Winifred 75
Tunnell, John 119
  Mary 117
Turner, Amies 115
  Amos 62, 74, 115, 145
  Ann 11, 36, 51, 77,
    85, 115, 123, 125,
    148, 164
  Ann Northington 155
    (2)
  Anne 41

203

Turner (cont.)
  Arthur 22, 77, 90, 99,
    102, 112, 115, 124,
    143, 154, 155, 164
  Ben. 95
  Benjamin 36 (4), 41
    (3), 45, 57, 58, 61
    (2), 63 (2), 66, 68,
    77, 85 (will)(2),
    93, 99 (will), 101,
    102, 119, 128 (3),
    140 (will), 141, 143
    (2), 150, 159, 165
  Betty 40
  Catherine 61
  Caty 61
  Celia 57 (2)
  Chacy 115
  Charlotte 115, 150
  Clear 113
  David 62, 74
  Edmond 147
  Edmund 94, 126, 147,
    150 (4), 155 (2),
    170
  Edwin 122
  Eliza 165
  Elizabeth 36, 41, 94,
    122, 123, 127, 140,
    159
  Elizabeth Bittle 128
  Etheldred 127, 143, 149
  Everett 164
  Fanny 77
  Hannah 41
  Harris 92
  Henry 30, 39, 85 (2),
    90, 127 (will)(2),
    128 (will), 159 (2),
    169
  Holland 102, 115
  Jacob 41 (2), 46, 62,
    64, 65, 68 (2), 70,
    74, 82, 94, 110, 111,
    117, 121, 123, 127
    (3), 132, 142 (2),
    143, 144, 146, 158,
    164
  Jacob Jr. 102, 166
  Jacob Sr. 102 (will)
  James 10, 15, 41 (will)
    (3), 42, 62, 77, 93,
    95, 102, 117, 125,
    126, 143, 150 (will)
    (2)
  James Jr. 7, 13 (2)
  James Sr. 7
  Jesse 36, 62, 63, 74,
    92
  Joel 99, 144
  John 22, 36 (2), 41,
    54 (2), 62 (will)(2),
    63, 65, 74, 90, 92,
    102, 112, 123, 125,
    128 (2), 144, 150,
    159, 165 (will)
  John Westray 145
  Jos. (or Jas.?) 116
  Joseph 57, 61 (will)
    (2), 62, 74, 76, 158,
    165, 170, 171
  Joseph (?) 54
  Joshua 123
  Josiah 125
  Kin 137
  Kinchen 167
  Kitchen 54

Turner (cont.)
  Lewis 92
  Littleton 77 (2), 97,
    108
  Lucy 42, 69, 145 (2)
  Martha 55, 94
  Mary 21, 36, 41, 62,
    76
  Mathew 36, 61, 63, 92
    (2), 140
  Mildred 141 (2)
  Milla 22
  Milly 127
  Nancy 95, 150
  Nanny 115, 122
  Nathan 39, 44, 79 (2),
    85 (2), 125, 155,
    165
  Nathaniel 91
  Parrot 102
  Pass. 125 (will), 130,
    148, 150, 168
  Patience 5, 126, 127
    (2), 142
  Peyton 150
  Polly 61, 125
  Priscilla 94
  Rebecca (Rebeckah,
    Rebekah) 40, 99, 125,
    127, 144, 155
  Robert 54
  Roger 61
  Sally 54, 140
  Sampson (Samson) 45,
    57 (will)(2), 61,
    113
  Samuel 93
  Sarah 5, 54 (2), 70,
    92, 101
  Simon 7 (2), 9, 10 (2),
    22 (will)(3), 24, 36
    (3), 41, 42, 63 (2),
    64, 69, 92, 107
  Simon Sr. 13, 41 (will)
  Sterling 150
  Susanna (Susannah) 118,
    127
  T. 92
  Temperance 94
  Thomas 22 (2), 36, 41
    (2), 49 (will)(2),
    55, 61, 70, 74, 75,
    76, 79, 82, 86, 88,
    90 (2), 91, 92 (3),
    94 (2), 97 (2), 99,
    100, 101 (2), 105,
    106, 107 (2), 110
    (2), 111, 112 (3),
    113, 115 (will)(4),
    118, 119, 120, 123,
    126, 128, 135, 138,
    139, 143, 149, 153,
    159 (3), 167, 169
  Walter 140
  Will 128, 159
  William 2, 3, 22, 33,
    36, 41(4), 46, 53,
    55 (3), 61, 62 (2),
    63 (4), 70, 77(will),
    80, 82, 90, 92, 93,
    95, 99, 127, 128,
    130, 159 (2), 169
  William and Henry,
    and Co. 128
  William Sr. 36 (will)
  Willie 145 (will), 147
Tyas, Ann 3

Tylaer, Edmund 29
Tyler, Edmund (Edm.) 22,
  29, 30, 32 (2), 34,
  35 (2), 38, 39, 41,
  43 (2), 44, 51, 52,
  58, 60, 64 (2), 73,
  98, 113, 120, 123,
  124, 130, 162, 164
  Edward 88
  Edward W. 167
  Elizabeth 120
  Esmund 42
  Jeremiah 88, 120
    (will), 129
  Martha 167
  Martha Kinchen 120
  Robert 31, 97
  William Jarrell 120
Tynes, West 113, 134
Tyus, West Jr. 158
Underwood, Elizabeth 15
  John 20, 23, 113
    (will)(2), 114, 124
    (2)
  Mary 113
  Mathew 79, 96, 113,
    124
Urquhart, John 139 (2),
  140, 146, 161
  Mary 112
  W. 52
  Will 61
  William 35, 49 (2),
    60, 62, 69, 80, 81,
    83, 92, 106, 112,
    116, 117 (2), 118,
    131 (2), 133, 135,
    136, 138 (2), 139
    (2), 146 (3), 147
    (2), 157, 161
Vance, Hugh 55
Vasse, Rachel 42
Vassel, Jesse 45
  Joel 24
Vasser, Ann 45
  Anne 67
  Benjamin 24 (will),
    30, 36, 113
  Bethia 27
  Dolly 24 (2)
  Dorothy 36
  Elizabeth 67
  Elijah 66
  Etheldred 113 (2)
  Jacob 15, 18, 24
  Jesse 67, 79, 108
  John 42
  Joseph 11, 16, 24,
    113 (will)(2), 114
  Lydia (Lyda) 45, 52,
    67 (will), 69, 79
  Margaret 45, 67, 79
  Marget 108
  Mary 45, 67, 79 (2)
  Nathan 2, 4, 18, 20
    (2), 24 (2), 25, 26
    (3), 27, 33, 45
    (will), 47, 52
  Robert 45, 79
  Tabitha 147
  William 24, 113
Vasser (?), Robert 4
Vaugan, Henry 84
Vaughan, Amy 44, 145
  Ann 138, 145
  Betsey 145
  Dorcas 44

Vaughan (cont.)
  Elizabeth 44
  Ephraim 44
  Fathe 44
  H. 22
  Henry 6, 10 (2), 18(2), 20, 23, 24 (2), 26, 29, 33, 35, 38 (2), 41, 44 (5), 45, 48, 100 (will), 101, 104, 138, 145
  Howell 100 (2), 104, 138
  James 44, 114, 134, 138
  John 138
  Lydia 116, 146
  Mary 44, 134
  Mary Briggs 44
  Phoebe (Phobe) 86, 114
  Polly 146
  Rebecca 79
  Sarah 44 (2), 79
  Seymour (Semour) 145 (3), 148, 154, 164 (2)
  Simon 117
  Thomas 44, 96, 98, 100 (2), 104, 109, 111, 113, 124 (2), 138 (2), 156, 167
  William 44 (will)(2), 46, 69, 79 (will), 91, 92 (2), 97, 109, 117, 138 (will)(2), 167
Vauhan (?), Henry 54
Vellins, Armstead 89
Vick, Ann 15, 38, 40, 62
  Anne 102
  Arthur 14, 40 (2), 82 (will)(3), 91, 101, 105
  Beda 40, 62
  Benjamin 166
  Betsey 146
  Burwell 140, 167
  Charlotte 140
  Council 102, 116
  Dorcas 102
  Edith 139
  Elizabeth 40 (2), 62, 74, 105, 119, 161 (2), 167
  Fanny 146
  Giles 102, 119 (2), 140
  Isaac 74
  Isabell 116
  J. 124, 139, 147, 148, 154, 163, 167
  Jacob 3 (2), 14, 24, 40, 74, 102 (2), 119 (will)(2), 140, 156
  James 9 (2), 10, 52, 70, 89, 147 (will)(2), 157, 160
  Jesse 96, 106, 116, 119, 120, 146, 147 (2)
  Jo. 84, 122, 125, 132, 133, 135, 136, 139, 140, 146, 151, 153
  Joel 116
  John 120, 163
  Jordan 120 (3), 160
  Jos. (or Jas.?) 115, 127 (2)

Vick (cont.)
  Joseph 24, 46 (will) (2), 52, 89, 94, 104, 106, 111, 116 (2), 118, 123, 129, 139, 147, 150, 162, 165
  Joseph (Capt.) 166
  Joshua 14, 40(will), 41, 62, 102, 119 (2), 161 (will)(3), 163
  Josiah 14, 84, 96, 98, 104, 116, 121, 132, 134, 137, 145
  Josiah (Capt.) 121
  Kirby 116
  Knowell 116
  Lewis 98, 102 (3), 128
  Littleberry 163
  Lucy 163
  Lydda 119
  Margaret 134
  Martha 14, 36, 140, 142
  Mary 156
  Mason 163
  Mathew 37, 42, 52, 74 (2), 102, 116
  Mathew Sr. 116 (will), 129
  Newit 140 (2), 141, 146, 162
  Noel 146
  Parks N. 147
  Patience 3, 24, 102, 119
  Patty 14, 146
  Peggy 105
  Peterson 163
  Piety 102, 119
  Pilgrim 102 (2), 128
  Priscilla 139
  Rebecca 147
  Richard 14 (will)(3), 16, 23, 24, 36, 53 (2), 102, 104, 119 (will), 147 (2)
  Richard Jr. 19
  Robert 23, 46, 74 (2), 120 (will), 121, 141
  Sally 102
  Samuel 82 (2), 105 (will), 108, 130
  Samuel Sr. 91
  Sarah 116, 119, 147(2)
  Selah 146
  Shadrack 82, 105 (2), 108, 119
  Silas 102, 119
  Simmons 116
  Simon 74 (2), 163(will)
  Thomas 74, 140, 142
  W. Burwell 102
  William 14, 40, 55, 62, 74 (will)(3), 75, 98, 102 (will), 104, 128, 140 (2), 141, 146, 161 (2), 167 (will)
  William Jr. 133
  William Sr. 140 (will)
Vinkles, John 12
Vitching, Martha 167
Waddell, Noel 147
Wade, Ann 93, 101
  Christopher 8, 26 (3), 30, 32, 92 (will), 99, 101
  John 93, 101

Wade (cont.)
  Martha 93, 101
  Samuel 93
  Sarah 93, 101
  Wilson 92, 101, 160
Wainwright, Mary 1, 2
  Thomas 109
Wakins, Mary 82
Wall, Ann 62
  John 165
  Sarah 50
Waller, Benjamin 58
  John 101
  John Benjamin 89
  Jordan 54
  Lucy 141
Walters, Elizabeth 4
Ward, William 153
Warren, Benjamin 25, 36 (2), 37, 158, 162 (will)
  Elizabeth 36
  Etheldred 118 (2)
  Faith 71, 74, 85 (will), 86
  Henry 71, 85, 140
  John 36 (will), 37, 158
  Joseph 44, 71 (will) (2), 74
  Martha 139
  Mary 162 (2)
  Michael (Michl.) 71 (2), 74, 85 (2), 86, 90, 111 (2), 115, 119 (2), 120, 166
  Nicholas 128
  Sally 162
Washington, A. 6
  Amos 111
  Arthur 8, 9, 22 (will), 23, 32, 34, 111 (will)(2)
  David 99, 109, 129, 148, 150, 171
  Easter 171
  Elizabeth 8 (2), 14, 22
  Etheldred 149
  Faith 8, 38
  Fil. 135
  George 22, 28, 31 (will)(3), 32, 33 (2), 40, 42, 55, 58, 62, 76, 79 (4), 99 (will), 100, 102, 109, 129, 133, 171 (will)
  James 3, 111
  Jesse 8, 38 (2), 46, 47, 111, 120, 129, 149
  John 8 (will)(2), 9, 28, 34, 38 (will), 40
  Joseph 28 (2), 30, 31 (2), 32, 52, 62, 63, 85, 89, 99, 111, 166
  Martha 98
  Mary 8, 22, 38
  Olive 111
  Robert 70, 94
  Sarah 22 (3), 28, 29, 99 (2), 100, 109
  Tamer 21
  Thomas 8 (2), 111, 129, 133, 149

Washington (cont.)
  William 28 (will), 29, 30, 32, 171 (2)
  Zebediah 109
Watkins, Benjamin 38
  John 19, 26
  Joseph 117
  Mary 107
Watkins (?), Mary 82-83
Watson, Alexander (Alex.) 3, 5, 61, 93
Weatherley, Jesse 10
Webb, Charles 14 (will) (2), 48
  Daniel 164
  Elizabeth 14 (2), 48
  John 14, 123
  Micajah 14
Wellens, Benjamin 123 (3)
  John 123 (will)(3)
  Lucretia 123
  Mary 123
  William 123 (3)
Wellings, John 16
Wellons, Anne 58
  Annemeriah 73
  Charles 65, 73, 74
  Elender 101
  Elenor 100 (2)
  Henry 73, 100 (will), 101
  John 62, 73 (will)(2), 74, 75
  John Sr. 86
  Mary 57, 58, 63, 73
  Robert 120
  Sarah 51
  William 101, 136, 149 (2), 153, 159, 164, 168
Wellons (?), John 16
Wells, Rebecca 150
Wentworth, James 119
West, Ann 24 (2)
  James 16
  Joseph 24 (will), 25, 26, 82
  Josiah 26, 33
  Josias 24 (2)
  Lucy 131
  Mary 24, 48
  Mercy 20
  William 82
  William (Capt.) 4
Westbrook, Ann 21, 112, 140, 151
  Anne 39
  Arthur 61
  Beck 115
  Beckey 39
  Benjamin 39
  Betsey 140
  Burwell 21, 107 (3), 117, 151, 159
  Celia 39
  David 93, 107, 151, 159, 162
  Demsey 32
  Diana 61
  Dolly 140
  Dorcas 107
  Elias 21, 58, 68 (will)
  Elizabeth 39 (2)
  Fason 61
  Gray 21
  Hannah 63, 94, 112, 151

Westbrook (cont.)
  Helen (Hellen) 69 (2), 70, 112 (will), 113
  Henry 26, 61, 69 (2), 70, 94, 112, 113, 157 (will)
  Henry J. P. 138
  Hilvia 39 (2)
  Honour 21 (2), 32
  Jack Tillar 138
  Jacob 21, 61, 107
  James 21 (2), 39, 52, 61 (will)(3)
  Jarret 140
  Jesse 32
  Joel 93, 107, 151
  John 21 (will)(2), 32, 39 (2), 61, 66, 90, 107 (will)(3), 131, 139 (will), 145
  John Person 107
  Joshua 39
  Lucy 107 (2)
  Mary 39, 61, 107, 115 (will), 151
  Mason L. 138
  Mial 39
  Miday 112 (will)
  Moses 21
  Phebe (Pheby) 61, 93, 107, 151
  Priscilla 39, 157
  Rebecca 112, 151
  Sally 138, 157
  Samuel 21 (will)(3), 39 (2), 41, 94, 107 (3), 110, 151
  Samuel H. 93
  Samuel Jr. 61, 66
  Samuel Sr. 61 (2), 66, 107 (will), 108
  Thomas 2, 7, 18, 21, 39 (will)(2), 40, 61, 69 (will)(2), 70, 138
  Thomas Jr. 18
  Turner 107, 151
  Widdis 39
  William 9, 21 (2), 39 (will), 41, 93, 110, 157
  William Person 157 (2)
Westbrooke, Burwell 136
  Hannah 93
  Henry 122
  Henry J. P. 132
  John 31
  Joshua 135
  Mason Simmons 132
  Parson 132
  Samuel 46, 93 (will), 151
  Turner 93
Wester, Benjamin 8
  Giles 145
  Sally 152
  William 37
  William Jr. 142
Westra, William 42, 89
Westray, Benjamin 7
  Mary 30
  William 33
Wheeler, Benjamin 142
  Jacob 110
Wheeler (?), Martha 79
Wheelis, Martha 79

White, B. 98
  Baker 32, 55, 59
  Benjamin 165
  Benjamin Jr. 138
  Mary 64
  William 105
Whitehead, Adolphus 133
  Alexander 143
  Ann 3, 6
  Arher Meade 133
  Arthur 3 (will)(3), 5, 6, 14 (will), 16, 17, 18, 127, 133, 157, 170
  Benjamin 3, 19
  Colin 60
  Elizabeth 17
  Harriet 133
  Isabel 17
  J. 146
  Jack Anthony 133
  James 171
  Jesse 14 (2), 79, 81, 82, 90, 91 (2), 92, 96
  Jesse (Capt.) 77 (2), 79
  John 17, 92, 106, 114, 127, 133 (will), 169, 170
  Lazarus 3, 14 (2)
  Lemuel Murder 133
  Lewis 3 (2), 5, 6, 17 (will), 18, 20
  Lewis Augustus 133
  Lucindy 133
  Mary 3, 17 (2), 19, 143 (will), 148
  Maximillan 133
  Meriam 133
  Mitildy 133
  Nathan 3
  Patience 117
  Patty 17
  Priscilla 60
  Sally 133
  Thomas 14
  Selah 14
  Temperance 60
  William 3 (2), 14 (2), 45, 80, 96, 105, 112, 130, 140, 157, 170
Whitehorn, Sally 167
Whitfield, Benjamin 119, 120, 147 (will)(3)
  Burwell 162
  Elisha 147
  George 120
  John (147 (3)
  Mary 120, 147
  Reuben 147 (2)
Whitley, Abridgton 82
Whitney, Amy 28
  Ann 70, 137
  Elisha 28, 56, 137, 139, 160
  Giles 56, 99
  Joshua 11 (2), 12, 28 (will)(2), 29 (2), 30, 39, 56 (4), 70, 124, 137
  Margaret 23
  Margery 28 (2), 56
Whittington, Howell 71, 102, 104 (2), 130
Wick, Josiah 112

Wiggins, Abrams 12
Wiggons, Abraham 55 (2), 61
  James 55
  John 55 (will)(2), 61
  Richard 55 (2), 61
  Thomas 11
  William 55
Wiliams, Blyth 70
  Mary 70
Wilkins, John 75
  Michael 62
  Robert 60, 71
Wilkinson, Elizabeth 101
  J. 115
  James 101 (2), 105, 112, 116 (2), 133, 135, 160, 166, 169 (3), 170
  Jane 148
  John 18 (2), 19, 20, 21, 22, 24, 28 (2), 29, 30, 44, 46, 52, 55, 56, 58, 60 (2), 61, 62, 66 (2), 77, 82, 87, 88, 100, 101 (will)(3), 103, 116, 130 (2), 146, 160, 161, 169 (will)
  John Lewis 169
  Mary 54
  Nathaniel 169
  Sarah 101
  William 148
  Willis 156
Willeford, Jesse 151
  Jordan 98
  Thomas 98
  see also Williford
William, Daniel 166
Williams, Absalom 113 (2), 166 (3)
  Ambrose 4, 16, 20, 21, 22 (2)
  Ann 19, 22, 77, 140
  Anne 19, 20, 110
  Apaphroditus 120
  Arthur 19 (will), 22, 109, 131
  Benjamin 14, 16, 17, 18, 19, 20, 24, 29 (2), 32, 33, 36, 37, 38, 41, 45, 46, 50, 73, 79 (2), 80, 112 (will), 121, 122, 133, 137, 140, 163 (2)
  Bly 17, 64, 65
  Burwell 163 (4), 167
  Chaplain (Chaplin) 3 (2), 5, 14, 17
  Chaplain (Chaplin) Jr. 3, 17
  Chaplin Sr. 17
  Charles 166
  Cowper 124 (2)
  Daniel 1, 2 (2)
  Dorcas 58
  Drewry 163 (2)
  Drury 79
  Edwin 137
  Egbert 163
  Eley 50 (2), 52, 163
  Elias 121 (will)(2)
  Elisha 2, 96, 167

Williams (cont.)
  Elizabeth 10, 38, 58 (2), 84, 94, 115, 121, 137, 147, 152 (2), 160
  Epaphroditus 4, 9, 23, 30, 71, 74, 127(will)
  Ephraim 120, 127 (2)
  Ethelbert Carr 112
  George 2, 37, 41, 43, 48, 152, 163, 166 (will), 171
  George Thomas 113
  Gilstrap 58
  Henry 93, 114, 160
  Isaac 50 (2), 52, 62, 65, 74, 76, 78, 87, 106, 118, 125, 132, 137, 166
  Isaack 80
  Jacob 14, 16, 38, 50, 56, 71, 76, 96, 98, 121, 127 (2), 158, 160 (2)
  James 113
  Jeremiah 163
  Jerry 96
  Jesse 50 (2), 52, 74, 87
  Jethro 58
  John 2, 110, 121, 124 (2), 130, 148, 163 (3)
  Jonah 50 (will), 52
  Jone 3
  Jordan 111, 153, 163 (2), 164 (2)
  Joseph 17, 137
  Joshua 2 (2), 58
  Josiah 166
  Kinchen 96
  Lawrence 132
  Lewis 50, 148
  Lucy 23, 163
  Marian 112
  Martha 16, 50 (2)
  Mary 14, 92, 112 (2), 122, 137, 163 (2)
  Mathew 3, 148
  Michael 63, 87, 89
  Naack 148
  Nathan 17 (2), 160
  Nathan Robert 58 (will)
  Nicholas 18, 56, 65, 76, 121 (2), 124 (will), 130
  Patience 122
  Polly 147, 163 (2)
  Rachel 143, 152, 166
  Rebecca (Rebkah) 17, 23, 167, 169
  Rhoda 96
  Richard 2, 12, 109, 148, 152 (will), 153, 168
  Richard Egbert 112
  Robert 18, 38, 45, 47, 58, 63 (2), 167 (will)(3)
  Sally 124, 137, 160
  Sarah 2 (will), 3, 4, 38, 63 (will), 96, 113, 132
  Silas 161
  Sion 41, 163 (will)(2)
  Solomon 2, 166

Williams (cont.)
  Thomas 2, 17 (will) (3), 38 (will)(2), 69, 140, 147
  Thomas (Capt.) 17
  Thomas Sr. 44
  Walton 38
  Will 59
  William 14, 17, 19, 20, 22, 35, 60, 69, 70, 78, 91, 93, 96 (will), 97 (2), 108, 110, 111, 124, 138
Wilson 50 (2), 52
Williamsburg, Turner 89
Williamson, Abigail 60, 61
  Absalom (Absolom) 7, 110, 138
  Ann 7 (2), 55, 62
  Arthur 7 (2), 35, 55 (will)(2), 60 (2), 89, 98
  Arthur Sr. 94
  Averilla 7
  Benjamin 7, 9, 25, 35, 54 (will), 55, 133
  Benjamin Weldon (Benjamin W.) 169 (3)
  Burwell 7 (3), 35, 50, 55, 56, 58, 62, 63, 77, 101, 102, 110, 116, 130 (will)
  Calia 144
  Celah 123
  Elizabeth 7, 45 (2), 54, 70, 77, 82
  Exum 7, 55, 94
  F. 94
  Francis 89 (will), 110
  George 56
  Hannah 3, 7 (2), 13, 93
  Howell 75
  J. 60
  Jacob 115 (2)
  James 54 (2), 58, 65
  Jesse 55, 60, 94, 138
  John 55 (2), 73, 89, 107, 115 (2), 120, 122 (4), 124 (2), 131, 133, 135, 136, 139, 140, 142, 144, 149, 150, 151, 152 (2), 155, 156, 164, 167 (2), 170
  Joseph 7 (will), 13
  Joshua 115 (w)
  Lewis 54
  Lucy 70, 77, 130, 170
  Martha 3, 29, 70, 77, 160
  Mary 7, 55, 66, 70, 77
  Mary ann 55
  Mathew 54, 113, 120
  Nancy 130 (2)
  Nanney 45
  Olive 7-8
  Person 89
  Polly 89
  Robbin 72
  Robert 36, 44, 57, 65, 115 (will), 123
  Robert Mickleberry 60
  Sarah 117
  Selah 115 (2)

Williamson (cont.)
  Silviah 7
  Stephen 45, 54, 58, 70
  Stephenson 77
  Thomas 2, 7, 8, 9, 10, 18, 32, 34, 35, 37, 111 (will), 116
  Thomas (Col.) 106
  Turner 55, 89
  William 7, 54, 114
Williford, Belah 98 (2), 102, 157
  Benjamin 19
  Charles 55
  James 98
  Jeremiah 98
  John 19 (will), 24, 116
  Johnson 98
  Jordan 98, 102
  Josiah 157
  Lucy 19 (2)
  Mary 19, 98 (2)
  Molly 115
  Mourning 19
  Nathan 19
  Samuel 157
  Sarah 98
  Susanna 157 (2)
  Thomas 19 (3)
  William 19 (2), 98 (will), 102, 157
  see also Willeford
Wills, Francis 1 (will), 2, 26, 48
  Goodrich 165
  Marthew 168
  Mathew 1, 6, 9, 11, 21, 23 (2), 26, 35, 48, 50, 60, 84, 88, 89, 90, 91, 93, 97, 98 (2), 121, 129, 142
  Temperance 1, 2, 48
  Thomas 1 (2), 48 (3)
  William 128
Willson, John 27, 103
Wilson, Elizabeth 161 (2)
  George 77
  James 82, 83, 90
  Pheeby 77
  Thomas 129
  William 77 (will), 79, 90
Winddom, John 145
Windham, Benjamin 93
  Edward 5, 32
  Eustace 73
  Jesse 73
Wittemore, Buckner 120
Wo (?), M. 63
Womack, James 108, 112
  James B. 149, 159
  Juliana 60
  Priscilla 90
  William 16, 60
  see also Wommack
Womble, Celia 36
  Jesse 40, 47, 50, 129, 133, 144, 145, 146 (2), 155, 156
  John 161, 163
Wombwell, Jesse 62 (will) (2), 63, 80
  Joseph 62
  Joshua 62
  Nancy 62, 80
  Sarah 62
  Selah 62, 80

Wommack, Carter 142 (2), 143, 168
  Elizabeth 142
  James 61
  Mary 107
  Thomas 142 (will), 143, 168
  see also Womack
Woobank, Robert S. 1
Wood, Anna 97
  Benjamin 31, 34, 46 (2), 97, 103
  Edmund 97
  George 46 (will)(2), 49, 63
  Hannah 34, 61
  Joel 97, 121
  John 84, 120
  Joseph 105
  Joshua 46 (2), 49 (2), 71, 72, 93, 97 (will) 103, 105
  Mary 46 (2), 51, 97, 108, 164
  Moses 46 (2), 51 (3), 72
  Pamelia 51
  Rebecca 97
  Sarah 97
  Thomas 46, 93, 118, 156 (2), 168
  see also Woods
Woodard, Ann 87
  Charles 84, 89
  Elizabeth 51, 84
  Jesse 84
  John 98
  Lydia 58
  Samuel 8, 58, 70, 83, 84
  Temperance 43
  William 84
Wooddard, Charles 84 (will)
  Elizabeth 84
  William 84
Woodlief, Martha 133
  Patsy 133
  Thomas 133
Woods, Joel 121
  Joshua 72
  see also Wood
Woodward, Charles 5
  John 89, 160
  Martha 5 (2)
  Mary 26
  Oliver 47
  Rueben 5
  Samuel 5 (will), 6
  Simon 26
  Temperance 70
Wooten, Ann 38
Wootten, Elizabeth 131
  Jane Exum 131
  Richard 59
Worrel, John 128
  Richard 123
Worrell, Ann 34 (2)
  Benjamin 34, 38, 70
  Cherry 116
  Elizabeth 34, 127
  Honour 53
  John 34, 66, 86, 107, 127, 132, 162, 166
  John Jr. 166
  Josiah 162
  Lewis 160 (3)

Worrell (cont.)
  Mary 11, 119
  Mathew 116, 119
  May 147
  Molly 116
  Nathan 34
  Nathaniel 38
  Richard 16, 28, 34, 38, 53 (3), 116 (will)(3), 119 (2), 166 (will)(2), 171
  Shadrack 116 (2), 119, 166, 171
  Tabitha 166
  William 28, 34 (will) (3), 38 (2), 88, 106, 116, 119, 166
Wray, Anne 67
  William 67
Wren, Richard 68, 72, 140
  William 140
Wrenn, Anna 113
  Jesse 113
  Richard 109
  William 109
Wright, Ann 112 (2)
  David 60, 68, 69, 70, 78, 90, 97, 110, 112, 114, 126
  Henry 112
  James 26 (will), 27, 60, 71 (will)(3), 72, 90, 94, 112
  Job 6 (2), 8, 11, 20 (2), 28, 31, 32 (2), 33, 35 (2), 38 (2), 40 (2), 41, 42 (2), 43 (2), 46, 53 (2), 56, 59, 76, 165
  Jobe 21
  John 26, 40, 71, 113, 115, 123, 131, 135, 138, 145
  Joseph 71 (2), 106, 113, 120, 123 (2), 136
  Martha 26 (2), 27, 71
  Mary 26, 87, 94, 114, 168
  William 112, 126, 135 (2), 142, 165
Wyche, Nathaniel 165, 171
Young, Francis Jr. 129, 131

www.ingramcontent.com/pod-product-compliance
Lightning Source LLC
Chambersburg PA
CBHW070256230426
43664CB00014B/2557